Defining Moments

ADVANCE PRAISE FOR *DEFINING MOMENTS*

———

"Faith-based travel can be a life-transformational experience for those who take these journeys. And according to neuroscience, our brains retain and use information that is personally experienced, better than when we read a book or watch a video. The McCarthys have assembled the book that helps you do it all, including preparation, highlight descriptions of significant sites in the world and agenda recommendations. Highly recommended."

John Townsend, Ph.D., *New York Times* bestselling author of *Boundaries*, Founder of the Townsend Institute for Leadership and Counseling, psychologist

"Thanks for doing this great work! Kim and I have raised our kids with the philosophy of "getting out of the bubble", seeking every opportunity to bring them to the mission field to engage the world that God has called us to serve in. This work gives great insights into how to do this for everyone. I believe that this book will be a great help to everyone who wants to see God transform their life by seeing His work in the world & will make people more equipped to serve God, being His agents of change."

Carl A. Moeller, former CEO, Biblica

"Defining Moments is essential to throw in your backpack when making the journey of a lifetime. This resource will turn vacation travel into pilgrimage by going behind the facts of each location to the stories and spiritual revelations forever embedded in these spiritually historic places."

Gabe Lyons, Founder of Q Ideas & Author of Good Faith

"*This* book is what every Christian should take with them when traveling to places of religious historical significance. An appreciation of what Christians did and sacrificed before us could exhort us all to be similarly faithful."

Brad Dacus, Founder & President, Pacific Justice Institute

"Even armchair travelers can be transported through this book to experience the Bible in a whole new way. After exploring the historical backgrounds of our favorite Bible stories, the McCarthys invite us to a time and place where we experience a parallel conversation of what God may have to speak over our own lives. This conversation can be especially powerful for small groups, as such conversations will empower transformational discoveries—all without ever leaving your living room!"

Christopher McCluskey, best-selling Author, podcast host, & Founder/President of Professional Christian Coaching Institute

"To suggest that Rick and Susan McCarthy are a dynamic duo would be a massive understatement. Not only are they the most qualified couple on the planet to write this book, they have also done an outstanding job. If you want to transform your travel from consumption to Kingdom impact, look no further. "Defining Moments" will absolutely get you there."

Dane Sanders, Author and Founder at Fastermind.co

"Rick & Susan McCarthy again go deeper with Kingdom expansion into various subjects and fields, either geographical or industrial, where no one even considers. Transformation is the only byproduct Rick seeks to cultivate in the endeavors where God leads him. This latest guide only exemplifies how taking a rather routine platform such as travel, and applying it into the Christian world, leads to another level of understanding and enrichment."

Jason Brown, Marketplace Chaplains

"Tired of just another cruise or exotic destination only for fun? Seen most of the world but missed the spiritual side of the ledger? Want to make your next travel experience Kingdom-focused? My friends, Rick and Susan McCarthy, were tired of the "next exotic destination" too, so they did something about it. They have traveled to over eighty countries and, after hundreds of thousands of miles, they have now captured their learnings into a comprehensive faith-based travel guide, like Fodor's and Lonely Planet for travel with a purpose. You will find out where you can go, what to expect, what to read ahead of time, how to create deep bonding for your travel team in advance, what to pack, how to pray and much more, including daily devotionals, archaeological and Biblical guides, and suggested songs to sing at each site! Rick and Susan have created a step-by-step, nothing left out guide for you to turn everyday travel into missional-focused, life-changing travel including Israel, Greece, Turkey, the Reformation and short-term mission trips. I highly recommend it!"

Greg Leith, CEO, Convene

"So many of us check our spiritual disciplines at the door when we travel. We rarely visit distant churches, often do not take time to read our Bible, and mostly fill our time with self-indulgence. "Defining Moments" will create a sea-change in how you approach your travels. Refueling your spiritual tank is as important as satisfying your physical rest needs. This book does such a fantastic job of making the pursuit of Christ on your vacation interesting, fun and valuable. You will never approach time on vacation the same way again."

Tony Ferraro, Founder/CEO of Twubs.com;
Author of *Killing Cows & How to Avoid Leadership Suicide*;
Strategist & Speaker

"As a Bible student, travel buff and one who stops at all historical markers along the road, this book hits all of my buttons. The McCarthys have compiled a tool to be used to both increase the head knowledge of these sites, but also my heart knowledge, as I journal and pray specifically at each location. Can't wait to plan my next trip using this book!"

Becky Turner, National Managing Partner,
The Barnabas Group

"I have been to Israel a number of times, and know that the stories of Bible heroes take on a new twist when we stand in their shoes and listen for God's revelation for us. This book takes that experience a step farther and sets the stage for you to apply those same 'aha' moments with God to your own life—while standing in the very spot that those Biblical figures once tread. Just invite the Holy Spirit into the experience, and be prepared for a life-changing interaction."

Bill Butterworth, Keynote Speaker to Fortune 500 companies & professional sports teams; Author of 36 books including *Building Successful Teams & Everyday Influence*; Coach; Ghostwriter; Founder, Butterworth Communicators Institute

"Most people come back from travel dragging bags and scrolling photos—on their mobile device—with no compelling narrative to share with friends and family. Trips are forgotten before the boarding passes for the next journey are printed. Rick and Susan McCarthy aren't from that tribe of travelers: they've gone to places rich in spiritual history, and allowed themselves to be impacted by the settings that were backdrops for great moments in God's story. Allow them to take you along in those itineraries, and coach you in finding the rich meaning that awaits the pilgrim who is looking for more!"

Bob Shank, Founder of The Master's Program; Cofounder of The Barnabas Group; Author of *Life Mastery, Total Life Management & Full Time*

"Defining Moments" is a revelational read. Literally. It breathes life into travel in ways that bring a deeper meaning and purpose to the experience. Page after page, it will help drive what we know to be true in our faith deeper down into our Spirit, turning the locations you travel to into lasting spiritual transformation.

Dean Del Sesto, CEO, Breviti Marketing; Speaker; Author of *Shift Your Thinking* series

DEFINING MOMENTS

THE TRANSFORMATIONAL
PROMISES OF
FAITH-BASED TRAVEL

RICK AND SUSAN McCARTHY

MOUNT
TABOR
MEDIA
AN IMPRINT OF
MORGAN JAMES

NEW YORK
LONDON • NASHVILLE • MELBOURNE • VANCOUVER

Defining Moments

The Transformational Promises of Faith Based Travel

All Scripture quotations, unless otherwise indicated, are taken from the *Holy Bible, New International Version*®, NIV®, Copyright © 1973, 1978, 1984, 2011 by Biblica Inc™. Used by permission of Zondervan. All rights reserved worldwide. www.zondervan.com The "NIV" and "New International Version" are trademarks registered in the United States Patent and Trademark Office by Biblica, Inc.™

Maps used by permission of The Interactive Bible, Bible.CA, who owns their copyrights. www.bible.ca

Published in New York, New York, by Mount Tabor Media, LLC, a branded imprint of Morgan James Publishing. Morgan James is a trademark of Morgan James, LLC. www.MorganJamesPublishing.com

Printed in the United States of America

ISBN 9781631952449 paperback
ISBN 9781631952456 eBook
Library of Congress Control Number: 2020909715

definingmomentsbook.com

Cover Design by:
Rachel Lopez
www.r2cdesign.com

Interior Design by:
Chris Treccani
www.3dogcreative.net

This book is dedicated to all the travelers before us who have left footsteps of amazing faith adventures and to our son, Patrick, and the significant footprints he left on our lives.

TABLE OF CONTENTS

FOREWORD

———

Every once in a while, someone writes a book solely out of the interest of those they write it for. In writing *"Defining Moments: The Transformational Promises of Faith-Based Travel,"* Rick & Susan McCarthy have set out to accomplish several goals: to encourage people to take faith-based vacations and turn them into Defining Moments that will shape their lives forever; to help people see the real possibility of not just having their *heads* filled with facts regarding a vacation spot but to have their *hearts* shifted and changed in ways they never imagined; to learn the practical ways of meeting God in powerful and personal ways that will restore, revive, and reenergize their faith; and finally to inform people of the important places in Christian history so they can be can strengthened and inspired in their faith.

I have traveled around the world, led trips to Israel using such Defining Moments teachings, and have been on a faith-based trip that was led by Rick & Susan to Greece and Turkey in the footsteps of Paul. Their passion for their faith, knowledge of Christian history and commitment to life transformation is why they wrote this book. I would highly recommend this book and the clear direction it gives for you to plan and execute a faith-based trip of your own. The Defining Moments they include are intended to move you to a *discovery* method of learning, rather than simply a *teaching* method that most tour guides and pastors use. If you want to plan a trip of a lifetime that will impact your family, friends, believers and nonbelievers alike, then I heartily encourage you to pick up and read *"Defining Moments: The Transformational Promises of Faith-Based Travel."*

—**Eric Heard**, Pastor of Stewardship and
Marriage Ministry, Mariners Church

PREFACE

A re you ready to leave your everyday life to meet God in exciting, scary, powerful, and new ways? Sometimes a change in environment is a gift to quiet the noise and to hear God's gentle whisper instead. We pray such trips will be a time for you to go deeper and refresh, restore, and reenergize.

You are going to travel halfway around the world. Do not stop there! *The most important part of the journey is that last twelve inches from your head to your heart!* Invite the Holy Spirit along on your travels.

There are many great pastors that lead great faith-based trips and offer great, Biblical, *head* teachings. Far too many of these pastors unknowingly rush you back on the bus and on to the next cool site without stopping to speak to your *heart*. Please do not *run* where Jesus or Paul *walked*!

We want you to not just *read* about a site and have a pastor *tell* you about what you are seeing. We want you to *live* it, touch it, smell it, experience it—and return as a different person. These are not just tours or places, but journeys of transformation.

Our heart is that *your* heart will be transformed by a personal, relevant encounter with the living God, that you have defining, life-changing, "Aha!" moments, where the Holy Spirit applies what you have just seen in walking around Corinth, for example, to your walk with Him today. The Bible and its history will become real people in real places with real meaning to your life today.

Our prayer for you is that this book will start you on new journeys, new possibilities and promises, new transformations. There is a vast difference between *knowing* Bible places and stories and *experiencing* our presence in those stories. Imagine yourself in that time and place, and then listen to the Holy Spirit showing you where you are today in that story.

For you *armchair travelers*, this book offers a rich combination of history book, Bible study and life-application opportunity. We encourage you to *read and learn with your head*, and then *listen and apply with your heart*.

Faith-based travel started in the Old Testament and continued in the New Testament. The faithful were making pilgrimages to Solomon's Temple 1,000 years before Christ. Deuteronomy 16:16 commands all Jewish males to appear at three annual feasts—The Festival of Unleavened Bread, the Festival of Weeks, and the Festival of Tabernacles—which Jesus faithfully obeyed. Wise men from the east traveled great distances to see the Baby Jesus.

Paul took three missionary journeys, including Greece, Turkey and Syria, and then he was later imprisoned in Rome. In Biblical times, pilgrims traveled often to places like Jerusalem for holidays ("holy days"). Today millions of people each year travel to religious sites. The World Tourism Organization estimates that approximately 330 million tourists visit the world's key religious sites every year. Faith-based travel includes pilgrimages, leisure trips, getaways, adventure and active travel, conferences, events, missions, humanitarian trips, and more.

The first year we were married, I suggested to Susan that we experience together a DreamMaster weekend developed by Bob Shank, founder of The Master's Program and cofounder of The Barnabas Group. I was single when I went through his rich, three-year Master's Program, and loved the idea of couples spending a weekend together communicating their individual and shared dreams for the future. By God's "coincidence," Bob led that year the very first facilitated weekend retreat for several couples, which was the one we joined.

I had always had a dream of writing a book on the great festivals of the world, like Carnival in Rio, Mardi Gras in New Orleans, and the Running of the Bulls in Pamplona. I realized that as I became a believer and my faith grew, God was redirecting my focus instead to *faith-based* travel. With our shared love of Jesus and travel, the weekend resulted in God giving us the dream of writing this book together. We roughed out a five-year plan that took over ten years to obediently complete, plus several more years before we made efforts to publish it.

Part of the inspiration for this book was that Susan, prior to our meeting, had experienced an amazing Israel trip, led by then-senior pastor, Kenton Beshore, of Mariners Church in Newport Coast, California, and she had experienced a lackluster Reformation trip. A key difference between those trips was the opportunity to go beyond the typical trip's emphasis on great teaching—*head knowledge*—to relevant, Holy Spirit-led, personal application—*heart experience*. Most trips show you all the history and then rush you back on the bus for twelve more stops that day. Our hope is that trip leaders will stay an extra 20–30 minutes at most sites to facilitate an opportunity to experience the relevance to you today of what happened at that site centuries ago. We wish you to have "Aha!" Defining Moments with God to enrich your trip and your life. If your trip leader only does the head teaching, you may concurrently use this book to have your own Defining Moments with God.

"But when He, the Spirit of Truth, comes, He will guide you into all the truth. He will not speak on His own; He will speak only what He hears, and He will tell you what is yet to come. He will glorify Me because it is from Me that He will receive what He will make known to you. All that belongs to the Father is Mine. That is why I said the Spirit will receive from Me what He will make known to you" (John 16:13–15).

Please note that out of reverence, we have chosen to capitalize all names and pronouns referring to God, Jesus and the Holy Spirit, as well as Bible, Cross, Word, Scripture, Eternity and Heaven; we have chosen not to capitalize references to humans, such as king, queen, pope, emperor, and archbishop.

Much of church history is not precise, so well-meaning theologians and researchers often contradict each other as to dates, doctrines, places. You may disagree with some of our heavily researched content, which we respect. Please know that our heart is simply to get it right, and mostly to in no way violate the Divinity of God, Jesus or the Holy Spirit.

Faith-based travel is an ideal way to connect intimately with fellow Christians while experiencing the roots and stories of your shared faith. Travel is the one thing that makes you richer *after* you pay for it.

CHAPTER ONE:

———

Preparing for Your Journey

WHAT?
WHY?
WHERE?
WHEN?
HOW?

"I will lead the blind by ways they have not known, along unfamiliar paths I will guide them; I will turn the darkness into light before them and make the rough places smooth. These are the things I will do; I will not forsake them"

(Isaiah 42:16).

Expectations for the Journey

The countries that the events of the Bible happened in are amazing places of history, but they are even more amazing places when you visit them in the company of the Holy Spirit. The revelations seen and heard throughout Israel are stimulating to the mind, but the revelations that the Holy Spirit of the one true God reveals are thrilling—*if* you are listening for them. Walking along the same roads as the Apostle Paul and understanding the culture of his time will forever change the paradigm that the Pauline Epistles are viewed from.

This book is written for those who want to experience *transformation*, not only by what God reveals to their *eyes* on these trips, but also what is revealed to their *spirits*. It is a guide for how to prepare for the experience, a spiritual roadmap marked by others' experiences and testimonies on this journey, and an invitation to the trip of a lifetime with the Holy Spirit.

Our friends, David and Elizabeth Sparks with Footstep Ministries, say it so well through their Mission of the *Four Es: Explore the Past, Examine the Scriptures, Experience the Culture, Engage in Worship and Prayer*. If you faithfully pursue each of those opportunities, you will be guaranteed a powerful experience!

The fact that Jesus, God the Father's own Son, slept and walked and ate here on this earth, on the very land you may see, is captivating. To walk up the same stone steps that the God of the universe walked up, to stand at the pool of Bethsaida where He healed the sick, to enter the tomb He may have been buried in. It is all very compelling.

But what is even more compelling is to remember the stories that unfolded on those sites and compare them to our *own lives today*. What parallels are there for us to discover? What can we learn from others traveling alongside us on this journey? What does God have to give us as we take time away from our jobs, families, and responsibilities just to walk in the same steps as Jesus, His disciples, and His apostles?

What does He want to say to us as we sit in the same kind of fishing boat as the disciples did, fearing that the storm would ruin them? What does He want us to understand about the saints that went before us that were used to edify the Church and God's Kingdom? What does He want us to experience as we walk the path that Jesus walked on His final, glorious, worship-filled entry into Jerusalem, only to be killed within the week?

What will He show us about the burdens in our own life as we pray in Gethsemane, where He knew fear and suffered to the point of sweating blood? What was He thinking as He carried His Cross through the streets of Jerusalem, or as He wept over His beloved city? When we are standing on the Mount of Olives where He ascended into Heaven, how does He want us to think about life, death, and our purpose on this earth? Who among us can say that these experiences are all so well known by reading God's Word that visiting them in person will not make them even more vivid in their faith walk?

In James 4:8, it says: "*Come near to God and He will come near to you. Wash your hands, you sinners, and purify your hearts, you double-minded.*"

It is only when we make this trip with an attitude of profound reverence that we will experience the closeness to God that He has planned for us here. It is by setting apart ourselves to be captivated at His feet that we will experience Him in a deeper way. We take our worries, concerns, pride, preconceived ideas, all of our sins, and anything that is not of God to the foot of the Cross. *"And we take captive every thought to make it obedient to Christ"* (2 Corinthians 10:5).

Since God has a specific plan for each one of our lives, know that He will have specific things to share with each person on their faith adventure trip. There will be site visits on this journey that are intimate and joyful and Spirit-filled for everyone, it seems, but you. The next stop, *you* will have a profound transformational discovery that *others* will not experience. Each site and story will have a different purpose and meaning for each person. As long as you are drawing near to God, dear one, know that He will keep His promise to draw near to you.

Site Authenticity

While many of the sites are mesmerizing to us because we know the events of Scripture truly happened at those places, there are many sites whose authenticity cannot be proven. Sites are usually classified as "A," "B," and "C" sites. An "A" site has fairly well-established authenticity. The Sea of

Galilee, the Mount of Olives, the Valley of Kidron, the Temple site and Jacob's Well all fall into this category. "B" sites are somewhat established, and a "C" site is an educated guess or tradition.

Do not make the mistake of throwing the baby out with the bath water, though, by regarding "B" and "C" sites as meaningless just because they are unproven. Far more important is what happened at or near each of the places. We are here to put ourselves into the same experience of the Biblical stories said to have happened in these places. Experiences and testimonies from the Word do not crumble with time, as buildings may. Even if the historical accuracy of a site is unknown, the churches that are built near that site to honor a particular Biblical event can bring us into a Spirit-filled remembrance of what God wants to reveal to us through that particular story.

We owe much to the groups that have risked their lives at times to preserve these sites. The Franciscans have led the struggle to keep the holy places of God holy. We draw inspiration to do the same within our *own* lives on this trip. Let us set ourselves apart, turn around our actions, direct them to the Father's will, love Jesus and love each other—that is how we set our own lives apart as holy, just as these places we will visit have been set apart.

This should not be a time of visiting as many sites per day as possible to "check them off our list." We will not be visiting holy places like museums, just to get a quick glance at an artifact or piece of art. The best way to savor this experience is through quality, not quantity. We will linger at each site, waiting on God to impress upon us what He has for each one of us there. We will see multiple tour buses come and go while we are being still before God—either lingering in prayer, sharing with each other a thought God has just revealed to our hearts, or worshipping and praising Him with an intimacy we may have never known before. As we experience these holy places, both physically and spiritually, we will experience adventure and excitement with the God of the universe who has planned a fascinating, captivating, and exciting time ahead of us, beyond anything we have ever experienced.

Our only job is to respond to God as He reveals His wonders to us. Enjoy the fellowship of your travel mates. God may use them in a big way to reveal Himself to you. Rest in the solitude of quiet time with Him—just the two of you with no one else around—as you find a hidden place at one of your favorite spots. Allow your emotions to express themselves freely and often as your heart is moved. Your authenticity compels others into freedom for themselves. Be generous with your time, conversation, and interest in the experiences of your group. You will be enriched in ways beyond your expectations, and you just may find new people that you count as family for Eternity. Since you will be spending Eternity with them, why not start to get to know them now?

Prayer for the Journey

Lord God, thank You for each person You have brought on this journey. Thank You for the amazing privilege of visiting the very lands that Jesus and His followers walked on. Set us apart for this journey. We repent of any uncleansed sin we are carrying with us. Set us apart in Your holiness for this journey. Please keep us focused on You. Keep our entire group in unity, just as Jesus is in unity with You.

Give us a love for each other, and give us a new depth for our love for You. Give us the power and strength to love Your Son as You do. Please let us have an encounter with Jesus that glorifies You and Your Body of believers. We pray over each person on the trip, that they would have the revelation and transformation that You have planned for them alone. We invite the Holy Spirit to be in every conversation on this trip, to inspire every thought, to encourage us to deeds of love for each other, and to enable us to worship You in spirit and in truth as we journey together. May we return home with enriched testimonies of whom You have shown Yourself to be in our life, so that we can inspire others into deep relationship with You. Amen.

Preparation for the Journey

Many details will have been planned and prepared for the physical aspects of this trip. Your travel agent has coordinated flight schedules, hotels, airport transportation, payment, and the list goes on. But these details account for only half of the preparation necessary for the transformational trip you are invited to participate in. *The most important preparation will take place in your heart.* The following steps to prepare your spirit for all God has for you on this trip will bless you before, during, and after the experience.

Reading Materials

In the Appendix, there is a Suggested Resources list of reading materials and videos. Our website has many resources available at DefiningMomentsbook. com/Resources. The books have been specially selected to help get you into the mindset of the stories that happened in the land you are visiting. What was the culture like? How can you relate these stories to your own life? What parts of Scripture will be most helpful for you to know? Are there any Bible studies that may get you prepared? The recommended resources for each trip will greatly enrich your experience.

Prayerful Mindset

It is important to begin asking God to prepare you for the trip several weeks before you leave. Ask Him to reveal anything to you that needs to be exposed and dealt with so you can enter this experience with a clean slate. Ask the Holy Spirit to do a mighty work. Ask to surrender to all that God has for you, because you do not want to miss a thing. If you are going with a mate or friends, pray together a few times before you go. If you are traveling with a group, pray together as a team at a few socials. You will find a Prayer Countdown schedule, *30 Days of Prepared Hearts,* in the section "Appendix: General," plus one modified for mission trips in its own section in this book that enables your group to pray for the same things on the same days, and includes specific Scriptures to pray over each day's subject.

Realistic Expectations

To paraphrase Rick Warren's famous opening line in *The Purpose Driven Life, this trip is not about you.* God will do amazing things in individuals as a result of transformational, faith-based travel, so *the trip is about Him and His purposes.* It is not about your comfort, your appetite, your likes and dislikes, your rest, your preferences, your shopping opportunities, or your own pace. It is about submitting and surrendering completely to the Holy Spirit, so that you can experience all that God has for you in this journey. Grace will be required, as you will be asked to get up when you are tired, eat things you are not familiar with, travel in cramped spaces and experience climates out of your comfort zone. If you want the comforts of home, stay home.

Be ready for new experiences of how things are done. Though many places will have people who understand English, there is a charm that comes with learning a few phrases in the native tongue that will melt hearts. Have small bills and change available for small needs, from purchasing bottled water to getting rid of bottled water. (Bathrooms are usually called W.C., for Water Closet, but have jokingly been referred to as With Cash since many require coins, and sometimes you even need to bring your own toilet paper.)

A Cloud of Witnesses

In some of the places you will be going, *you are the closest thing to a Bible most people will ever experience.* You are ambassadors of Christ and witnesses to the joy of walking with Jesus, no matter what circumstances you are in. Be kind, love the unlovable (especially if they are in your group!), and be humble. You have an opportunity to advance the Kingdom in every kindness you exchange with strangers, be they tour operators, airline ticket agents, bell boys, or bus boys. This is your platform on which to practice the fruits of the Spirit: love, joy, peace, patience, long-suffering, gentleness, goodness, faith, meekness, and temperance. Also, realize that this is a human society, not a utopia. In other words, no one on this trip is perfect, including yourself. Make allowances for each other, holding each other up in love.

Group Etiquette

The biggest blessing you can give the group is to *be on time*—always. Synchronize all watches with the leader's, and commit to being where you are expected to be at all times, whether it is reconvening after bathroom breaks, free time at museums, photo opportunities, or meals. If you are easily distracted during your free time, bring a watch with an alarm to remind you to get back to the group. Do not wander off, especially not to shop outside of free time because you will affect the group schedule. Your guides will give you plenty of time and advice on shopping. You will not miss a thing by following their recommendations.

Also, during lecture times and journaling periods, do not talk. You may not think that anyone can hear you, but they can, and you are disturbing their concentration to gratify your own needs. Act like you are in a movie theater (or not, depending on how you act in a movie theater).

Team Bonding

You are about to go through some very intimate experiences with your faith on this adventure. It is beneficial to get together with the people you are going with to start to get to know them *before* you travel. Get together once a month for fellowship and prayer. Share with each other your concerns and your expectations. Invite each other to discuss the reading materials that you have chosen to read, and what you are getting from them.

Additionally, the most important thing you can do to bring the hearts of the travelers together is to *meet every night after dinner during the trip,* in a place that enables a private conversation for your group, and include two components:

Affirmation Times

So many times, we hear about what other people are doing in their lives and feel admiration for them. Rarely do those thoughts make it to the spoken realm. During affirmation time, travelers are invited to tell the group about things they have learned specifically about other individuals in the group that they admired or were encouraged by. There is no order and every person does not have to participate.

For the leader, this time may feel awkward or uncomfortable as your group is embarking into unknown territory. What if no one gives an affirmation? What if there is nothing but silence? Give it time. The ball may start rolling slowly, but once it gets going, people jump on the affirmation band wagon who you did not even know were listening.

You are encouraged to be vigilant about scheduling and keeping this time together. While this may sound insignificant, the results in team building are astounding. You will encounter resistance to this committed time together, as there will be many times that travelers, and even leaders, are tired and would rather skip this nightly gathering. People are in an exciting city and want to go adventuring, or they want to take a nap due to jet lag. If it is at all possible, keep the commitment to this meeting. The investment is definitely worth the reward of the hearts of travelers drawing together. Many groups feel like family after doing this during a trip, and the unity that God made us to feel for each other is greatly enriched with this tool. Additionally, sharing insights brings others to their own insights and participants experience a "domino effect" while sharing their revelations for the day.

Sharing "Aha!" Moments

The other part of these nightly meetings is to share the things that truly touched your own heart with the rest of the group. Did God say something to you that touched you today? Was there a time and site where you discovered something wonderful about yourself or your relationship with God? What did you let go of at one of the sites that you had been carrying around awhile? Start with the questions "*What did you see?*" and "*What did you learn?*" Sharing these minor or major revelations with each other also results in a snowball effect. As each person hears what the other is discovering, they build it into their own experiences and the team's "Aha!" moments grow exponentially.

Again, unless you have experienced this dynamic, it may not seem like a big deal. However, once your team gets going on this task, the entire team goes deeper into what God has for them on the journey.

Staffing Your Faith Adventure

Select a Tour Guide Operator. This person and their company will coordinate your trip schedule, lodging, transportation, and most meals for your entire adventure. Additionally, they will provide a guide that accompanies you throughout the trip and gives your group the historically relevant information for each site. The guide may or may not share your beliefs. For example, in Israel most of the guides are Jewish, yet know the New Testament and worship songs better than many of the travelers. Good luck trying to convert them—likely every Christian tour group has also tried!

In Greece and Turkey, unless you select an agent that is part of a Christian ministry, it is likely the guide will know only about the *historical* facts and have little *Biblical* knowledge. Select an operator that has been personally recommended by someone that has used them. Depending on the country, the quality of operators varies, so conduct the necessary background research before you go.

Let your tour operator know well ahead of time that you will be conducting teaching times for up to an hour, depending on the teachings you choose from this book. Most tour groups get off and on the bus very quickly, some spending only fifteen minutes at each site. Let your operator know that you are going to fewer places and spending longer times at each place, and ask if there is a space that you can reserve to give your group a place to sit in comfort and shade while they listen to the teaching and write in their journals.

If you are conducting your trip on your own, please research or contact every historical site you plan to visit beforehand. Visiting hours, mandatory reservations, and holiday closures are constantly being revised. Let them know the exact date that you plan to visit and whether you are traveling in a large group. Many of these sites are happy to provide groups with knowledgeable guides, but only if they know that you are coming.

Select a Trip Teacher. This book will enable anyone from a pastor to a layperson to lead your group into transforming experiences through the teachings included in each section. You may be blessed with a pastor that will take this on, and completely customize the site lesson with his gift of teaching. Or you may have a volunteer trip leader that tenderly reads the lessons included verbatim. Either way, it is the Holy Spirit that is in charge of taking you deeper into the heart of God. Know that you will be well cared for. It is important that the teacher take the responsibility of incorporating all of the essential components of the transformational moments that are outlined for each site.

Select a Trip Coordinator. This person is responsible for taking care of all the details of the trip. They are the liaison with the travel agent and tour guides, the "go-to" person for questions on schedules and travel situations that come up. The trip coordinator needs to be flexible, calm, and gracious no matter what is going on around them.

Select a Team Shepherd. There will be many spiritual surprises revealed on your trip. Along with that comes a need to have someone to talk with to both share these revelations and to process them. Make sure your group selects a "Shepherd" for the journey. It can be a pastor, but it does not have to be. It should be a mature believer, gifted in shepherding people into the deeper places of their faith. It is suggested that this person be available in the hotel lobby in the evenings.

Select a team Worship Leader. Find someone in your group who is a gifted singer, or who will take responsibility for prerecording worship songs and bringing a CD player and printed lyrics. Worship will bring you into the heart of God in a way that allows deep intimacy while you are on this journey.

How to Use This Book at Site Visits

There is always a **Historical Significance** and **What To See** section for each site in the book. These sections give the relevant current and historical facts for the specific locations. Groups should read this ahead of time to familiarize themselves with the site before they hear their guide's teachings. There are also **Scripture** references (where applicable) that will show the group where each particular site is mentioned in the Bible. Where it is relevant, there is also a teaching section called "Defining Moment." In some sites, there are several teachings to choose from, depending on the needs of each particular group. They are labeled by subject category to help the leader discern the most appropriate teaching for their individual trip. This information should *not* be shared with the group ahead of time as they are meant to be experienced "in the moment" of the site visit. These teachings have the greatest effect when applied in the following manner:

Defining Moment:

These vignettes align the spiritual stories of the sites with the current-day experiences of the travelers and should be read out loud to the group. There are spiritually relevant questions in italics at the end of each teaching for the group to consider during their Journal Time. These questions will enable the group to leap from just learning about the site to actually interacting with what God has to reveal to them personally at each place. After the teaching is read, the group should have at least ten to fifteen minutes to go off in silence and reflect on the questions that were raised in light of their own lives. During this time, they should write down their thoughts and any ideas God is revealing to them. The leader should provide Journal Time for all travelers specifically for this purpose.

Share Time:

The group reconvenes and is invited to take another ten to fifteen minutes to share with each other what they learned about their own lives while reflecting on the specific questions for that site. Not everyone will have a chance to share every time. In every group, there will be dependable 'sharers' that enjoy consistently participating. There will also be quiet folks that need to be gently invited into the conversation. The more diverse and complete the sharing during this time, the richer the transformation that will occur for individuals.

Not every person will connect with every site. There will be someone at each site with a great "Aha!" moment, while others experiencing the same teaching will come away with little insight. Do not judge the site by what is seen. Do not be discouraged if the leader's expectations for sharing are not always met. The capacity for the Holy Spirit to transform according to the unique experience of each traveler is astounding, and much of the transformation comes *afterward,* while people are mulling over what they have heard from others. That is why a wide range of experiences and sites is necessary to fully serve the needs of the entire group.

It is also necessary to have consistency in the Journal Time and Share Time at each site. Even when the leader may feel uncomfortable with prolonged silences, or pressured to get the group back on schedule, keeping committed to these times will affect the transformational moments for the group in a greater way than anything else done on the entire trip. Making the deadline to get into a museum will probably not be remembered a decade later. Hearing God reveal a condition in a person's heart that He wants to bless will become part of a testimony that may live on for decades.

Do not be fooled into "keeping the schedule" if it means sacrificing the transformational moments that the Holy Spirit has for your group.

Prayer:
A group prayer is suggested for each teaching, and even more powerful Spirit-led group prayers are encouraged.

Worship Song Recommendations:
While there are relevant songs suggested for each teaching, you are strongly encouraged to put together your *own* song book that is familiar to *your* group. There is one traditional hymn and one contemporary worship song choice for each teaching, but your travelers will get far more out of the experience if they are able to worship with lyrics that are already familiar and meaningful to them. Your team worship leader will need to put a song book of lyrics together for either the suggested songs or those that you choose for your trip. This template is given as a menu for you to choose which "course" you would prefer to start and end with. Maybe your group wants to start with "dessert" and use Prayer and Worship first. Or, you may want to read the Scripture references before anything else. Please use the material in the order that serves you best. We trust that God will lead you in the order best for your group.

Travel Tips
Packing: Most tours allow for one piece of luggage and one carry-on bag. Less is always more when traveling internationally. Pack as lightly as possible, keeping most valuables at home. Weather can be highly changeable, especially in spring and summer, so be prepared for anything. Check the long-term forecast on the web before you go. Know that, in many holy places, women must cover their shoulders and legs, and even men cannot wear shorts. Bring a modesty wrap to prepare for those situations. There is a *Packing List* in the *Appendix* to help you plan.

Bring essential toiletries, medications, eyeglasses, and a change of clothes in your carry-on bag in case your checked luggage is lost. If you are getting new shoes for the trip, break them in beforehand with lots of walking. Remember sunglasses, a hat, and sunscreen. Consider packing moist towelettes for warm days.

Put your name, contact information, and destination addresses inside your bags, in case the luggage tags come off. If traveling with a companion, consider each putting some belongings into the other's suitcase in case one gets lost.

Luggage: Airlines are constantly revising their luggage allowances, so check with your carrier for specifics. There are inexpensive, fairly accurate hand-held luggage scales that consist of a strap and an electronic reader the size of a candy bar. They are small enough to take with you in case you plan to do a lot of shopping and do not want any surprises at the airport coming home.

Because your bags will be handled by bellmen most of the time, you will want to follow a few guidelines. Do not bring expensive luggage. You will be in very modest countries at times, and the temptation can be great for baggage handlers. Do not pack anything that you would miss if it were stolen. You will be separated from your luggage for long periods with many bus drivers, baggage handlers, and hotel bellmen having complete access. There is little recourse if you discover something missing.

Travel Safety: Airport security can be especially thorough overseas. When transferring through airports, such as Heathrow, you may have to go through security all over again, and it might be much more intense.

Pickpockets are waiting for you, so carry your passport, purse, and only the credit cards you plan to use, in a travel wallet that can be carried underneath your clothing.

Use discretion when taking photographs; if you are in doubt, ask permission beforehand. Some military will require you to hand over your camera if you have taken pictures that could compromise safety.

Currency: Find out if there are any meals and incidentals, such as bottled water, that are not covered by your tour and plan accordingly. Many countries welcome U.S. currency, but will give you change in their local currency, so bring plenty of small bills ($10, $5 and $1s). You can order the local currency in your hometown given a couple weeks' notice. You may be able to negotiate better bargains if you pay in the local currency. Use a currency calculator app to determine the amount you would like to bring.

Shopping: Where there are shopkeepers that want your business, some English is often spoken—which means almost everywhere! When bargaining for an item, do not appear too anxious. Be ready to walk away and have them follow you. Never accept the first price as the actual price. In many cases, you can buy the item for half of the asking price.

Telephone and Internet: Check with your tour operator before you go. Most hotels have Wi-Fi either free or for purchase. Even some tour buses offer Wi-Fi at no cost. Skype is very helpful overseas for keeping in touch with family. It is also great to call U.S. based toll-free numbers when you need help with travel changes or challenges. Call your wireless provider before you go to understand their overseas rates. Some carriers charge a minimal amount to receive and send texts. You can also get packages for data without getting cell phone coverage. It is worth spending time with them on the phone before you go to understand your particular options.

Electric Appliances: The electric current overseas is usually 220-volt and requires special adapter plugs that vary by country. Once you have the correct plug, you will most likely need a converter to run your 110-volt appliance. If you have very high voltage appliances, like hair irons, you will need a special converter that can handle the intense load. You can also buy dual voltage hair irons that only require an adapter plug. Walmart has good, inexpensive adapters and converters.

Eating: Much of the food will be new to you. Ask your tour guide if you need to use caution in eating fresh, uncooked vegetables and fruit. Consider bringing meal bars or dried fruits and nuts along to eat between mealtimes in case you are hungry.

Physical Exercise: You will be doing a lot of walking, so prepare your body (especially your feet) by taking lots of walks before your trip to condition your body.

Cultural Tips:
- Resist the temptation to be a reformer.
- Accept things are usually smaller than in the U.S.
- Driving is hectic, but life is slower.

- The standard of living is lower.
- People appreciate you learning and using even a few words in their language.
- Be friendly (as an ambassador of the U.S.) and Christ-like (as an ambassador of Heaven).
- Remember you are in a foreign land that is *their* home, so if you want the comforts of home, please stay home!

Now, you are ready to embark on your journey. Get ready for the time of your life!

CHAPTER TWO:

———

Israel, The Holy Land

"The Word became flesh and made His dwelling among us. We have seen His glory, the glory of the one and only Son, who came from the Father, full of grace and truth"
(John 1:14).

Introduction to Israel: The Holy Land
See **Appendix:** Israel: The Holy Land
- Major Archaeological Finds, New Testament
- Jesus' Teachings, in Biblical Order
- Jesus' Parables, in Biblical Order
- Jesus' Miracles, in Biblical Order
- Jesus' Disciples
- Resurrection Appearances
- Harmony of the Gospels by Region

- Jerusalem Occupiers: Old Testament and New Testament
- Suggested Resources: The Holy Land
- Map: First Century Israel
- Map: Modern Israel Today
- Map: Ancient Jerusalem

The ancient land of Israel is a testimony, evidence of the greatness God did there, a testimony of truth. As each layer of the many archaeological tells are peeled away, more of these people and their culture are revealed to us and more of the Bible is confirmed for us.

The majority of Jesus' three-year ministry was spent in the triangle of Chorazin, Capernaum, and Bethsaida, on the northern shore of the Sea of Galilee. He likely never traveled more than 100 total miles from Jerusalem during His lifetime, yet He has over two billion followers two millennia later!

The Crusades were a series of military expeditions which established and maintained a European Christian presence in the Holy Land from 1099–1291. The First Crusade captured Jerusalem on July 15, 1099. The Second Crusade in 1147 brought in reinforcements to continue to control this territory. The Third Crusade lasted from 1189–1192.

The Ottomans, Turks, and other Muslims controlled the small, neglected land of Israel from the 1500s until the end of World War I. Jerusalem's present Old City walls were built by Suleman the Great in 1538.

In World War I, the Allies wanted Jewish financing (e.g., Rothschilds) *and* Arab desert fighter support, so they promised Jews a homeland and promised Arab king Abdulla concessions. (For more, read "Lawrence of Arabia" and "The Source.") General Allenby, in defeating the Ottoman empire, captured Jerusalem without a battle. The 1917 Balfour Declaration was intended to establish a national homeland for Israel and to recognize Palestinian's historical connection to the area. The result, the British Mandate for Palestine, actually created no clear resolution.

In World War II, the Jews sided again with the Allies due to their fear of Hitler and, ironically, to learn warfare tactics they would later use against the British who trained them. After the war ended, the British pulled out on

September 1, 1947, and the United Nations partitioned the land into Jewish and Arabic states, including a "No Man's Land" in the international city of Jerusalem. The Jews concurred, the Arabs did not, leaving the Jerusalem Jews under siege. On May 14, 1948, after the War of Independence, David Ben Gurion (namesake of the airport), proclaimed the independent State of Israel, named Jerusalem as the capital, and placed Arabs in refugee camps, a move which led to the launching of the P.L.O. (Palestine Liberation Organization).

Jerusalem remained a divided city from 1948–1967, with Israel controlling the west, Jordan the north and south, and a border through the middle. Israel developed the west far more than the Arabs did their territory, but Jewish hearts were with the eastern Old City. When attacked in the 1967 Six-Day War, Israel reunited the city and gave free access to the holy places to all religions for the first time. The holy places remain open to all peoples today.

Israel—with five million people, approximately twenty percent of whom are Arabs—could fit into California sixteen times over. Jerusalem has over 900,000 residents as of 2017—sixty percent Jews, thirty-eight percent Muslims, and just two percent Christians and others.

BETHANY

Historical Significance:

Bethany was a safe place for Jesus, only two miles southeast from the plotters in Jerusalem, but where He was always welcomed by Lazarus, Mary, and Martha. It sits on the eastern slope of the Mount of Olives surrounded by the hills of the Judean desert. Today, it is a small Muslim village by the Arabic name al-Eizariya, (Lazarium, or Place of Lazarus), preserving its connection to Jesus raising Lazarus from the dead here. It was the final station on the road from Jericho to Jerusalem.

Mary sat at Jesus' feet while her elder sister Martha served food and drink. Mary humbly and lavishly expressed her deep devotion for Him and anointed His head and feet with a pint of expensive perfume (worth a year's wages) from an alabaster jar at Simon the Leper's home, unwittingly preparing Him for burial, and outraging Judas Iscariot.

Jesus cursed the fig tree for bearing no fruit, though full of early leaves, in this place. It was nearby that His disciples got an unbroken colt, the foal of a donkey, for His Palm Sunday entrance, and was also where He ascended to Heaven.

In John 11, Jesus delayed two days before returning to heal His friend Lazarus—knowing Lazarus was already dead—testing Mary and Martha's faith until He called Lazarus out of the tomb after four days. He spoke Lazarus back to life just as God spoke Creation into life. This miracle again infuriated the Pharisees and the Sadducees (chief priests) in Jerusalem, who now also plotted to kill Lazarus.

It is likely Jesus spent each night of Passion Week through Thursday in Bethany, at the home of His dear friends Mary, Martha, and Lazarus.

What to See:

Near **Lazarus's tomb**, required by Jewish custom to be located outside the city walls, there is a Franciscan church and a minaret. Just uphill sits a **Greek**

Orthodox church. You walk down twenty-four narrow stone steps into the antechamber where the shortest verse in the Bible tells us *"Jesus wept"* (John 11:35) and into the tomb itself, six and a half feet squared (approximately the size of Christ's tomb).

Scripture:
    Mathew 21:17, 26:6–13
    Mark 11:1, 11–14, 19, 14:3–9, 16:19
    Luke 10:38–42; 19:29, 24:50–51
    John 11:1–47, 12:1–11
    definingmomentsbook.com/resources

Defining Moment . . . Lazarus's Tomb

> *"Meanwhile a large crowd of Jews found out that Jesus was there and came, not only because of Him but also to see Lazarus, whom He had raised from the dead. So, the chief priests made plans to kill Lazarus as well, for on account of him many of the Jews were going over to Jesus and believing in Him"*
>
> (John 12:9–11).

What was it like to be Lazarus? You are friends with Jesus, He hangs out at your house, you get sick and die, you are hanging out in Heaven for a couple of days, you get put back into your earthly body, people flock to your town to see you because you have been resurrected, and then the local religious leaders decide they are going to kill you. It is such an unbelievable plot that a movie could not pull it off, yet it really happened. God's plots are much more interesting than man could ever create.

Maybe the question that begs to be asked is, "What was it like to be the chief priests?" You see the power of God happen in your own domain—a man is raised from the dead. Instead of dropping to your knees with awe, you decide to have that man killed so people will not leave your religious institution and start believing in Jesus. That was just a precursor to where they were really headed—killing Jesus to stop the mass exodus of people leaving to believe in Him.

It is easy to look at these men with horror and judge their despicable plans. How dared they think that they can squash God's Glory by killing the resurrected Lazarus? Did they even understand that they were contending with God Himself by doing this?

But what about the ways that *we* have attempted to squash God's Glory by planning to exterminate something that *He* has done? It seems impossible that anyone does that today, but think about how these examples shadow the same squashing of God's Glory:

When God heals someone miraculously, but we attribute the healing to medicine.

When God saves a person in an accident, but we credit "luck."

When God gives a person divine revelation, but we tell the person that God does not speak to people in this day and age.

Here is a real-life example: Shannon was facing the second divorce in her life. She did not know God well, but she knew He hated divorce. She asked Him for a black-and-white answer whether or not she should divorce. Within thirty-six hours, He had sent her a new job to move to, back in her home state, a new home to live in, and an unexpected poem mailed by a distant acquaintance that talked about leaving a relationship with grace . . . in black and white. This was the beginning of the most profound faith experience that Shannon could ever imagine. She went on to experience a deep, true, intimate relationship with Jesus where He keeps showing up in amazing ways.

A couple of years later, she was in a conversation with a pastor in her church about how God shows up. When she shared her testimony, he told her that those things were unconnected coincidences, and that cults were started by people thinking they heard God. He told her that it was not God showing up, and that He does not do that today.

Other examples occur in seminaries across America where future pastors are taught that miraculous healings only occurred in Jesus' time and are not something that God does today.

As God watches lost people attempt to squash His Glory, what is He feeling? Contempt? Rage? Or is it pity and compassion? Is there a way to lovingly uncover those parts of our hearts that are so focused on our *own* mistaken ideas of who God is so we can celebrate who He *really* is? Is there a way to be the voice of truth to ourselves and others when we mistakenly squash God's Glory because of our own agendas?

Journal Time:

Have you experienced God's Glory being squashed? How did you feel? How did you react?

Share Time:

Talk about the ways that you have witnessed God's Glory. How can we love others into the place of *celebrating* His Glory instead of *denying* it?

Prayer:

Lord,

How glorious You are. We are so grateful for Your Glory and that it is not our actions that can stop Your Glory—it is so much bigger than we could ever imagine. Please, Lord, help us to revere and celebrate Your Glory. We want to stand in awe of it. Please, Holy Spirit, show us when we are squashing God's Glory in any way. Please give us the words and attitude into loving the people around us into a place of experiencing Your Glory for all that it is. We adore you.

In Jesus' name,

Amen

Worship:

"To God Be the Glory"

"Let the Glory of the Lord Rise Among Us"

BETHLEHEM

Historical Significance:

Bethlehem in Judea, town of David, meaning "house of bread," formerly known as Ephrath (or Ephrathah), is a small village five miles south of Jerusalem off the Hebron road in the hill country of Judah. The lambs for Temple sacrifices were born and raised here.

Rachel the Matriarch, wife of Jacob and mother of Joseph and Benjamin, wept for her children on the outskirts, where her tomb is found.

Ruth and Boaz's courtship happened here during the wheat and barley harvests, after Ruth followed her mother-in-law, Naomi, here.

David was born here and later anointed king of Israel by Samuel, called to shepherd the nation instead of his father's flocks. He later longed for water from the well near the gate of Bethlehem. Three men then risked their lives to break through Philistine lines to get the water for their king, but David refused to drink it because of the risk they had taken (2 Samuel 23:15). David's grandson, Rehoboam (928–911 BC), fortified Bethlehem.

God used the pagan emperor, Caesar Augustus, to fulfill Micah 5:2, when he decreed a census that required natives Joseph and Mary to travel to Bethlehem to be registered. The prophet Micah foretold around 800 BC that the Messiah would come from Bethlehem. They only moved to Nazareth due to the insecurity generated by the Herodian dynasty (Matthew 2).

Such an ordinary place for such an extraordinary event. Jesus was born here and laid in a stone (not wood) manger, a feeding trough for animals; a practice still used by shepherds today. In the nearby fields, the lowly shepherds were selected as the first to be told of His birth and to see Him in a cave like they might sleep in. They were descendants of the priestly tribe of Levi and were tending the holy, sacrificial sheep that needed to be perfect, though the shepherds themselves were too lowly to be allowed in the Temple courts. Remember that king David was originally a shepherd. When you realize how close Jerusalem is to Bethlehem, you have to wonder, since they would have seen the *same* star, why *no one* came from Jerusalem to meet the Messiah?

Bethlehem is where God chose to be one of us, because He wanted us to be His so badly. He did not stay distant. What does it mean to *you* that He came to be like you, to be with you, to love you forever?

The wise men later lavished gifts on Him in His house, not that night at the manger. King Herod the Great of Judea, threatened by a potential king by *right* as opposed to him being king by *might*, ordered all boys two years old and under in Bethlehem be killed, but Joseph had already taken his family to Egypt. Herod *also* murdered his wife, three sons, mother-in-law, brother-in-law, and uncle.

What to See:

Today controlled by Arabs, Bethlehem is sometimes too dangerous to enter, and people prefer to instead stop at one of two enclosed **shepherd's fields** (one Greek Orthodox, one Roman Catholic), from which you can see the town's light-colored houses and towers terraced over two hills. As we sat in one field hearing our pastor say, "and the shepherds were tending their flock," a young boy and his sister "coincidentally" walked just below us with their sheep, and the pastor lost us, as we all jumped up to snap pictures. As we know, "Coincidences are God's way of remaining anonymous." The boy would throw pebbles at the sheep to get them to come back to his safety, just like Jesus invites us back to His safety. Just like the shepherds praised Jesus' arrival in the fields nearby, we can praise Him in song here.

Rachel's tomb is to the right of the road into Bethlehem from the north.

Take Manger Street to the left at the fork and detour around the town center east to the large square in front of **The Church (Grotto) of the Nativity,** with its ancient, fortress-like walls. In 325 AD, emperor Constantine built a beautiful basilica above the grotto that is the world's oldest church. It is still preserved and used, and is one of the largest churches in the Middle East. The large portal was bricked up, so one could not enter on horseback, so we humbly bend over to enter it today. The grotto (cave) is beneath the altar. Fifteen lamps burn constantly, maintained by Greek

Orthodox, Armenian Orthodox, and Roman Catholic priests. A star marks the traditional spot where Jesus is believed to have been born.

Next to the Church of the Nativity is the mid-twentieth century **Statue of St. Jerome** (aka Hieronymus, or Geronimus in Latin) at the **Church of St. Catherine of Alexandria**, built over the ruins of a Crusader church in 1882. Jerome was the second most voluminous writer in ancient Latin Christianity, after St. Augustine. He studied Hebrew with Jewish converts, and took the unusual position that the Hebrew version, not the Greek Septuagint, was the inspired test of the Old Testament. He translated the Vulgate (the authoritative version for Catholics until the twentieth century) over thirty years in a cave below the Church of the Nativity. He was later judged severely by Luther for his strict asceticism. He died near Bethlehem in 420 AD.

Also: remnants of two aqueducts which brought water from Solomon's pools to Jerusalem.

The **Herodium**: possibly Herod's tomb, has been found near Bethlehem.

No matter what day of the year you are here, say, "Merry Christmas" to someone!

Scripture:
Genesis 35:16–20
Judges 17:7–13
1 Samuel 6:1–13
2 Samuel 23:14–17
Micah 5:2
Matthew 2:1–18
Luke 2:1–22
definingmomentsbook.com/resources

Defining Moment . . . The Church (Grotto) of the Nativity or The Shepherd Fields Outside of Bethlehem

What was it like to be Mary? The God of the universe sends an angel to tell you that the Savior of the world is going to be born through you. Imagine the expectations she must have had. Put yourself in her place. What would you have imagined? Her expectations could have been huge. Did she think that, along with this amazing favor from God, she would have every need met? What was it like for Mary to end up in a cave with animals and all that comes along with them? Was she scared? Was she uncomfortable? Was she disappointed? What emotions were swirling around her while the most amazing event in history was happening through her?

The Bible does not tell us much about Mary's emotions, but what it does tell us speaks volumes. Listen to the last verse in this passage:

And there were shepherds living out in the fields nearby, keeping watch over their flocks at night. An angel of the Lord appeared to them, and the glory of the Lord shone around them, and they were terrified. But the angel said to them, "Do not be afraid. I bring you good news that will cause great joy for all the people. Today in the town of David a Savior has been born to you; He is the Messiah, the Lord. This will be a sign to you: You will find a Baby wrapped in cloths and lying in a manger."

Suddenly a great company of the Heavenly host appeared with the angel, praising God and saying, "Glory to God in the highest Heaven, and on earth peace to those on whom His favor rests."

When the angels had left them and gone into Heaven, the shepherds said to one another, "Let's go to Bethlehem and see this thing that has happened, which the Lord has told us about."

So they hurried off and found Mary and Joseph, and the Baby, who was lying in the manger. When they had seen Him, they spread the word concerning what had been told them about this Child, and all who heard it were amazed at what the shepherds said to them. ***But Mary treasured up all these things and pondered them in her heart***
(Luke 2:8–19).

The word *but* is what makes this verse about Mary's reactions even more interesting. People around her were *amazed*, and the word *but* seemingly excludes Mary from amazement . . . she was *treasuring* instead. Imagine being a teenager set on a donkey at nine months of pregnancy, being far away from your mom and sisters while giving birth for the first time and still living in a place of "treasuring."

Many times, in our walk with God, there are expectations that come along with what God calls us to. How do we stay in a place of "treasuring" what *God* has called us to when it is the complete opposite of *our* expectations? For example, a young woman, Clair, saw Zach and heard a whisper in her heart from God that this man would one day be her husband. A woman in their church that did not even know either of them had seen them together in a vision as husband and wife, long before they started dating. There were many other confirmations that God had chosen them for each other. They began dating, married a year later, and eventually pastored a large church. The path was rosy, until their marriage began to crumble under the strain of ministry. Clair began to question if God was calling them to be married. This was not the favored path she expected.

So, what do we do as Christ followers when we know God has called us into an amazing adventure, but it is not going as *we* expected?

We hopefully do what Mary did: we *treasure*. We look with jaw-dropping wonder at what God is doing that is amazing, we allow our hearts to be filled with awe, and we *ponder* that, just like Mary did. It does not say that she pondered the cold night, the stinky animals, or the long journey. She did not go into denial and play Pollyanna. She treasured where God was showing up.

Journal Time:

What is happening in *your* life right now that looks different than you expected it would? Are there any ways that you are disappointed in the lot that God has given you in this situation? How have you handled it? Are there times your heart has reacted like Mary's and you were able to stay in a place of "treasuring" despite the unmet expectations you had?

Share Time:

Share with one another your stories of both victories and defeats as you moved forward in a situation where your expectations were far different than what God allowed. (Trip Shepherd's note: If there are fellow travelers that need to process through a difficult situation that comes up during this time, make sure you circle back with them.)

Prayer:

Father God,

Thank you for the heroes in the Bible that model for us those ways of relating to You that are so blessing. Thank You for Mary, who shows us how to treasure You even when things looked far different than she might have imagined. We cannot imagine how You were training her up for a lifetime of experiences that differed from what she imagined, culminating in the Cross. Please give each of us strength and faith, as You did Mary, to keep our eyes on You and the bigger picture of what You are doing instead of insisting things go the way that we expect. Give us humility. Remind us of the ways that we have been angry with You over dashed expectations, and give us the gift of repentance and the sweet fragrance of being in awe of You and Your work in us, and trusting You above our expectations. We love You and adore You.

In the name of Jesus,

Amen

Worship:

"Away in a Manger"

"Joy to the World"

"Angels We Have Heard on High"

"O Come Let Us Adore Him" (or any Christmas carol)

BETHSAIDA

Historical Significance:

Bethsaida, meaning "house of fishing," was a small hillside town central to Jesus' ministry, east of the Jordan River, and just north of the Sea of Galilee. The fishermen brothers, Simon Peter and Andrew, were from here, along with Philip, with their partners James and John from nearby Tabgha. As Bethsaida was a mile from the Sea of Galilee, the brothers later moved to Capernaum, which is located right on the lake.

Jesus healed a blind man in His second laying on of hands just outside the city. He later rebuked it (along with nearby Chorazin and Capernaum on the shore, all within three miles of each other) for not repenting despite their witness of more miracles than any other area—the feeding of 5,000 men late in the afternoon near Bethsaida (the only miracle in all four Gospels) and ten miracles in Capernaum! (See *Appendix—Jesus' Miracles in Biblical Order.)*

Philip the tetrarch rebuilt Bethsaida, renaming it Julias after Caesar Augustus's daughter, Julia.

What to See:

Little exists today of Bethsaida (only recently discovered), Chorazin, or Capernaum. Today Bethsaida is oddly over a mile from the Jordan River and even farther from the Sea of Galilee.

Scripture:

    Matthew 11:20–24, 14:13–21

    Mark 6:30–44, 8:22–26

    Luke 9:10–17

    John 6:1–15, 12:21–22

    definingmomentsbook.com/resources

CAESAREA BY THE SEA (CAESAREA MARITIMA)

Historical Significance:

Not to be confused with inland Caesarea Philippi, also named after Caesar Augustus, Caesarea by the Sea (Caesarea Maritima) was, for over five centuries, the Gentile and governmental home of the Roman procurators over Samaria and Judea—including Pontius Pilate during Jesus' time (26–36 AD), and Felix and Festus during Paul's time (52–60 AD). Founded in the early third century BC, it was made important in 22 BC by Herod the Great, who reigned from 36 BC–4 AD. He loved to defy nature through building magnificent spaces such as Masada and the Temple Mount, including building in this place a palace extending out into the Mediterranean.

An aqueduct carried water nine miles to here from the base of Mount Carmel, and sewers were flushed out by the sea. It was a large, sophisticated, and magnificent city, known for the splendor of its buildings and great harbor (rivaling Alexandria's, larger than Rome's and Athens's) near the Via Maris (Way of the Sea trading route). Intended to be the most Roman (Gentile) city in Israel, it was the Roman capital of Israel until the third century AD. Jesus was born under this Herod (ironically a half-Jew), who then killed all the male babies in Bethlehem. Jesus died under another Herod: Herod Agrippa, the grandson of Herod the Great.

The port was designed to bring Roman culture *to* Judea. With God's sense of humor, Christian culture was brought to Rome *from* Judea! Years later, starting with Paul sailing away on missionary journeys from Judea, and later to Rome to his imprisonment and death, Christianity spread from the Jewish people to Gentile peoples. God had allowed Herod to be a tool for creating a seaport to spread the Gospel. What Herod thought was to *his* (short-term) glory was actually to *God's* (eternal) Glory. The city and seaport are gone, but Christianity is not.

The married apostle Philip the Evangelist, one of the seven deacons of the Jerusalem church, was the first to preach here and moved here for over twenty years along with his four unmarried daughters who had the gift of prophecy. Paul stayed with them at the end of the third missionary journey before heading sixty miles southeast (two days) to Jerusalem and being arrested according to the Lord's will.

After Cornelius's and Peter's visions, Simon Peter came from Joppa to Cornelius's home and preached the Gospel from the account of John's baptism through Jesus' Resurrection. Cornelius was a God-fearing Gentile; the first Gentile convert, a centurion in the Italian Regiment. Cornelius and all his companions received the gift of the Holy Spirit and were baptized with water. Peter initially felt that he should refuse to stay at Cornelius's home, since it was against Jewish law to visit or eat with a Gentile, but then the Holy Spirit showed him that God does not show favoritism. Later, Peter was criticized by the Judaizers, and stopped fellowshipping with Gentiles, and was then rebuked for this by Paul.

These people did not need Peter to come to Cornelius's home, for they already had Philip. Peter needed to come here to learn something he could not learn anywhere else: *Israel* does not need you; *you* need Israel to learn something you could not learn anywhere else. God took Peter out of his comfort zone to teach him that all people matter. He then entered a Gentile's home, ate with them, ate non-Kosher food as in his vision, baptized Gentiles and stood up to criticism from his fellow Jews! This is similar to how Elijah, prior to confrontation with the pagan prophets of Baal on Mount Carmel (I Kings 18:16–19:12), first experienced God's power, provision, faith, and fear. How has God prepared *you* for what He had in store for you?

Paul visited here three times, the last when he was imprisoned for two years at the palace of the procurator Antonius Felix after the Zealots and chief priests plotted Paul's death in Jerusalem.

The high priest Ananias, and his lawyer, Tertullus, came five days later to Caesarea, the Roman headquarters of Samaria and Judea, to convince the governor, Antonius Felix, to kill Paul. They accused him of being a Nazarite sect leader and of desecrating the Temple. Felix was so incompetent that Nero withdrew his role two years later. Felix's second wife, Drusilla of Judea—both had divorced prior spouses after their affair began—was the daughter of Herod Agrippa I, who was eaten by worms and died.

Felix was torn between needing, by law, to acknowledge the rights due to Paul as a Roman citizen, and wanting the approval of the large Jewish community. Felix kept meeting with Paul for two years, hoping for a bribe. His replacement, Festus, wanted to release Paul, but had no choice but to send him to Rome due to Paul's appeal to Caesar. First, king Herod Agrippa II who was allied with the Sadducees, who ruled over the territory northeast of the Sea of Galilee, was consulted while visiting with his sister, Bernice (later the mistress of emperor Titus). He also concluded that Paul would have been set free had he not appealed to Caesar. (Herod and Bernice's father, Agrippa I, had fallen deathly ill in the theater at Caesarea by the Sea after beheading James and imprisoning Peter.)

In 66 AD, a slaughter led to riots that began the Jewish Revolt. During this Revolt, Roman soldiers destroyed the Temple in 70 AD and massacred the remnants of the Jewish people at Masada in 73 AD. The soldiers entered the land through the port of Caesarea by the Sea. Ironically, they destroyed Jerusalem as a symbol of Judaism and yet, today Jerusalem stands, and Caesarea lies in ruins. You can walk along the beach and the ruins and see millions of small to large stones, representing the broken pieces of Herod's dream. He lived only for himself and his glory. Who are *you* living for? Will people later pick up broken pieces of *your* dreams?

The Third Jewish Revolt, or Bar Kokhba Revolt, began here and lasted from 136–132 BC. It was led by Simon bar Kokhba, who proclaimed himself the Messiah. He led 400,000 fighters, and declared a State of Israel for two years before the Romans killed 580,000 Jews and razed 50 towns and nearly 1,000 villages. It is likely the Romans killed a greater percentage of Jews than even Hitler did. The Arabs came to Caesarea by the Sea in 639, Crusaders arrived in 1099; the Arabs returned in 1187 followed by more Crusaders in 1228.

It is now a booming resort town, about thirty miles north of Joppa (Japha today), near Tel Aviv.

What to See:
As you drive north here from Tel Aviv or Joppa through the Sharon Valley and Plain, you will notice climate and vegetation similar to southern California,

with vineyards, eucalyptus (from Australia), pecans, pines, oranges and palms.

Excavated and reconstructed remains of the harbor, raised aqueducts (built by the 10th Roman legion's slaves in 25 BC), city fortifications, a bathhouse, a mammoth fortified gate, a hippodrome, large statues, an ancient synagogue with mosaic floors, the foundations of Herod's palace, and the partially restored, oldest Roman amphitheater. Voices from the stage would be carried by the winds from the Mediterranean to the back row of the 4,000 seats it contained. The reconstructed framework is visible, and to the north, the remains of the entry and another theater can be seen. Today's beautiful view of the Mediterranean Sea from the theater would have been blocked in Christ's time by the backstage area. A block of limestone with an inscription naming Pontius Pilate as the governor of Judea, the first physical evidence of his existence, was unearthed here in 1961.

Scripture:
    Acts 8:40, 9:30, 10:1–11:18, 12:19–23; 18:22, 21:8–16, 23:22–35, 24:1–17, 25:1–26:32, 27:1
    definingmomentsbook.com/resources

Defining Moment . . . Caesarea by the Sea Amphitheater
Have *you* ever been falsely accused? Have you ever had a close friend or family member say something about you that was not true, but held on to their story for reasons that did not even make sense?

Think about what Paul must have been feeling above. He is out there preaching, converting, and bringing the Holy Spirit to thousands, then, in the midst of doing God's work, he is imprisoned. Many come before the court over the several years of his imprisonment and wrongfully accuse him. No one can back up their stories. On top of it all, he is being kept in prison because the guy in charge thinks he can get a bribe out of him.

You are most likely visiting the ruins of the theater in Caesarea by the Sea. As you explore its nooks and crannies, take a look at the small stone cells that are underneath the theater. Paul could have been imprisoned in a cell that looked much like the one you are seeing. Not only was he falsely accused, but he was probably very uncomfortable for the two years he was imprisoned here.

What did Paul do? He was unwavering in his truth, not succumbing to the lies that were being told about him. He kept repeating the truths about himself, even after being called insane (Acts 26). We might read this and reply, "Of course, he refuted those lies. They were lies!" But how often do we hear lies and start to believe them? Even those we love may make accusations against us based on past wounds in their own hearts that have nothing to do with us—until we start agreeing with them.

Sheila had been a strong, successful career woman at the top of her game. She was fearless in negotiations with multi-million-dollar companies. She married a man that seemed too good to be true and found out that he was. Only weeks into the marriage, allegations came her way accusing her of being incompetent, unreasonable, and worthless. The accusations fell on deaf ears at first, but after a couple of years, Sheila started to believe them. Her identity was affected to the point that she was unable to do her job and serve her ministries well. She started to believe the lies.

Know that Satan has no power over us *until* we start to agree with him. Eve was not in any trouble as she listened to Satan tell her the lie that if she ate the fruit of the tree of knowledge she would be like God, knowing good and evil. Her trouble (and ours!) only began when she *believed* the lie and acted accordingly.

Paul was so strongly rooted in his identity in Christ that nothing, not even lies from the rulers of the land, shook his understanding of who God made him to be and what he believed about God and about himself. How do we follow Paul's example?

Journal Time:
What lies have you believed about yourself that need to be refuted? Are you willing to renounce them? Just as Paul refuted his lies, he replaced them with truth. For every lie you list, list a corresponding truth.

Share Time:
Pair off and read your entire lists to each other.

Say, "The lie is that _____, but the truth is that
_____." Do this over *every* lie. After everyone is finished, share
your experiences with the group. What did it feel like to call the lie out in
front of a witness and replace it with the truth?

Prayer:

Father God,

*We are so grateful that You are Truth for us. Thank You for revealing those
lies that are not from You. Thank You, even more, for revealing the truth which
is from You. Lord, we renounce as a group any agreements we have made with
these lies. Please separate them from us as far away is the east is from the west.
Please keep whispering Your truths over us, not so much so we can feel better
about ourselves, but so that we can live out the true identity that You have given
us and irresistibly invite others to enjoy the same freedom in Your Kingdom. We
adore You!*

We pray this under the Blood and in the Name of Jesus,
Amen

Worship:

"Voice of Truth" by Casting Crowns
"O God of Truth"

CAESAREA PHILIPPI/BANIAS AKA BARNVAS

Historical Significance:

The northwestern part of Israel in the Old Testament was the center of Baal worship and later, worship of Greek fertility gods. It was nearby in Dan where Israel's then-king Jeroboam built the high place and the golden calf when the two tribes split that angered God. Pagans believed its cave was the entrance to the underworld, the gates of hell, where fertility gods lived during winters. Caesarea Philippi was originally called Caesarea Paneas, in tribute to the Greek cultic god Pan whose shrine was there and who inspired immoral activities to invite their god back each year, only twenty-five miles from Galilee's religious communities.

Not to be confused with Caesarea by the Sea, also named after Caesar, emperor Augustus gave the city to Herod the Great in 20 BC, who passed it along to one of his sons, along with Antipas and Archelaus. Philip the Tetrarch (not a king), then honored Roman emperor Tiberius Caesar (and himself) in the naming of his capital after he rebuilt it in 2 BC, and stationed a Roman legion here, north of the Sea of Galilee, near the foot of Mount Hermon. The Banias River was one of the three headwaters of the Jordan River: since life comes from God, lots of water must be where the gods live, particularly Baal, so they located such pagan worship centers near water sources, and worship continued toward Greek gods.

This is the farthest north Jesus ventured in His public ministry. It was here that Jesus, a year and a half into His ministry, brought the disciples on their first mission trip, to basically a red-light district, and then asked them: "Who do the people say the Son of Man is?" *The most important man in history asked the most important question in history!* Notice He does not declare it, He invites us in. Who do *you* say He is?

Peter first replied, "You are the Christ, the Son of the living God."

Jesus then promised Peter, "On this rock I will build My church, and the gates of hell will not overcome it." Catholics say the rock is Peter, the first pope; Protestants say the rock is Peter's confession. Jesus was also, confrontationally, declaring that His church would replace these pagan fertility gods.

Clearly Jesus wanted more than a retreat with them before going from there to Jerusalem to die: He wanted them to take on the power of the devil in the very world they lived in, to storm the gates of hell. His church would not just defend against Satan (aka Beelzebub), who wintered in Hades, but would attack hell, and not hide in our Christian churches, fellowship, and schools. Where in *your* life are the gates of hell found? When it comes to the battle against evil today, are *you* on the offense or on the defense? Do *you* accept sin that ruins people's lives or confront it? Are *you* politically correct or do you proclaim truth without shame of your Lord? Sixty million Evangelicals in the U.S. should be making a difference in our culture!

The boy with seizures (and his believing father) was healed from the demon by Jesus after the disciples lacked the prayer and faith to first heal him. This was after the Transfiguration just northeast of Caesarea Philippi on Mt. Hermon.

What to See:
The Grotto of Pan was popular for worship due to the abundant springs flowing into the Jordan River. There in the Grotto of Pan was a rocky cliff whose carved niches formerly housed statues and idols of immoral fertility gods. Extensive, ongoing archaeological excavations have uncovered remnants of a palace, a synagogue, and a bath house.

Scripture:
Matthew 16:13–20, 17:14–21
Mark 8:27–30, 9:14–29
Luke 9:37–43
definingmomentsbook.com/resources

CANA

Historical Significance:

Cana of Galilee is the site of Jesus' first miracle, somewhere in the hill country west of the Sea of Galilee, at the wedding feast He attended with His mother, Mary. He came out of thirty years of obscurity in mocked Nazareth to speak the transformation of six stone jars of the sort used for ceremonial cleansing, by turning the added water into about 150 gallons of very fine wine, the highest quality usually served at the *beginning* of a feast, not toward the *end*. We know He loves a good celebration, and that He was sent to prepare the eternal feast of joy in Heaven.

Jesus also healed the royal official's son in Capernaum—all the way from Cana. The official and his family believed.

The disciple Bartholomew (or Nathaniel) lived here.

What to See:

There are two sites that commemorate this miracle. **Kfar Cana** is the more popular, en route from Haifa to Tiberias. The Franciscans maintain a Roman Catholic parish church (Cana's Wedding Church) built in 1880 on peaceful grounds surrounded by groves of pomegranates and olives. There is a replica of a Jewish water jar from that era.

Chirbet Cana is six miles from Kfar Cana, north of Nazareth, consisting only of ruins on a hill and an ancient cistern.

Scripture:

John 2:1–11, 4:46–54, 21:2
definingmomentsbook.com/resources

Defining Moment . . . Kfar Cana

Collaboration with the God of the universe is fascinating. In the midst of His power and might, He could do anything He wants with a wave of His hand, but instead He invites us to interact with Him.

In 1 Kings 22:20–22, God has a job that He wants taken care of on earth, and it has to do with yet another battle against Israel. He calls a meeting of the Heavenly hosts and asks them what they think should be done. Several ideas are given, but one angel makes a suggestion to send a lying spirit to do the job. God agrees and tells the angel to carry out that plan, and the battle is won.

But why did God hold a meeting with angels when a move of His right hand could have made the battle go the way he wanted? He builds relationship through collaboration.

Another curious collaborative conversation occurs between Mary and Jesus in Cana:

> On the third day, a wedding took place at Cana in Galilee. Jesus' mother was there, and Jesus and His disciples had also been invited to the wedding. When the wine was gone, Jesus' mother said to Him, "They have no more wine."
>
> "Woman, why do you involve Me?" Jesus replied. "My hour has not yet come."
>
> His mother said to the servants, "Do whatever He tells you"
> (John 2:1–5).

When Mary asks Jesus to fix the problem, He replies that His hour has not yet come. This implies that Mary indeed knew that there was an hour coming, and she knew it was not yet, but she asked anyway. Jesus basically says no. Mary, totally ignoring Jesus, said to the servants, "Do whatever He tells you."

At some level, this feels like disobedience on Mary's part. The God of the universe basically tells her that it is not time for Him to help out in the way she is asking. But when Mary keeps pushing, Jesus gives in like a good son, and turns water into wine.

What does this interaction say to us about asking God to move on a situation? Jesus was God, so He must have known in advance how this would all unfold. Why did He include this story in the Bible? What is He revealing to us in this story?

Journal Time:

Is there a situation in your life that you would like to collaborate with God on? Sit with an open heart and mind and ask Him what your part is and what His part is. How can you collaborate with an end to His Glory on this opportunity in your life?

Share Time:

Share with each other about what God is putting on your heart that He wants to collaborate on with you. What is He asking you?

Prayer:

Lord,

You amaze us. That You have a desire to collaborate with us seems too rich for words. Thank You for being so interested in building relationships with us and using collaboration to do that. Lord, we want to learn to collaborate with You. We want to hear Your whispers inviting us into confronting the battles in our lives that You see. Lord, please help us to know the difference between our part and Your part. Please keep us from over-stepping our bounds in handling those things that only You can handle, but also keep us from not showing up to do our part. Show us Your ways, O One!

In Jesus' name,

Amen

Worship:

"Your Word is a Lamp Unto My Feet"

"Just a Closer Walk With Thee"

CAPERNAUM

Historical Significance:

Jesus spent over half of His public ministry based in this major city on the northwestern shore of the Sea of Galilee, about two miles southwest of the mouth of the Jordan River, likely living with Simon Peter, Peter's wife, his mother-in-law and his brother, Andrew. Capernaum was a Roman military outpost that straddled an important international caravan trading route, the Via Maris or Way of the Sea, which stretched from Mesopotamia to Damascus and over to the Mediterranean and down to Egypt. Isaiah had prophesied the Messiah would live by the way of the sea (Isaiah 9:1).

The ill servant of the centurion built a synagogue here (Luke 7). Gamla synagogue was here, where Jesus preached. It was also the location of the village of Nahum, named after the prophet, and the birthplace of Petrus. Once a volcanic lake, the Sea had large basalt deposits.

Jesus called the tax collector, Matthew (Levi), from the customs toll house, taught in the synagogue, and preached Salvation to thousands. The most miracles by far (ten) happened here:

- Healing of the centurion's servant: Mark 8:5–13; Luke 7:1–10
- Healing of Peter's mother-in-law, Mary, on the Sabbath: Matthew 8:14–15; Mark 1:29–31; Luke 4:38–39
- Healing of two blind men: Matthew 9:27–31
- Jairus's daughter raised from death: Matthew 9:18–19, 23–26; Mark 5:22–43; Luke 8:41–42, 49–56
- Healing of mute, possessed man: Matthew 9:32–33
- Healing of paralytic: Matthew 9:1–8; Mark 2:1–12; Luke 5:17–26
- Healing of bleeding woman: Matthew 9:20–22; Mark 5:25–34; Luke 8:43–48
- Temple tax coin in fish's mouth: Matthew 17:24–27
- Healing on Sabbath of man with evil spirit: Mark 1:21–28; Luke 4:31–37

- Healing official's son in Capernaum while Jesus was in Cana: John 4:46–54.

It was in Capernaum that Jesus told the parable of the bridegroom (Matthew 9:14–15), the parables of new cloth and new wine (Matthew 9:16–17), the parable of the lost sheep (Matthew 18:10–14; Luke 15:3–7), the parable of the unmerciful servant (Matthew 18:21–36), and the parable of the debtors and the money lender (in the Pharisee's house; Mark 7:36–50).

Jesus called six disciples from this area-Andrew, James, John, Peter, Matthew, and Philip—and may have sent the Twelve out from here (Matthew 10:1–42).

Jesus rebuked Capernaum and correctly prophesied its demise (along with nearby Bethsaida and Chorazin) for its unbelief and for not repenting after the witness of so many miracles (see *Appendix-Jesus' Miracles in Biblical Order*). Nothing of significance remains of any of these cities today. How many of *us* today are like these cities, who have seen miracles and heard teaching and *still* do not know Him?

What to See:

There is no city today, just the first- through fourth-century ruins of Tell Hum by the sea, discovered in 1905 by German archaeologists. A pink-domed, white Franciscan monastery is surrounded by palms and eucalyptus trees. Underneath the monastery is the foundation of a third century synagogue built on the ruins of another synagogue that may date to the first century, in which Jesus may have preached. Peter's house has been found here based on an inscription uncovered. The Star of David, seen on some tombs, indicating they are waiting for the Messiah, only originated as a symbol for Jewish people after the fourteenth century. There is also an olive press, made of black/porous/round basalt rock, which symbolizes the weight Jesus carried and how He was pressed out (Messiah means anointed with olive oil).

Scripture (in addition to miracles and parables above):
Matthew 4:13–14,18–22, 9:9–12, 10:2–5, 11:2–7, 20–24
Mark 1:16–34, 2:1–22, 3:1
Luke 4:38–40, 5:27–32, 7:18–24, 10:15–16
John 2:12
definingmomentsbook.com/resources

Defining Moment . . . Capernaum By the Sea

"From everyone who has been given much, much will be demanded; and from the one who has been entrusted with much, much more will be asked"
(Luke 12:48).

The people of Capernaum had been given much. They were blessed by Jesus' teachings and miracles, yet they did not respond, staying stuck in their old ways. In fact, more recorded miracles occurred in Capernaum than in any other city.

Then Jesus began to denounce the towns in which most of His miracles had been performed, because they did not repent. 'Woe to you, Chorazin! Woe to you, Bethsaida! For if the miracles that were performed in you had been performed in Tyre and Sidon, they would have repented long ago in sackcloth and ashes. But I tell you, it will be more bearable for Tyre and Sidon on the day of judgment than for you. And you, Capernaum, will you be lifted to the Heavens? No, you will go down to Hades. For if the miracles that were performed in you had been performed in Sodom, it would have remained to this day. But I tell you that it will be more bearable for Sodom on the day of judgment than for you"
(Matthew 11:20–24).

Even in today's culture, we see evidence of God's miraculous healing power. However, even after hearing firsthand accounts of these miracles, relatively few people give God the glory and give their lives to Him. If it were the healing power of God restoring the sick that guaranteed faith, the three cities above would have had the most powerful faith base of any in Jesus' day. God provided the miracles, but the missing component had to come from the people: repentance.

Repentance is the flashpoint that puts our faith into action. God showing up in power in our lives is the first step; but if we do not respond with repentance, we will go nowhere with Him.

The word *repentance* is a military term meaning "to turn around." We do this with God's help, not out of condemnation but out of joy. Many people in today's world see repentance as drudgery that carries guilt, shame, and condemnation. They run from it like the wind. The opposite could not be more accurate. "Repentance" is really a huge *gift* from God. It is the sign on the highway that tells us a cliff is coming up—turn around or you will fall off the cliff and hurt yourself! People do not ignore those kinds of road signs, and we have an opportunity to see repentance for the true gift that it is. When we truly repent, God truly forgives us and erases our sins. We become white as snow through the amazing process of repentance and God's promise to forgive us.

Journal Time:
How have you viewed repentance up until now? Have you seen it as a gift or a liability? In what areas of your life have you avoided repentance? Why?

Share Time:
Talk about the gift that repentance (or making a U-turn) really is. Share with each other examples of where repentance was either avoided—and the costs that were incurred—or embraced, and the blessings that ensued.

Prayer:
God,

We long to be a Church who is repentant. We do not want to be like Capernaum, but we want to be a people who turn around from evil and glorify You with our entire beings. Dad, please help us to see repentance for the gift that *it really is. Help us to treasure it and use it on a daily basis so that we can be made a holy people with lives that are a living sacrifice to You. It is only through Your power that we can achieve this. Please help us to do our part as You do Yours.*

In Jesus' name,
Amen

Worship:
"Purify My Heart"
"Change My Heart"

DEAD SEA

Historical Significance:
The Dead Sea is also known as the Ancient Sea, Sea of Sedom, Sea of the Arava (or Arabah), Last Sea, Eastern Sea, and the Sea.

The River Jordan flows out of the southern Sea of Galilee (along with the Zarqa River, Arnon Stream, and many dry streams) down into the Dead Sea, which has no outlet and, therefore, nothing living in or around it. Masada is southwest of the Dead Sea. The kingdom of Moab was to the southeast, and the hills of Judea to the west. The ruins of Qumran (site of discovery of the Dead Sea Scrolls) is near the northwestern edge.

Sodom and Gomorrah were located around the south. When God let burning sulfur rain down on those cities, Abraham's nephew, Lot, escaped with his daughters, while his wife was turned into a pillar of salt after looking back in disobedience to the Lord.

Ezekiel predicted the sea would one day become fresh with many fishermen.

What to See:
The Dead Sea is about forty-five miles long and eleven miles wide. At 1,300 feet *below* sea level, it is the lowest spot on earth. It is very deep in the north and rather shallow in the south. Its eastern shore is part of Israel's eastern border.

It is fun to float in the clear, clean Dead Sea because the high salinity (six times higher than the ocean) and mineral (twenty-seven percent salt, calcium chloride, magnesium and potassium) content of the water multiplies the buoyancy for all body types. Be careful not to float face down or get water in your eyes as the minerals are fatal to the lungs, damaging to the eye, and bitter and nauseating to taste. A thorough shower is needed afterward. There are hot sulfur springs on the western side.

Scripture:
> Genesis 14:3, 10
> Numbers 34:3, 12
> Deuteronomy 3:17
> Joshua 3:16, 12:3, 15:2, 5, 18:19
> Ezekiel 47:8–12
> Mark 1:4
> Luke 3:20
> definingmomentsbook.com/resources

Defining Moment . . . The Dead Sea

You will most likely visit the Sea of Galilee on this trip: a life-giving body of water that is fed by the Jordan River. Its southern end is also an outlet that serves as a continuation of the Jordan River which culminates in the Dead Sea, which has no other outlet.

When you visit the Sea of Galilee, you will notice the prodigious amount of fish it still produces to feed the surrounding population. The Dead Sea, however, is true to its name: dead. There are no life forms—either plant or animal—in the entire sea. The Dead Sea has the fresh water of the Jordan River flowing into it; however, it has six times the salt level of ocean water. There is absolutely no water flowing out of it. Any life that comes in contact with the water for a long period of time suffers from osmotic shock and dies.

The Dead Sea does give us a great analogy, however, for our own spiritual lives. When we have life flowing into us and service for our Lord flowing out of us, we are like the Sea of Galilee—full of life and healthy. When we have life flowing into us and nothing flowing out of us, we tend to stagnate like the Dead Sea. We are made to be life-giving to others through service, relationships, encouragement, help, and hundreds of other ways we are able to pour into the lives of others. When we choose not to let that life flow through us to others, it is not good for *us*. It can be damaging and even life draining.

Remember the words the Lord Jesus Himself said: *"It is more blessed to **give** than to **receive**"* (Acts 20:35). The giver has even greater joy than the receiver.

Journal Time:

Think of the times in your life that you have been the most fulfilled. What were you doing? Were you being life-giving to another? What is it in your life that gives you the most joy? How has God used it to be life-giving? Are you struggling with being a "Dead Sea" that is not pouring out to others at this point in your life?

Share Time:

Talk with each other about what it feels like to be life-giving to others. When do you feel most alive and fulfilled? What are the circumstances that enable you to feel more like the life-giving Sea of Galilee and less like the Dead Sea?

Prayer:

Lord,

How we long to be life givers for You. Thank You for the life You continually fill us up with. You give us every resource possible so that we can be filled up to pour out on to others. Help us, Lord, not to be Dead Seas. We want to enable life, not destroy it. Show each one of us the specific ways that You want us to pour out into lives of service and love. Help us to realize the great joy both You, and we, experience as we have the privilege of coming alongside others.

In Jesus' name,

Amen

Worship:

"Take My Life and Let It Be"
"Brother, Let Me Be Your Servant"

DECAPOLIS
(ACROSS THE BORDER IN SYRIA/JORDAN)

Historical Significance:

The Decapolis was an unofficial confederation of ten free pagan and semi-pagan cities that reflected high, sophisticated Roman and Greek culture in an otherwise Jewish and Aramean region mostly east and southeast of the Sea of Galilee. In Greek, "deka" means ten and "polis" means city. Only Scythopolis is in modern-day Israel. Damascus is the capital of Syria. The other eight cities are east of the Jordan River in modern Jordan. They were mostly founded between 323–63 BC. They used the Roman plan of a grid of streets around a center.

Although the cities were nominally grouped together, their cultural practices were still quite different. For example, the Jews disagreed with the Greeks' practice of homosexuality, while the Greeks disagreed with the Jews' practice of circumcision.

Sometimes known as the "Land of the Seven," it represented the seven pagan nations driven from Israel by Joshua. Jews avoided this region believing it was dominated by the devil and pagan fertility gods.

Jesus ministered to the Gentile majority here in lieu of His usual focus on the Jews in Palestine. His miracle of healing the demonic man by casting the demons into a herd of pigs (forbidden by Jewish dietary laws), as reported in the Gospels of Matthew, Mark, and Luke, happened outside Gerasa, one of the cities of the Decapolis. They also experienced the feeding of the 4,000 and the healing of the deaf and mute man.

Jesus went to the pagans in the east to confront the power of evil. The feeding of the 5,000 (Mark 6:39–43) was in Capernaum to the Jews, with twelve baskets left over representing the Twelve Tribes of Israel. The feeding of the 4,000 (Mark 8:1–8) was in Decapolis to the Gentiles, with seven baskets left over, representing the seven nations. It was here that a man possessed by demons, who gave his name as Legion, lived in tombs in a grotto cave adjacent to a gradual hill. The hill lead to a cliff over the Sea of Galilee where the demons were cast into the 2,000 pigs (Mark 5:6–20) which then rushed down a hillside into the lake. This shows us Jesus immediately confronting evil, and the people did not like it. (Pigs were sacred to pagan fertility rites like lambs were to Jewish rites).

On this eastern, non-Jewish side, Jesus told the man who had been possessed to "*go home to your own people and tell them how much the Lord has done for you, and how He has had mercy on you*" (Mark 5:19), while telling those He healed on the western, Jewish side *not* to tell others, so as to not draw even greater crowds nor the attention of the Jewish leaders at this time.

The disciples, who had faced another storm (Mark 4:37–41) as they were coming fearfully to this unclean, pagan, eastern side, were terrified and awoke Jesus who was sleeping in the stern. He then rebuked the wind and waves (representing the power of evil). The wind and the waves completely calmed, showing us that both nature *and* demons obey Him!

Many others came for healing when Jesus returned (Matthew 15:29–31). He calls us also, as ambassadors, to be His people in a culture that does not hold His values. This pagan area actually became the strongest of the early Church, starting with the ministry of *one* changed life. That man cleansed from the impure spirits had more passion and personal experience than he had knowledge.

Control of the region shifted from Roman to Byzantine to Christian through the centuries, and most of the cities housed bishops of the faith.

Gerasa and Scythopolis are still inhabited. Damascus and Amman (formerly Philadelphia) are capitals. Most of the other cities have been located and are being excavated.

Scripture:

Matthew 4:25, 8:28–34, 15:29–31
Mark 4:37–41, 5:1–20, 7:31–8:10
Luke 8:26–39
definingmomentsbook.com/resources

Defining Moment . . . Jerash's Archaeological Site

Did you ever notice that sometimes when Jesus healed a person, He told them not to tell anyone, and then other times He told them to tell everyone? When Jesus was healing in Jewish cities, He asked the healed not to tell anyone because it was not yet time for the religious leaders to be stirred up to want to kill Him. We see the angst in them every time they found out that Jesus had healed yet another person.

Decapolis, however, was a group of pagan cities. When Jesus healed the demonic man in this area, Jesus told him to stay and tell everyone about his healing, even though the man wanted to leave his home and go with Jesus.

By going into Decapolis, Jesus went into an area full of lost people. He did not wait for them to come to Him. Jesus equipped this man with a testimony of complete healing, knowing that he would be used mightily—even though he was by himself in a pagan land, left alone to testify to others about Jesus and what He had done for him. What a calling!

Journal Time:

Ask Jesus to put on your heart the lost people that He wants you to go to. It could be a neighbor, a friend from work, or a country. Who does He want *you* to come alongside? How does He want you to minister to them?

Share Time:

Who are the people that God is bringing to mind that He wants you to minister to?

Prayer:

Lord,

We pray for the lost that Jesus has reminded us of in our Journal Time. We pray that their hearts will be open when they are ministered to, and that they will fall in love with Jesus.

In Jesus' name,

Amen

Worship:
"Bringing in the Sheaves"
"I Love to Tell the Story"

EMMAUS

Historical Significance:

Midday on Easter Sunday, after the empty Tomb had been discovered, Cleopas and another disciple were on the road from Jerusalem to Emmaus. By divine intervention, they did not recognize Jesus as the man who walked with them. They urged Him to stay with them at their destination and broke bread together, at which point they recognized Him, and He disappeared. They realized their hearts had been burning as He "opened the Scriptures" to them during the walk. They returned immediately to Jerusalem and the eleven apostles to share the Good News and to hear He had also appeared to Simon.

Two places north of Jerusalem along the Nablus Road in the Judean hill country are possibly Emmaus: al-Qubeiba and Amwas, both ruins of settlements dating from Roman, Byzantine and Crusader periods. Al-Qubeiba seems more likely, as its eight-mile straight line distance from Jerusalem—versus fifteen miles to Amwas—approximated the sixty stadia (seven miles) the disciples are said to have walked.

A church built on the ruins of a Crusader church, which has lovely stained-glass windows and bells, is a great place to celebrate communion with little cups made of olive wood, commemorating where the risen Christ broke bread with His apostles.

Scripture:

Mark 16:12
Luke 24:13–35
definingmomentsbook.com/resources

EIN GEDI

Historical Significance:

Ein Gedi, meaning "spring of the wild goat," is an oasis with a freshwater spring, plants, and trees, midway off the western side of the Dead Sea.

When Saul was hunting for David with 3,000 men, David and his men hid in a cave here, and David cut off tassels from Saul's robe to prove that he had gotten so close that he could have killed the king if he had wanted.

David, though already anointed by God, was determined not to take the kingship from Saul, but to wait for God to give it to him. Temporarily Saul felt remorse, but soon decided again to kill David, who had not expected the repentance to last.

It is believed that David wrote many Psalms here, including Psalms 57 and 142 (prayers for deliverance from enemies), while hiding here.

Solomon's beloved likened him to "a cluster of henna blossoms" from Ein Gedi's vineyards.

What to See:

Driving through the Judean wilderness and arriving at Ein Gedi kibbutz makes the vision of an oasis very real. There is a small hiking trail from which you can view the caves of Ein Gedi and walk into the deep crevices of the oasis to view the stream, waterfall, date palms, vineyards, aromatic and medicinal plants, and the cave—a favorite site of David's.

Scripture:

2 Chronicles 20:2
Joshua 15:62
1 Samuel 23:29, 24
Song of Solomon 1:14
Ezekiel 47:10
definingmomentsbook.com/resources

Defining Moment . . . Ein Gedi

Imagine what it must have been like to be in David's shoes at the time
he was camping out at Ein Gedi. A man who you love is after you to kill
you, because God has anointed you to be the new king. While you already
have the appointment, you are waiting on God to make the final placement,
and are being chased for your very life. How do you cope when you have
an enemy that is coming after your life with a vengeance? If you are David,
you write psalms.

Psalm 142, a song of David, when he was in the cave, a prayer

I cry aloud to the LORD;
I lift up my voice to the LORD for mercy.
I pour out before Him my complaint;
before Him I tell my trouble.
When my spirit grows faint within me,
it is You who watch over my way.
In the path where I walk
people have hidden a snare for me.
Look and see, there is no one at my right hand;
no one is concerned for me.
I have no refuge;
no one cares for my life.
I cry to You, LORD;
I say, "You are my refuge,
my portion in the land of the living."
Listen to my cry,
for I am in desperate need;
rescue me from those who pursue me,
for they are too strong for me.
Set me free from my prison,
that I may praise Your name.
Then the righteous will gather about me
because of Your goodness to me.

What is fascinating about David's prayer is that he asks to be set free from prison, not so that he can be comfortable, not so that he can be safe, but so that he can praise God's name. He then wants other believers to gather around him because of God's goodness to him.

David is at the end of his rope, but instead of the ultimate outcome being about him, he makes it about God. His hope is not in *himself,* but in God alone.

Journal Time:
What would you feel like if your mentor or someone that you used to trust turned on you and wanted to kill you, and you felt that there was no one to protect you except God? What is going on in your life right now that you feel all alone in? Is there any situation that you feel is trying to destroy you, and only God can save you? Write a psalm, just like David did, pouring *your* heart out to God. Tell Him what is going on in your heart and how He alone can save you.

Share Time:
Read some of your psalms aloud to each other.

Prayer:
Lord,

Thank You that You alone are our refuge. It is You that we trust in. Please meet each of us in the areas of our lives that we are being attacked in. Please protect us and comfort us when we feel alone in our battles. Please give us strength and the knowing that it is You who will protect us and save us when we cannot save ourselves. We trust You. We will praise You in the middle of the battle, because You are our God, and You alone can save us. Keep our focus on praising Your name.

In Jesus' name,

Amen

Worship:
"Let Everything That Has Breath Praise the Lord"

"I Am Trusting Thee Lord Jesus"

SEA OF GALILEE

Historical Significance:

Also known as: Sea of Tiberias, Lake (or Sea) of Kinneret—from the Hebrew word "kinnor" meaning harp or lute, due to the lake's harp-like shape—and Lake of Gennesaret (by Luke).

Much of Jesus' ministry happened in this region in the northern Jordan Valley, particularly along the northern shore. It is the location of the homes of the majority of the disciples (eleven, eight of whom were fishermen—see *Appendix*), and the majority of miracles and parables occurred or were related here. In Jesus' day, there were 240 villages, cities, and towns around the Sea, all of which had at least one synagogue and usually a school. Tiberias is midway on its western shore.

The Jordan River flows into the Sea of Galilee from the north. From there, it flows out of the southwestern tip of the Sea of Galilee and empties into the northern part of the Dead Sea. The Ten Decapolis cities were to the east and southeast in a non-Jewish region. The Golan Heights, named after one of the cities of refuge in Joshua 20:8, extend beyond the eastern shore and included nine of the cities.

The northern shore had the three cursed cities of Capernaum, Chorazin, and Bethsaida—home of five of His disciples—along with the Mount of Beatitudes, where the Sermon on the Mount was delivered. In the region is the site of the feeding of the 5,000, and of many healings. The majority of Jesus' three-year public ministry happened in this triangle. They are cursed, because they witnessed so much, yet believed so little and never repented.

The lake is 15 miles long, 7–9 miles wide, 165 feet deep, and 650 feet *below* sea level, but is not salty like the Dead Sea, an even lower spot. All around is rich vegetation and hills full of flowers in spring.

Jesus slept in the back of the boat while these *seasoned* fishermen were so fearful of high waves. At first, they thought He did not care, then they were too fearful of Him to understand that even the wind obeys Him (Mark 4:35–41).

Jesus (and Peter) also later walked on water here (Matthew 14:22–31). He asked them when they woke Him up, "*Why are you afraid?*" After all, they had the God of the universe in their boat! Why are *you* afraid, since you also have the God of the universe in *your* boat? I imagine that in the years ahead, whenever the disciples would again have fears and questions, Jesus might have subtly just looked at or pointed toward the lake as a reminder.

Most fishermen feared the sea as a symbol of the abyss and did not even know how to swim, yet Peter had the courage to get out of the boat, saying by that action, "*I want to be like You, my Rabbi.*" Jesus calmed the storm (Mark 6:45–52). God is also powerful enough to calm *my* storms, but sometimes He calms the storm and sometimes He just lets the storm rage while He calms my soul.

Note that Jesus saw them struggling with the oars when it became dark, but waited six to eight hours ("shortly before dawn") to walk out there to help. So, He often allows us to struggle first ("about to pass them by" before He immediately responded to their call and they realized "their hearts were hardened"). Also, note they ended up in Gennesaret, (not Bethsaida), so sometimes He allows us to end up in a different place than *we* were aiming for.

Jesus helped them make huge catches of fish here: 153 fish, representing the 153 nations then ("all of the world"). They were expert fishermen. The lessons show that we will need much practice to be followers of Jesus and though we may not always appear to be catching anything, we must keep casting our nets in faith.

There were four people groups in Galilee, Land of the Twelve Tribes:
- Orthodox Jews: The obedient, Torah-knowing Sadducees and Pharisees were mostly unsurprisingly in the northern, unbelieving triangle of Chorazin, Capernaum, and Bethsaida.
- Zealot Jews: The fierce, anti-Rome killers of Romans and Herodians from Gamla in the northeast, later took their last stand at Masada in 73 AD. They wanted Jesus to be a warrior king, not a "Love your neighbor" Savior.

- Herodian Jews: The secular Jews near Tiberias worked with the Romans and were wealthy friends of Herod, including the unclean Zacchaeus; they were the "lost sheep."
- Pagan Gentiles were from the Decapolis east of the Sea, aka "the far country."

What to See:

Today it includes resort hotels, spas, and beaches. The area, much larger than you likely imagined, is abundant with olive trees, pine trees, poplars, and wheat. The lake is still the source for a third of all water pumped throughout Israel.

You can take a "**Jesus boat**" ride (replica built on a larger scale than the originals) from Tiberias or Capernaum to the Yigal Allon Center at **Kibbutz Ginosar**, where, during the severe drought of 1986, two marine archaeologist brothers on the western shore found and preserved a first century, humble fishing boat made from twelve types of wood, similar to those boats used by Jesus and several of his disciples.

An abundance (twenty-two species) of fish—including carp, mullet, sardine, and catfish—are still caught by nets today. Fishing is as important an industry as it was during Jesus' time. Violent storms and sudden winds form a wind tunnel, caused by the surrounding hills, that still often churns the lake up in the afternoons after usually calm mornings. What are *your* storms and fears today? What does the calm lake say to *you*?

definingmomentsbook.com/resources

The Mount of Beatitudes, originally called Mount Eremos, the traditional site where Jesus chose His twelve disciples and later preached the Sermon on the Mount—which started with the nine Beatitudes—sits on the northwestern shore. This was His first sermon to all of His disciples and the crowds about His heart and His life, as until that point, His focus had been on healing, to get their attention for this *next* season of teaching. The feeding of the 5,000 occurred on the northeastern shore, where Jesus healed the multitudes. In 1937, Franciscan Sisters built a church with a domed roof, marble altar, arched porches, and a fabulous view of the Sea. It is a holy site, so please dress with no knees or shoulders showing.

Scripture:
Matthew 4:18–22, 5:7, 8:23–34, 11:20–24, 13, 14:22–31
Mark 1:16–20, 3:13–19, 4, 5:1–20, 6:45–53
Luke 5:1–11, 8:1–39, 13:18–19
John 6:1–25, 21:4—11
definingmomentsbook.com/resources

Defining Moment . . . A Boat on the Sea of Galilee

Then He got into the boat and His disciples followed Him. Suddenly a furious storm came up on the lake, so that the waves swept over the boat. But Jesus was sleeping. The disciples went and woke Him, saying, "Lord, save us! We are going to drown!"

He replied, "You of little faith, why are you so afraid?" Then He got up and rebuked the winds and the waves, and it was completely calm. The men were amazed and asked, "What kind of Man is this? Even the winds and the waves obey Him!"
(Matthew 8:23–27).

As we read this account of the storm that happened on the Sea of Galilee, it is easy to be tempted to judge the disciples for their unbelief. The Sea of Galilee, though calm most of the time, can have raging storms with huge waves. This boat was full of fisherman who knew the difference between when there was danger on the sea and when it was just a little rocky. They were truly frightened. As we read this, we know that Jesus is God, they knew that Jesus is God, and that we all know that He is going to save them. To see them go to a place of fear makes their faith feel shallow, and Jesus called them out on it.

Let us compare it to our faith if we were in the same situation. You are in a boat with Jesus. He is asleep. A huge storm and waves come up. What do you say to Him? Pause and really think about what you would do.

Now think of the storms that come up in your life right now. Are you responding to them in the way that you just thought you would if you were really in a Sea of Galilee storm? The God of the universe is in your boat. He is sitting right beside you; you know He is God, and He is in control.

How do you react when you hit that financial storm and are in danger of losing your home? What about that job that may go away? Or that illness that pops up out of nowhere? The God of the universe is in your boat, and He will not let it sink, so what are you afraid of?

Journal Time:
What are you afraid of? What is causing you to stay in a place of anxiety? What do you want to let go of, right now, on the Sea of Galilee? What have you built up in your mind as bigger than God that you want to confess and repent of and give to God right now?

Share Time:
Share with each other those things that you have been afraid of that you are releasing to God during this experience.

Prayer:
Lord Jesus,

Please forgive us for our lack of faith. It is so easy to judge others, like the disciples, for their crisis of faith, and yet we are too blind to see it in our own selves. We are handing over the fears that we have journaled about to You. We recognize You as the God of the universe who is in our boat. We have nothing to fear. You are right beside us, and no matter how big the waves get, You are in control. Thank You for calming the waters and saving us. We love You.

In Your holy name,

Amen

Worship:
"Lord of All"

"I Am Trusting Thee, Lord Jesus"

GIDEON'S SPRING

Historical Significance:

Also known as: Ain Jalut, the Spring of Goliath, or the Spring of Harod, meaning "trembling"—either for the fearful Israelites or the panicked Midianites.

Southwest of the Sea of Galilee, at the foot of Mount Gilboa, is the freshwater spring where Gideon (or Jerub-Baal) and his 32,000 men camped only four miles from the 132,000 Midianites. The Lord wanted the victory to be clearly His, not that of his "mighty warrior," Gideon, so He sent more than 22,000 fearful Israelites home. We meet Gideon in Judges 6 hiding in a cave, certainly not a mighty warrior. He *wants* to be, but sees himself as "least" until the Lord says, "I will be with you."

Then the Lord further selected just 300 soldiers of the remaining 10,000: those of fighting readiness who "lapped" the water when drinking—on their left knees, swords in their right hands, looking left and right, while cupping water in their left hands, prepared for any emergency. (The others put down their swords and got on their hands and knees to drink like a dog). God then used unconventional methods and weapons—Gideon listened to the enemy to gain confidence, then, using trumpets, shouting, and broken jars, he made the Midianites turn on each other in confusion and fear. The ensuing victory, clearly through God's power alone and not Gideon's, took place north in a valley by the Hill of Morch.

What to See:

This is an "A" site, known to be exactly where the story occurred. Gideon's Spring represented a watershed moment of decision for Gideon and his men. Are there places in *your* life where He let you also know that only *He* can accomplish such victories through *you*? This could be a place for you to internalize, believe, and hold God's plan for you.

Scripture:

Judges 6–8
Hebrews 11:32
definingmomentsbook.com/resources

Does God Still Do Miracles Today?

In Judges 6–7, we see how God took Gideon's 300 men and defeated the Midianites' 132,000 men. God used unconventional weapons and methods to achieve His purpose. He had Gideon listen to the enemy to gain confidence. He had them use trumpets, shouting, and broken jars to imply a large army surrounding the Midianites, to make them confused and afraid. He had their panic result in turning on each other with swords.

Clearly, the message to Gideon, his men and all Israel was that they—and we—could only accomplish the great victories we desire through His power, His ways.

There is an interesting parallel in the story of modern-day Israel: the Yom Kippur War of 1973 (also known as the October War). It is so called because it began on the Day of Atonement, Yom Kippur, the holiest day of prayer and fasting in the Jewish religious calendar. Egyptian forces from the south, and Syrian forces from the north, financed by Saudi Arabia, Kuwait, and Libya, surprised Israeli forces at noon on Saturday, October 6, 1973.

Why was this similar to Gideon facing the Midianites? In the Suez along the Bar Lev line, just 500 Israeli soldiers faced 80,000 Egyptian soldiers. In the Golan Heights, for the first 48 hours, just 150 Israeli tanks and 600 soldiers faced 1,400 Syrian tanks and 60,000 soldiers. The combined Egyptian–Syrian air force outnumbered the Israelis two to one.

The Israeli forces were initially overwhelmed. Within two days, the Egyptians had crossed the Suez Canal and moved fifteen miles inland, while Syrian troops had advanced by the same distance into the strategic Golan Heights in northern Israel. The Israelis managed a miracle.

1) They counter attacked and pushed the Egyptians back across the Suez and advanced within forty-two miles of Cairo, the Egyptian capital.

2) Israeli forces pushed the Syrians back and advanced within thirty-five miles of Damascus, the Syrian capital!

For Israel, each war is a fight to the finish—death or glory! For the Arab nations, a loss means they have survived to fight another day.

Why were the Syrians only able to seize one Israeli fortification on Mount Herman, a key electronic surveillance base, with such overwhelming odds and surprise in their favor? Most Israeli troops were home with their families celebrating this most solemn day; TV and radio stations were closed; the roads were empty. God had also protected Israel in the swift victory in the 1967 Six-Day War, which sadly resulted in overconfidence: the military and intelligence credited their *own* strength and smarts. Despite warnings from king Hussein of Jordan and the CIA, Israel chose not to mobilize reserves, which would require forty-eight to seventy-two hours.

Syria had three oversized infantry divisions, 930 tanks, and 900 artillery pieces in forward positions facing the Golan Heights, plus two armored divisions and 460 tanks held in the rear, protected by 30 batteries of anti-aircraft missiles. Israel only held the Golan Heights with 177 tanks, an infantry division, 44 artillery pieces, and a SAM battery. Thus began the largest tank battle since World War II! In the northern Golan, on October 9, Israeli tanks, reduced to a few dozen, annihilated about 200 Syrian tanks. Though the Israelis were out of ammunition and still awaiting complete mobilization of the reserves, the Syrians halted their attack.

In the Southern Golan, on October 6, Israel had about forty tanks outnumbered by seven Syrian brigades. Lt. Zvika Greengold, who faced a Syrian tank brigade alone, fought them off for twenty hours with a single tank until help arrived.

On October 7 at 3 a.m., Israel intercepted a radio message by a Syrian brigade commander: "I see the whole Galilee in front of me. Request permission to proceed."

One of many miracles then occurred as the Syrians, seeing things progress so well, feared a trap as in 1967, and halted. This gave the Israelis time for complete mobilization, to regroup, and to resupply by a massive U.S. airlift.

So, does God *still* do miracles today? Does He *still* use unconventional methods to achieve His victories? Just like the Midianites over 3,000 years ago, God led Israel to defeat far superior numbers by letting them listen to the enemy and making the enemy confused and afraid to the point of panic!

Side Note: The United Nations only acted by finally ordering a cease fire on October 24, once it was clear *Israel* was going to win on *both* fronts. By then, Israel held the entire western side of the Suez Canal, had destroyed 1,100 Syrian (Russian) tanks and had completely surrounded Egypt's Third Army!

An estimated 2,700 Israelis, 3,500 Syrian and 15,000 Egyptians were killed in the fighting. Egypt lost 1,000 tanks, Syria 1,150 and Israel 400. Egypt lost 325 airplanes and 42 helicopters; Syria, 135 and 13; Israel, 105 and 5. The Israeli navy incurred no losses, sinking seven Egyptian and five Syrian missile boats, four Egyptian torpedo boats, and several coastal defense boats.

One more thing. Both Syria and Egypt somehow considered themselves victorious!

Defining Moment . . . Gideon's Spring

In Judges 6:12, the angel of the Lord calls Gideon—who is hiding in a wine press—"Mighty Warrior," but he responds in 6:15 *"my clan is the weakest in Manasseh and I am the least in my family."*

The Lord answered, *"I will be with you and you will strike down all the Midianites, leaving none alive"* (verse 16). To jump ahead to the ending, note that of the 132,000 Midianites, 120,000 died when faced with Gideon and his 300 men: *"Mighty Warrior,"* indeed!

Did you know that the God who created you also has a name for *you*?

"I have summoned you by name, you are Mine "(Isaiah 43:1).

He called David *"a man after my own heart"* (Acts 13:22).

He called Peter *"the rock"* (Matthew 16:18).

He changed Abram's name to Abraham (Gen 17:5).

He called the disciples James and John *"Sons of Thunder"* (Mark 3:17).

God's name for you may be big and powerful. Like Gideon, your first response may be to say, "No, not me, I am the least" and embrace the old, small, negative names you have for yourself to keep Him away—like hiding in a wine press with the hordes waiting outside to attack.

If it is a *nice* name you hear, that *might* not be it.

If it feels *scary* and you want to push it away, that probably *is* it!

Not all of you will get your name immediately—it may come now; it may come later; it may be confirmed for you in some manner.

Rick's story: When going through this experience of listening for God's name for him, Rick sat by the stream at Gideon's Spring and heard the whisper "Builder of Men" over him. Because he regularly mentors and is in accountability groups with men, he thought he might be making the name up in his own mind and wanted to wait for confirmation. When others asked him about his God-given name, he did not share and said it was still coming. However, when he got back on the tour bus with the rest of the group, he started talking across the aisle with a pastor on the trip who he did not know before. The pastor nonchalantly said to Rick that he saw him as a "Builder of Men." That was all the confirmation it took for Rick to know that it was the Lord and not his own imaginings that came up with that God-given name.

Journal Time:

Take some time now in silence and solitude—try to just *listen* for His name for you. Try to clear your mind of everything else. Try to not speak to Him— *just be; abide in Him.*

Share Time:

Share with others what you have heard in your private time with the Lord. What name has He given you?

Prayer:

Father,

We pray over every person on this trip, that they would clearly hear the name that only You have for them. Give them confirmation, in only the way that You can, that gives them the gift of knowing that the name comes from You, who created them. Please, Lord, help each of us to live up to Your name for us through Your power, and not our own. Give us courage and perseverance to use Your name for us to Your Glory.

In Jesus' name,

Amen

Worship:
"He Knows My Name"
"As the Deer"

GOSPEL TRAIL, AKA JESUS TRAIL

There is a forty-mile walking trail in northern Israel for some of the two-thirds of tourists to Israel who are Christians and might want to *walk* in Jesus' footsteps rather than just *drive*. You can also ride horseback part of the way and take a "Jesus boat" ride on the Sea of Galilee at the end. The trail heads south from Nazareth, across gentle green hills, past grazing livestock, through both Jewish and Arab towns, ending in Capernaum on the sea.

It begins at Mount Precipice with its beautiful views, where, according to tradition, Jesus was nearly thrown off a cliff by a mob after He was rejected by His own town of Nazareth. The path heads to Mount Tabor and its Franciscan church, said to be the site of the Transfiguration, when Jesus became radiant while speaking to Moses and Elijah.

A side trail goes to Cana, site of Jesus' first miracle, turning water into fine wine at the wedding feast. It now features the nineteenth century stone Wedding Church. The path then passes by the bases of the double extinct volcanoes, the Horns of Hattin, where it is believed Saladin's Muslim army defeated the Crusaders in 1187.

Next is Migdal, the ancient town of Magdala, said to be Mary Magdalene's home, and Tabgha, where the Church of the Multiplication of Loaves and Fishes commemorates feeding the multitudes. The trail passes close to banana and pear trees by the Mount of Beatitudes, and ends in Capernaum.

Due to the region's very hot summers and very wet winters, it is best to travel this trail in March, April, September, October, and November. Enjoy the sounds of songbirds, the smells of wild dill, and the times of reflection. The entire trail is designed to be walked over four days.

definingmomentsbook.com/resources

JAFFA/JOPPA AKA JOFFA

Historical Significance:

Mythology says that it is named for one of Noah's, sons, Japheth, who built it after the flood. It is one of the oldest port towns in the world, dating back to Canaanite times.

Joppa, a natural harbor, was the main seaport for Jerusalem. Jonah sailed from here to Tarshish in disobedience to God's call to go to Nineveh.

During the reigns of kings Solomon and David, the majestic cedars from Lebanon (Tyre/Phoenicia) were sent through Jaffa en route to Jerusalem for the first and second Temple construction. Later, the city was controlled by the Hellenists and then by the Romans.

Peter raised Dorcas (Tabitha) from the dead after arriving here from an incredibly successful ministry in Lydda, near the location of the Ben Gurion International Airport. Here also he had his vision on Simon the Tanner's roof about the Gentiles, represented as a sheet coming from Heaven filled with animals for food. He left with the believers to meet Cornelius in Caesarea. God overcame Peter's ego and gave him the powers to heal, to speak, and to raise from the dead. What barriers keep *you* from hearing God's voice?

Roman soldiers killed 8,400 citizens and burned the city during the First Jewish Revolt.

Today the capital Tel Aviv ("Hill of the Spring"), founded in 1090, Israel's second largest city, lies to the north on the Mediterranean coast, and includes the ancient port city of Jaffa. With a population of 400,000, it is the center of commercial, industrial, and cultural activity. Forty percent of Israel's population live within ten miles of Tel Aviv.

What to See:

Jaffa today has many partially restored Canaanite and medieval buildings and other historical sites, with a monument to the story of Jonah and restored Egyptian gates that are about 3,500 years old. The Roman Catholic **St.**

Peter's Church, run by Franciscans, and **St. Peter and St. Tabitha** Russian Orthodox church, built in 1894, are on the grounds of the **Greek Orthodox Monastery of Archangel Michael**, serving Romanians and Russians, and is considered the traditional site where Peter had the vision. St. Tabitha's tomb is considered to be below the chapel. **Immanuel Church** (1904) holds Lutheran services.

Scripture:
Joshua 19:40, 46
2 Chronicles 2:16
Ezra 3:7
Jonah 1:1–3
Acts 9:32–10:48
definingmomentsbook.com/resources

JERICHO

___

Historical Significance:

Jericho was one of the oldest cities of the ancient world, dating as far back as 7,000–10,000 BC, populated from the Middle Stone Age, and blessed with abundant fresh water, temperate weather, and a strategic location at the crossroads to Jerusalem on the eastern side of the Jordan.

Jericho was the first city Joshua conquered, by marching his troops around for a week with priests blowing trumpets until on the seventh day the walls came down. The harlot Rahab hid Joshua's spies here, in return for saving her and her family.

Elisha and Elijah served in Jericho. Herod the Great built a winter palace here. The story of The Good Samaritan happened on the road to Jericho.

The traditional site of Jesus' three temptations by Satan in the Judean wilderness is close by: The Mount of Temptation, where a monastery was somehow built into the mountain. Jesus converted the chief tax collector, Zacchaeus, here, when he called him down from a sycamore-fig tree and healed Bartimaeus of blindness.

What to See:

Jericho is an Arab city today, with extensive **excavations** (eighty feet high, nearly ten acres wide) northwest of the modern city that have revealed relics from Neolithic, Chalcolithic, Early and Middle Canaanite periods. You must see **Elisha's Spring**, across the road from Tel Jericho, Herod's Winter Palaces, a water tower, and wells built of stone and mud dating back to 7,000 BC, as well as palaces from the Maccabean and Herodian eras, a large burial site, and a sixth century synagogue with mosaic floor. No ruins of the walls that came tumbling down have been found near this lovely, green oasis of trees; among them orange, lime, grapefruit, apple, and date, and plants, mainly grape, cucumber, and tomato. Many flowers are surrounded by brown desert.

Scripture:

Joshua 2, 5:13–6:26
1 Kings 16:34
Matthew 20:29–34
Mark 10:46–52
Luke 10:30–37, 18:35–43, 19:1–10
Hebrews 11:30–31
definingmomentsbook.com/resources

JERUSALEM (OVERVIEW)

Historical Significance:

Jerusalem has many names: meaning, ironically, "City of Peace" in Hebrew, is also called Zion, or the Golden City. Her Arabic name means "the holy": Al Quds. Jerusalem is a sacred city in the land of Judah in the Judean hills, the City of David, the capital of ancient Israel, the only city called the "city of our God" (Psalm 46:4). For a "City of Peace," it has been conquered thirty-nine times (thirty-seven times from the vulnerable north that has no natural defenses) and destroyed seventeen times!

It is a focal point for Jews, who claim heritage back to Abraham's son by Sarah, Isaac; for Christians, dating back to Christ; and for Muslims, claiming heritage back to Abraham's son by the servant Hagar, Ishmael. Pilgrims from all three faiths, even today, come from afar to walk the holy city. While it is *important* to Christians and Muslims and not essential to our faith, it is *essential* to Judaism.

Jeremiah 3:17 says, *"At that time they will call Jerusalem The Throne of the LORD, and all nations will gather in Jerusalem to honor the name of the LORD."*

North is the wealthy Upper City, Hellenistic Jewish suburbs with the Damascus Gate, the entrance from Syria. *West* is Herod's luxurious western palace, with rich mosaics, large pools, elaborate gardens and three huge watchtowers overlooking the city. Here is likely where he decided to kill the male babies of Bethlehem, and where Jesus was interrogated by Herod Antipas; the Jaffa Gate, the entrance from port of Jaffa; the priestly area, the Garden Tomb, Calvary, and the Church of the Holy Sepulchre.

South is Mount Zion today, the South Gate with its entrance for pilgrim masses, and the Armenian Church over Caiaphas's Palace. *East/southeast* is the poor area, the Lower City, along the Western Hill, where Jesus healed a blind man by placing mud in his eyes, symbolizing the many in Jerusalem who were blind to Jesus. Here as well is the majestic royal palace of

Babylonian (Gentile) rulers, and the Kidron River at the foot of the Mount of Olives. All buildings were required to be built of different colors of rock for the different hills.

There were four tower fortresses for the Roman garrisons, including Antonia Fortress, named after Herod the Great's patron, Marc Antony, adjacent to the Temple Mount.

Jerusalem is first mentioned in Egyptian documents from the twentieth century BC. It became a fortified city with a complete water system by the eighteenth century BC. It has been occupied by Canaanites, Israelites, Babylonians, Persians, Greeks, Romans, Byzantines, Arabs, Crusaders, Mamelukes, and Turks.

It is first mentioned in the Bible in Genesis 14:18 when Abraham meets Melchizedek, the king of Salem, thought to be an abbreviation for Jerusalem. Then in Genesis 22:2 Abraham offers Isaac as a sacrifice during God's test on Mount Moriah, where Solomon built the First Temple (2 Chronicles 3:1).

Jews know it as the site of the two temples, and mentioned Jerusalem 667 times in the Old Testament, pray facing Jerusalem—and when in Jerusalem, pray facing the Temple site, and consider the Wailing Wall to be their holiest site. The Jewish holy cities are Jerusalem, Hebron (in the West Bank), Tiberias, and Safed.

Christians know it as the place where Christ had His Last Supper, Crucifixion, burial, and Resurrection, where the Church was born at Pentecost, and where He will return to judge the living and the dead.

Muslims consider it their third holiest site after Mecca and Medina, at one time being told by Muhammad to pray bowing toward Jerusalem. They believe their prophet Muhammad ascended a ladder to the throne of Allah from here.

Jerusalem is seen as the world's place of final judgment and redemption. Medieval maps and the Italian poet Dante placed it at the center of the universe.

Jerusalem was conquered and its residents killed by the tribe of Judah.

David made it his capital, brought the Ark of the Covenant, and reigned here thirty-three of his forty years (1010–970 BC). This was four centuries after the Israelites returned under Moses' successor, Joshua, as the Jebusites had continued to control the city. At that time, the city only included the spur of land south of the Temple Mount outside today's walls. David purchased the threshing floor of Araunah the Jebusite, where Solomon's Temple later sat.

Solomon reigned here over a time of peace and prosperity for thirty-nine years (970–931 BC), and built the Temple. King Nebuchadnezzar of Babylon ransacked and burned Jerusalem in 586 BC, and the people were exiled to Babylon, making them yearn for Jerusalem.

Egyptian pharaoh Shishak attacked the city and plundered the Temple in 926 BC. King Joash of Judah set aside funds to repair it in 835 BC. King Jehoash of Israel attacked, tore down the city walls, and took the Temple treasures to Samaria.

Herod the Great started constructing his temple in 20 BC, which Jesus visited both as an infant and at age twelve. At both the beginning and the end of His public ministry, He cleansed the Temple. He healed a man at the pool of Bethesda nearby.

During Passion Week, Jesus rode a donkey down the Mount of Olives, through the Valley of Kidron, and up into Jerusalem, entering through the Sheep's Gate to foreshadow His becoming our Sacrificial Lamb. They cried "Hosanna," which means "deliver me," as a *political* statement not a *religious* statement. Even though Sunday was lamb selection day (Exodus 12), they were *not* wanting delivery of another sacrifice—not understanding, again, that God had indeed selected His Lamb. The palm branch symbol had been on their coins from the latest Jewish independence back to the Maccabees.

Jesus cried that week: grieving over Lazarus' death in Bethany, over Jerusalem upon entering Sunday, and over His burden in the Garden of Gethsemane late Thursday night.

Back on the Mount of Olives, He told of the destruction of the Temple and later prayed in the Garden of Gethsemane before His betrayal and arrest. He washed the feet of His disciples and served the first Lord's Supper. He was tried, crucified, buried, and resurrected; and appeared before disciples and other followers here.

Jesus ascended to Heaven from the Mount of Olives. The Holy Spirit came down on Pentecost when the Church was born. Peter and others preached the Gospel message in the Temple. Stephen was stoned to death just outside the city wall with Saul watching. Saul, a fanatic of the Law, was commissioned by Jewish leaders to pursue Christ's followers in Tarsus, but was converted en route. He returned fourteen years later as Paul, a fanatic of grace, for the first Church Council. At the end of his missionary journeys, he returned here, only to be arrested and taken to Rome.

Jerusalem and the Temple were destroyed by Titus in AD 70, as foretold by Jesus, and then again by emperor Hadrian in AD 135. The present city walls were built by Suleyman I during the Turkish Era (1617–1917), followed by the British Era (1917–1948), the Jordanian Era (1948–1967) and independence in 1967.

Short History of Jerusalem:

3000–1000 BC: Canaanites to Abraham and Isaac, Egyptian exile, Moses, Joshua, Judges, Saul, David, the Ark of Covenant, and the Temple Mount.

1000–980 BC: Israelites to David and Solomon and United Kingdoms, religious and political center, Rehoboam, Jeroboam, Israelites to the north, Judeans to the south.

600 BC: Hezekiah and Assyrian exile for Israelites, Nebuchadnezzar and Babylonian exile for Judeans, Temple burned.

600–500 BC: Persian king Cyrus allowed Israelites to return, yet only some did, second Temple and city rebuilt, Ezra and Nehemiah.

300–150 BC: Hellenists, Alexander the Great captures city from Persians, Hanukkah, and purification of Temple.

150–60 BC: Hasmoneans, independent rule.

60 BC: Romans, Pompey, head of Roman army, captures city.

48–37 BC: Romans, Temple Mount reconstructed and expanded by king Herod.

66–70 AD: Romans, Great Revolt, Titus, Temple destroyed.

300–600 AD: Byzantines, Christian rule under emperor Constantine, monasteries, churches, pilgrimages.

600–630 AD: Persians, Persian occupation, then Byzantine occupation, Jews massacred.

640–1100 AD: Early Muslims—captured by Caliph Omar (not mentioned in Koran), Dome of the Rock (691 AD).

1100–1200 AD: Crusaders—Christian Europe's religious revival, captured in 1099 and massacred Jews/Muslims, recaptured by Muslims in 1187 and converted churches to mosques, agreement in 1229 AD for Muslims to keep Temple Mount and Crusaders to keep the rest of the city (lasted only fifteen years).

1250–1500 AD: Mamelukes, Turks ruled Egypt, city now third holiest Muslim site.

Scripture:
Genesis 14:18–27, 22:1–18
Judges 1:7–8
1 Samuel 17:54
2 Samuel 5:4–24:25
1 Kings
2 Kings
1 Chronicles
2 Chronicles
Ezra
Nehemiah
Psalms 51:18, 79, 122, 128:5, 137, 147
Song of Songs 6:4
Isaiah 1–4, 37–38, 44:24–28
Jeremiah 33:16, 38:28–39:9
Lamentations 1
Ezekiel
Daniel 6:10, 9
Joel 3:16–17
Zechariah 2:1–4, 8, 12, 14
Matthew 2:1, 4:25, 15:1, 16:21, 20:18, 21:1–28:15
Mark 10:33–34, 11:11–16, 27, 15:41
Luke 1:5–25, 2:21–50, 4:9–12, 5:17, 9:31–51, 13:33–35, 18:31–33, 19:28–24:12, 33–53

John 2:13, 23, 3:1–21, 4:19, 5:2, 7:10–10:39, 11:55, 12:12–20:31

Acts 1:3–8:3, 8:14, 9:26–30, 11, 12:25, 13:31, 15:1–30, 20:22, 21:12–23:32, 25:15–24

Romans 15:19, 25–28

1 Corinthians 15:4–7

Galatians 4:25–26

Hebrews 12:22

Revelation 3:12, 21:2, 10

What to See:

Today, **Jerusalem,** the ancient capital of Judea is the State of Israel's capital. In 1996, Israelis celebrated the 3000th anniversary of Jerusalem as the capital of Israel, which despite many years of conquest against it, was never the capital of any other country, religion, or people.

It contains the small **Old City**, which is less than one percent of Jerusalem's total size, and is surrounded by high fortified walls and ramparts, along with the modern New City, including the Knesset, Israel's Parliament; Yad Vashem, the Holocaust museum; Hebrew University; and the model of the Old City as it was in Jesus' era. The Old City has four quarters (Jewish, Muslim, Christian and Armenian), eight gates, the Temple Mount and the Western or Wailing Wall. Under Jordanian (Arab) rule until 1967's Six-Day War, Israel now rules the Old City, where the Jewish population has doubled since.

The **Jewish Quarter** to the southeast, between Dung and Zion Gates, was rebuilt after reunification in 1967 following the nineteen years of Jordanian rule. Within are the Western Wall remains, the Cardo, a restored main street from the sixth century Byzantine era that runs from Damascus Gate to Mount Zion, the Tower of David Museum, ancient synagogues, and **Hezekiah's (or Siloam) Tunnel** under the Temple Mount. This tunnel is worth a tour, although you would walk partially in the dark, in water up to your ankles. It is not for claustrophobics, often just the width of your shoulders. The 600-yard-long construction started at both ends and miraculously met in the middle within four feet of each other, and is the basis of a story in James Michener's *The Source*. Built in 700 BC by king

Hezekiah to protect the water supply from invading Assyrians and channel the water from Gihon Springs outside the city walls into the Pool of Siloam within the walls, it was where the blind man was sent by Jesus to wash the clay from his eyes and came back seeing.

The **Muslim Quarter**, to the northeast from Damascus to Herod's, Lion's and Dung Gates, has the colorful, vibrant marketplace, the Temple Mount, and parts of the Via Dolorosa.

The **Christian Quarter** to the northwest from Jaffa to New Gate to Damascus Gate, has the Church of the Holy Sepulchre (considered by many to be the holiest site in Christendom), many churches, monasteries, and some of the Stations of the Cross on the Via Dolorosa. It is quieter and wealthier than the Muslim Quarter due to the better educational system.

The **Armenian Quarter** to the southwest from Jaffa to Zion Gates has Ramparts Walk, St. James Monastery, Armenian Museum (commemorating the slaughter of one-third of the Armenian people during World War I), beautiful pottery, and the Tower of David, today it is a seventeenth century mosque built on earlier ruins.

Prayer:

Lord Jesus,

You are our Savior who has healed our many physical, emotional, and spiritual maladies. We thank You that Your heart identifies with our suffering as it did with that of the lame man. Help us to see what You see—any areas of our lives today where we have chosen badly, either consciously or unconsciously. Show us what we need to confess and where we need to turn around so that true, permanent healing can begin in the deepest parts of our lives.

In Your precious name,

Amen

Worship:

"There is Healing in His Name"
"This is Where the Healing Begins"

JERUSALEM: BETHPHAGE

Historical Significance:

It was the day after Jesus was anointed with perfume by Mary, at her home with Lazarus and Martha, in Bethany, two miles southeast of Jerusalem. Fulfilling the prophecy in Zechariah 9:9, Jesus deliberately started Passion Week with the Triumphal Entry on Palm Sunday—on a donkey colt with its mother (Matthew 21:1–3). The donkey symbolized humility and gentle peace (as opposed to a war horse) and Davidic royalty (2 Samuel 18:9, 1 Kings 43–44). That no one had ridden it added a religious use (Numbers 19:2). This served to provoke the Jewish leaders.

Bethphage ("house of the early figs") is mentioned in the Talmud, not in the Old Testament, and only here in the New Testament. As Jesus descended the Mount of Olives, He wept for His beloved Jerusalem and its people, who celebrated His arrival with palms and shouts of "Hosanna"—only to crucify Him a few days later! His tears showed that He knew His beloved citizens of Jerusalem did not understand His entire mission—that of peace and submission to the Father. The palms that they waved were actually symbols of the Zealots as they entered into warfare. Peace was the furthest thing from *their* minds, as they looked to Jesus to fight their *earthly* battles instead of to save their *eternal* souls.

What to See:

Off the Jericho highway on the eastern slope of the Mount of Olives lies the **Church of Bethphage and a Franciscan monastery** built in 1883 on the traditional site of Jesus' mounting the colt at the start of the Triumphal Entry into Jerusalem.

Scripture:

Zechariah 9:9 (quoted in Matthew 21:5 and John 12:15)
Matthew 21:1–9

Mark 11:1–10
Luke 9:28–44
John 12:12–16
definingmomentsbook.com/resources

Defining Moment . . . The Franciscan Church in Bethphage

Even though the Scriptures told the Jews who Jesus would be when He came (The Prince of Peace), they had their own ideas of why He was coming. They had been so persecuted by the Romans that they were just sure the Messiah would arrive and overcome the injustices that the Romans had inflicted on them. When Jesus did not show up like they expected Him to, they no longer thought He was the Messiah.

We would like to think that we would not have fallen for the same deception if we were alive in Jesus' time. The problem is, we still suffer from this malady today. Many of us have a certain idea, birthed in our own minds, of who God is and what He is supposed to do for us. The problem is, when He does not show up like we expect, we think He is not moving.

We forget that God's number-one goal is to spiritually form us into the true identity He has given us to live out eternally. That spiritual formation does not come about from telling God how we want our lives to turn out, and then watching Him deliver on our prayer requests like the candy man. *Spiritual formation comes from suffering.* Before you disconnect at hearing this bad news, let me remind you of the many examples that God gives in the world that use stress to build things up:

- Our muscles do not get bigger without stressing them. When we lift weights, it tears down our muscle fibers. Our bodies build them back up stronger than they were before.
- The best wine in the world is made from stressed vines that do not get the most water. The vines that get more water get overburdened with fruit that is not the best quality. The underwatered, stressed vines produce less—but higher quality—fruit.
- Steel is only made strong once it is heated to high levels. Molecular changes solidify the metal to make it incredibly strong, but only after it has been put through immense heat.

We make suffering into a bad word. It conjures up pain and difficulty in our minds, and we avoid it. God is not asking us to enjoy suffering, but He does want us to appreciate that in His hands, it will be used to glorify the Kingdom. *"And we know that in all things God works for the good of those who love Him, who have been called according to His purpose"* (Romans 8:28).

Here is an example:

Julie's father was an alcoholic who put the family through incredible suffering. There were even near-death experiences as a result of his drinking. When Julie was twelve, her mother had divorced her father. Within the next couple of years, her mother married a Christian man who adopted and loved her and all of her siblings as if they were his own. Julie finally had the stable, Godly father that she had always dreamed of. When she became a woman, Julie was being courted by a widower with two teenage children. Many women would have been intimidated by the situation, but because of Julie's past, she was unafraid to marry this man and pour herself into these children. God used her suffering to equip her to be a huge blessing. It did not mean that life was perfect but that she was perfectly prepared to be a blessing.

How is God inviting *you* into the precious experience of using *your* suffering for *His* Glory?

Journal Time:

Think about the times that you have suffered. What did it bring out in you? How did God turn your suffering into a blessing for His Kingdom? Is there an area of suffering that you are going through now? How can you hold it differently, seeing it as a future blessing instead of focusing on the current pain?

Share Time:

Encourage each other with accounts of how God used your suffering for His Glory. Uplift those in the group that are dealing with suffering now, helping them focus on God's plan instead of their own pain.

Prayer:

Jesus,

Help us with our warped view of suffering. We confess that we run from it and can be afraid of discomfort in our lives. Thank You for the promise that in all things You work for our good. Help us, through Your power, to chase after our spiritual formation ahead of those things that make us comfortable. Keep us from wanting Your blessings more than wanting You and Your deepest work in us. We need You to authentically get to this place, and we are trusting You to take us there.

In Your name,

Amen

Worship:

"Blessed Be the Name of the Lord"

"Who Will Suffer With the Savior?"

JERUSALEM: CALVARY (GOLGOTHA)

Historical Significance:

Calvary (Latin, Calvaria, a bald place) or Golgotha (Aramaic) (*skull* is *gulgolet* in Hebrew) or Place of the Skull (Greek, found in Matthew 27:33) is the place just outside the city walls, near the Damascus Gate, where our faith is founded—the death and Resurrection of Jesus Christ. Everywhere in Israel points here, to the fulfillment of the promise made to Abraham fifty miles south. The hill may have looked like a skull, or it may have been so named due to the many executions there. Jesus was crucified along with two criminals (appropriately being identified with sinners in his brutal death for us). One of the two accepted His gift of Salvation, and the other rejected it.

His outer garment, under garment, belt, sandals, and head garment were divided between the four executioners, as was their right, unknowingly fulfilling the prophecy of Psalm 22:18.

The customary wooden sign listing the condemned man's charge said, "King of the Jews" in Aramaic, (a wider regional language of the Jews, used as well as Hebrew), Latin (the language of Rome), and Greek (the common language of the Roman empire). Pilate mocked the Jewish leaders, for they wanted Jesus killed for only *claiming* to be "King of the Jews."

John was the only disciple at the Crucifixion. The rest were hiding in fear, even though Jesus had prophesied forty-three times (in the four Gospels) about his death, Resurrection, and Second Coming. John was joined by Mary, Jesus' mother, who Jesus then entrusted to John for the balance of her life, instead of to the care of His own brothers; Mary Magdalene; and Mary the wife of Clopas, mother of James the Younger and Joses.

Weakened from His beatings, He had carried a beam of His Cross, weighing thirty to forty pounds, part of the way, until Simon of Cyrene helped Him.

He cried out to His Father in Aramaic, "*My God, My God, why have You forsaken Me?*" and later declared: "*It is finished!*" in victory. His suffering was for about three hours to fulfill other prophecies, not the more common two to three days. It then went dark for three hours when He was taken down from the Cross. The priest would blow the shofar for the lamb's death at 3 p.m.

The tall, thick curtain of the Temple that separated the Holy Place from the Most Holy Place was torn in half. It symbolized that Christ had entered Heaven and that *we* may now enter God's presence *directly* (Hebrews 10:19–20). Love had conquered!

Joseph of Arimathea, a city twenty miles northwest of Jerusalem, was one of the seventy-one judges of the Sanhedrin (like Saul). Joseph of Arimathea was a rich, secret disciple of Jesus who had just built for himself an unused, expensive tomb in a garden very near Calvary. Accompanied by Nicodemus, he courageously asked Pilate for Jesus' body for burial in his own tomb. The tomb had an antechamber in front, a burial chamber in the rear, and a disc-shaped stone that rolled in an angled channel to seal the entrance.

Before dawn on Sunday, while the men remained in hiding after observing the Sabbath, Jesus' mother Mary, Mary Magdalene, and Salome, the wife of Zebedee and mother of James and John, went to the Tomb to anoint Jesus' body. They also did not expect the promised Resurrection. They found the stone rolled away—not to let Jesus *out*, but to let them *in*! An angel of the Lord and then Jesus (disguised as a gardener) appeared. When the women told the disciples, Peter and John raced to the Tomb, to also find it empty. Do *you* live today truly knowing the Tomb is empty and that He is alive? Do you share that Good News with others?

What to See:

The traditional site of the Tomb has been the Church of the Holy Sepulchre (see next listing), which is believed to be on the site of a first century cemetery. What matters to us is the Person, not the place, for *"He is not here; He is risen,"* meaning our faith rests on His Resurrection not on where it happened. Even if this is not Jesus' Tomb, I know there is one nearby, and I know it is empty! See His unbelievable humanity and humility; He is so near, just like the Gardener. May we never be the same again.

However, **The Garden Tomb** site is also believed by many to be the original burial Tomb for Christ, given by his secret follower Joseph of Arimathea. Burials were both nearby (John 19:20) and outside (Hebrews 13:12) the city walls. There is another site adjacent to a rock face that looks like a skull, with a carved, unfinished, twelve foot by twenty-two foot empty Tomb with a groove in front for a rolling stone to close up the entrance. You can enter the Tomb as did the women and Peter. There are gardens, where the Gardener spoke to Mary Magdalene, who then experienced the quickest five seconds from deepest despair to deepest joy! The Garden Tomb has numerous seating areas to sit and reflect, or gather as a group or privately, a viewing platform, and a chapel in which to take communion.

Solomon's Quarry, where stones were carved to build his Temple, was north of the city as is this limestone outcrop.

The area near **Skull Hill** was known as the **Place for Stoning**. Jews threw people over a cliff and then stoned them if they survived the fall (St. Stephen's Church is nearby). Romans crucified people along busy highways as a warning to others, and this was by the roads to Jericho and Damascus.

In 1867, when Israel was part of the Turkish empire, a Greek man digging to find a water cistern found a hole full of skulls and bones and abandoned the ancient burial place. In 1883, a British soldier and Bible scholar, General Gordon, saw from a friend's home on the city wall a skull-like rock face that could be Golgotha. After his murder in Khartoum, interested British Christians bought the land in 1894 from the Germans, and founded an association to maintain it as "a sacred, quiet spot." They were required to build a wall separating it from the Muslim cemetery. Volunteers for an English foundation live on-site for short periods to maintain it.

John's Gospel mentions a garden by Joseph's tomb where Mary Magdalene mistook the "gardener." Water was necessary due to the hot summers. This site has several water cisterns to collect winter rains, including the third largest in the city, along with a wine press suggesting a vineyard. The garden was restored by removing the earth and rubble in the 1890s. On Easter Sunday, successive services continue from before dawn until midday in six languages.

Scripture:
Matthew 27:32–28:15
Mark 6:29, 15:21–16:8
Luke 23:26–24:8
John 19:16–20:18
Acts 2:29
definingmomentsbook.com/resources

Defining Moment . . . The Garden Tomb

As Christ was preparing to leave His best friends and disciples, He knew that they would remember Him but that in their humanity they may not remember Him for the things He so lovingly longed for them to focus on. As much as Jesus wants us to remember our victories in Him, our human side recalls our failures far more than He wants us to. Yes, Peter would remember Him healing his mother-in-law and surprising him with gigantic boatloads of fish, but he also might ruminate on his own weaknesses. He might remember the time he fell into the water because, as he was walking on it, his faith wavered, or the time he told Christ he would never deny Him. What does Jesus remember about these times? Our God promises that He *separates us from our failures* (Psalm 103:12), so He is probably remembering how excited He was to see Peter get out of the boat and run to Him, or how at Taghba Peter told Him three times that he loved Him and would feed His sheep. Jesus remembers the good things.

Journal Time:

Jesus has a heart for us to remember the awesome parts of who He is in our lives. He came in a human body to experience all that we are, with all the joys and hardships, beauty and ugliness, victories, and defeats that this world offers. To remember that He came in this bodily form, answer, "What does His body mean to you?"

On our trip to Israel together, to Rick, it meant that He came in a body like ours, and He will give us a new body in Heaven. To Susan, it meant that His body achieved victory over death, and He achieved victory over every fear, turning it into joy. What does His body mean to *you*?

As we think of Christ's blood that was shed for us, we often focus on the sadness and the regret of how He was treated on earth, and we are overcome by confession of our part in crucifying Him. While our Lord treasures our repentant hearts, His real plan was for us to rejoice because our names are written in the Book of Life! The shedding of His blood enabled eternal life for us. Answer the question, "What does His blood mean to you?"

To Rick, it meant that He experienced far more sadness and despair than we, so we would not have to face an Eternity of sorrow. To Susan, it meant that she will never fall out of God's hands. What does His blood mean to *you?* May Christ's body and blood bring remembrance to you of how very much He loves you.

Share Time:

Break off into groups of two. You will be serving communion to each other.

As God helps you reveal your answers above, tell your partner what Christ's body is to you. Now, take the flatbread that represents His body, and serve it to your partner, speaking back the words describing what Christ's body means to that person. Have your partner then do the same for you.

Repeat the process of speaking back the words that Christ's blood means to your partner, as you serve him or her the wine. Have your partner then do the same for you.

You will now never experience communion the same again! Without ever discussing it, and every time since, whenever we take communion, Rick serves Susan, reminding her what Jesus wants her to remember, and then Susan serves Rick, reminding him what Jesus wants him to remember.

Prayer:

Lord,

Thank You for separating us from our failures. Thank You for remembering what is best about us. Help us to remember who You really are to us. We long to be one with You and the Father as You prayed before You left the earth. Keep us remembering those things that You revealed to us today. Thank You for dying on the Cross for us, for rising again in victory and for the gift of eternal life that nothing can take away from us. We celebrate You and remember You with great joy.

    In Jesus' name,
    Amen

Worship:

    "Were You There When They Crucified My Lord?"
    "Christ the Lord is Risen Today"
    "He is Risen"

JERUSALEM:
CHURCH OF THE HOLY SEPULCHRE

Historical Significance:

In the Christian Quarter of Jerusalem is one of the most sacred places in Christianity. The Church of the Holy Sepulchre is the traditional site for Jesus' Crucifixion, burial, and Resurrection at Calvary. Here is the rocky outcrop, a quarry in which the wealthy hewed their tombs, some still visible inside the church, outside what was then the city wall and away from places of residence, as Jewish Law prohibited burials within the holy city.

Constantine built a basilica over a former temple of Herod's, Calvary, and the Tomb. This basilica was later destroyed by infidels, which contributed to the start of the Crusades. The present structure was built in 1149 by Crusaders after their conquest of Jerusalem. Six different groups share the church today: Greek Orthodox, Roman Catholic (Franciscan order), Armenian Orthodox, Syrian Orthodox, Coptic, and Abyssinian Orthodox Christians.

What to See:

The **tenth through fourteenth Stations of the Cross** are located inside this complex of chapels and churches presided over by multiple faiths.

10th Station: Roman Catholic chapel. After climbing the steep stairway just inside to the right, you will see a floor mosaic on the right commemorating Jesus being stripped of His clothes.

11th Station: To remind us of Jesus allowing Himself to be nailed to the Cross, a large fresco depicting this event is behind the altar.

12th Station: Greek Orthodox chapel with Altar of the Crucifixion. A narrow stairway leads up the traditional Hill of Calvary to the Rock of Calvary beneath the altar, where one can touch the site where the Cross was allegedly erected. The rock is visible through the glass cases on either side of the altar.

13th Station: A small altar commemorates Jesus' body being removed from the Cross.

14th Station: Remembering Jesus' burial anointing is the Stone of the Anointing, also called the Stone of Unction, downstairs ahead of the main entrance.

The Holy Sepulchre is to the left inside white marble walls, the burial Tomb (or sepulchre) represented by a marble slab. It is believed the original slab is under this one.

Sixty Ethiopian monks live in mud huts on its roof, trying to maintain their small community.

When visiting this site: please no knees or shoulders exposed.

Scripture:
Matthew 27:35–60
Mark 15:22–16:1
Luke 23:33–24:1
John 19:17–20:1
definingmomentsbook.com/resources

Defining Moment . . . The Church of the Holy Sepulchre
Your itinerary most likely will include *either* the Garden Tomb OR The Church of the Holy Sepulchre. Use the "Defining Moment . . . The Garden Tomb" in the prior section here.

JERUSALEM:
CHURCH OF SAINT PETER IN GALLICANTU

Historical Significance:

Jesus' *Jewish* trial consisted of a preliminary hearing by the respected former high priest, Annas, followed by a trial by the high priest, Caiaphas, (a Sadducee who was Annas's son-in-law), secretly upstairs in his home along with the entire Sanhedrin. Then the Sanhedrin council's official special session at dawn on Friday of Passion Week to make the death sentence legal—for treason, not blasphemy, as he was originally charged.

Even though Annas was deposed after nine years by the Romans, the Jews and the Romans still recognized his authority. Annas was followed in office by five of his sons and his son-in-law, Caiaphas. Annas still had a great deal of influence, which is why they first took Jesus before him. How fair a trial was possible in front of Caiaphas, who had been part of the earlier plot to kill Jesus, saying it would be more expedient for one man to die—no matter how innocent—than the entire nation? He was more focused on the political solution than on guilt or innocence. Ironically, in 70 AD, the nation died anyway.

Jesus' *Roman* trial consisted of Governor Pontius Pilate's initial trial, followed at Herod the Great's magnificent palace, by Herod Antipas's trial, then by Pilate's final decision.

The Sanhedrin (high court) consisted of seventy-one Pharisees and Sadducees from three courts including the Court of Priests (representing high priests and their male descendants), Court of Elders (representing the wealthy), Court of Pharisees (representing the masses), and Teachers of the Law (perhaps also Saul of Tarsus). The Romans gave them great authority but not the right to determine capital punishment, except in cases where a foreigner entered the Temple. They never met at night, so after the pretrial where Jesus "blasphemed" by admitting who He is, He was placed in this dungeon by the priests until early morning without telling the Pharisees or the Elders, so the priests would have the majority vote.

Peter entered Caiaphas's courtyard while Jesus was being tried, beaten, and scourged upstairs. The servant, doorkeeper, and others recognized the Galilean with his different accent and accused him of being "*with that Nazarene.*" Peter later three times denied knowing Jesus, and, as prophesied, in all four Gospels, the rooster crowed (*gallicantu*). Peter then "*went outside and wept bitterly.*"

While Peter may be easily criticized for falling after walking on water and for denying Christ those three times, *we* should have the boldness to be the only one to try to walk on water toward Jesus, the only one to strike the servant of the high priest with a sword in Gethsemane, and one of only two—John being the other—not to flee in fear after Jesus' arrest.

What to See:

This church was rebuilt in 1931 by the Assumptionist Fathers, an Augustinian Catholic order, over what is considered to be the high priest Caiaphas's house on the eastern side of Mount Zion, among pine, olive, cypress, and pepper trees. The ancient steps outside on the left that have been excavated were likely those Jesus took en route to Caiaphas's palace. Neil Armstrong, the first man to walk on the moon, declared that visiting Caiaphas's house was "the best moment of my life."

While we do not know if Jesus was actually imprisoned in the cold, damp dungeon deep below the church, it is a great place to contemplate His night of suffering for our sake, and to sing praises of love and gratitude to Him. Some believe Caiaphas's house was more likely at the top of the hill.

Scripture:

Matthew 26:31–35, 57–75
Mark 14:27–31, 53–72
Luke 22:31–34, 54–62
John 11:45–53, 13:31–38, 18:15–27
definingmomentsbook.com/resources

Defining Moment . . . Church of St. Peter in Gallicantu

The steps that you are walking down behind this church are likely the same steps that Jesus walked as he was en route to be judged by Caiaphas. It is hard to imagine the pain that He was in. He knew what was coming, not just from an earthly standpoint, but also in realms that we cannot even imagine. Often, we are horrified as we think of the suffering on the Cross and the humiliation and physical torture that occurred. But that torment was but a fraction of what was coming. Jesus was about to take all the sins of the world on His shoulders, which separated Him from His Father. That was a torment that we probably will not ever fully understand, because if Jesus really allowed us to see the sacrifice that was involved, we probably could not bear it.

As we stood in the pit underneath the church that Jesus was likely imprisoned in, we are horrified by the punishment that He took on for us. Standing in Jesus' shoes, though, what must it have been like to be dragged into this pit under false accusations? The Jewish leaders had been plotting this for some time, and now they had enough false witnesses to make their case. Jesus did not call down condemnation and judgment on His accusers—though He could have. He did not agree with nor argue against their false accusations, either. He stuck to His mission that the Father had set before Him, leaving His accusers to their own sin. He never called out their lies about Him. He knew their origin, and He was headed to victory over sin.

Journal Time:

Think of a time that *you* have been falsely accused. How did you respond? What was the price that you paid? Ask God to show you how you can learn from how Jesus handled false accusations.

Share Time:

Share with one another the leadings that you are getting from God on how to handle false accusation. Share with each other experiences you have had and where you have handled them well and where you have not. Encourage each other to forgive your false accusers, and leave them in God's capable hands.

Prayer:

Lord,

Thank you for taking the punishment for our sins. Thank you for showing us how to handle false accusations. Lord, we confess that we have not handled false accusations in ways that surrendered them to You in the past. Forgive us for the lies that we have believed, the vengeance that we have taken, and the toxic thoughts that we have ruminated on. We want Your ways, not our ways. Show us Your way to forgiveness and freedom.

In Jesus' name,

Amen

Worship:

"Create in Me"

"I Need Thee Every Hour"

JERUSALEM: DOMINUS FLEVIT CHURCH

Historical Significance:

On Palm Sunday of Passion Week, Jesus looked across the Kidron Valley as he rode the colt down from the western slope of the Mount of Olives. Seeing His beloved Jerusalem, knowing the misguided hearts of the people, and the future destruction of the Temple, He wept over it. He grieved over how they had turned the Temple, God's dwelling place, into a den of thieves. On Thursday night, He would return to Gethsemane at the bottom of the Mount of Olives to pray tears of blood as He cried out to His Father. When Jesus returns in glory, the Mount of Olives will be split in half, and His people will finally lament over what they did to Him (Zechariah 14:4).

What to See:

By AD 400, there were twenty-four convents and monasteries located in Jerusalem. A small, sixth century Byzantine chapel and monastery was built. Today the tear-shaped Dominus Flevit Church ("The Lord Wept"), built by the Franciscans, features large windows over the altar with a view of Jerusalem. This is the traditional site where Jesus may have wept.

Scripture:

Isaiah 22:4
Luke 13:34–35, 19:37–44
definingmomentsbook.com/resources

Defining Moment . . . Dominus Flevit Church

"Jesus wept." It is the shortest verse in the Bible, but it is also where we get to see the compassion of our Lord.

There is a great movie called *The Visual Bible: Matthew*. Bruce Marchiano is the actor who portrays Jesus. He wrote about the experience of making the movie in his book *In the Footsteps of Jesus: One Man's Journey.* Before each scene, Bruce asked Jesus to share with him exactly what He was feeling and thinking when He was living it. When Bruce asked Jesus about the passage below, He described being brokenhearted, as if He was jilted by someone He loved very much. Hearing that perspective gives us a whole new framing of Jesus weeping with a broken heart as He said the following:

Woe to you, teachers of the law and Pharisees, you hypocrites! You shut the door of the Kingdom of Heaven in people's faces. You yourselves do not enter, nor will you let those enter who are trying to.

Woe to you, teachers of the law and Pharisees, you hypocrites! You travel over land and sea to win a single convert, and when you have succeeded, you make them twice as much a child of hell as you are.

Woe to you, blind guides! You say, 'If anyone swears by the Temple, it means nothing; but anyone who swears by the gold of the Temple is bound by that oath.' You blind fools! Which is greater: the gold, or the Temple that makes the gold sacred? You also say, 'If anyone swears by the altar, it means nothing; but anyone who swears by the gift on the altar is bound by that oath.' You blind men! Which is greater: the gift, or the altar that makes the gift sacred? Therefore, anyone who swears by the altar swears by it and by everything on it. And anyone who swears by the Temple swears by it and by the one who dwells in it. And anyone who swears by Heaven swears by God's throne and by the one who sits on it.

Woe to you, teachers of the law and Pharisees, you hypocrites! You give a tenth of your spices—mint, dill, and cumin. But you have neglected the more important matters of the law—justice, mercy and faithfulness. You should have practiced the latter, without neglecting the former. You blind guides! You strain out a gnat but swallow a camel."

Woe to you, teachers of the law and Pharisees, you hypocrites! You clean the outside of the cup and dish, but inside they are full of greed and self-indulgence. Blind Pharisee! First clean the inside of the cup and dish, and then the outside also will be clean.

Woe to you, teachers of the law and Pharisees, you hypocrites! You are like whitewashed tombs, which look beautiful on the outside but on the inside are full of the bones of the dead and everything unclean. In the same way, on the outside you appear to people as righteous but on the inside you are full of hypocrisy and wickedness.

Woe to you, teachers of the law and Pharisees, you hypocrites! You build tombs for the prophets and decorate the graves of the righteous. And you say, 'If we had lived in the days of our ancestors, we would not have taken part with them in shedding the blood of the prophets.' So you testify against yourselves that you are the descendants of those who murdered the prophets. Go ahead, then, and complete what your ancestors started!

You snakes! You brood of vipers! How will you escape being condemned to hell? Therefore I am sending you prophets and sages and teachers. Some of them you will kill and crucify; others you will flog in your synagogues and pursue from town to town. And so upon you will come all the righteous blood that has been shed on earth, from the blood of righteous Abel to the blood of Zechariah son of Berekiah, whom you murdered between the temple and the altar. Truly I tell you, all this will come on this generation.

Jerusalem, Jerusalem, you who kill the prophets and stone those sent to you, how often I have longed to gather your children together, as a hen gathers her chicks under her wings, and you were not willing. Look, your house is left to you desolate. For I tell you, you will not see me again until you say, "Blessed is he who comes in the name of the Lord"
(Matthew 23:13–39).

Prior to reading Bruce's experience, I always saw Jesus seething with anger as He spoke the words above. Hearing Him weeping as if He has been rejected by the love of His life gave me an entirely different perspective of His love and compassion.

Journal Time:

Jesus' heart was broken, but He longed to "gather Jerusalem's children together, as a hen gathers her chicks under her wings." Even though Jesus' compassion was available, Jerusalem declined it. They wanted to earn the Kingdom through works instead of surrendering to Jesus. Watching as outsiders, we can judge their folly. However, are there areas of your *own* life that Jesus wants to pour compassion over, yet *you* are declining? Is there an area where you are trying to use legalism to fix yourself, rather than surrendering to Jesus and His compassion? Ask the Holy Spirit to show you just one of those areas, and then give Jesus permission to pour His grace and redemption and compassion into that place in your heart. Or, do you have a story already of giving Jesus that freedom to pour His compassion over you?

Share Time:

Share your stories either of where you need Jesus' compassion or of where you have received it already. Encourage those who are having a hard time receiving Jesus' grace. Remind them to renounce any lies of shame, guilt, self-sufficiency, or unbelief that are keeping them from reveling in the compassion of Jesus.

Prayer:

Lord,

You wept near here because of our sins and our rejection of You and Your holiness. Help us to shed tears of heartfelt repentance. Help us to daily connect with Your compassion and give You permission to free us from our past mistakes, and to trust You alone with our future.

(Continue to pray for any individuals in the group that are struggling with this).

In Jesus' name,
Amen

Worship:

"All to Jesus I Surrender"
"Come Thou Fount of Every Blessing"

JERUSALEM: ANTONIA FORTRESS

Historical Significance:

One of four tower fortresses for the Roman garrison stationed in Jerusalem, the Antonia Fortress, named after Herod the Great's patron, Marc Antony, is adjacent to the Temple Mount.

When he was in Jerusalem, Pilate, the Roman governor of Judea from 26–36 AD, (whose official residence was on the coast in Caesarea by the Sea) usually stayed in Herod the Great's magnificent palace on the western side of the city, near the Jaffa Gate.

When there were threats of an uprising, as during Passover with so many Jews in town, he likely took up residence in the Antonia Fortress, the powerful Roman military citadel just northwest of the Temple. The Gospels tell us Jesus was tried, accused, crowned with thorns mocking Him as a false king, and condemned at the Roman governor's official palace, the Praetorium.

Scourging, or flogging, involved a whip with several leather strips with scraps of lead and bones tied to the ends. The Jews limited the blows to thirty-nine, while the Romans' lack of limits often resulted in death. Pilate hoped the flogging would be enough for the Jews, so he could release Jesus, who he knew was no rebel. Pilate thrice pronounced Jesus' innocence (John 18:38, 19:4, 19:6).

Pilate and Herod (whose headquarters was on the Sea of Galilee in Tiberias and who was also in Jerusalem due to the Passover crowds) were rivals until this very day, so Pilate first sent Jesus to Herod, under whose jurisdiction Jesus was. Herod was curious to meet this man he had heard so much about, but then he sent Jesus back to Pilate.

Years later, king Herod had James killed, and arrested Peter during the Feast of Unleavened Bread, delaying trial until after Passover. An angel awoke Peter, who was chained between two soldiers and peacefully sleeping before his likely execution, and they escaped. They were probably held in the Antonia Fortress.

Even later, Paul was also arrested by two Roman centurions and 200 soldiers when a Jewish crowd at the Temple tried to kill him. He spoke to the crowd in Aramaic from the steps leading into the barracks. The tower overlooked the Temple, with the fortress being connected to the Temple at the northwest end by two flights of steps.

What to See:
See "Via Dolorosa" Station #1. The Franciscans today maintain the **Church of the Flagellation** (with a large crown of thorns above the sanctuary) and the **Church of the Condemnation and Imposition of the Cross**.

You can see rough carvings on the flagstones of geometrical patterns in what was likely the outer courtyard, where the Roman soldiers played the Game of the King.

Scripture:
Matthew 27:1–2, 11–31
Mark 15:1–20
Luke 23:1–25
John 18:28–19:16
Acts 12:1–10, 21:31–22:30
definingmomentsbook.com/resources

Defining Moment ... The Churches of Condemnation and Imposition of the Cross and of the Flagellation
The Antonia Fortress is most likely where Pilate judged Jesus and where he used a water basin to wash his hands clean of the guilt of what he was about to do.

> "When Pilate saw that he was getting nowhere, but that instead an uproar was starting, he took water and washed his hands in front of the crowd. 'I am innocent of this man's blood,' he said. 'It is your responsibility'"
>
> (Matthew 27:24).

Pilate was sentencing an innocent man to death, but his real focus was on his own circumstances and finding a way to rid himself of his own guilt for what he was doing.

Contrast that scenario with one that Jesus went through just the night before. Though He was absolutely innocent and knew that the Crucifixion was near, *His* focus was on His disciples. Jesus, like Pilate, calls for a basin of water. But instead of "washing his hands" of the human race, He did something that absolutely shocked His disciples.

> *It was just before the Passover Festival. Jesus knew that the hour had come for Him to leave this world and go to the Father. Having loved His own who were in the world, He loved them to the end. The evening meal was in progress, and the devil had already prompted Judas, the son of Simon Iscariot, to betray Jesus. Jesus knew that the Father had put all things under His power, and that He had come from God and was returning to God; so He got up from the meal, took off His outer clothing, and wrapped a towel around His waist. After that, He poured water into a basin and began to wash His disciples' feet, drying them with the towel that was wrapped around Him*
> (John 13:1–5).

Headed for excruciating pain, Jesus' focus was on those He loved and on serving them. He knew where He was going (back to God). He fully focused on loving and serving those around Him.

Journal Time:

Two water basins were used in less than twenty-four hours—one to serve *oneself* and one to serve *others*. Ask the Holy Spirit to show you where He is calling *you* to serve others, even though the road ahead may be unknown to you. Also, journal about any areas that He reveals to you where you have been self-serving that He is calling you out of.

Share Time:

Share with each other thoughts that the Holy Spirit gave you about serving others. Where is He calling you to serve those around you?

Prayer:

> *Dear Lord,*
>
> *Thank You for choosing to serve us. Your love for us and the lavish ways that You care for us is beyond our hearts' capacity to imagine. Lord, we want to walk in Your footsteps and serve others, even when the road ahead is scary or unknown. We want to care more for others than we do for our own selves because You fill us with Yourself and give us the Father's perfect love to pour out on others. Keep us from serving out of hearts that are legalistically choosing what we think is right. Instead, we want to serve out of a heart of true love, like You did. Thank You for guiding us onto the paths of serving others that You have whispered to us through the Holy Spirit. Please give us faithful, moldable hearts to follow You and trust in Your ways.*
>
> *In Jesus' name,*
> *Amen*

Worship:

> "If We Are the Body" (Casting Crowns)
> "What Wilt Thou Have Me to Do?"

JERUSALEM: GETHSEMANE

Historical Significance:

From Gat, meaning press, and Shimonim, meaning olives. Jesus was greatly pressed in Luke 22:44, agonizing prior to arrest and death to the point of sweating drops of blood like olive oil. An olive press is made of black, porous, round, basalt rock, which symbolizes the weight Jesus carried and how He was pressed out (Messiah means "anointed with olive oil"). *We* were the press, the millstone around His neck; *He* was the olive who took the weight of our sins to hell for six horrific hours.

After the Last Supper, Jesus crossed the Kidron Valley to the east with His disciples to a favorite place of solitude and prayer—the Garden of Gethsemane, an olive orchard on the lower slopes of the Mount of Olives, looking back at His beloved Jerusalem. This is where He experienced great agony, and went away to pray three times; he sweat blood; He was tempted by Satan and comforted by angels. Here He was disappointed three times to find Peter, James, and John sleeping. Here, he was betrayed by Judas to an armed mob, and healed Malchus's ear and protected the disciples, who then abandoned Him before He was led off to trial and Crucifixion. He had known his enemies would come from the city, so he could have easily escaped by taking a ten-minute fast walk up the Mount and disappearing into the open desert.

Gethsemane means "oil press," a place for squeezing oil from olives, a pressing Jesus truly experienced here. On Maundy Thursday, He encountered Satan and his hordes at the cave instead of encountering His Father. The first great battle of the world occurred in the Garden of Eden with Satan battling Adam and Eve. The second great battle occurred in this Garden of Gethsemane with Satan battling the second Adam—Jesus. The third and last great battle is foretold in the book of Revelation.

What to See:

In 614 AD, the Persians demolished the fabulous fourth century **Basilica of the Agony, Church of All Nations.** A fourth century Byzantine basilica, a small eighth century church, and a larger, black-domed Crusader church also stood on the site. Tradition calls the light-colored limestone, on which our Lord's tears and sweat may have fallen as He prayed, the Rock of Agony. Jesus was both human like us (*"take this cup of suffering away from Me"*) and divine (*"not My will, but Your will be done"*). What are *you* going to surrender to God's will that you are holding on to?

The current basilica was built by Roman Catholics from sixteen nations between 1919–1924. The cupolas are decorated with beautiful mosaics, lots of gold, and windows of translucent alabaster covered with lattice work that only allows dim light inside. The façade has a magnificent mosaic with much gold representing Christ's offering of His and the world's suffering to His Father. On the peak near the Cross are two deer—*"As the deer pants for streams of water, so my soul pants for You, O God"* (Psalm 42:1). This is a dangerous place to visit—you can *never* again have *not* been here. There is no turning back for you after this!

The **Grotto of Gethsemane** (aka Grotto of the Betrayal) also has the sunken courtyard of the Tomb of Mary, commemorated since the fifth century by some as her burial place.

Olive trees lack rings to determine their age, unlike other trees, so we do not know how old the eight ancient trees are that are still in the grove of Gethsemane, which is owned by the Vatican today. Olive trees do not die, but just keep producing new shoots. Most likely they are descendants of the original trees, although they are very old. Monks keep the Garden vibrant.

Scripture:

Matthew 26:36–56
Mark 14:32–51
Luke 22:39–53
John 18:1–13
Hebrews 5:7
definingmomentsbook.com/resources

Defining Moment . . . Gethsemane

Then Jesus went with His disciples to a place called Gethsemane, and He said to them, "Sit here while I go over there and pray." He took Peter and the two sons of Zebedee along with Him, and He began to be sorrowful and troubled. Then He said to them, "My soul is overwhelmed with sorrow to the point of death. Stay here and keep watch with Me."

Going a little farther, He fell with His face to the ground and prayed, "My Father, if it is possible, may this cup be taken from Me. Yet not as I will, but as You will."

Then He returned to His disciples and found them sleeping. "Couldn't you men keep watch with Me for one hour?" He asked Peter. "Watch and pray so that you will not fall into temptation. The spirit is willing, but the flesh is weak"

(Matthew 26:36–41).

Imagine Jesus taking his very closest and dearest friends with Him during His darkest hour. Peter, James, and John were asked to go with Him to Gethsemane and keep watch immediately before Jesus was to be taken into custody. Though they were willing, as Jesus said, their flesh kept failing them. The phrase immediately preceding is a curious one: "Watch and pray so that you will not fall into temptation." He could have admonished them to pray so that they would not fall asleep, but I wonder if Jesus was much more concerned with the temptations that were coming their way during His Crucifixion.

In this statement, I can imagine Him saying to them that they will be tempted to abandon Him, to doubt Him and His power and promises, and to have second thoughts about the paths they had chosen for the past three years. "Watch and pray so that you will not fall into temptation." This part of the story could be understood as Jesus needing them to stay awake and pray for Him, but that does not fit the Jesus we know. He always makes it about us, and He knew that the days ahead were going to be a severe trial for

His best friends. He wanted them to pray to keep them from being tempted into dark places that they would deeply regret. It was all about them and how much He loved them.

Journal Time:

Is there a place in *your* life where Jesus is asking you to *"watch and pray so that you will not fall into temptation"*? This is not about condemnation from our Lord, but it is about Him knowing our weaknesses and having compassion on us. He wants to walk through those weaknesses with us, and we have a part to play in that—to pray that we will not fall. He knows that, like His best friends, *our* spirits are willing, but our flesh is weak. He wants to set us up for victory, not remorse. He loves us. Where is He revealing temptation in your life for you to pray over?

Share Time:

Share within your group areas that the Lord is inviting you to pray over so that you do not fall into temptation. This can also be done by breaking up into small groups.

Prayer:

Lord Jesus,

Thank You for Your constant care and love for us. Thank you for facing the Cross. Thank You for Your compassion on us. Lord, like Your best friends, our flesh is weak though our spirits are willing. Please continue to whisper over us those places that need praying over so that we do not fall into temptation. We lift up every one of them revealed here today. We give them to You and Your Resurrection power. We trust in Your saving grace alone.

In Jesus' name,

Amen

Worship:

"There is a Redeemer"

"I Surrender All"

JERUSALEM: KIDRON VALLEY

Historical Significance:
The Temple Mount is to the west, and the Mount of Olives is to the east of the Valley of Kidron. The original eastern entrance to Jerusalem was through the Horse Gate here.

Hezekiah, the "second Solomon," was a religious reformer who purified everything unclean, including the incense altars, from the Temple in the middle of the seventh century BC.

King David fled through here but ordered the Ark of the Covenant be sent back to Jerusalem, where it belonged as the symbol of God's covenant with Israel. He wept as he left, just as his descendant, Jesus, would weep as He entered Jerusalem for Passion Week. The crowds were sad to see David leave and joyous to see Jesus arrive.

At Jesus' arrest in Gethsemane at the foot of the western slope of the Mount of Olives, all His disciples fled, and the soldiers and Jewish leaders took Him across the valley to Caiaphas's house.

What to See:
Jewish graves (buried underground with a tomb above and pebbles on the top like a wreath), had windows for twenty-four-hour memorial candles. The holiest, oldest, and largest Jewish cemeteries are at the base of the eastern side of the three hilltops on the Mount of Olives. Christian graves are further down. Muslim graves are at the base of the western side just below the Temple site.

Scripture:
    2 Samuel 5:6–8, 15:23–26
    1 Kings 1:38–41
    2 Chronicles 29:16, 30:14
    Jeremiah 31:40

Joel 3:1–2
Matthew 26:57
Mark 14:53
Luke 22:54
John 18:1, 12–14
definingmomentsbook.com/resources

JERUSALEM: MOUNT OF OLIVES

Historical Significance:

East of and 300 feet higher than Jerusalem, the three hilltops of the Mount of Olives stretch out for a mile at a height of 2,700 feet, which is 200 feet above the height of the Temple. As well as the magnificent views of the Old City and the Judean hills, one can see across and above the Kidron Valley and overlook the route to Bethany, Jericho, and the Judean desert where Satan tempted Jesus. The Mount of Olives was formerly covered with olive groves on its summits and gentle slopes.

The glory of the Lord paused here upon leaving the corrupted Temple in 591 BC. Solomon set up an altar here to Molech, the detestable god of the Ammonites, and to Chemosh, the false god of the Moabites, around 550 BC.

Jesus taught here of the signs of His coming and the end of the age; the parable of the ten virgins; the parable of the talents; the parable of the sheep and the goats; and the parable of the watchful servant. He spent much time here as He often stayed with friends nearby at Bethany, walking along a ridge up the hill to Bethphage (roughly the modern road) and along another ridge to the city and back each evening.

He paused here before riding down on a donkey and entering Jerusalem on Palm Sunday, and wept over His beloved City of David, which would reject Him. It was at the foot of this mount in the Garden of Gethsemane where, on Maundy Thursday, He endured His brutal agony and suffering for us and then gave Himself up to be arrested and executed. He later ascended to Heaven from the top of this Mount.

Zechariah prophesied that one day, Jesus would supernaturally deliver His people, stand on the Mount of Olives, and split it in two from east to west.

What to See:

There are three paths down from the top, all ending at Gethsemane. You may see, among other sites:

Dominus Flevit Church, shaped like a tear to represent Jesus' tears over Jerusalem (see separate listing).

Basilica of the Agony, Church of All Nations, adjoining the Garden of Gethsemane, built in 1924 (see separate listing).

The Church of the Pater Noster, built on the traditional site where Jesus taught the Lord's Prayer to His disciples. The Lord's Prayer is inscribed in sixty-two languages in tile with beautiful borders. One of the first church buildings, this church was originally built by Constantine in the fourth century as the Church of the Ascension in anticipation of Jesus' return, with a slab in the center inscribed with the Lord's Prayer in Arabic. Here also is the cave of eschatological teaching, where Jesus revealed to His disciples things concerning the end times.

Viri Galilae Church is the Greek Orthodox Monastery of Little Galilee.

Tower of the Ascension Church is owned by a Russian Orthodox convent.

Church of Mary Magdalene, with its onion domes, is a Russian Orthodox church and convent.

The Mosque of the Ascension, originally built in 378 AD as the Church of Ascension. There is still a small, circular church within the mosque's grounds. This church was the model for The Dome of the Rock in the seventh century and was converted into a mosque in the twelfth century. It is built around a rock that, legend says, was imprinted with Christ's footprint when He ascended. If this is not the actual spot, it is very near to it. As Muslims also believe the "prophet" Jesus ascended, they allow Christian churches to have services there once a year only on the Feast of the Ascension.

The **Jewish Cemetery** is on the western slopes, so they believe they will be first in line when the Messiah comes, while Christians believe He already came and ascended to Heaven from there. The Muslim graves are opposite the Kidron Valley, *below* the Temple site, believing that will keep the Messiah out.

Scripture:

    2 Samuel 15:30, 32

    1 Kings 11:7

    Ezekiel 11:23, 43:1–2

    Zechariah 14:1–11

    Matthew 6:9–13, 21:1, 18, 24:3, 25:1–46, 26:30

    Mark 11:1, 12:20, 13:3, 32–37

    Luke 11:2–5, 12:35–40, 19:11–29, 37, 21:37, 22:3, 24:50–51

    John 8:1

    Acts 1:9–12, 21:38

    definingmomentsbook.com/resources

JERUSALEM: MOUNT ZION (UPPER ROOM)

Historical Significance:

Mount Zion is different than the original City of David, on the eastern hill to the south. This Mount Zion, on the western hill, is where the Lord's Supper, post-Resurrection gatherings of the disciples, and the gift of the Holy Spirit to the disciples at Pentecost are remembered. The name is a synonym for Jerusalem, for the Heavenly Jerusalem.

Jesus had apparently made prior arrangements to use a room in the house of a wealthy man to celebrate Passover with His disciples. He sent Peter and John ahead to prepare the place where He would wash His disciples' feet, share a meal, reveal Judas as His betrayer, and lead the rest in the new covenant of eating the bread and drinking the wine. He offered the third of the four cups, the cup of Redemption and Salvation, saying this is the new covenant in His blood, said that He loved them, invited them to be His spiritual Bride, and offered them the cup to drink to accept His gift. He alone knew the price was so high that, in Gethsemane shortly after, He asked His Father to remove the cup from Him. Ultimately all but one of the disciples would also die painful deaths due to the cup *they* had accepted.

"Upper Room" does not necessarily mean upstairs; it could mean a room in the Upper City, southwest of the Temple Mount.

After the Resurrection, the third person of the Trinity, the Holy Spirit, sought out Jesus' disciples, and at Pentecost breathed new life into their once fearful hearts.

What to See:

There is a courtyard opening from the Zion Gate, which was scarred in the 1948 fighting and left as a memorial. A stairway leads to the Upper Room above a Jewish shrine with a view over to the Mount of Olives and back to Jerusalem. The present church was built by Crusaders in the twelfth century. When the Byzantines enlarged it, they called it "Holy Zion" to associate it with Isaiah's prophecy, perhaps when Mount Zion received its name.

Scripture:

Matthew 26:17–30
Mark 14:12–26
Luke 22:7–38
John 13–17
Acts 1:4–9, 12–14, 2:1–4
definingmomentsbook.com/resources

JERUSALEM:
TEMPLE MOUNT (DOME OF THE ROCK)

Historical Significance:

God may have gathered the dust to create Adam from this site. Abraham met the king of Salem, Melchizedek, here around 2,000 BC, and later climbed Mount Moriah (Zion) prepared to obediently sacrifice his son, Isaac, which is why the Temple was later erected here. God instead had provided a ram in the thicket, so it is named Mount Moriah for "God will provide." Animal sacrifices here were later replaced by Christ's offering—again, God will provide! Where do you see God providing today for *you*?

David captured the city and made it his capital, to unite the Twelve Tribes into a single nation around 1,000 BC, and brought the Ark of the Covenant here. God said David had too much blood on his hands to build a holy Temple and instructed his son, Solomon, to build it around 960 BC to specific plans and adjacent to the king's palace.

Nebuchadnezzar and the Babylonians destroyed Solomon's Temple in 587 BC and exiled the conquered Jews. They returned and built a second, less grandiose Temple from 536–516 BC, but the Ark had been lost by then, and it was destroyed by the Greeks in 168 BC. This Temple was eventually replaced by Herod the Great's grand temple, modeled after Solomon's original Temple, beginning construction in 20 BC.

To accommodate hundreds of thousands of pilgrims, Herod doubled the size of the Temple complex to the length of 1,200 feet and width of 800 feet by expanding the land to the south by first building a series of large retaining walls filled with earth. The south wall was up to 200 feet high! One wall, the Western Wall, is not actually a wall of the Temple, but was built to protect his lower infill. He added a beautiful colonnade along all four sides and a porch above the south colonnade, the Royal Stoa, with marble columns and a tile roof, where early Christians met as "the Church" referred to in Acts. Jews believe the third and final Temple will be built here when their Messiah comes.

The Temple was built with three types of marble and was one of the world's most glorious buildings of its time, where God Himself lived. As Christians, *we* have become His glorious Temple, as He now lives in us!

The second Temple had separate entrances and courts for priests, royalty, Gentiles, Jews, and women. Jesus said, *"My house will be a house of prayer for all nations"* while throwing out the moneychangers from the Court of Gentiles immediately after His triumphal entry (Mark 11:15–17). He was confronting the authority of the Sadducees, who were supported by the Romans, and their economic system. Jesus generally was unopposed by the Pharisees or the average Jew. He was angry that the Jews thought it acceptable to disrupt Gentiles from their opportunity to worship God. Today, Muslims disrupt Jews and Christians from worshipping on the Mount.

The Court of Women was a rectangular center where worship services were held separately, the closest that women were allowed to the Temple. West of the Court of Women was a ramp to a holy altar made of uncut rocks per God's commandments in Exodus. To its left, the Court of Israelites, for Jewish men to perform sacrifices around the clock. Four inner courts were Nazarite, for those who had taken a vow of separation; Wood, for sacrifices; Oils, for incense offerings; and Lepers, so they could participate without mixing with the crowds.

The entrances were narrower than the exits, so one would slow down, approaching prayerfully. The Temple Mount was a series of inner and outer courts with the Holy of Holies in the center behind gold doors and an enormous curtain veil (torn in half at the moment of Jesus' death) protecting God's very presence. Only the high priest, and only on the Day of Atonement, would enter. Jesus entered from the east as prophesied.

The Temple stones—which were over ten feet high, eleven feet thick, and forty-five feet long and weighed over a million pounds each—were so carefully shaped that even today a credit card cannot be slipped between them. Like the Temple stones, God has carefully shaped each of *us* and fit us together into a strong community, and God's *spiritual* house will last forever.

East was Golden Gate, facing the Mount of Olives, the main ceremonial entrance, which is underground today; the gate was later replaced by a higher gate. This is where Peter and John, upon entering to pray, were stopped by a beggar; they had no money to give him, and gave him what they had—Jesus—and healed the man.

Northeast was Sheep's Gate and the Pools of Bethsaida just outside the walled city.

Jesus was circumcised here at the age of eight days, and found in "*My Father's house*" when He was twelve years old after his parents realized during their return from the Feast of the Passover that He was missing. He was later tempted by Satan to "throw yourself down" from the highest point of the Temple. Much of His teaching involved the Temple.

He cleansed the Temple at the beginning of His ministry according to John and again at the end of His ministry on Monday of Passion Week according to Matthew, Mark, and Luke. Pilgrims needed to buy animals fit for sacrifice and exchange their money into the local currency for the annual Temple tax. The public Court of Gentiles, several acres in size, had been turned into a loud marketplace, disrespectful of the sanctity of God's dwelling.

Jesus cast out the "*den of thieves.*" Jesus was reminding the Temple authorities that God cared for Jew and Gentile alike and had desired for all people to be allowed to worship there (Isaiah 56:7). They did not learn, for Paul was later threatened with death for bringing a Gentile into the areas reserved for Jews (Acts 21:27–32). Do *you* still create walls between other believers?

When Jesus said He could tear down this Temple and rebuild it within three days, He meant *His body* would die and be resurrected. They thought He meant the *actual* Temple and charged Him many times over this blasphemy. Actually, the Roman general Titus conquered Jerusalem and took months to destroy the Temple in 70 AD. In 637 AD, the Arabs captured the city and built a mosque modeled after the Holy Sepulchre.

Jews considered this Temple the legitimate central home of the God of Israel, the only place where prayers and sacrifices could be offered directly to God. However, some Jews believe it had been defiled and was doomed to be destroyed by the Romans and then replaced by a purer third Temple not built by a heathen. The Holy of Holies contained the Ark of the Covenant with the Ten Commandments tablets. It is speculated that they could even today be buried under the rubble from the destruction of the First Temple.

Pharisees Versus Sadducees:

The Hebrew word for *Pharisee* means "separated." These were religious conservatives, favored by common people, who promoted oral law, were often called rabbi ("*my teacher*"), and taught that all Jews should observe Ttemple purity laws outside the Temple. The Hebrew word for *Sadducee* means "just ones." These were Temple priests from the class of wealthy, Judean aristocrats who were dominant in society, politics, and religion, and controlled the Temple's services due to their cooperation with the Romans. They tolerated the Hellenism that the Pharisees opposed. They disappeared after the 70 AD Temple destruction.

Sunnis Versus Shiites:

The essence of Islam (*submission*) is that there is one true God that Muslims ("one who submits to God's will") need to believe in and serve based on the Qur'an's teachings. Their prophet Muhammad, a wealthy trader, was born around 570 AD in Mecca, fifty miles from the port city of Jeddah, Saudi Arabia. When he was roughly forty years old, he began to believe that he was selected by God ("Allah") to be his last and only Arabian prophet, Christ's successor. He claimed that he had received a vision from God. Many subsequent revelations he wrote on palm leaves and flat rocks in a cave that were recorded centuries later in the Qur'an.

Failing to reach many and with his life at risk in 622 AD, his message changed from *inviting* people into his religion to *forcing* people to believe through brutal ways, called "conversion by the sword." His tribesmen were fierce, with the result that most of Arabia had converted by Muhammad's death in 632 AD, only ten years later! He married many times, with extensive documentation of troubles within his harem—yet most Muslims consider him sinless, the "holy of holies."

The rift between these two Muslim sects began as soon as Muhammad died, as he had no son to succeed him as caliph (or spiritual and political leader), only one daughter. The Sunnis chose his closest advisor and friend, Abu Bakr, while the Shiites preferred his son-in-law, Ali, and named him Abu's successor. Bakr was soon succeeded for the Sunnis by his close advisor, Omar, who captured Arabia and then captured the rest of Persia, Egypt and Israel (then known as Palestine) in 637 AD. Over the next thirty years, they extended their reach into parts of Europe, north Africa, and central Asia. Such a choice: if you converted, your taxes were eliminated, including the high tithe to the Roman church; if you did not convert, you were slaughtered. Sunnis usually prevailed in their violent interactions. They differ in some rituals involving prayer and holidays.

- *Sunnis* represent eighty to ninety percent of the 1.5 billion Muslims worldwide today; their extremists are Al Qaeda, ISIS, the Taliban, Boko Haram, and the Muslim Brotherhood; they see no need of clerical intermediaries other than for religious guidance and pray directly to Allah, believing in separation of church and state (hence Saud Arabia's more secular government); they often see shrines, icons, antiquities, and religious art as heretical and are destroying priceless works of art.
- *Shiites* are in majority only in Iraq, Iran, Bahrain, and Azerbaijan today; their extremists are Hezbollah and Hamas; these fundamentalists have Ayatollahs and Imams in a centralized clerical hierarchy as their spiritual and political leaders, which explains why Ayatollahs have ruled Iran since the Shah was deposed during the revolution. Some Saudis consider Shiites to be even more heretical than Jews and Christians.

Syria has a Sunni majority ruled by a Shiite minority. Iraq under Saddam Hussein had a Shiite majority ruled by a Sunni minority, which was reversed after forty years by their first democratic elections, and resulted in the intrusion by Al Qaeda and ISIS.

What to See:

The Temple site is dominated by The **Dome of the Rock,** likely the most contested site in the world. Jews and Christians call it the Temple Mount, while Muslims call it the Noble Sanctuary (Haram al-Sharif). When Israel captured it back from Arabs in the 1967 War, they turned the keys back over to the Grand Mufti because of the prior agreed policy of status quo to all religious sites. Today it is administered by Jordan, with security provided by Israelis.

The thirty-six-acre site on top of Mount Moriah represents one-sixth of the size of the Old City. Said to be one of the most beautiful mosques in the world, the exterior tile has varied shapes and designs in a stunning shade of blue. The dome and wide surrounding area are done in plates of aluminum impregnated with 700 kilograms of gold (donated in the 1960s by Jordanian king Hussein) which reflect sunshine from many views throughout Jerusalem and nearby.

The altar of burnt offering inside the Dome where Isaac was nearly sacrificed is sixty feet by fifty feet by four feet tall. In the center is the Foundation Stone, with dark wood railing around it. Jews believe the hole in the rock leads to a cave where the Holy of Holies would be found. There are beautiful Persian rugs and stained-glass windows looking like jewels throughout. Muslims wash their feet in special fountains before entering. The Dome is used for individual worship, and the much smaller Al-Aqsa Mosque nearby is used for group prayers.

There are six gates on the western side and three on the northern. The best bronze in the world from Corinth was used in the gate called "Beautiful," worth more than all the other gates combined. The Damascus Gate, the largest and most impressive of the entrances to the Old City, leads to Al Wad (formerly king Solomon's) Street which goes through the Old City. Dung Gate, with its large hand-carved stone blocks, is the closest to the Western (or Wailing) Wall. On the eastern side looking toward the Mount of Olives is the closed-up Golden Gate near where Solomon's Portico was. Jesus entered this gate as a youth of twelve and then on a donkey at the age of thirty-three on Palm Sunday.

Muslims built The Dome of the Rock in the late seventh century AD as their first major sanctuary to commemorate their belief that the angel Gabriel accompanied their prophet Muhammad to Heaven from this spot. They converted Solomon's Stables (now thought to have been used as such by the Crusaders instead), under the southeastern courtyard to a Muslim prayer hall, El-Marwani.

The famous **Wailing (Western) Wall**, built by Herod in 20 BC and visited by ten million annually, is actually the only remaining section of the retaining wall that supports the foundation under the esplanade below the Temple site. It represents just sixty-five of over 500 yards of the original length. Weighing 500 tons, it is forty-five by sixteen by fifteen feet in size. The Temple was the place where God dwelt among His people, the Israelites.

The huge blocks in the lower section were left by Titus in 70 AD, to show future generations the greatness of the Roman soldiers who had destroyed the rest of it. It is called the "Wailing" Wall, to the dismay of Jews, as Jews lament their dispersion and weep over the ruins. From 1948–1967 under Jordanian rule, they were not ever allowed here, and at the end of this period, mosques and many homes were razed to create the present plaza.

Jews pray and wail there because of the destruction of the Temple and to await the Messiah to return to bring in the Messianic Era, filling the cracks with their hand-written prayers. Men and women pray in separate stations as in a synagogue. This is the closest Orthodox Jews will approach the Temple, fearful of accidentally stepping on the sacred, inner sanctum Holy of Holies in the defiled, destroyed Temple. The Holy of Holies was where the Ark of the Covenant was kept and only the high priest was allowed to enter, on pain of death.

Muslims claim the Wall to be part of their Al-Aqsa Mosque. The path to the right leads up to the Mograbi (Mughrabi) Gate, through a covered wooden bridge. This thirteenth century gate was nearest to the eight-sided Dome of the Rock, and was the sole entrance to the compound for non-Muslims. Jews and Christians are "forbidden" from praying on Temple Mount. This controversial policy that "Muslims *pray* on the Mount; non-Muslims *visit* the Mount" causes regular disturbances when enforced by Israeli guards.

Scripture:
>   Genesis 14:17–18, 22:1–19
>   2 Samuel 6:1–19, 18:18
>   1 Kings 5–8
>   1 Chronicles 22
>   2 Chronicles 3–7, 36:18–19, 36:23
>   Ezra 2:68–6:22, 10:1–44
>   Matthew 4:5, 12:8, 12:12, 12:16–22, 21:12–16, 23:37–39, 24:1–31, 26:55, 26:60–61, 27:40, 27:51
>   Mark 11:11–17, 12:35, 13:1–27, 14:57–59, 15:29, 15:38
>   Luke 2:41–49, 4:9–12, 18:10, 19:28–23:56
>   John 2:13–25, 8:20, 10:23–39
>   Acts 1:6–8, 3, 6:14
>   definingmomentsbook.com/resources

Defining Moment . . . The Temple Mount

Abraham was set to sacrifice his son here at the Temple Mount. We read that story with horror at times, but we forget that God knew how it would end. *He* knew that Abraham would obey Him. *He* knew that He would call off the sacrifice and that Isaac would be unscathed. The only one who did not know all of that was Abraham. Sometimes I am curious about what God knowingly allows in *our* lives. He uses situations to mold us and shape us, but He also uses them to show us where we really are with Him. It is one of the ways that we can see that we have really grown in Him. Otherwise, how do you really measure growth?

Abraham now *knew* that he really did trust the Lord. For the rest of his days, he could remember that when the Lord asked something of him that did not make any sense, He would provide. That day the Lord provided a ram caught in a bush for the sacrifice in place of Isaac. The Lord provides, and He knew that Abraham needed to know that he finally understood it.

Abraham did not have the greatest record of trusting God. He started out great, packing up everything he and his family knew, in order to go to a foreign land at God's command, when he was seventy-five years old. But then he found himself in a land where he was afraid his wife's beauty would mean his death—so that pharaoh could keep her—so he lied and said that she was his own sister. That is not really trusting God. In Genesis 15:8, Abraham asks God, "*How do I really know that all these promises are going to come true?*" God reconfirms with a vision, but then soon after, Abraham jumps back into not trusting God by listening to his wife instead of to God's promises—and Abraham sleeps with her maid to bear him a son, Ishmael.

Finally, Isaac, his son, is promised and born when Abraham is 100 years old. Abraham must have started trusting God a little more when he was able to save his nephew, Lot, from the destruction in Sodom and Gomorrah. However, another incident of lying about Abraham's wife being his sister occurred in yet another land, again because he was afraid the beauty of his 100-year-old postmenopausal wife would cause his death when the land's leader wanted her for himself. Again, his trust in God's provision was at an all-time low, even though God did provide for him in all of those situations. Abraham really did need to know that he trusted in God's provision after this track record, and this experience with Isaac and the altar proved that— to *him*.

The Lord knows that He will provide, but He wants *us* to know that, just like Abraham did. God turned the very thing that Abraham lacked into the very thing he became known for. In the end, Abraham's life stood for trusting God, and he was listed as a "hero of the faith" in Hebrews 11.

Journal Time:

Journal about some of the times that the Lord has provided for *you*. Make a list. Now make a list of the areas that you are waiting on for the Lord's provision. Pray and ask the Lord to keep you strong in your trust of His provision, just as He provided for Abraham.

Share Time:

Share with each other about some of the ways that God has provided for you. Encourage each other with your testimonies of God's great favor.

Prayer:

Jesus,

We are in awe of the ways that You bless us with your provision. It is so much grander and more glorious than the ways that we contrive to provide for our own needs. Please forgive us all for the times in our lives that we have trusted ourselves instead of You. We praise You and bless Your name for the many ways You have provided for us in the past. Please keep us in that spirit of praise. We thank You ahead of time for the way that You are going to act on our behalf for all of the situations that we have journaled where we are awaiting Your provision. We know that You are acting in our best interests, even when we do not see behind the scenes where You are working. Help us to trust You, and show us evidence of our trust in You, just as You did for Abraham.

In Jesus' name,

Amen

Worship:

"Come Thou Fount of Every Blessing"
"Shout to the Lord"

JERUSALEM: VIA DOLOROSA

Historical Significance:

The Way of Sorrows (or Grief or Suffering), today in the Muslim Quarter, represents the Old City east–west street on which Jesus carried His Cross from His trial to His Crucifixion. There are nine stations today on the road, with the last five inside the Church of the Holy Sepulchre (see separate entry). It is designed more by faith than by history—not all are accurately located, as real events were assigned to locations along a path to celebrate His steps.

The earliest reported pilgrimage path dates to the Byzantine era, proceeding on Maundy Thursday from the top of the Mount of Olives through Gethsemane into the Old City at the Lions' Gate (a.k.a. St. Stephen's Gate). St. Stephen was stoned to death here, just outside the city walls, with Saul watching. From there, the path led past the Church of St. Anne (the mother of Mary). Built in 1138 AD over a crypt said to be where Mary was born, it is one of the best-preserved Crusader churches, with great acoustics.

On we go to the Church of the Holy Sepulchre. In the fourteenth century, the Franciscans designed a devotional walk to follow Jesus' steps.

As each Gospel only has one or two lines about this walk, much is based on tradition only, such as Jesus' three falls (Stations 3, 7, and 9) and two of his four encounters (Stations 4 and 6). This route assumes the Praetorium was next to the Antonia Fortress in the northeast near the modern Lions' Gate. Roman governors like Pilate generally stayed in Herod's palace on the southwestern hill, but it is possible Pilate stayed near the fortress in the event of an uprising.

What to See:

Unlike other street signs in English, Hebrew and Arabic, the name Via Dolorosa is used consistently. The path is loved and crowded as it winds through the bazaar with vendors calling out to you from their open shops lining both sides of the street. The streets of Jesus' day lie buried under layers from the city's many destructions over the years.

1st Station: Commemorating the trial at the Praetorium before Pontius Pilate, His condemnation, and His scourging. Three nineteenth century Roman Catholic churches represent the first two stations—**Church of the Condemnation and Imposition of the Cross**, the **Church of the Flagellation** (built in the 1920s), and **Church of Ecce Homo.**

2nd Station: Remembering Jesus' replies to Pilate, who had greeted Jesus' appearance before him with "Ecce homo!" which means "Behold the man!"

3rd Station: Representing Jesus' traditional first fall, adjacent to then nineteenth century Polish Catholic Chapel (built by Armenian Catholics, at one time used as a Turkish bath).

4th Station: Representing an encounter with Mary, the mother of Jesus, this station is at a nineteenth century Armenian Orthodox chapel.

5th Station: Commemorating Jesus' Biblical encounter with Simon of Cyrene, adjacent to the **Chapel of Simon of Cyrene** (built in 1895 by the Franciscans).

6th Station: Representing the medieval Catholic legend that a noble woman, Veronica, wiped the sweat from Jesus' face with her veil, which was then imprinted with His image. (This is not the same as the post-Crucifixion face and body image known as the Shroud of Turin.) In the late nineteenth century, Greek Roman Catholics built the **Chapel of the Holy Face** or the **House of St. Veronica.**

7th Station: Representing Jesus' second fall, this station is adjacent to a small Franciscan chapel, built in 1875, at the major junction with the north–south road.

8th Station: Remembering Luke's telling of Jesus' sermon to the weeping, pious women of Jerusalem, adjacent to the **Greek Orthodox Monastery of St. Charalampus.**

9th Station: Representing Jesus' third fall, this station is off the Via Dolorosa path at the entrance to the **Ethiopian Orthodox Monastery** and the **Coptic Orthodox Monastery of St. Anthony**, above the Chapel of St. Helena (part of the Church of the Holy Sepulchre).

The 10th through 14th Stations of the Cross are located inside the **Church of the Holy Sepulchre** complex of chapels and churches presided over by multiple faiths. (See separate Church of the Holy Sepulchre listing.)

Every Friday afternoon, Franciscans from the monastery at the first station lead a procession along the Via Dolorosa. Various reenactments are also presented periodically.

Scripture:

Matthew 16:24, 27:11–33
Mark 15:1–22
Luke 23:1–30
John 18:28–19:17
definingmomentsbook.com/resources

JORDAN RIVER

Historical Significance:

The Jordan River, meaning "go down," is Israel's largest river and the world's only to flow mostly *below* sea level. It follows a speedy, winding, 156-mile path (seventy miles as the crow flies) from the snow-capped peaks of Mount Hermon at 9,000 feet above sea level 25 miles to the northwestern Sea of Galilee and continues from the southeastern end 65 miles to the depths of the Dead Sea 1,400 feet below sea level.

That drop of over 10,000 feet accounts for its name and speed. It mostly had steep banks, a swift current, and dense vegetation that hid wild animals. The river bed has shifted many times, and today it is generally a narrow stream less than fifty feet wide. It originates from the Hasbani, Dan, Banias, and Snir Rivers and is joined by many other rivers including the Yarmouk. It is mentioned nearly 200 times in the Bible.

It was the eastern border of Israel. Gideon stopped the Midianites from fleeing by taking control of the Jordan. Elijah, who had crossed to the east side to hide from king Ahab, and Elisha walked across it on dry land. David also had crossed it when being pursued by his scheming son, Absalom.

The fast-flowing waters were at flood stage when Israel was ready to cross and possess the Promised Land. Choosing between trusting or disobeying God's plan and power, the priests fearfully carried the Ark of the Covenant to the river's edge, put their toes in, and watched in wonder as the fierce waters stopped flowing and parted. Do *you* trust God enough to put your toes in and obediently cross the scary barrier He has in front of you?

John the Baptist, who Muslims also consider to be a prophet, preached a message of repentance out in the desert here. Many journeyed an entire day from Jerusalem to see John. Jesus, too, came in anonymity and humility to be baptized by John (into His death and into His new, resurrected life) before launching His public ministry.

Jesus later commanded His disciples in turn to *"Go and make disciples of all nations, baptizing them in the name of the Father and of the Son and of the Holy Spirit, and teaching them to obey everything I have commanded you"* (Matthew 28:19–20). Baptism does not save us; it is, however, an act of obedience identifying us as set apart, part of our testimony of faith.

As a water source and natural boundary, the Jordan River has been a source of dispute between Syria and Jordan, and since 1922 has served as the border between Israel and Jordan. When you view the land on both sides, you notice the revealing contrast between the lush greenery cultivated over years on the Israeli side and the desert on the Syrian and Jordanian sides.

Scripture:
Numbers 34:12
Deuteronomy 1:1–5, 3:20, 26–28, 4:21–26, 9:1, 12:10, 31
Joshua 1:1–11, 3, 4, 12:7, 13, 14:3, 16–19, 22–24
Judges 3:28, 5:17, 8:4, 10:8–9, 12:5–6
1 Samuel 13:7
2 Samuel 10:17, 19:41
2 Kings 2:6–14, 5:1–14, 6:1–7
Jeremiah 12:5
Zechariah 11:3
Matthew 3, 14:15, 25, 19:1
Mark 1:4–11, 3:8, 10:1
Luke 3:1–22, 4:1
John 1:6–42, 3:26, 10:40
Romans 6:3–5
Acts 2:38–39
definingmomentsbook.com/resources

What to See:
The **Greek Orthodox Monastery of St. John the Baptist,** five miles east of modern Jericho, has the traditional place of Jesus' baptism on its eastern bank, where the Israelites crossed the river on dry ground and invaded the land under Joshua's leadership. The Franciscans, Syrians, Copts, and

Abyssinians also have baptismal sites along the Jordan. Chuck Smith of Calvary Chapel helped build the site at Degania with a cemented slope and handrails down to the river for baptisms.

Defining Moment . . . The Banks of the Jordan River

As soon as Jesus was baptized, He went up out of the water. At that moment Heaven was opened, and He saw the Spirit of God descending like a dove and alighting on Him. And a voice from Heaven said, 'This is my Son, whom I love; with Him I am well pleased'
(Matthew 3:16–17).

The river that you stand next to is the very same river where Jesus was baptized. While we do not know the *exact* spot, we know He was here. Can you imagine what it was like to be one of Jesus' disciples, watching Heaven open and the Spirit of God descending?

It makes me wonder about what else was going on up in Heaven when Jesus got baptized. Were the angels rejoicing? Was there singing going on? Luke 15:10 tells us that when just one sinner repents, there is rejoicing in the presence of the angels of God. Imagine what was happening up there that we could not see when Jesus went up out of the water. We know Jesus' Father chose to speak audibly, declaring His love and affirmation of His Son.

If you have given your life to the Lord and repented of your sins, Heaven has had that *same* party of rejoicing for you. I am curious as to the words of affirmation that your Father in Heaven has for you, as you are one of His sons and daughters now. Ask the Holy Spirit to help you to hear His voice. He made you and loves you. He has something to affirm you for, just as He did with His Son here.

"The LORD your God is with you, the Mighty Warrior who saves. He will take great delight in you; in His love He will no longer rebuke you, but will rejoice over you with singing" (Zephaniah 3:17).

Take a few moments and listen for the affirmation that He wants to speak over you. What "joyful song" is He singing to rejoice over you?

Journal Time:

What did God whisper to you? If you did not hear any words or phrases come up in your heart, what would you dream of your Heavenly Father speaking over you? We sometimes yearn for words of affirmation from our parents, teachers, or spouses. It is OK for you to yearn for those words from your Father in Heaven. Journal what you have heard, or would like to hear.

Share Time:

Give each other the gift of hearing what you have sensed God was speaking over you, or what you would like to hear Him say about you.

Prayer:

Dear Father God,

Thank You so much for bringing us here to the river Jordan. Thank You for quiet, still moments where we can listen for Your whispers over us. Please forgive us for the times that we have ignored or have been too busy to listen to both the challenging and the affirming words that You have spoken to us. Lord, we long to keep ourselves tuned in to You. Please give us the gift of the Holy Spirit's revelation of Your words to us.

In Jesus' name,
Amen

Worship:

"Awesome in This Place"
"Be Thou My Vision"

MASADA

Historical Significance:

Masada (Metsada, meaning "stronghold" or "fortress" in Hebrew) is a natural mesa in Judea, fifteen miles north of Sodom, two and a half miles from the western shore of the Dead Sea, built by Jonathan the Hasmonean as a refuge in times of danger in the middle of the second century BC. David may have fled here ten miles south from En Gedi after confronting Saul.

In 37–4 BC, paranoid Herod the Great built an eighteen-foot wall across the top and added a three-level winter palace with hot and cold baths, making it the largest fortress in the world at that time and one of the strongest in Judea. They dammed a wadi and diverted water ingeniously to storage cisterns.

Masada was part of a line of fortresses along his escape route to Moab, and was to be his last refuge in the event the Jews turned against him, or if Cleopatra of Egypt persuaded Mark Antony to have him killed, yet there is no record he ever stayed there. Jewish historian Josephus said it had sufficient supplies for thousands of men for ten years.

Jewish rebel patriots (Zealots) retreated here and seized it in 66 AD at the beginning of the First Jewish Revolt against Rome. This war ended with the Romans taking back Jerusalem and destroying the Temple. The Zealots, commanded by Eleazar, had built an inner wall of timbers and dirt to absorb the Romans' battering ram. After a three-year siege, the Romans set fire to this wall in order to gain entry.

The Roman army captured the "impenetrable" fortress on April 16, 73 AD, after thousands of slaves built a ramp to the top. Josephus says that the Romans found only two women and five children alive. He says 960 others had killed each other and set fire to the fortress, leaving only their food and weapons so the Romans would know they had not starved or run out of the means to fight, preferring death rather than slavery to the Romans. Each father killed his own family; then ten were selected by lot to kill the men; then one selected by lot in turn killed the remaining nine and then stabbed himself. Masada symbolizes Israel's survivor fervor even today of "never again."

The Zealots mistakenly focused on *earthly* freedom and sinned by committing suicide. The questions for us are:

1. Do *you* live your faith with such active devotion?
2. What enemies are trying to break down *your* walls to take *your* spiritual freedom?

What to See:

Israel's most famous and important non-Biblical archaeological site is Masada. With eight fortified Roman camps linked by a wall that surrounded it, Masada is imposing and tells a powerful story. It includes lots of walking over rough terrain to view the enormous siege ramp, walls, towers, gates, the magnificent two-level Northern Palace, other palaces, a bathhouse with original tile, living rooms, a synagogue, an impressive aqueduct and water system, storehouses, ramparts, pottery, weapons, and coins to be viewed at the site.

The mountain is 1,430 feet above the Dead Sea, 130 feet above sea level, 1,900 feet long, and 650 feet wide. You can walk—minimum forty minutes for the very fit—via two steep trails (one is called the Snake), or you may take a cable car up and down.

Scripture:

1 Samuel 24:22
definingmomentsbook.com/resources

MOUNT OF BEATITUDES

Historical Significance:

Jesus gave the Sermon on the Mount here, beginning with the Beatitudes (eight declarations of blessedness) and ending with the wise and foolish builders. This new law, just like the old law in Exodus 19, was delivered on a mountain. "Blessed" means more than "happiness"—it is a spiritual joy, regardless of our circumstances.

What to See:

There is no agreed tradition of where exactly Jesus delivered His Sermon on the Mount. It likely is in the northwest corner of the Sea of Galilee, as Jesus "*entered Capernaum*" (Luke 7:1) after his talk. The Mount is only about 350 feet high. In 1938, Italian Catholics built a beautiful, octagonal church and hospice on the top, open daily, and featuring an eight-sided dome listing the eight Beatitudes given by Jesus in the Sermon. A hill to the west is considered the traditional spot for Jesus' feeding of the 5,000. Another Catholic Church there commemorates that miracle.

Scripture:

Matthew 5–7 (longer Sermon on the Mount)

Luke 6:20–49 (shorter Sermon on the Plain; verses 20–22 are the Beatitudes, while verses 24–26 are the negative counterparts)

definingmomentsbook.com/resources

Defining Moment . . . Mount of Beatitudes Catholic Church

When Jesus saw His ministry drawing huge crowds, He climbed a hillside. Those who were apprenticed to Him, the committed, climbed with Him. Arriving at a quiet place, He sat down and taught His climbing companions. This is what He said:

"You are blessed when you are at the end of your rope. With less of you, there is more of God and His rule.

"You are blessed when you feel you have lost what is most dear to you. Only then can you be embraced by the One most dear to you.

"You are blessed when you are content with just who you are—no more, no less. That is the moment you find yourselves proud owners of everything that cannot be bought.

"You are blessed when you have worked up a good appetite for God. He is food and drink in the best meal you will ever eat.

"You are blessed when you care. At the moment of being 'care-full,' you find yourselves cared for.

"You are blessed when you get your inside world—your mind and heart—put right. Then you can see God in the outside world.

"You are blessed when you can show people how to cooperate instead of compete or fight. That is when you discover who you really are and your place in God's family.

"You are blessed when your commitment to God provokes persecution. The persecution drives you even deeper into God's Kingdom.

"Not only that—count yourselves blessed every time people put you down or throw you out or speak lies about you to discredit Me. What it means is that the truth is too close for comfort and they are uncomfortable. You can be glad when that happens—give a cheer, even—for though they do not like it, I do! And all Heaven applauds. And know that you are in good company. My prophets and witnesses have always gotten into this kind of trouble."

—Eugene Peterson in *The Message*

We have a very different view of what it means to be "blessed' in American/Western European culture. Materialism usually tops the list of what blessing means, followed by career, social status, and sometimes health. Jesus turns that notion upside down. In this version of the Beatitudes from *The Message* by Eugene Peterson, Jesus says that you are blessed when:

- you are at the end of your rope
- you feel you have lost what is most dear to you
- you are content with just who you are—no more, no less
- you have worked up a good appetite for God
- you care
- you get your inside world—your mind and heart—put right
- you can show people how to cooperate instead of compete or fight
- your commitment to God provokes persecution
- people put you down or throw you out or speak lies about you to discredit Me (Jesus)

There is a group of people I know that represent, almost item for item, the entire list above. They are a group in eastern Congo that is ministered to by Un Jour Nouveau/Africa New Day. They have suffered the effects of genocide (the fallout from the far lesser Rwandan genocide), starvation, disease, gender violence, and homelessness. Yet, when I visit them, they are in such deep relationship and dependence on Jesus that the light of their faith is almost blinding. The most memorable New Year's Eve "party" of our lives was an all-night church servcie there filled with singing, dancing, and truly unbridled love and joy.

In my homeland's "blessed" materialistic culture, I see limited dependence on Jesus and bright lights of faith are few and far between. Meeting with these saints in the Congo is like going from a dimly lit room into the blinding sun in terms of faith and intimacy with God. I leave the Democratic Republic of Congo thinking that the reality is that *I* am from a poor country and *they* are the rich ones. This is the counter-intuitiveness of our Lord, which is what the Beatitudes is all about. We think we know what blessing is, but in reality, we are deceived.

That deception goes back to the very beginning, when Eve believed the devil's promise. In the original Hebrew, Satan promised Eve that she would know the difference between "blessings and curses" if she just ate the forbidden fruit. It was a lie, and Satan knew it. We humans can never fully discern between blessings and curses, because we are easily deceived. We look at immediate gratification instead of the long-term development of who Christ is making us to be eternally. We choose comfort over character when left to our own devices.

We are forever indebted to our Lord for showing us the truth about blessings through this passage.

Journal Time:

Journal about an example in your life where you thought you were going through a difficult time and it really turned out to be a blessing, or vice versa. Did you ever choose a "blessing" (i.e. a dream job, relationship, etc.) that really turned out to be a "curse"?

Share Time:

Share with each other examples in your lives of mixing up "blessings" and "curses." Is there anything you would like to bring before the group that feels like a curse right now that you can see God turning into a blessing? Encourage each other in how God will be blessing you through your current challenges.

Prayer:

Dear Jesus,

How we long to choose what You would choose for us. Lord, please give us Your desires for our hearts. Please give us the blessing of wanting what You want for us and running from what You do not want for us. Thank You for turning what the enemy means as curses into amazing Kingdom blessings. Help us, dear Lord, to daily put our trust in You and not in ourselves. Help us to seek You more than we seek blessings from You.

In Jesus' name,

Amen

Worship:

"Jesus, What a Beautiful Name"

"It is Well with My Soul"

NAZARETH

Historical Significance:

Nazareth, *Natzrat* in Hebrew, means branch or shoot, just as we are Jesus' branch; the name is also the reason Jesus and His followers were called Nazarenes. Nazareth is still a small village surrounded by stony fields in the southern hill country off the beaten track in Lower Galilee overlooking the Jezreel Valley, midway between the Sea of Galilee and the Mediterranean Sea. Nazareth was first populated in the Early Canaanite Period and depopulated when Jews were expelled after the Byzantine victory over the Persians in 614 AD.

In a cave here, Gabriel, the messenger of God, bade Mary an election to carry Jesus, which she accepted, saying, *"May your Word to me be fulfilled."*

This is where Jesus returned to from his exile in Egypt, where He spent His boyhood and early manhood prior to launching His ministry. It was a lowly, poor, obscure life, in an apparently despised place (per Nathaniel's question, *"Can anything good come out of Nazareth?"*). Jesus preached His first recorded sermon here among people who knew Him well and was greeted with anger and an attempt to kill Him by stoning.

The Crusaders erected a three-nave church that was destroyed by 1263. The Franciscans, residents since 1620, built a small church in 1730, above the grotto that is said to be the spacious cave in which Jesus' family lived.

What to See:

An Arab town of 78,000 today (sixty-nine percent Muslims, thirty-one percent Christians), built over the ancient village of Nazareth, very little of which is visible today. Set on a quiet hill in the middle of the bustling modern city, the old section consists of an energetic bazaar, narrow curving roads with numerous steps, churches, monasteries, a souk (market), and many small courtyards. All streets are built on hills. The **Franciscan monastery** is in the center of the old town.

Nazareth Village, operated by Arab Christians with strong ties to U.S. evangelical churches who send short-term missionaries here to work, is a fifteen-acre re-creation with primitive stone structures built by hand, reminiscent of the first century, with shepherds, farmers, carpenters, spinners, etc., in period dress doing daily chores as they would have during Jesus' time here.

Tradition holds that the synagogue where Jesus preached is the room next to the **Melkite Greek Catholic Church.** Archaeological finds are still being recovered, including the base of a watchtower, pools, a stone quarry, a crushing stone and agricultural terraces. Since scholars estimate only 1,000 people lived here when Jesus' family did, the discovery of an ancient wine press carved out of a large hillside rock makes one wonder if perhaps Jesus used this very same press and played on this hill.

Dominating the village is the **Basilica of the Annunciation**, said to be the largest church in the Middle East, built between 1955 and 1969, preserving the outline of the prior Crusader church on the traditional site of the angel speaking to Mary. The church features a magnificent rose window, an altar built over an ancient altar, and sitting areas to meditate. No exposed shoulders or knees please.

Church of St. Joseph—built by the Franciscans in 1914.

Scripture:
    Matthew 1:18–25, 2:19–23, 4:13, 13:53–58
    Mark 6:1–6, 14:67, 16:6
    Luke 1:26–38, 2:39–52, 4:16–30
    John 1:45–46
    Acts 24:5
    definingmomentsbook.com/resources

Defining Moment . . . Nazareth Village
Father God certainly continued His counterintuitive ways with the places that He allowed Jesus to exist in the world. The King of Kings was born in a barn with all of the smells and discomforts that you can imagine. Have you

ever slept in a barn with the noises and excrement that waft through the air? He was then hunted by Herod to be killed as a baby.

Then He was given a hometown, Nazareth, that archaeologists think had a population of 150, was half pagan, and was despised by Jews in neighboring cities. Jesus came from the "wrong side of the tracks," and God would not have it any other way. The prestige of the world means nothing to our God. He is not necessarily against the posh trappings of this world; they just do not have lasting Kingdom value.

Being in a relationship with all people, especially the poor and lowly, is what Jesus came for. To be in a real relationship with those classes meant that you had to understand their plight, walk in their shoes, and do life with them. It reminds me of a book I read, *The Cause Within You*, by the pastor of The Dream Center, Matthew Barnett. Jesus asked him to go live in the most dangerous, drug infested, violent park in his Los Angeles neighborhood. He only stayed twenty-two hours, but he was forever changed by living just one night with the poorest of the poor—materially, physically, and spiritually. He came out of that experience equipped with a heart for the lost to an extent that he had never known before, and a faithfulness to God's call on his life that was strong and sure. He got firsthand experience that living with the poor actually enriched him.

Journal Time:

Have you ever spent time with the poor—either physically, relationally, or spiritually? Journal about the gifts that God gave you through that experience. If you have never been among the poor, have you read stories or seen movies that brought out emotions you did not expect? Journal about what was happening in your heart. What have you learned about serving?

Share Time:

Share about what God has shown you in your experiences with or about the poor.

Prayer:

Lord,

Thank You for leaving the comforts and entitlements of Heaven to be with us. Thank You for serving the least in the world in ways that astound us. Please help us to follow Your lead, Jesus. We long to serve like You did, to have impact like You did. In John 14:12, You say: "Very truly I tell you, whoever believes in Me will do the works I have been doing, and they will do even greater things than these, because I am going to the Father." Lord, we take these words by faith. Equip us to serve in even greater capacity, through You.

In Jesus' name,

Amen

Worship:

"Take My Life and Let It Be"

"Brother, Let Me Be Your Servant"

QUMRAN

Historical Significance:

The Dead Sea Scrolls (third century BC to first century AD, in Hebrew, Greek and Aramaic) were discovered in the summer of 1947 by one of three Bedouin goat shepherds in one of several caves in the mountains and cliffs near Qumran, in the remains of a second-Temple-period Jewish settlement and Roman fort overlooking the northwestern shore of the Dead Sea. Climbing after a stray goat, he saw a small opening in a cave, threw a rock in, and heard it break pottery.

Only ten jars were still intact, some with their lids securely on, and eight were empty. Muhammed left the original three scrolls hanging in his tent for months before locating an antiquities dealer from Bethlehem to broker them for less than $100 to the Syrian Orthodox Monastery of St. Mark's in Jerusalem. Eventually all the scrolls were bought and donated to the Israel Museum in Jerusalem.

Cave IV, now enlarged, where the largest quantity of scrolls came from (thousands of fragments), is only 100 yards from Qumran. A Jewish sect, the Essenes, had settled their community here in 31 BC, and later, becoming fearful of the advancing Roman military in 68 AD, put several hundred of their scrolls in jars of pottery and hid them in nearby caves. The scrolls were written mostly on leather, papyrus, and parchment from dried animal skins sewn together, though two were on copper. The people who stayed were massacred by Roman soldiers on their way to Jerusalem to crush the First Jewish Revolt. Those Jews who had left joined the Jewish rebels who had captured Masada and were killed there in 73 AD.

It is considered the greatest archaeological and manuscript discovery of modern times. About one-third of the documents are Biblical, including much of the Old Testament books most quoted in the New Testament (thirty-six scrolls from Psalms, twenty-nine scrolls from Deuteronomy, and twenty-one scrolls from Isaiah) along with a complete twenty-four-foot-long scroll of Isaiah (the nearly intact Isaiah Scroll) and fragments of every Old Testament book except Esther. They are copies 1,000 years older than any previous discoveries and reflect the great care and reliability taken to stay true to the original. Area ruins include the defense tower, the scriptorium where they wrote and the community dining hall.

Scripture:
Deuteronomy 32:43
Joshua 6:5, 15:62
2 Chronicles 26:10
Daniel 2:18
Joel 2:23
Luke 9:35
definingmomentsbook.com/resources

TABGHA

Historical Significance:

Tabgha, an Arab contraction of the Greek name meaning "seven springs," is in the north Ginosar Valley just below the Mount of Beatitudes. Tabgha has the small bay, Simon Peter's Landing Place, where the springs flowing into the Sea of Galilee make the water warm and ideal for fishing.

It was near here that Jesus likely first called Peter, whom Jesus sought out after meeting him in Judea, into full-time commitment, and called James, John, and Andrew to follow Him and be *"fishers of men."* This area is believed to be the small harbor where they kept their boats. Peter, Andrew, John, James, and Philip all came from the area of Tabgha/Bethsaida/Capernaum.

This is the traditional site of the miracles of the multiplication of the loaves and fishes—the feeding of the 5,000—and then the feeding of the 4,000 (whose counts both excluded the women and children). It is likely instead that the feeding of the 5,000 happened in a remote area outside Bethsaida on the northeastern shore, and the feeding of the 4,000 happened in the Decapolis region on the southeastern shore (whose crowd would have included both Jews and Gentiles). Both miracles reveal the Good Shepherd's power and compassion, giving physical *and* spiritual nourishment.

The feeding of the 5,000 is the only miracle recorded in all four Gospels. Jesus tested Philip's faith (who was from Bethsaida), but, like the others, he failed his test. The twelve baskets were possibly the lunch baskets of the twelve apostles. Jesus had come here often after John the Baptist was arrested, when the Jordan Valley was no longer safe.

Some of the disciples had further betrayed Jesus' Great Commission by returning here as fishermen after His death. Jesus restored Peter from the guilt of denying his beloved Christ three times, asking him three times, *"Do you love Me?"* He then commissioned Peter to *"Feed My sheep."* Peter, still thinking it was all about him, said, *"Depart from me, I am a sinful man."*

It was the third of four Resurrection appearances to His disciples, this time also including Thomas, Nathaniel, James, John, and two others, where their obedience to let down the nets resulted in the miraculous catch of fish. Now they were ready to walk away to follow Jesus, not in their own strength anymore.

What to See:

The rocky shores are probably very similar to what they were in Jesus' day. There is a beautiful, gray stone church built by the Franciscans in 1933, the **Church of the Multiplication of Loaves and Fishes**. The present church was built over the remains of a 350 AD church with a well-preserved, fifth century mosaic floor. The mosaics are a lovely display of plant and animal life in addition to the celebrated one of two fish flanking a basket of loaves directly in front of a huge stone altar said to be where Jesus laid the bread to bless it.

Scripture:

Matthew 14:22–32; Mark 6:47–56; Luke 5:1–10 (Fishers of men)

Matthew 14:15–21; Mark 6:30–44; Luke 9:10–17; John 6:1–15 (Feeding of the 5,000)

Matthew 15:29–39; Mark 8:1–10 (Feeding of the 4,000)

John 21:1–23 (Catch of fish/restoring Peter)

definingmomentsbook.com/resources

Defining Moment . . . Church of the Multiplication of Loaves and Fishes

Imagine that you are Peter. You had a pretty tormenting situation where your best friend and teacher, Jesus, told you that you would deny Him three times. You were absolutely certain you would never do that! Within twenty-four hours, you then deny three times that you are with Him. You have not had a conversation with Jesus about it, and you are feeling very troubled about this unfinished business. Satan is heaping lies on you—"You cannot serve Him now. You are not worthy of being His friend. It is over. You have wasted three years of your life and you ruined it." And then, this happens:

Afterward Jesus appeared again to His disciples, by the Sea of Galilee. It happened this way: Simon Peter, Thomas (also known as Didymus), Nathanael from Cana in Galilee, the sons of Zebedee, and two other disciples were together. "I am going out to fish," Simon Peter told them, and they said, "We will go with you." So they went out and got into the boat, but that night they caught nothing.

Early in the morning, Jesus stood on the shore, but the disciples did not realize that it was Jesus.

He called out to them, "Friends, have you not any fish?"

"No," they answered.

He said, "Throw your net on the right side of the boat and you will find some." When they did, they were unable to haul the net in because of the large number of fish.

Then the disciple whom Jesus loved said to Peter, "It is the Lord!" As soon as Simon Peter heard him say, "It is the Lord," he wrapped his outer garment around him (for he had taken it off) and jumped into the water. The other disciples followed in the boat, towing the net full of fish, for they were not far from shore, about a hundred yards. When they landed, they saw a fire of burning coals there with fish on it, and some bread."

Jesus said to them, "Bring some of the fish you have just caught." So Simon Peter climbed back into the boat and dragged the net ashore. It was full of large fish, 153, but even with so many the net was not torn. Jesus said to them, 'Come and have breakfast.' None of the disciples dared ask Him, 'Who are you?' They knew it was the Lord. Jesus came, took the bread and gave it to them, and did the same with the fish. This was now the third time Jesus appeared to His disciples after He was raised from the dead."

When they had finished eating, Jesus said to Simon Peter, 'Simon son of John, do you love Me more than these?'"

"Yes, Lord," he said. "You know that I love You."

Jesus said, "Feed My lambs."

Again Jesus said, "Simon son of John, do you love Me?"

"He answered, 'Yes, Lord, You know that I love You.'"

Jesus said, "Take care of My sheep."

The third time He said to him, "Simon son of John, do you love Me?"

Peter was hurt because Jesus asked him the third time, "Do you love Me?"

He said, "Lord, You know all things; You know that I love You'"

Jesus said, "Feed My sheep. Very truly I tell you, when you were younger you dressed yourself and went where you wanted; but when you are old you will stretch out your hands, and someone else will dress you and lead you where you do not want to go." Jesus said this to indicate the kind of death by which Peter would glorify God. Then He said to him, "Follow Me!"
(John 21:1–19).

Did you notice that just as Peter denied Jesus three times *before* His Crucifixion, Jesus gave him three opportunities to declare his love for Him *after* His Resurrection? Jesus did not heap shame, or guilt. or judgment on Peter. He did not go over the blow by blow of the denials. Just as He had said to Peter at Gethsemane, *"the spirit is willing, but the flesh is weak,"* He knew Peter was weak, and He was not going to punish or humiliate him for that human flaw. He decided to remind Peter of the truth, and of what the Lord was calling him into: feeding His sheep. Even with Peter's imperfections, He knew that if Peter loved Him the Holy Spirit would come and empower him to feed His sheep. Jesus was about truth and vision.

Have you ever heard of the book *StrengthsFinder 2.0*? The premise is that corporate America spends most of its time looking at the weaknesses of its employees and trying to help them get better in those areas. The companies that are really successful do the opposite. They spend most of their effort looking at the strengths of their employees and figuring out how to use those gifts more fully to make the company better. If you take an employee weakness and spend $1,000 in resources to get it up to par, you might get your $1,000 back. If you spend the same $1,000 to leverage the greatest gifts that same employee has, it is likely you will get your investment back many times over.

Jesus was a wise investor. *He* knew that Peter loved him. He just wanted *Peter* to know. The vision that Jesus had for Peter to serve Him was far greater than anything that Peter could have imagined. Jesus set him free to live out that vision by focusing on Peter's strengths (loving Jesus) instead of his weaknesses.

Journal Time:

Is the Lord calling *you* into an encounter like He did with Peter? Is there an area of guilt or shame that the enemy keeps calling you into? Are you going to listen to Satan's voice or to Jesus? What is Jesus calling you to let go of—and what is He calling you into? Spend a few moments in silence, allowing the Holy Spirit to minister to you. This is more about you *listening* to Jesus rather than you *speaking* to Him. Record whatever He puts on your heart.

Share Time:

What did you hear? What are you willing to let go of? What are you willing to embrace?

Prayer:

Dear Lord Jesus,

Wow, what a loving God You are! Thank You for this example of how You loved Peter back into his calling. Thank You that You are not a god who shames, humiliates, and accuses us. You are a God that lifts us up out of our mistakes, sees who the Father made us to be, and helps us to stand in that identity. Please take every bit of shame and guilt revealed today and do with it what You did to Peter's shame. Take it away with Your love. Please take every calling revealed here today and infuse it with Your power and strength. Make us all fit for who and what You have called us to be. Thank You, Lord. We are amazed by how Your love is boundless. We are speechless and in awe of You.

In Jesus' name,

Amen

Worship:

"Thank You Lord"

"Amazing Grace"

TIBERIAS

―――

Historical Significance:

The Sea of Galilee (the popular name) is actually a lake, also known by John as the Sea of Tiberias, likely the official Roman name, and known by Luke as the Sea of Gennesaret. The city of Tiberias is on the western shore of the Sea, one of four holy Jewish cities (along with Jerusalem, Hebron in the West Bank, and Safed). It was founded by Herod Antipas in 17–20 AD as the capital of Galilee, and named after emperor Tiberius Julius Caesar, Rome's emperor from 14–37 AD (during Jesus' ministry). Tiberias contained an active cemetery within its walls, and was considered unclean as a result, yet it was the seat of famous Talmudic scholars as well as being the seat of the Sanhedrin, where the Talmud and the Mishna (two of the most important Jewish books) were written, and thus became a holy town to Jews.

During Passion Week, Herod Antipas left his main headquarters in Tiberias for the Passover in Jerusalem, where his rival, Pilate, tried to rid himself of Jesus' case by sending it to Herod.

Tiberias was destroyed in 1033 AD by the great earthquake, and later became the first town to be freed in the current State of Israel.

What to See:

Lower Tiberias is a modern, lakeshore town, 700 feet *below* sea level, while Upper Tiberias is 600 feet *above* sea level, where most of the hotels and healing, therapeutic spas, and mud baths (some lakeside) are for multi-day visits to the region. See ancient hot baths, many famous burial sites of scholars and rabbis, several ancient sites from Roman and Crusader times, date palms, and bougainvillea. View a beautiful sunrise over the Golan Heights, just as Jesus must have many times.

Scripture:

The town is not specifically mentioned in Scripture, but the Sea of Tiberias is referred to in Mark 1:16, Luke 5 and John 6:1, 23 and 21:1.

definingmomentsbook.com/resources

CHAPTER THREE:

Paul's Journeys

Then Ananias went to the house and entered it. Placing his hands on Saul, he said, "Brother Saul, the Lord Jesus, who appeared to you on the road as you were coming here has sent me so that you may see again and be filled with the Holy Spirit." Immediately, something like scales fell from Saul's eyes, and he could see again. He got up and was baptized, and after taking some food, he regained his strength. At once he began to preach in the synagogues that Jesus is the Son of God. All those who heard him were astonished and asked, "Is not he the man who raised havoc in Jerusalem among those who call on this name? And has not he come here to take them as prisoners to the chief priests?" Yet Saul grew more and more powerful and baffled the Jews living in Damascus by proving that Jesus is the Christ

(Acts 9:17–22).

Introduction to Paul's Journeys:

See *Appendix* Paul's Journeys

- Letters Written by Paul, in order of writing date
- Themes of Letters Written by Paul, in Biblical order
- Paul's Traveling Companions
- Major Archaeological Finds, New Testament
- Timeline of Paul's Life and Journeys
- Biblical References to Places in Greece, Turkey and Cyprus
- Suggested Resources: Paul's Journeys
- Map: Paul's First Missionary Journey
- Map: Paul's Second Missionary Journey
- Map: Paul's Third Missionary Journey
- Map: Paul's Trip to Rome

There is no one else in the Bible or in Christian history, other than Christ, who has had more impact on our world than the Apostle Paul. Sometimes called the "cofounder" of Christianity, more books have been written about Paul than about anyone else except Jesus Christ.

While we know well *Jesus'* life and ministry, there is much to learn from a better understanding of this man from Tarsus. This introduction will serve as an attempt to compile a linear summary of his life from many resources to further acquaint you with this remarkable man before we look at Paul's journeys city by city. It is nearly impossible to give a true chronology of Paul's life, as scholars still debate the order and the years of certain events.

Paul called himself the chief of all sinners, the least of all saints, and was forever grateful for his transformation through the gift of grace. The more we understand how dark his prior life was, the more we will understand his gratitude for grace. He has been called "the apostle of grace." No one's past is too dark—no one is beyond hope.

Paul is a true example and hero of our faith, yet he also was an imperfect man, just like you and me. Only Christ Jesus lived a perfect life. We can learn from each of them. Paul's life and faith are so amazing and inspiring, yet we also can learn hope from his weaknesses. He was the Church's greatest missionary and first theologian, expanding on Jesus' spoken word in writing. He took Christ's message to the Gentiles, the future of the Church.

There are five primary reasons to look at Paul's life:

- He was the first Western missionary.
- He was used by God to move Jesus' story from a sect within Judaism to a world religion.
- His letters are the first and most important interpretation of Jesus' mission (as the Gospels are just narratives of Jesus' life).
- His letters dominate the New Testament (thirteen of twenty-seven books; they are arranged longest to shortest, not chronologically).
- His is the most distinctive voice in Christian theology throughout the ages.

He was also very controversial, as he called himself an apostle (he saw the risen Lord, but without witnesses), and he claimed apostolic authority. He was a radical thinker who challenged all—male and female, rich and poor, Jew and Gentile, free and slave—to be brothers in Christ. He called it a religion for *sinners*, while most religions required *holiness* first.

Paul always points us toward Jesus, not himself. He never told us he was born in Tarsus, was on the road to Damascus, was blinded by light, was a Roman citizen, used to be called Saul, and was a tent maker. These were all covered in Acts by Luke, not in Paul's writings. It is possible that the Jerusalem church got ahead of God's timing by replacing Judas with Matthias instead of Paul.

As we shift now from Israel, the eastern world, to Greece, the western world, more than geography changes. Westerners learn in the *Greek* tradition of words ("God is strong"), while easterners learn in the *Hebrew* tradition of pictures and metaphors ("God is my rock").

Saul of Tarsus, Paul of the World:

Saul was born circa 5 AD, an Israelite in Tarsus, a Roman province of Cilicia, a dozen miles from the northeastern corner of the Mediterranean Sea, in southeastern Asia Minor: Turkey today. Paul was born with the Hebrew name of Saul, the name of Israel's first king. His mother died when he was nine. His father was a successful tentmaker, from the tribe of Benjamin; from his father he inherited Roman citizenship. They were both well respected Pharisees, fanatic believers of Jewish nationalism and Moses' Law. He would have received an international education just living in cosmopolitan Tarsus. We know little about his youth and have no Biblical descriptions of his appearance. We know much more about his thoughts than we know about him.

By the age of thirteen, Saul was an expert in Scriptures and the history of Israel. He had come to Jerusalem at a young age to be trained as a (legalistic) Pharisee under Gamaliel, the most honored rabbi and scholar of the first century, with the goal of being one of the seventy-one men of the Great Sanhedrin (Supreme Court). He spoke at least Hebrew, Aramaic, and Greek. It appears Saul never married or had children.

After Pentecost, these pious Jewish leaders were furious and fearful that crucifying Jesus had not stopped thousands of Jews from embracing Christianity, and felt their power was threatened. Saul listened with fury to the uneducated fisherman, Peter, speak of Jesus, unaware that soon they would both be planting churches all over the world.

Stephen

Stephen, a young Christian, was a deacon in a community of Greek Jews speaking in the Temple precincts and acting with authority in Jerusalem—and perceived to be enemies of the Torah and the Temple. Less than two years after the Crucifixion, he was accused by the Sanhedrin (or Council) of worshipping someone other than God—a dead man! He likely debated a young, knowledgeable officer of the Council, who hated the name of Jesus, approved of his stoning, and held the robes of Stephen's murderers at his execution—Saul.

Try to understand what Saul's life was like then as a fanatical Pharisee, trying desperately to faithfully follow hundreds of manmade laws from daily rituals to Sabbath restrictions. Focusing on such obedience pushed his true heart farther *away* from God. Father, convict us and forgive us when we also unknowingly act like Pharisees, substituting *our* laws for *Your* laws.

Stephen was the first Christian martyr, worthy to die for Christ while his ministry was just launching (circa 34 AD). He was confronted with false charges and false witnesses in front of the Sanhedrin and gave one of the most powerful sermons in history (Acts 7:1–53), declaring that the worship of God was no longer restricted to the Temple, and declaring a risen, crucified Lord. These were both blasphemies that *must be stopped* in the eyes of the Pharisees. (In Deuteronomy, a man hanged was accursed by God, so a crucified Messiah was an unacceptable oxymoron.)

Stephen Stoned

Governor Pontius Pilate, who had held Jesus' trial, had authorized the Jews to commit capital punishment by this time. He would have been at his headquarters in Caesarea by the Sea now that the Passover had ended. Saul must have been one of those defeated in debate by Stephen in the synagogues of the Cilicians and must have been affected by his sermon, his angelic face, his Godly traits (servant leader, witness, and judge) and his words of forgiveness when Saul witnessed Stephen's stoning. Ironically, Saul's beloved teacher, Gamaliel, had just advised the Sanhedrin to leave the believers alone.

According to the Torah, Stephen was taken outside the city wall (like Jesus was), probably just below the northwest corner of the Temple wall in the Kidron Valley. There is a small chapel there today. He was dropped down a hill at least twice his height by the accusing witness, landing on his back. As he was still alive, the second witness dropped a heavy stone on his chest over his heart. Still alive, Stephen (again like Jesus in Luke 23:34) cried out, "*Lord, do not hold this sin against them,*" and was then hit by stones thrown from all until he died. They silenced a *messenger*, but the *message* remained.

Foreign (Greek), Christ-following Jews fled Jerusalem (to Damascus, Samaria, Phoenicia, Cyprus, and Antioch) after Stephen's stoning and further persecution. By trying to *eliminate* this new faith, the Jewish leaders actually *spread* it to the world! The "Way" did not require following the Law or circumcision—their pathway led directly to Salvation through a man, Jesus of Nazareth, making Gentiles equal to Jews!

This resulted in unrest in places like Damascus, where the synagogue leaders beseeched the high priest in Jerusalem for help. He recommended the Pharisee called Saul go to **Damascus** to stop the spread of this heresy by arresting the Christ followers. (Rome had granted Jewish authorities the rights of extradition in 132 BC.) After twenty days of no strong drink and no haircut, he went to the Temple and cut his hair as an offering before heading off, prepared to use words, beatings, imprisonment, and murder.

Around 34 AD, Saul was struck, at midday, three times by a blinding, silent light, followed by a roar from the Heavens. He had been traveling 170 miles over eight days with Jude and other companions, on the road to Damascus in the Roman province of Syria. Christ appeared to him and asked Saul why he persecuted Him. His conversion took but an instant, yet his sanctification grew throughout his lifetime. The men with him *heard* the voice but *saw* nothing.

He was told to go on to Damascus, a city with a large Jewish population, and wait, still blind, desperately dependent for the first time in his life. Repentance (from the Greek *metanoia*) means "to change one's mind." Saul went from hating a dead Christ to loving a living Jesus. Remember, he had likely heard Jesus preach in public before and would have hated what he had heard. He had probably also been affected by the bravery of the believing prisoners and by the way Stephen had died: angelic and forgiving.

Ananias

Ananias (meaning "Favored of the Lord"), possibly a bishop, was the chief Christian disciple living in Damascus. Ananias was sent by God to Straight Street (where Saul had been praying and fasting for three days in what must have been an agonizing reappraisal of this Jesus) to welcome him as a brother into the faith—Saul, the feared *enemy* of all Christians! Saul's sight was restored, and the Holy Spirit filled him.

Ananias commissioned him to carry Jesus' name to both Gentiles and Jews, and then baptized him, eighteen months after Jesus' death and Resurrection. Saul, now called Paul, considered himself the least of Christians, having so persecuted the Christ followers. But he was a changed man, perhaps the most transformed in all of world history. He wants the same for you today!

Paul had learned Scripture better than most at an early age, but did not know the Author of it all until that point. The last time Paul was in Damascus, he was blaspheming Christ and arresting believers. Now he returned to preach Christ, eating and staying with these believers. He baffled the Jews in Damascus (the oldest still inhabited city in the world today) by weaving Old Testament Law and prophesies into their fulfillment in Christ.

Paul began teaching the Gospel in the synagogues after spending several days with the disciples. Like Moses, David, Joseph, Elijah, and John the Baptist before him, God met him more personally and powerfully during a season of solitude and obscurity in the desert. He *"went away to Arabia"* before returning to Damascus. He says three years, perhaps as long as the disciples trained with Jesus. Later, around 35 AD, he went up briefly to **Jerusalem** to meet with Peter (Cephas). To first learn humility, though, Paul started by escaping the plotting Jews who now, for the first of many times, wanted to kill *him*. This escape was via a wicker fish basket hanging by a rope from a window in the exterior city wall!

Paul then stayed with Peter and his wife for fifteen days in Jerusalem—*imagine* the conversations these two had! The younger, former fisherman, Peter, was schooling the older, highly educated rabbi. Peter was most likely in his late twenties, while Paul was in his mid-thirties, an age difference that was opposite for teachers and students in that rabbinical culture. He also met with Jesus' stepbrother, James, who was emerging as the head of the Jerusalem church. To protect Paul from a death plot, the apostles sent him back to his hometown of Tarsus, through Caesarea by the Sea. Paul was to reach the Gentiles and Peter the Jews.

Imagine Paul sailing to his hometown of **Tarsus** after his conversion, to his father, also a Pharisee, and to his Jewish community, who had seen him as a hero. His father may very well have disowned him—after all, he had left to *stop* these new followers of the Way and had come home as *one* of them!

Years of Silence

Paul does not appear in Scripture again for another ten to eleven silent years, though we know he spent time as an independent missionary in northern Syria and Cilicia around 35–45 AD, proclaiming the faith he had once tried to destroy. It is likely that during this time he was given the thorn or splinter in his flesh: a handicap to keep him humbly dependent on God, that he later called his "*blessing in disguise*." They did not need *him* yet, but he learned he needed *them*. He learned humility in his over ten years of preparation. He said, "*I am crucified in Christ*" in Galatians 2:20, knowing that "I" in Greek means his "ego." He was in his mid-forties when he finally got called into service for a twenty-year career.

Joseph Barnabas, a Jew from Cyprus, was sent to **Antioch** in Syria, 300 miles north of Jerusalem, where followers were first called "Christians," a term intended as ridicule. The Christian experience is filled with irony: over 1.7 billion people in our world today call themselves by that "mocking" word that both unites and divides. His name had been changed from Joseph to Barnabas, meaning "son of encouragement"—which is what he was sent to do for them. He had sold all his land and possessions and given them to the Jerusalem apostles. He partnered with "Paul" (in Greek versus "Saul" in Aramaic, as he was from the tribe of Benjamin, whose most famous ancestor was the first king of Israel, Saul). The names appear interchangeable, Saul in a Jewish setting, Paul in a Gentile setting.

Paul worked with leather, canvas, and cilicium: a woven, felt-like cloth Tarsus was known for. Cilicium is from the long hair of black goats, and still used by Bedouins today to make strong tents that shed water. Paul's job as a tentmaker included making and mending tents, cloaks, awnings, and sails. Barnabas worked with precious stones and metals. It was not unusual for a rabbi to practice a trade, so he could offer teaching without a fee and set an example (2 Thessalonians 3:7–10).

Barnabas went 120 miles to Tarsus and brought Paul back to Syrian Antioch for a year. Barnabas and Paul took the offerings from the Antioch church to aid the prophesied famine victims in Jerusalem. The chief priests did not understand why Paul brought no prisoners. The disciples did not believe he was really one of them now. It was Barnabas who vouched for him to the apostles, accepting him as a brother.

Most believers in Jerusalem still valued circumcision in the Law, since Jesus came to *fulfill* the Law (not *destroy* it). King Herod Agrippa, the part-Jewish grandson of Herod the Great, (who had rebuilt the Temple and ruled in Jesus' day), was beloved by the favored Sadducees, Zealots, and Pharisees. He arrested and beheaded James, the son of Zebedee, the brother of John. Romans favored beheading. The Torah favored stoning, the way Stephen was martyred. Herod then took Simon Peter captive, but God executed a jail break, and he fled Jerusalem before he could be executed after that Passover ended. Herod executed the guards and went to Caesarea by the Sea; he was then eaten by worms when he sought to be worshipped as god.

Rome's Pax Augusta ("the peace of Augustus," the emperor when Jesus and Paul were born) had made land and sea travel safe just in time for Paul's journeys.

FIRST MISSIONARY JOURNEY
(45–48 AD, ESTIMATED)

(Acts 13:4–14:28)

1,400 Miles

Antioch, Cyprus, Perga, Pisidia, Antioch, Iconium, Lystra, Derbe, Lystra, Iconium, Pisidian Antioch, Pamphylia, Attalia, Antioch.

Barnabas, Paul, and John Mark (Barnabas's cousin, who would later write the second Gospel and in whose mother's home the early Church met) were faithfully sent out from Antioch in Syria ("Little Rome") after Peter's vision to offer the Gospel to the Gentiles. They sailed in early spring down the Orontes River, then from the port of Seleucia to the copper island of **Cyprus** (Barnabas's hometown), preaching in synagogues west/southwest around the island from Salamis (with its thin, sandy coastline) to Paphos, the third largest island in the Mediterranean. There they encountered a Jewish false prophet/magician and attendant to the proconsul of Cyprus, Sergius Paulus from Pisidian Antioch. Paul called the sorcerer "*son of the devil*," and blinded him in his first recorded wonder through the power of the Holy Spirit.

The renegade Jewish occultist feared losing influence if the governor of this provincial capital converted. The proconsul believed. The Scriptures, after this first miracle, now call him "Paul," and no longer "Saul," as he took the name of his first recorded convert. Barnabas also yielded control to Paul here, as the order of their names was reversed in Scripture.

Continuing onto the large Roman province of Galatia to **Perga**, the capitol of Pamphylia (a coastal province between Lycia and Cilicia; today the Turkish Riviera with beautiful waterfalls, majestic even in ruins), John Mark returned to Jerusalem, possibly resenting Paul for taking over leadership from his cousin.

Long and Effective Journey

Paul and Barnabas headed 100 miles uphill over seven days to the cosmopolitan Roman colony of **Pisidian Antioch** with its seven hills surrounding the 4,000-foot high flatlands, again preaching with authority the Good News in the synagogues until large crowds believed, which caused the *Jewish* leaders to challenge them. Paul told them they would now share the message with the *Gentiles* instead. The Jewish leaders were deaf to the message that Christ had fulfilled over sixty major prophecies from the Old Testament.

This was the first of many times where their message was well received and God began a great work, only to get the enemy's attention.

Paul and Barnabas walked 100 miles southeast to the huge metropolis of **Iconium**, where a Roman bridge still stands over the valley, and founded the second thriving Asia Minor church, but left disciples behind to continue to spread the already spreading Word. The same thing happened there: upon hearing they were to be stoned, they walked twenty-five miles southwest to **Lystra** (probably Timothy's hometown), in Lycaonia in the Roman province of Galatia, a Roman colony like Antioch.

Paul healed a cripple begging just inside the city gate, but the people mistook them for gods (Barnabas as Zeus, the father of gods and man; Paul as Hermes, the god of communication) and prostrated themselves. The priest of Zeus began preparing to sacrifice a bull to Paul. Lystra was the town where legend had it that Zeus and Hermes had come in human form to see Bacchus, and the nonbelieving townsfolk had been turned into frogs. Paul told them to bow for no one except the true, living God that he knew well enough to call "Father." He had reached these pagans without mentioning Israel, the covenant, or the Law: only by telling them of Jesus.

Just like Jesus hearing adoring "*Hosanna*" one day, shortly followed by "*Crucify Him*," when some Jews followed from Antioch and Iconium to stir things up, Paul was beat up one night, stoned, knocked unconscious, and left for dead in a ditch outside the city. Paul probably remembered Stephen's stoning as he received this taste of his own medicine.

All Paul cared about was preaching the truth, not about himself. He called *both* what happened in Iconium (escaping before a beating) and in Lystra (*not* escaping the stoning) "divine rescue." The next day they traveled sixty miles southeast to **Derbe** (home of Gaius), where impatient crowds had been waiting to hear their message, then backtracked counterclockwise the long way back through dangerous **Lystra** and **Iconium**, and then sailed back to their home base of Syrian **Antioch**, strengthening, encouraging, and appointing older men as elders and other men and women to faithful service.

They returned to find more unrest. Jewish legalists, including Pharisees from Judea, were again inciting the people, outraged by these occurrences:

- Teaching that baptism in Jesus is enough and circumcision was not needed;
- Preaching directly to pagans without mention of Israel;
- Nothing was required of believers other than belief in the Resurrection;
- Gentiles and Jews eating unclean food together.

Stephen, who had been stoned, had at least remained tied to the synagogue. Antioch sent representatives to Jerusalem for help nineteen years after Pentecost. Paul, Barnabas and Titus also went to settle doctrinal questions at the most important council in church history, the **Jerusalem** (or Apostolic) **Council** in 49 AD, traveling through Phoenicia and Samaria.

Titus was a Gentile believer, a result of the Gospel being shared with non-Jewish people. He served with Paul the longest (twenty years), and mediated Paul's relationship with the Corinthians who were practicing immorality. Titus later became the first bishop of Crete and was the recipient of Paul's personal letter on the qualities of a good leader (Titus). While Paul and Barnabas did the preaching, he was otherwise a full participant in their ministry. Some were upset that Titus was still uncircumcised and would not extend fellowship to him, believing Gentiles must first become Jews before becoming Christians.

Pharisees of the circumcision party, the Judaizers, passionately defended the Law and accused Paul of creating a church outside of the Lord God. Paul countered that requiring Titus to be circumcised would be adding the Law of Moses to Jesus' Gospel, minimizing it as incomplete. Simon Peter, who had dined with the Gentile Cornelius in Caesarea, argued that the

Gentile believers should be accepted equally by the Jewish believers. He pointed out that the legalists expected of others what they could not even do themselves—live the *entire* Law. Paul said God would not have allowed their miracles if they were preaching the wrong Gospel.

Peter, a pillar of the Jerusalem church, the genial fisherman, supported Paul and spoke, saying that king Herod Agrippa had killed James, John's brother, to satisfy the Jews since he saw him as different. The Roman emperor had threatened to expel the Jews over these public differences about Jesus. James the Just, the stepbrother of Jesus, the first bishop of Jerusalem, then commissioned Paul and Barnabas to go forward with sharing the Gospel to the Gentiles, *separate* from the synagogues. James, Peter, and John continued to preach to the Jews *within* the synagogues.

Return

They then returned with a letter to their beloved at **Antioch** along with two Church leaders: Judas (called Barsabbas) and Silas (Silvanus). It said the Gentile believers need not be circumcised, but then appeared to contradict itself by urging them to follow other parts of the Law: four mild restrictions about idols, fornication, strangled animals, and blood. In a sad step backward, both Peter and Barnabas later stopped dining with Gentile Christians after the Judaizers showed up again. Paul later opposed Peter to his face in public. Paul's letter to the Galatians was written to correct the erroneous teachings of the Judaizers.

Today, worldwide there are 160 Christians for every Jew.

SECOND MISSIONARY JOURNEY
(49–51 AD, ESTIMATED)

(Acts 15:39–18:22)

2,800 Miles

Antioch, Syria and Cilicia, Derbe, Lystra, Iconium, Phrygia and Galatia, Troas, Philippi, Thessaloniki, Berea, Athens, Corinth, Ephesus, Caesarea, and Antioch.

Barnabas, the Levite, would speak to the group a little and then minister individually by singing, comforting, and praying. Paul was truly able to speak with conviction to all no matter their race, faith, stature, gender, or age. But within a month of their return, this vital duo parted, with Paul leaving in anger.

Paul was now teaching with even more confidence after the experience in Jerusalem. He would start in each new city by preaching in the synagogue, proving Jesus was Christ by quoting the Old Testament prophecies. Some Jews and many Gentiles would believe. Then other Jews would be envious, and they would riot.

The letter from the Jerusalem church required abstaining from unchastity and foods sacrificed to idols, strangled, or bloody. The Gentile believers would not be required to observe the rest of the Law, including the feasts.

Paul was furious that some Christian converts from Judaism were still trying to add Laws to Jesus' message and to separate Jewish and Gentile believers over unclean foods, putting Titus, among others, outside their fellowship. He now went beyond saying the Torah was no longer needed, to saying it was a curse if one relied on the works of the Law.

Barnabas Leaves

When Barnabas wanted to bring John Mark along again, Paul, still upset that John Mark had left them on the prior journey, disagreed, and instead left with Silas, a fellow Roman citizen who spent three years with Paul on this journey across the High Anatolian plateau for **Lystra through Syria and Cilicia**, strengthening the churches. Silas later joined Paul in Rome.

Barnabas and his cousin, John Mark, left for Cyprus, where Barnabas was born. Cyprus was the first stop he had made with Paul on the first missionary journey a few years before. Was God's plan to divide and multiply? One team of two preachers became two teams of two. In lieu of reconciliation, God doubled His impact through two powerful teams: Paul and Silas, and Barnabas and John. It could never be the same again for Paul and Barnabas. Paul's heart was more for church planting, while Barnabas's heart was more as an encourager for man.

Remember that John Mark later wrote the straightforward, chronological Gospel of Mark, the shortest of the four, presenting Jesus as the Son of God. He wrote largely from Peter's preaching. He clearly persisted beyond his youthful mistake due to Barnabas's investment in mentoring him.

Paul's only authority now was Jesus: no man, no congregation, no church council. His plan was to preach in the cities, form churches, and then move on, leaving the responsibility to the city churches to then share the Gospel to the surrounding villages.

Beginning with cities they had already visited, they went to **Iconium, Derbe, Lystra, and Pisidian Antioch**, intending to go west, on to Ephesus in Asia. In Lystra, which was governed as a Roman colony, with few Jews and no synagogues, they met a young native, Timothy (Greek for "one who honors God"), with a Jewish mother and a Greek Agnostic father. Timothy would often serve as Paul's envoy. As Paul wanted to bring him along westward as his first disciple to spread the Good News to Agnostics, Jews and Gentiles, he had Timothy circumcised, so the Jews would be open to his message. Timothy had learned great life lessons from his mother, Eunice, and grandmother, Lois. The Holy Spirit stopped them from entering Asia and instead pointed them north through Phrygia, at a pace of twenty miles a day.

Luke Joins Paul

Luke, from Antioch, the author of Acts, seems to have joined them in Troas, as Acts 16:10 starts referring to "*we*." Luke would later journey with Paul to

Rome, on the voyage where they were shipwrecked on Malta and Paul was imprisoned in Rome. After Paul died, Luke wrote his Gospel account as well as The Acts of the Apostles.

Paul had a vision in the crossing seaport of Troas, an area twelve miles southwest of Troy. Troy was the city that the Romans traced their origins to, and was located on the northwest coast of Asia Minor. Paul's vision beckoned him from Galatia to Macedonia (northeast Greece today). They sailed the northeast Aegean Sea to the island of **Samothrace**, where the statue of the Winged Victory, now in the Louvre Museum in Paris, was discovered. They reached the mainland port of **Neapolis** ("new city"), then walked ten miles to **Philippi**, a Roman colony in Macedonia with gold in the mountain to its west.

Lydia from Thyatira, a wealthy, religious, purple cloth merchant, heard their preaching while praying down by the river on the Sabbath and was baptized along with her family. It was the first conversion in Europe. She invited them to stay with her.

Paul Jailed

Here also, some weeks later, Paul exorcised a possessed, fortune-telling slave girl. This upset her owners, who had profited from her "prophecies." They brought Paul and Silas before the anti-Semitic Roman authorities, who ordered them stripped, beaten with rods, and imprisoned in stocks (Timothy and Luke may have been considered Gentiles and were left free). What a start for Silas's ministry!

Paul and Silas sang hymns loudly until an earthquake struck at midnight, opening all the doors and releasing all the chains. The jailer, thinking all had escaped, prepared to kill himself (as his life would be demanded in place of that of an escapee), until Paul assured him all were accounted for. Because Paul was free enough in Christ to stay, loving the jailer who had beaten him, the jailer asked, "*What must I do to be saved?*" He took them home, cared for their wounds, fed them, and was baptized with his family.

The magistrates freed them in the morning, but Paul pointed out they had illegally and publicly beaten and imprisoned Roman citizens without a trial. The alarmed authorities went to the prison and apologized, asking them to leave, but not before Paul had converted a wealthy and well-connected businesswoman (Lydia), a lower class slave girl, and a middle class jailer, leaving Luke to disciple them for a few months. Note that he chose to not declare himself a citizen *before* the flogging—they likely remembered this when years later, again amidst prison suffering, he wrote in his letter, "*Rejoice in the Lord always.*"

They walked along the Via Egnatia to **Amphipolis**, **Apollonia** and then **Thessaloniki**, debating for three weeks in the synagogue. This road was part of 50,000 miles built for the Roman military—tightly packed sand and gravel over which a pavement of hewn stones was set in a gentle convex curve for draining. Again, while some Jews believed, others were upset, so the believers asked them to leave.

They moved on fifty miles to **Berea**, a beautiful city between the ocean and Mount Olympus, the supposed home of Greek gods and goddesses, where the Jews in the synagogue were more receptive, examining the Scriptures daily to verify truth, until the vindictive Jews from Thessaloniki came all that way just to cause trouble. Silas and Timothy stayed this time, while Paul sailed south to ancient **Athens**, shortly thereafter to be rejoined by them.

Though well past her glory days, Athens was still full of academics and philosophers. Greeks value good debate, wit, and public speaking, so people came from all over to hear their preaching. Paul was angry with all their idols, and argued with Jews and Greeks, Epicureans and Stoics, until he was invited to share his new ideas at their meeting at the Areopagus (Greek; Mars Hill in Latin). Noting their altar to an "unknown God" to hedge their spiritual bets, he told them of the true, known God: the Creator of all of us, not the one created by human hands.

Not Received Well

They were mostly indifferent to his message of a Resurrection, and he left, not because he was forced to this time, walking west fifty miles to **Corinth**, population then at 200,000, never mentioning a church plant in Athens. An amazing sermon filled with truth and enlightenment cannot change a closed heart. What irony—the smart Athenians were blinded to the message, yet the sinful, worldly Corinthians received it. The more lost or weak we are, the more we need God.

Celebrating the 800th anniversary of Rome's founding, emperor Claudius (41–54 AD) renewed the old religions and expanded the pomerium, the ancient city boundary within which only Roman gods could be honored. The synagogue of Aquila and Priscilla was on the Aventine on a hill that had been outside the boundary, but was now inside, and the congregation was disbanded. Some emigrating Greek-speaking Christian Jews were teaching that Salvation through the Messiah had spread throughout the world, His death making Gentiles equal to Jews. The Jewish leaders were outraged, since *they* were the chosen people.

The traveling Jews prophesied famine. The citizens abroad, facing a grain shortage, demanded food from the emperor, who then expelled the "Christus," Jewish followers of Christ. Aquila and Priscilla sailed for Corinth from Brindisi and paid taxes to practice their leather and canvas trade in the public markets there, arriving about six months before Paul arrived on this second missionary journey.

As he neared Corinth by land from the east at the end of the second day, Paul saw the Acrocorinth, a monument to the dead gods, a rock 2,000 feet high housing sacred prostitutes (priestesses). A small temple of Aphrodite (Venus), the Greek goddess of love and sex, was at the peak, expanded by cells and chambers. Paul likely entered at the Isthmian Gate at dusk, climbing all the next day, going for the higher northern summit. Heavy winds preceded a storm. He had a vision where he cried out to God for His heart to preach nothing but Christ, and Jesus appeared, telling him for the first time to not fear and to continue.

Priscilla

Priscilla met Paul in the marketplace and was excited to finally find fellow Christ followers, including an apostle who witnessed Jesus after the Resurrection. She invited Paul to live in their home and share the business, so he would be allowed to work—and preach—at his bench in the markets.

Timothy went north with a letter to the new church at Thessaloniki (1 Thessalonians) and later returned. Second Thessalonians was written to them about six months later. Silas left to join Peter in Antioch without warning, and told Titus of all the churches started in Galatia (in the region of Turkey's capital today, Ankara), former cradle of the Hittites, and in Macedonia and Achaia. Titus headed from Antioch for Corinth, sent by Barnabas, who was tired and had stopped traveling.

Christ Followers Increasing

The synagogue was losing Jews to the now three churches. They banned Paul from the synagogue. He spoke less in public, focusing more on training teachers to continue on after he left. Then they locked him in the synagogue, preparing to charge him and seek the death penalty. The proconsul of Achaia (Rome's name for Greece), Lucius Julius Gallio, in his tribunal at the bema, freed Paul, and after eighteen months, they left Corinth, first having sent a sharp letter to the Galatians and several congregations in the northern area of Asia Minor.

If Gallio had found Paul guilty, the provincial governors would have had a test case as he visited other areas. Gallio validated Christianity, nearly three centuries before Constantine did, in the second most important trial in history after Jesus' trial.

Aquila, Priscilla, and Sosthenes sailed to **Ephesus** to start a church. Apollos, a passionate, learned Jewish believer from Alexandria, came to Ephesus schooled in Scripture. Priscilla and Aquila took him and taught him the Gospel more fully. He was prepared now to fill Paul's rather large preaching shoes and moved on to Achaia (the Roman province with Corinth as its capital). Churches had been founded by the Ephesians as far away as **Laodicea, Pamukkale/Hierapolis,** and **Colossae.**

Silas stayed in Corinth to minister, while Paul, Timothy, and Titus sailed further on to Antioch in Syria, as Paul wanted to get to Jerusalem via Caesarea by the Sea. He was furious to have heard, upon Titus's arrival in Corinth, that Judas Barsabbas had for six months been effectively preaching the need for circumcision, in the very towns in Galatia that Paul had planted churches.

Barnabas had thought Paul would head directly to Galatia, not first to Jerusalem and Antioch. Paul had decided to collect from all the Gentile churches he had started in Galatia, Macedonia, and Achaia to give to the poor in Jerusalem. In Jerusalem, Paul passionately asked James to control Barsabbas abroad, which James could not do.

Back in **Antioch**, after 2,800 miles on this journey, Paul learned that Peter had been preaching there after he had left, and that he was no longer welcome. Peter, Silas, and John Mark had gone to Rome. Paul visited the ailing Barnabas and reconciled after all those years apart.

Paul and others had come so far in such a short time, as fewer than 100 people in the Old Testament were described as having the Spirit within them, and, now, since Pentecost, *every* believer had the Holy Spirit in them!

THIRD MISSIONARY JOURNEY
(52–55 AD, ESTIMATED)

(Acts 18:23–21:17)

2,700 Miles

Antioch, Galatia and Phrygia, Ephesus, Macedonia and Greece, Troas, Miletus, Jerusalem.

Paul left west from **Antioch** through the Seleucian Gates with Timothy, stopping throughout **Galatia and Phrygia** (for the fourth time through **Derbe, Lystra, Iconium,** and **Pisidian Antioch**) overland toward Ephesus in Asia Minor to encourage his churches and disciples along the way. After receiving his letter, the strong Galatian warriors were like scolded children needing their (spiritual) father's love and forgiveness. They became even more obedient.

They were welcomed into Aquila and Priscilla's home in **Ephesus**, where their new church met after nine months apart. For two years daily in the rented lecture hall of Tyrannus's local philosophy school, Paul focused on training teachers after three months and another rejection in the synagogue. Once trained, Paul sent them off to strategic centers throughout Asia Minor—north to Smyrna and Pergamum, northeast to Philadelphia and Sardis, east to Magnesia and Tralles. The locals in each major city then spread the Gospel to the surrounding countryside. He wrote 1 Corinthians toward the end of this stay in the spring.

This was his longest stay in one location. Ephesus had all of the benefits of a major trade city—and all of the vices; a ripe harvest field in Paul's eyes.

He introduced Lydia to Priscilla as her spiritual mother, one who had led worship, the first woman to speak in the Spirit in public. He then asked Priscilla to exercise her greater maturity and share with Lydia her God-given gift of prophesy, edifying the Church.

Paul sent armed men from northern Galatia to Jerusalem, fighting their way against thieves, to the Temple to distribute the offering to the poor.

Barsabbas claimed Gentile money was an abomination in this sacred city. James warned Paul not to bring any further collections himself, as Jerusalem was too dangerous for him.

Paul sent Timothy and Erastus (Corinth's director of public works) to **Corinth** by way of Macedonia where there had been fighting among the multiple factions of the Church during the two years since they had left. He visited churches along the way in **Thyatira, Troas, Samothrace, Neapolis, Philippi, Amphipolis, Apollonia, Thessaloniki, Berea, Thebes, and Megara.**

Paul had also sent Stephanas to Corinth before Pentecost in the spring of 55 AD, with a letter to all the churches there in response to their questions about church members suing each other and committing sexual immoralities. He admonished them, told them he had sent Timothy, and promised to return. Some questioned why they should imitate Paul.

Back in **Ephesus**, Luke, the physician, tended to Paul and his various ailments. Timothy rushed straight back from Corinth to tell Paul he was held in contempt after false "apostles" had misled the people with flattery.

Paul wrote another letter before winter from Philippi in Macedonia for Timothy to take to the Corinthians (Second Corinthians), asserting his authority in Christ and challenging them to be reconciled again to God.

Paul received a letter from Lydia after she had met Simon Peter and Silas in Philippi. Peter told her that James thought Paul should never return to Jerusalem and that all the Galatian men had been circumcised. He remained through the Ephesian Games and Pentecost.

Demetrius, a silversmith making shrines of the goddess Artemis (the Greek name for the Roman goddess Diana), saw his business decline, as Paul had warned against gods made by humans. Joining craftsmen, priests of Artemis, and citizens, they seized Gaius and Aristarchus, created chaos, and shouted in the largest amphitheater in the Greek world for two hours: "*Great is Artemis of the Ephesians.*"

Artemis ("the many breasted") had by tradition fallen down from the sky, a gift from Zeus. So, I wonder who worships the revered Artemis/Diana still *today*? In his later letter to the Ephesians, Paul had to warn of a new type of idolatry—greed and covetousness. This was only the second time that

Paul had been opposed by Gentiles, the first being on his first journey when he cast out the demon from the soothsayer in Philippi. Paul wanted to talk to the crowd, but the disciples did not let him.

Escape to Greece

Timothy, Luke, and Priscilla helped Paul escape and flee through Macedonia and into Greece: **Smyrna, Pergamum, Troas, Macedonia, Neapolis, and Philippi**. For three months in the winter of 56 AD, Paul picked up another collection for the Jerusalem poor. He intended to go to Achaia and Corinth, then Jerusalem, Rome, and Spain. In Rome, seventeen-year-old Nero had succeeded the poisoned emperor Claudius. Soon Christians thought Nero might be the antichrist and Paul felt led to go to Rome.

After three months in **Corinth**, Paul discovered another plot to kill him in Jerusalem. He went with Timothy, Gaius, and others back via land to Macedonia, even though sailing would have gotten him to Jerusalem more quickly. Luke was by his side again from this point until the end. Paul wrote his letter to the Romans: the longest epistle and powerful Magna Carta of the Christian life. He said he would come after taking the offering to Jerusalem, hopefully in time for Pentecost, and sent the deaconess Phoebe to deliver the letter.

Before sailing, they stayed in **Troas** for a week after the Feast of Unleavened Bread. The last night, Paul preached until midnight, always eager to share the Good News. A youth, Eutychus, fell asleep and died when he fell out the third-floor window ledge (Acts 20:7–12)—the first recorded instance of a sermon going too long for the listeners! (When giving a speech, I sometimes open with: "My job is to speak and yours is to listen, but if you happen to get through *before* I do, I would appreciate your letting me know.") Well, Eutychus certainly let Paul know! God raised Eutychus from the dead, but that is not the end of the story. Paul resumed teaching until daylight—my guess is that no one fell asleep *that* time.

He sailed to **Mytilene, Chios, Samos,** and **Miletus** (one of the world's oldest cities, thirty miles south of Ephesus), sending for the Ephesian elders for a final farewell to them, then on to **Cos, Rhodes** and **Patara** (the birthplace of St. Nicholas; no longer a port today) where they changed from a small, coastal ship to a larger seagoing vessel; below Cyprus to **Tyre** (his first visit to Phoenicia). While Paul was in Smyrna for a week to unload cargo, he was again warned in a premonition from the Holy Spirit not to go on to Jerusalem.

TRIP TO ROME
(57–59 AD, ESTIMATED)

Arrest and Imprisonment

By 56 AD, Paul ended this third missionary journey and landed at Caesarea by the Sea after several weeks traveling by way of Ptolemais. He walked sixty-five miles southeast over hills to **Jerusalem** just before the Passover, spending a week at Philip the Evangelist's home along the way. Philip also warned Paul not to go to Jerusalem. It was Timothy's second time there and had been six years since he had seen James. Almost thirty years prior, Jesus' disciples had also warned *Him* not to go back to Jerusalem.

Paul was received warmly and was thrilled to hear that many thousands of Jews had believed.

James, the brother of Jesus, author of the letter of James and leader of the Jerusalem church, faced a dilemma: The Jews were under a murderous siege by the Romans. Believers were subject to the same by the Jews. Jewish believers were coming to celebrate the Pentecost. He was the sole remaining apostle, wanting to protect them, and Paul had proudly brought him the offering from the churches in Achaia and Macedonia—in unacceptable golden coins emblazoned with the face of a false god, Nero.

James told Paul to cleanse the coins of the Gentile taint, and to use the money in the service of the Law by spending them in the Temple. It was a test, since Paul had spoken years before of the "*curse*" of the Law. Paul submitted to his authority and asserted his belief that the Law was holy and delightful to him and that he considered himself "*blameless under the law*"; except for the Law, he would never have known about sin and what is right! Peace between them at last—twenty-three years after they had shared the Lord's Supper together.

God is, indeed, a God of restoration and reconciliation. Paul himself then even went through the week-long Levitical purification rites with four

Nazirites—his first time in the Temple since he had debated Stephen there twenty-five years prior.

This is a great lesson for any of us traveling to serve in a foreign land. We need to be culturally sensitive. Paul always tried to be "*all things to all men.*"

Another Plot

Paul stayed too long, and word got out he was there. One more time, the Jewish people were threatened, so they planned to kill him in the Court of the Gentiles, assuming he had brought a Gentile into the Temple area, and lying that he had told Jewish converts to forsake Moses. As they began beating him, the commander of the Roman centurions arrested him, thinking he was an Egyptian terrorist, bound him with two chains, and carried him to the Antonia Fortress overlooking the Temple Mount from the northwest.

He spoke honestly and humbly in Greek to the commander and in Aramaic to the Jews, from the fortress's staircase: another lesson for us to speak the language of our listeners. But, also speaking in truth, he lost the Jews when he said the Gentiles were important to God, as the Jews' need to feel superior exceeded their receptivity to the message. God had protected him from birth with his Roman citizenship, so he was not flogged.

The next day, the commander released him and brought him before the Sanhedrin and the high priest, Ananias, noted for cruelty and later assassinated by his own people during the revolt against Rome.

How frustrating it must have been for Paul to face his greatest opposition in the holy city of Jerusalem, whose streets and people he knew so well. He just focused on being obedient, leaving the results to God. That night, Paul had a vision where the Lord said, "*As you have testified about Me in Jerusalem, so you must also testify in Rome*" (Acts 23:11).

Then over forty Zealots plotted with the chief priests to kill Paul when he was being led to Herod's palace. Upon warning by Paul's sister's son, he was taken thirty miles northwest during the night by 200 soldiers, 70 horsemen, and 200 spearmen to the procurator of Judea's palace in Caesarea by the Sea, where he remained for years. His mission was not yet finished, the race not yet fully run, until he shared Christ in Rome.

The high priest, Ananias, and his lawyer, Tertullus, came five days later to Caesarea by the Sea, the Roman headquarters of Samaria and Judea, to convince the governor, Antonius Felix, to kill Paul, accusing him of being a Nazarene sect leader and of desecrating the Temple. (Felix was so incompetent that Nero withdrew him as governor two years later). His second wife, Drusilla of Judea, (both had divorced prior spouses after their affair began) was the daughter of Herod Agrippa I, who was eaten by worms and died.

Felix was torn between needing, by law, to acknowledge the rights due to Paul as a Roman citizen, and wanting the approval of the large Jewish community. Felix kept meeting with Paul for two years, hoping for a bribe. His replacement, Festus, wanted to release Paul, but had no choice but to send him to Rome due to Paul's appeal to Caesar. First, Herod Agrippa II, who was allied with the Sadducees and ruled over the territory northeast of the Sea of Galilee, was consulted while visiting with his sister Bernice (later the mistress of emperor Titus). He also concluded that Paul would have been set free had he not appealed to Caesar. Herod and Bernice's father, Agrippa I, had fallen deathly ill in the theater at Caesarea by the Sea after beheading James and imprisoning Peter.

Paul, as a Roman citizen, had insisted on his right to be tried in Rome before the emperor, Nero. The Jews had wanted him transferred back to Jerusalem for a show trial. (James was stoned five years later, after Annas, the high priest, charged him with transgressing the Law). His long-planned trip to Rome was now funded by the state!

The Jewish leaders killed Stephen and tried many times to kill Paul— all because their authority was threatened. They felt justified, unaware of the true God above and of the evil Satan had placed in their hearts. In *Mere Christianity*, C.S. Lewis said: "A proud man is always looking down on things and people; and of course, as long as you are looking *down*, you cannot see something that is *above* you."

Sailing for Rome

Luke (again using *"we"* in Acts 27) and Aristarchus of Thessaloniki sailed for Rome in 59–60 AD with Paul (since it was not a military vessel) under

Julius, a kind, good centurion in the Imperial Regiment, through the Phoenician port of Sidon, under the lee of Cyprus, off the coast of Cilicia, Pamphylia, Myra in Lycia (southwestern Asia Minor), changing ships, past Cnidus, under the lee of Crete off Salmone to the small bay of Fair Havens (south central **Crete**).

Paul warned—and was ignored by—the centurion, the ship's owner, and the captain not to chance reaching Phoenix harbor, a better winter port forty miles to the west, on Crete. A violent northeaster pushed them southwest away from the shoreline. At the end of October or early November, after fifteen days out of control, with no sun by day or stars by night, throwing cargo (including wheat from Egypt) overboard, hungry, and exhausted, all 276 people aboard survived when they ran the ship aground on **Malta** (known as Melita by the Greeks and Romans; fifty-eight miles south of Sicily) in what is known now as St. Paul's Bay, where they then stayed for three months.

This was apparently Paul's *fourth* shipwreck! They were so fortunate that the Maltese were "unusually kind."

Gathering wood for a fire, Paul was bitten by a venomous viper. The native people (Phoenician in ancestry) of Malta concluded he was receiving justice for being a murderer, which showed that they, though not evangelized at this point, at least understood about a divine judge. When Paul shook the snake off into the flames and was not harmed, they concluded that he was a god. The chief official Publicus's father was sick. God chose to not let the physician, Luke, heal him, but to let Paul access the power of the Great Physician to heal the man.

They went for ten days via another Alexandrian grain ship on to **Rome,** the greatest city in the world at that time, sailing via Syracuse (in Sicily) and Rhegium to Puteoli, an important port and arsenal city. Puteoli, a commercial port on the north shore of Naples Bay, was just below Mount Vesuvius, which twenty years later would erupt and bury Pompeii and Herculaneum in mud, lava and fiery ash. Julius allowed Paul to stay and preach for a week. They then walked north inland in the early spring of 61 AD on the Forum of Appius, met on the Appian Way by a delegation of Christians from Rome.

Paul lived in a rented house between the Forum and the Campus Martius with John Mark for two years under house arrest, in chains and with a guard. Many palace guards heard his teaching and his dictating letters. Again, the synagogue leaders were not convinced, but many Gentiles were! He never stopped speaking and was never freer, despite the chains! In his letter to Philemon, Paul called himself "a prisoner of Jesus," not of Rome. Nero was not present for a trial, as he had ordered his mother killed and then spent eighteen months in southern Italy.

Rome consisted then of about one million citizens and one million slaves. Claudius's former edict for all Jews to leave Rome had lapsed or been revoked, as many Jews were living there again, along with many Christians.

Paul wrote thirteen books of the Bible (see *Appendix: Letters Written by Paul*); four believed from Rome while under his first imprisonment there. In order, they were Colossians (Colossae, a nominal city in Asia Minor), Ephesians (a circular to all churches in the area), Philemon (a believer from Colossae), and Philippians. They were letters to church communities and individuals. Along with the Gospels and Acts, they form the heart of the New Testament. Those he wrote to knew him and had heard him preach many times, so he focused on mistakes or misunderstood issues. Most of the New Testament was written in the context of Judaism; Paul saw Christianity to be the fulfillment of Judaism.

Paul's primary theological themes were Grace (God's love is unearned through Christ's sacrifice), Justification (a legal-like pardon from the sentence of sin and death), Reconciliation (relational restoration between God and man) and Redemption (deliverance from the slavery of sin and the Law). He also taught and wrote regularly on Righteousness (right relationship with God based on faith), Salvation (deliverance and restoration) and Sanctification (process of becoming more holy, Christ-like).

Released from Prison

He was released around 62 AD and presumed free for four years, when he wrote 1 Timothy (to the spiritual son he had left in Ephesus) and Titus (a Gentile convert who had served with Paul at Ephesus during the third missionary journey, then preaching on the island of Crete). It had been about twenty-six years since *Saul, the persecutor*, had been turned into *Paul, the preacher*, on that road to Damascus.

A possible fourth missionary journey (62–64 AD) between his two Roman imprisonments may have included Spain, Crete, Miletus, Colossae, Ephesus, Philippi and/or Nicopolis.

A great fire started on July 18, 64 AD (two to three years after Acts concludes), in the Circus Maximus and wiped out two-thirds of the city during the next nine days. Needing a scapegoat, emperor Nero blamed and killed innumerable Christians, including Peter (more proof the Gospel had spread here) in many cruel ways. Contrary to popular legend, the Colosseum was not completed until approximately 70–80 AD, after Nero's death in 68 AD, so he did not have Christians eaten by lions there.

Paul was a Roman citizen, so he was imprisoned again, this time bound in heavy chains at nearly sixty years of age, facing a death sentence for being not just Christian but a leader. Paul was an urban evangelist, teaching in the cities and letting them then spread the Word out to the country. Perhaps there is a lesson for us today to refocus on the cities instead of the suburbs.

Only Luke, also an old man, stayed with him. Paul asked for Mark and Timothy to come. He wrote 2 Timothy (who was still in Ephesus) from the Mamertine dungeon, fatherly instructions to the beloved he took under his wing at such a young age, aware of his impending death. He was beheaded outside the city with a sword around 65 AD. Appropriately for all of his journeys, he was buried alongside a highway, today the Basilica of St. Paul, erected over an earlier memorial to him that dated to Constantine.

End of the Story

The story that began thirty years prior on the road to Damascus ended in Rome. The church that numbered in the hundreds now numbered in the tens of thousands throughout Asia and Europe, including Rome, the center of the world! Paul had traveled (mostly by foot) up to 30,000 miles. Five times, he had been whipped with 39 lashes, and he had been stoned as if to death. Paul had fought the good fight, finished the race, kept the faith, and looked forward to the Crown of Righteousness.

Ironically, in perhaps the first scandal of the Olympics, Nero received a victor's wreath despite not finishing the race. In 67 AD, the heavy thirty-year-old entered himself in a ten-horse chariot team; though he did not even finish, the judges gave him the prize. He rewarded the Greeks by exempting them from taxation (some things never change, huh?).

Paul's recurring themes as we have experienced his heart were Salvation by grace through faith; the doctrine of the Holy Spirit; the new man at war with the old man; darkness (Satan) to Light (Jesus); and the divine mystery of Christ in you. Times have changed, but *the message remains the same*. This represents an unfinished story for each church generation to keep adding chapters to.

The church grew to be over two billion people today. Paul's journey is *our* life's journey.

PAUL'S EPISTLES

It appears Paul's letters were written in approximately this order:
Galatians
1 and 2 Thessalonians
1 and 2 Corinthians
Romans
Philemon
Ephesians
Colossians
Philemon
Philippians
1 Timothy
Titus
2 Timothy
See Appendix for:
Letters Written by Paul in order of the Writing Date
Themes of Letters Written by Paul, in Biblical Order

Cultural Context:

To the Jewish believers, truth was *Jesus*, and the focus was relationship with Him. To the Greeks (and Romans), truth was what *my* mind could comprehend. (Personally, I do not want a God so small that *I* can understand His every thought).

Luke was the only Gentile author in the New Testament. Paul and John were rabbis who had memorized the entire Torah. They spoke truth into the *hearts* of the Greco-Roman world, not just into their *heads*. Intellectual wrestling allows *detachment*; a touched heart involves *commitment*. The Greek world then is very relevant to the world we live in today—that is why we identify with Paul's epistles. "Med" from Mediterranean means "middle of earth," representing the importance of the region at the time.

Consider the miracle of this story. These religious, working-class kids from Galilee encountered Jesus and took the Good News to Asia Minor, Greece, and Rome, converting most to Christ within just two generations. That is like sending six kids from Barstow to places like San Francisco and seeing them totally change the culture in a short time.

Socrates's philosophy was "To do is to be," while Plato's was more like "To be is to do." As Christians, we want to first focus on the *being*, abiding in Christ constantly. Then our *doing* will be a natural expression of our love for Him, our obedience to Him, and our gratitude to Him.

The Greeks and Romans worshipped many gods, though *none* were connected with morality. They could not imagine why religion would have anything to do with how you live your life. Each of their gods was associated with a capital city that would celebrate them at least annually with two-week festivals including drunkenness and orgies.

Only Artemis (Diana to the Romans) is named in the Bible—the others are assumed in the letters. John, the pastor to Asia Minor, directly confronted their gods by relating Jesus' miracles he had witnessed. God also took supremacy over the Egyptian gods, one by one, through the plagues.

During the early church, the transition had begun from worshipping the gods to worshipping the emperors, so both were revered at the time. The emperors started by strongly suggesting they be treated as divine, and later killed people who did not worship them that way.

Greek History in Brief

2700–1100 BC Minoan Civilization, seafaring, Cretan king Minos; weak militarily; similar to Egyptians; known for frescoes and bright blue pottery with aquatic life images; built Palace of Knossos and labyrinth legend; weakened by the Thera volcanic eruption, earthquake, and tidal wave.

1600–1100 BC Mycenean Civilization, warriors; built hilltop fortified cities.

1200–800 BC Dark Ages, little historical information available (that is why it is called the Dark Ages).

800–500 BC Archaic Period, beginnings of Greek alphabet, language and civilization; Trojan War legends based on Homer's *Iliad* and *Odyssey* (written in the 800s about the 1200s); colonization around the Aegean Sea to the boot of Italy and north African coast.

480–430 BC Classical Period, a.k.a. *the Golden Age of Pericles,* a time of peace, prosperity, and the building of many Athenian monuments; Philip II of Macedonia in the north "unites" southern cities by force; Persians defeated in naval battle off Salomis.

330–42 BC Hellenistic Age, beginnings of universalism and value placed on sharing of ideas; Alexander the Great's campaigns to Asia Minor, Middle East, and north Africa; areas conquered divided into four section at his death.

42 BC–476 AD Roman empire, Julius Caesar assassination results in civil war with Brutus and Cassius losing to Octavian and Marc Antony at Battle of Plains at Philippi. Roman Republic falls, is replaced with Roman empire with Caesar Augustus as emperor; a time of corruption and immorality; attacks by northern invaders.

325–1453 AD Byzantine empire, a.k.a. *The New Roman empire,* Constantine made Constantinople (Istanbul, the center of Greek Orthodoxy) the Roman capital, called bishops to Nicea (resulting in Nicene Creed); declared Christianity to be an official religion in the empire at the Edict of Milan in 313 AD.

1299–1821 AD Ottoman Turkish empire, weakened Europe subjected to Islam.

1821–present Hellenic Republic, quasi-independence from Turks, Otto of Bavaria made king; independence in 1830; after World War II captured Aegean Islands returned to Greece in 1947; shift from monarchy to two-party republic in 1967; citizenship exchange of one and a half million Greeks in Turkey with 800,000 Turks in Greece.

Roman emperors

Julian Dynasty

Caesar Augustus   27 BC–14 AD   Luke 2: census at Jesus' birth

Tiberius	14–37 AD	Jesus' death and Resurrection
Caligula	37–41 AD	
Claudius	41–54 AD	Exiled Jews from Rome
Nero	54–68 AD	Early persecutions; Gamla revolt

Flavian Dynasty:

Vespasian	68–79 AD	
Titus I	79–81 AD	Vespasian's son
Domitian	81–96 AD	Vespasian's son
Nerva	96–98 AD	
Trajan	98–117 AD	
Hadrian	117–138 AD	

The historian Titus Flavius Josephus switched sides from the Jews to the Romans after Vespasian's siege of Gamla. Vespasian adopted him, and gave him the family name. Titus subdued a major Jewish revolt at Caesarea by the Sea, Jerusalem, and then Masada. Domitian killed untold numbers of Jews.

TURKEY

Turkish History:

Did you know that seventy-five percent of the New Testament happened in Turkey (Asia Minor)?

Turkey's history includes Alexander the Great, the Apostle Paul, and Caesar Augustus, along with Hittites, Persians, Greeks, Romans, Crusaders, Ottomans, and others. Today it sits with Greece to the west and Syria/Iraq to the east, partly in southeastern Europe and mostly in southwestern Asia (Anatolia to the Greeks; Asia Minor to the Romans), along the Aegean and the Mediterranean Seas. Turkey and Greece are the setting for most of the New Testament after the four Gospels, but infamous Istanbul (formerly Byzantium or Constantinople) is actually not mentioned in the Bible.

The Garden of Eden (Genesis 2) is believed to have been in eastern Turkey at the convergence of the Tigris and Euphrates Rivers in Mesopotamia over 10,000 years ago. Noah's Ark (Genesis 7–8) is believed to have landed on Mount Ararat, a 17,000-foot-high volcano, 5,000 years ago. As it is by far the highest mountain in the Middle East, it is likely the first land to emerge out of the Great Flood. The Ark was the size of a football field, half the size of the Titanic, four stories tall, yet made entirely of wood.

We first meet Abraham, known as the father of all believers, the first to claim God as the one true God, in Genesis 11 at age seventy-five. It is believed that he was born in a cave near Sanliurfa. He is patriarch to Jews, Christians, and even Muslims (referred to in their five daily prayers as "God's friend.") Thirty miles southeast, by Harran, is the place believed to be where God first spoke to Abraham (Genesis 11:31–12:1); an important crossroads later abandoned during the Crusades. Its ruins were rediscovered by Lawrence of Arabia in the early 1800s.

The Persians conquered all of Asia Minor (aka Anatolia) in 547 BC and dominated the area bounded by the Black Sea to the north, the Mediterranean Sea to the west and south, and high mountains separated it from Asia to the east. For 200 years, they ruled the region, until Alexander the Great's father, Philip II of Macedonia, united all of Greece (except Sparta) and conquered Thrace in 335 BC. His son, Alexander the Great, died in Babylon at age thirty-three in 323 BC. Many Jews came here after the exile, since Israel was still under foreign domination. Jewish communities were formed that Paul would later visit.

The contrast between Asia Minor and Israel must have been difficult for arriving Jews. *Israelites* were a simple, poor, hard-working people with plain homes, unpaved streets, water carried from springs or wells, and utilitarian public buildings. The *Gentiles of Asia Minor* were wealthy and educated, enjoying beautiful architecture, homes with elaborate floors and artwork, paved streets, sewers, running hot and cold water, and many large public buildings. Scholars estimate that there were 80,000 followers of Jesus by the year 100 AD, and that just a century later *most* people in Asia Minor were Christian!

Initially the center of the Roman empire was in the fertile west with its capital in the major crossroads of Pergamum, but it was moved just before Jesus' time east to the major harbor of Ephesus. The mountains of Ararat in eastern Asia may be the resting place of Noah's Ark. The Hittite empire ruled here around 2000 BC until the coast was colonized by Greeks around 1200 BC, while the Lydians continued their civilization in the interior of the peninsula.

King Attalus III of Pergamum gave the province to the Romans at his death in 133 BC, resulting in complete Roman control of Asia Minor.

Historical Periods

Hittite	Abraham to David	2000–1000 BC
Phyrgian/Lydian	Monarchy	1200–500 BC
Persian	Return from Exile	500–330 BC
Hellenistic	Between Old and New Testaments	330–133 BC
Roman	Jesus and Early Church	133 BC–300 AD
Byzantine	Developing Church	300–700 AD

The Apostle Paul established several churches during his extensive travels here on his second and third missionary journeys, particularly in Ephesus. Jesus told the disciples to *"go to the ends of the earth."* We know that at least five disciples (John, Peter, Philip, Andrew, and Thaddeus) preached here as well as Paul, Timothy, Luke, Barnabas, and others.

John addressed messages of commendation, complaint, and correction in chapters two and three of the Book of Revelation (meaning "unveiling") to Seven Churches in western Asia Minor—Ephesus, Laodicea, Pergamum, Philadelphia, Sardis, Smyrna, and Thyatira (Lydia's hometown). All were on the Via Maris, the important trade route from Egypt and Babylon to Greece and Rome.

In 330 AD, the Roman emperor Constantine made Byzantium his capital, renaming it Constantinople. His successor, Theodosius I, converted, and made Christianity the official religion of the Byzantine empire. The church had grown from around 3,000 believers at the time of Christ to around thirty million by this time! The city fell to the Crusaders in 1204 AD and was pillaged.

In 1453 AD, the Ottoman Turks, led by Mehmet II, conquered Byzantium and changed the city's name to Istanbul, the capital of the Ottoman empire, an Islamic nation. The Ottoman empire's power peaked during the time of the sultan Suleyman the Magnificent in the mid-1500s.

In 1908, the Young Turks revolted against sultan Abdul Hamid to force constitutional and parliamentary rule. After allying with Germany in World War I, Turkey became a republican parliamentary democracy, replaced traditional religious laws with secular laws, and changed their alphabet from an Arabic script to a Latin script.

In 1945, Turkey joined the United Nations and, in 1951, NATO. Today, the population is eighty percent Turkish and twenty percent Kurdish, almost one hundred percent Muslim (mostly Sunni). It is moderately developed. A visa is required along with your passport, except for shore excursions to Ephesus. There are 3,000 Christians in Turkey today out of a population of 84 million.

Electric current is 220 volts (requiring a converter or adapter plugs). Many sites are located on hills with many steps.

Asia Minor gods

Asclepius (Aesculapius)—healing

Aphrodite—love and beauty

Apollo—light (the sun), and music

Artemis (Diana)—marriage and fertility (unique to Ephesus) otherwise the moon, chastity, childbirth, and the hunt

Athena—wisdom

Demeter—grain and fertility

Dionysus (Bacchus)—wine, orgies, fertility, and theater

Hades (Pluto)—underworld

Hermes—messenger

Hestia—hearth and home

Pan (goat)—fertility

Zeus (Jupiter)—king of gods

(They sure covered their bases with at least four separate fertility gods!)

Turkish Customs

Turkish baths (*Hamam*): cleanliness is emphasized in Islam, but the Turkish bath is also a social place for young and old, rich and poor. Traditionally, women used the bath at different times than men did. The bath is used for important occasions like wedding preparation for the groom and for the bride, a baby's fortieth day, circumcisions, and house guests.

Various Customs:

- People love to congregate in coffee houses (*Kahve*), sometimes smoking hubble bubble pipes (*nargile*).
- Superstitious people carry little blue glass stones (*bonchuk*) to guard them from the evil eye.
- It is considered rude to pick your teeth or blow your nose in public.
- It is also rude to point the sole of your shoe at someone.

definingmomentsbook.com/resources

ANTIOCH (ANTAKYA)

Historical Significance:

At least fifteen other cities of the ancient world were called Antioch. Known today as Antakya, it was best known as Antioch of Syria (or Antioch on the Orontes, the Roman capital of Syria). Pisidian Antioch a.k.a. "little Rome" was a separate city. Antioch once ranked just behind Rome and Alexandria, Egypt in the Greco-Roman world, vital from military, commercial and cultural standpoints, with a population then of 500,000, versus 125,000 today. It is just north of Syria in the Hatay province of southern Turkey.

After Stephen was stoned, many Christians fled Jerusalem to Antioch, among other cities. Christ followers were first called "Christians" here (Acts 11:6), and many non-Jews were first accepted into the early Church here. The first known relief offering was sent from here to the famine-struck Christians in Jerusalem. Antioch was second only to Jerusalem as a major center of the early Church.

Due to the Church's growth, Barnabas was sent to investigate. He traveled 120 miles to Tarsus to get Paul and return to Antioch, where they worked together for a year. They were commissioned on their first missionary journey here and returned to Antioch at its conclusion after the first Jerusalem Council. Their disagreement separated them at the beginning of the second missionary journey, and Paul took Silas through Asia Minor and Greece before returning again at its conclusion to a cool welcome. Paul also departed on his third missionary journey from Antioch.

Peter (Cephas) also visited Antioch, as it had strong communities of Greek-speaking Jews and Christians. In Galatians 2, written from Antioch, Paul confronted Peter about requiring Gentile converts to follow certain Jewish practices such as circumcision. Peter had backed off from fellowshipping with Gentiles as equals due to the vocal pro-circumcision contingent.

What to See:

While prestigious and prosperous in the Byzantine era, and a beacon for learning and culture, Antioch suffered through several earthquakes and three different Persian attacks involving its capture and/or burning. Unfortunately, little remains of Antioch to be seen today, only a wall of the ancient hippodrome. The Orontes River still flows through the city.

Hatay Archaeology Museum is the second largest **mosaic museum** in the world, featuring well-preserved Roman floor mosaics. There are remains of a castle built by one of Alexander the Great's generals.

The cliffside **St. Peter's Grotto** is believed to be where both Paul and Peter preached. It is a mile above the city, one of the world's earliest memorials to Peter. In Galatians, it is said they met, as an early Church at risk, in a cave (grotto), likely with an escape tunnel. Every June 29, there is a service in remembrance of Peter.

Scripture:

Daniel 11:7
Acts 6:5, 11:6, 19–30, 13:1–3, 14:26–15:3, 15:30–41, 18:23
Galatians 2:11
2 Timothy 3:11
Revelation 2:6
definingmomentsbook.com/resources

EPHESUS (KUŞADASI)

Historical Significance:

The marble city of Ephesus was originally a major trade route, commercial and religious center, a chief Aegean port, and capital of the Roman province of Asia. With a population of 250,000, Ephesus was on the Aegean Sea, forty miles south of Izmir, then three miles from the Aegean Sea via the Cayster River. Alluvial deposits and earthquakes around the Cayster River filled in the port, destroying most of it and bringing mosquitoes and malaria to Ephesus, causing it to lose its importance and prosperity. Today Ephesus is on the sides of a fertile valley about eight miles inland from the resort port of Kuşadası (with 300 days of sunshine each year).

A Greek city was first built here about 1000 BC. The Temple of Artemis at Ephesus (the Greek name for the Roman goddess Diana) was one of the Seven Wonders of the Ancient World and drew nearly a half million pilgrims from all over the world to its festivals. Because Artemis was deemed so powerful and protective of her temple, people from all over the world deposited their riches there for safety. These riches were then loaned out at usurious interest rates. The temple was built of the finest marble with joints finished in pure gold. It was burned down in the fourth century BC, rebuilt, then abandoned when Christianity became the empire's official religion, and was then used as a quarry.

Artemis of the Ephesians was revered for fertility, served by the largest collection in the Roman empire of religious prostitutes, pagan priestesses, sorcerers, magicians, cultists, charlatans, and frauds. While temples in some cities were safe asylums, the entire city of Ephesus was a sanctuary city, so you can imagine the types of people who were attracted to come here.

From 100 BC to 100 AD, Ephesus was the world capital of the slave trade. During the first and second centuries, Ephesus ranked only behind Rome, Alexandria, and possibly Antioch of Syria in size in the Roman empire, and was number one in importance in all of Asia Minor. It is possible Luke studied medicine here (or perhaps in Pergamum).

The city of Ephesus had a central sewer (eight feet by five feet) under the main street along with central heating and central cooling (via water cascading down) and hot and cold running water.

On his second missionary journey, Paul stopped briefly en route from Corinth to Jerusalem, and left Priscilla and Aquila behind to minister to the Ephesians. They discipled Apollos, who was already a great teacher but required further Christian training.

After Apollos left for Corinth, Paul returned on his third missionary journey to turn Ephesus into his headquarters, spending three years teaching the Good News, first in the synagogue, then daily in the rented lecture hall of Tyrannus (a Greek teacher or philosopher), training teachers to send throughout Asia. He would have taught during the heat of the day when the philosophy students were away. People took his sweaty handkerchiefs to heal others. He wrote 1 Corinthians (packed with corrective theology, superb logic, and apostolic diplomacy) in the spring of the third year. At the end of his third missionary journey, in haste to return to Jerusalem, he called for the elders to come to Miletus to meet him to warn them against false teachers, but he bypassed Ephesus.

A Jewish chief priest with seven sons tried it Paul's way, to exorcise "in the name of Jesus." The demon said he knew Jesus and Paul, but not them, and tore their clothes off and sent them out naked into the street. The word was out, and magicians threw their tools into a bonfire.

It was in 56 AD, at the end of Paul's long stay here, that the silversmiths started a riot because Paul's preaching was hurting their sales of silver shrines, charms, and statuettes of Artemis's likeness. If his teachings were true, then Artemis was worthless, and Ephesus's entire belief system, economy, and lifestyle could collapse. In the Great Theatre (which seated 24,000, a tenth of the city's population), they chanted "Great is Artemis of the Ephesians" like a synchronized sports chant for two hours. We do not know if Paul ever visited the theater, but we do know he could quote plays.

Paul wanted to go in to speak to the crowd, even if they were in a frenzy, and to rescue their captured traveling companions, Gaius and Aristarchus from Macedonia, but his friends and the Romans convinced him not to. It is a healthy indication that his followers were not afraid to disagree with him and that he was not afraid to listen. Paul then left for Corinth in Macedonia.

While we know Paul preached in a synagogue for the first three months, (the book of Acts refers to a Jewish community and synagogue in Ephesus), few Jewish inscriptions and no Jewish artifacts or synagogue remains have been unearthed.

John the Baptist had disciples here. Paul picked twelve of the feisty ones to train for three years, just like Jesus did.

Paul likely wrote 1 Corinthians and part of 2 Corinthians, and possibly Philippians, Philemon, and Colossians from Ephesus (more likely from Rome). Ephesians (written 60–61 AD from imprisonment in Rome) was likely a letter circulated to several churches, since Ephesus is not specifically referenced in the greeting. Ephesus is mentioned twice in 2 Timothy.

Paul appears to have returned to Ephesus after his first imprisonment in Rome (65–66 AD). After heading to Nicopolis, he was arrested and taken to Rome again to be tried and beheaded.

The Roman emperor Domitian demanded that people worship him as a god and insisted that everyone, including his wife, call him lord or god. Naturally, the Ephesians built huge structures dedicated to their latest king of the gods including a temple with a twenty-seven-foot statue of him visible from the sea upon approach. Anyone who did not annually say publicly in front of its altar, "Caesar is lord" would be killed.

John left Jerusalem (likely after Peter and Paul's deaths) for Ephesus in approximately 65 AD, where he preached until exiled to the island of Patmos, where he penned the book of Revelation in a cave. Ephesus is the only city Paul visited that was mentioned in Revelation. God said it had forsaken its first love, but promised paradise for those with repentance. After exile, John lived the rest of his years back in Ephesus, where he wrote the Gospel of John and the three letters of John while supervising the churches of Asia and exhorting the local assembly *"Little children, love one another,"* as they had replaced relationship with dogma and doctrine.

Of the ten disciples after Judas (suicide) and James (martyred), John is the only one to die a natural death and the last to die. He is buried in the Church of St. John the Theologian, not far from Ephesus.

John may have taken Mary, the mother of Jesus, with him. It is uncertain if she died and was buried in Ephesus or in Jerusalem. There is some dispute as to whether John of Patmos was the same person as John the disciple and/or which John took care of Mary at Jesus' request.

In 431 AD, the Council of Ephesus, the third Church Council, was held here, declaring Jesus as both fully human and fully divine and recognizing Mary as "mother of God."

What to See:

Ephesus is the largest, most impressive, **best-preserved ruins** site of Turkey (visited daily by thousands). The ruins showcase much of the ancient world with baths, silversmith shops (visualize where Demetrius the silversmith sold his silver shrines of the goddess Artemis/Diana), statues (including Artemis), temples, marble streets, fountains, the agora, and monuments galore.

The first two cities were completely destroyed. The city we see today (discovered in the 1860s) was built in the fourth century BC by Alexander the Great's successor, Lysimachus. Only ten percent has been uncovered to date, mostly by Austrian and Turkish archaeologists. The valley you drive in through used to be part of the Aegean Sea.

Outside was the city dump where they would discard live, unwanted babies to die, up to fifty daily. Slave merchants would sort through the abandoned babies for possible future merchandise; Christians would rescue the living and bury the dead.

You will enter up top through the Magnesian Gate, with a Roman bath just inside for one to clean up upon entry, and slowly be guided downhill—past the **Odeum** (Odeon), which was a concert hall; the Senate building, centrally heated; terraced houses with beautiful mosaic floors; the agora; the steam-heated **Baths of Scholastica**; the gymnasium, the **Temple of Hadrian,** and the **Fountain of Trajan.** Imagine Marc Antony and Cleopatra riding the wide, colonnade-bordered marble streets in royal procession where you can still see ruts from Roman chariots.

Like at Philippi, there are carvings in the pavement of a circle with lines through it like pizza slices. Next to it, incorporated into the design, are the Greek letters "ΙΧΘΥΣ," which means "Jesus Christ, God's Son, Savior." There is also a paving stone with carved symbols of a fish and a Cross, an unobtrusive way that believers identified themselves to other believers. How do *you* testify your belief to others in ways they could identify *you* as a Christ-follower?

The Library of Celsus, built around 125 AD as a memorial to the former governor of the province of Asia, housed 12,000 scrolls that were destroyed when the Goths sacked the city in 262 AD. Its façade, adorned with columns and statues, remains today. It took sixty-five years to excavate and is considered one of the most magnificent ruins in the world. It was the third largest library after Alexandria and Pergamum.

You can, by paying an additional admission fee, view the seven best Roman terraced villas, the largest of which was 10,000 square feet. There is a symbol on the lower road leading from the harbor of a heart and an "x" with an arrow pointing to the brothel at the crossroad by the library.

Stand on the stage of the 100-foot high **Great Theatre,** the largest theater in antiquity with a capacity of 24,000 people, with its amazing acoustics, where Paul preached, condemning pagan worship, during his third missionary journey stay in 53–55 AD. Walk up to the top for an amazing view, looking out on the remains of the Arcadian Way that once led from the theater to the harbor (four miles away today), then lined with columns and statuary. Hold a worship service. The gorge to the left of the theater is the fault line that shifted through fifty-three days of aftershocks, when an earthquake destroyed the theater in the 4th century AD.

View one of the Seven Wonders of the Ancient World, the **Temple of Artemis at Ephesus**. Artemis, (Roman Diana) was the daughter of Zeus in Greek mythology. The temple was a massive 450 feet long by 220 feet wide, with 120 columns that were sixty feet high. Only a single column remains today, which was recently restacked.

A thirty-five-foot-wide, marble-paved, pillar-lined street led up from the harbor into the city, the road Paul would have used to enter the city though the northern gate (Magnesian).

The Ephesus Archaeological Museum in Selçuk has an impressive collection of the Hellenistic and Roman statues, carved reliefs and artifacts discovered at the Ephesus ruins, including a rare statue of Artemis.

The Basilica of St. John the Theologian is inside in the Seljuk-style castle on Ayasuluk Hill that was built to protect it. Presumed to be where John died and was buried, and where many were baptized. Byzantine emperor Justinian built a domed, Cross-shaped basilica in the sixth century to replace an earlier church over John's traditional tomb. In the eighth and ninth centuries, after the cathedral was destroyed by Arab raiders, the defensive walls were built to protect it from Arab raiders. A baptistery, central pool, and chapel covered in frescoes of the saints have been excavated.

Kuşadası (population 70,000 today) also preserves excellent examples of Ottoman and Turkish mosques in the centrum.

The House of the Virgin Mary, six miles from Ephesus in a nature park on Bulbul Mountain, may be where Mary died after coming to the area with John. A church combining her house and grave was built in the fourth century AD. It has been visited by two Catholic Popes and by Muslims, who also believe in the virgin birth, and see Mary as the mother of one of their prophets, Jesus. Only the center and one room are open to visitors. It is possible the Council of Ephesus was held here in 431 AD, determining Mary should be called "bearer of God." It was the Cathedral of Ephesus originally, housing the bishop in an adjacent palace. The spring that runs under the house is believed by some to have healing properties.

Scripture:
   Acts 18:18–20:1, 20:16–38
   1 Corinthians 4:11–13, 15:32, 16:8
   Ephesians
   1 Timothy 1:3
   2 Timothy 1:18, 4:12
   Titus 3:9
   Revelation 1:11; 2:1–7
   definingmomentsbook.com/resources

Defining Moment . . . the Basilica of St. John the Theologian

Think of John's funeral. The Romans were probably relieved he was dead, and his friends knew where he was going—a win for both sides. Do *your* friends know where *you* are going? Is there an opportunity to witness to them about your Eternity? Rick has prepared a letter to have read at his funeral. He infused his gift of humor into the first line by starting with "I have gone to great lengths to gather you all here today." But the letter ends up taking a much more serious tone, inviting each person at his funeral to join him in the Kingdom of God. It is his last attempt to evangelize those people he loves, whom he wants to spend Eternity with, along with his Lord.

Journal Time:

Spend a few moments asking God to help you be the evangelist He made you to be. What brings out fear in evangelism situations? What makes you bold?

Share Time:

Share with the group an evangelism idea that you have, such as sharing with a specific person God has put on your heart. Have the group pray over you to give you boldness and humility as you approach the conversation.

Prayer:

Lord,

You have commissioned us to go to the ends of the earth and make disciples of all nations. Lord, apart from You, we can do nothing, but, empowered by You, we can boldly, lovingly invite people into the Kingdom just as You did. Lord, give us the words, through the Holy Spirit, to be bold evangelists. Keep us from our fears and from judging our "performance" based on whether or not someone invites You into their lives that we can see. Instead, keep us focused on the bigger picture, that we have obediently spoken truth into their lives, and it is now up to You and the Holy Spirit to bring them to a mature faith.

In Jesus' name,

Amen

Worship:
"Stir in Me"
"I Love to Tell the Story"

Defining Moment . . . The Ruins of Ephesus

Paul opens his letter to the Ephesians with a prayer, praising God for blessing us with every spiritual blessing. He goes on in verses 4–14 to elaborate on the rich spiritual inheritance that is sealed within each believer. But, in verses 17–19, he says,

> *I keep asking that the God of our Lord Jesus Christ, the glorious Father, may give you the Spirit of wisdom and revelation so that you may know Him better. I pray also that the eyes of your heart may be enlightened in order that you may know the hope to which He has called you, the riches of His glorious inheritance in His holy people, and His incomparably great power for us who believe.*

The implication is that even though they, as believers, possessed amazing redemption, power, and authority *sealed into them* (v. 13–14), they did not yet know how rich they truly were. Paul was praying that they would know the riches of their glorious inheritance, because they did not quite own it.

I am reminded of the slaves during the Civil War that were set free when the north won. In the moment the victory occurred, they had their lives back, just as we believers get our lives back through Christ. However, there were remote farms that were successful in keeping their slaves completely secluded from the outside world, so that they never knew that their freedom had been won. Some of those slaves were illegally kept for twenty years. They did not even know, much less fight for, the freedom that was legally theirs.

How many of us, as believers, stay in that place of *not really* knowing that we are indeed free? Are we living free lives? Do you awake each morning anticipating an amazingly powerful day, because the supernatural protection, provision, and guidance of the Creator of the universe is going to give you your best life, all day long? Or, do you look out on the day focusing on the things that you dread: feelings of being overwhelmed and under supported;

challenges that you really do not want to face; work that you really do not have the energy to do; relationships that you do not see much hope in? There is a richer life that is already sealed inside of you, but like the slave, you must know about it so you can own it and live in it.

Today, we as believers know that we are saved and set apart for eternal life with our Father. Yet, how many of us really know and live in the riches of the glorious inheritance that is ours through Jesus Christ?

Journal Time:

Take time to ask the Lord to reveal to you those things that are keeping you from living in the complete freedom that is already yours through Christ Jesus. What would enable you to live in that truth and experience those riches on a daily basis?

Share Time:

Share with the group ways that you want to surrender into the richness of redeemed life that is already yours. What do you need to leave behind in Ephesus that is keeping you from living the abundant life Christ died to give you? What is it that you need to take from here to live in that truth?

Prayer:

Father God,

Today we pray that very same prayer over ourselves that Paul prayed over the Ephesians so long ago. Give us the Spirit of wisdom and revelations so that we may know You better. We pray also that the eyes of our hearts may be enlightened in order that we may know the hope to which You have called us, the riches of Your glorious inheritance in the saints, and Your incomparably great power for us who believe. We surrender to You all the lies we have believed from the enemy about our lives. We embrace the truth about our inheritance and the rich, abundant life for which Your Son, Jesus, died that we might have. We stand firm in the authority that Jesus gave us when He conquered death and rose from the grave. Keep us conscious, Lord, of our freedom each minute of our day. Let us live lives that are irresistible to those that do not know You as they witness the inheritance that we are enjoying in this life, much less the next. Let them seek

You out just to hear more about this amazingly abundant life that is theirs for the taking.

In Jesus' name,

Amen.

Worship:

"Seek Ye First"

"Come Thou Fount of Every Blessing"

LAODICEA (PAMUKKALE)

―――――

Historical Significance:

At the north–south crossroads between Sardis and Pergamum and the east–west route from the Euphrates to Ephesus, Laodicea was the wealthiest city in Phrygia during the Roman era. It was recognized for banking, medical schools, textiles, sheep, a special cloth, and a therapeutic eye salve. It is ten miles from Colossae. It lacked an adequate water supply.

Paul never visited it, though it was a branch of Ephesus (as were Hierapolis and Colossae) and mentioned in Colossians and Revelation. It was condemned for being lukewarm (spiritually bankrupt). Along with Hierapolis, Laodicea is listed as the center of Epaphras's work.

What to See:

There are few ruins or signs to guide you here: The Northern Necropolis, the Temple of Apollo, and Roman baths and theater. **Herapolis** (Hierapolis or Pamukkale), the Roman spa six miles away, offers more impressive ruins.

Scripture:

1 Corinthians 16:19
Colossians
Revelation 1:11, 3:14–22
definingmomentsbook.com/resources

PERGAMON (PERGAMUM, BERGAMA)

Historical Significance:

Pergamon, known today as Bergama, was a trading, artistic, and cultural center in northwest Asia Minor, a rival of Alexandria and Ephesus, capital of a large and powerful pre-Roman kingdom. It is in western Turkey, sixty-five miles from Izmir (formerly Smyrna), built on a cone-shaped hill. It had the second largest library in the world.

After Egypt stopped supplying papyrus, parchment was created from untanned sheep calves and goat skin here. The word *parchment* comes from *pergamene,* representing this kind of leather. The first paged book was introduced here.

The church reached here very early, and the first execution of Christians by Romans happened here. One of the Seven Churches addressed in Revelation, it was both praised and criticized. It was the official center of Roman emperor worship in Asia, a place of persecution for those who refused to worship Caesar "where Satan has his throne," but Christ will be sufficient for their needs.

What to See:

Pergamon is certainly one of the best-preserved ancient sites in Turkey, with remains mostly from Hellenistic and Roman times. There are four separate places to visit, each with its own entrance fee. **The Asklepion** (oldest known healing center in Asia Minor), **Hellenistic Acropolis** (with its pagan temples 1,000 feet above the town), **Red Hall Temple/Basilica** (Temple of Serapis), and the **Bergama Archaeological Museum.**

You will want to see the famed (mentioned as the "Throne of Satan" in Revelation) **Altar of Zeus's** foundations and the amazing view from the theater carved out of the Acropolis's side. The Library once held 200,000 parchment volumes.

Also: **Homonym Church; Church of Pergamon; Royal Gates; Temples of Athena and Trajan; Agora; Grand Theater; Gymnasium; Health Center; Library** (second only to Alexandria's).

Scripture:

Revelation 1:11, 2: 12–17

definingmomentsbook.com/resources

PHILADELPHIA (ALAŞEHIR)

Historical Significance:

Philadelphia (Alaşehir today) sits on a hill in a grape region overlooking the royal road: a commercial gateway, seventy-five miles east of Smyrna (Izmir), twenty-eight miles southeast of Sardis (Sart). The original city of brotherly love was founded by Attalus II.

Like Smyrna, Philadelphia was one of only two churches addressed in Revelation that received only praise (for being faithful) and no condemnation from God. They were assured of an honored position at the Second Coming by receiving the name of God.

What to See:

Little remains to be seen due to repeated earthquake damage, except for the ancient wall and the remains of a Byzantine basilica in town.

Scripture:

Revelation 1:11; 3:7–13
definingmomentsbook.com/resources

SARDIS (SART)

Historical Significance:
The capital of the ancient kingdom of Lydia, a city of great fame and wealth, was ruled by king Croesus. It was captured by Alexander the Great in the fourth century BC, then by the Romans in the second century BC. The Acropolis was a natural citadel rising 1,500 feet along Mount Tmolus. The Acropolis is near the village of Sart. Coins were minted and wool dyed first here.

The most picturesque of the Seven Churches addressed in Revelation, it was known as being alive, but was judged by God as dead. The few who overcame would be assured of eternal life. John warned the Christians here to *"Wake up! Strengthen what remains and is about to die, for I have found your deeds unfinished in the sight of my God."*

What to See:
There is a third century, marble-paved synagogue; a Roman gymnasium; and House of Bronzes. The temple of Artemis was three times the size of the Parthenon in Athens! Ruins include the famous **Temple of Artemis** with its huge columns (commissioned in the fourth century BC by Alexander the Great) along the Pactolus River with an early Byzantine church.

Scripture:
Revelation 1:11, 3:1–6
definingmomentsbook.com/resources

Defining Moment . . . Synagogue of Sardis
God had plans for Sardis and its church, which started centuries before Christ came. Way back in 586 BC, when Nebuchadnezzar conquered Assyria, many Jews who were exiled from Jerusalem were brought to Sardis. It is out of this same group of Jews that the church of Sardis was eventually

formed. I am sure the Jews who were originally exiled from their beloved Jerusalem never dreamed that God had such a purpose in moving them— but He did.

Journal Time:

Spend some quiet time with God. Ask Him to show you a time in your life when you were going through challenges that you did not think could possibly bring glory to God. Then, think of how you later saw that it was all a magnificent part of His plan.

Share Time:

Share with your group an experience where God allowed you to see that something that seemed very difficult in your life ended up being a great blessing to you or to others. Also, share any difficult situation that you are going through now that you want to invite God to use to His Glory.

Prayer:

Father God,

How precious You are to us, and how we are amazed at the wonder of Your ways. We confess that we have doubted You at times when we have experienced turmoil in our lives. We repent and are choosing to praise You, regardless of the circumstances in our lives, for Your ways are Holy and not easily understood by us, but we do know that they are always righteous and good and loving. Lord, we want to do what You have told us in 1 Peter 4:12–13, where Peter prayed: "Dear friends, do not be surprised at the fiery ordeal that has come on you to test you, as though something strange were happening to you. But rejoice inasmuch as you participate in the sufferings of Christ, so that you may be overjoyed when his glory is revealed." Thank You, Lord, for all the times in Your Word when we get to see that trials were used by You to magnify the Kingdom. We want to be part of that, and we thank You for the privilege of participating with You in Your redemption plan. We lift our praise and adoration to You at all times and in all circumstances, celebrating the glory of Your will.

In Jesus' name,

Amen

Worship:
   "Complete"
   "I'm Trading My Sorrows"
   "I Surrender All"

SMYRNA (IZMIR)

Historical Significance:

Smyrna (Izmir today) was a prosperous port at the head of a long, narrow gulf, closely aligned with Rome, with a Jewish population hostile to Christians. Legend says it was founded by the Amazon race in the third millennium BC and that the epic poet Homer was born here. The Greek geographer, Strabo, called it the world's most beautiful city. Located thirty-five miles north of Ephesus, Izmir is Turkey's second most important port and third largest city (population of three million).

Like Philadelphia, Smyrna was one of the two churches addressed in Revelation to only receive praise and no condemnation from God in the shortest message. God said it was rich and would receive the crown of life, even though it was then poor and persecuted.

What to See:

Little remains from the Roman times beyond the **agora** (or forum) and the **Church of Smyrna** (Polycarp, Bishop of Smyrna, was martyred in the second century). However, it is central to visiting Ephesus, Sardis/Sart, Miletus, and Didyma by land.

Scripture:

Revelation 1:11, 2:8–11
definingmomentsbook.com/resources

TARSUS

―――――

Historical Significance:

Known primarily as Paul's hometown, Tarsus was the capital of the province of Cilicia in southeastern Asia Minor, a center of culture, commerce, and learning. Like Ephesus, it was a port city, accessed by the Cydnus River; modern Berdan River, or Tarsus Cayi in ancient times, it is located ten miles inland from the northeastern corner of the Mediterranean Sea today. Tarsus's population today is under 200,000.

Cleopatra's barge, with its purple sails of royalty, made its way down this river to greet the successor to Julius Caesar, the visiting Marc Antony, in 41 BC, forty years before Paul's birth. Cleopatra dressed like the goddess Aphrodite. She and Marc Antony then conspired to divide Rome between them.

Cicero lived here as proconsul of Cilicia in 51–50 BC. Julius Caesar visited in 47 BC. Over the years, Tarsus was conquered by Romans, Byzantines, Arabs, Seljuk, and Ottomans.

Paul was headed to Damascus—with the intention of arresting all Christ followers and bringing them to Jerusalem—when Christ blinded him and asked, "*Saul, why do you persecute Me?*" Paul then went to Damascus, still blinded, and fasted and prayed for three days, until Ananias, obedient to a vision, came to greet him as a brother. Ananias then baptized him and commissioned him to carry Jesus' name to Jews and Gentiles alike.

What to See:

Most of the ancient ruins from Hellenistic and Roman times lie unexcavated today, as the modern city was built ten feet above them. You can see **St. Paul's Gate** (a.k.a. Cleopatra's Gate) and the church built as a memorial over what is traditionally considered Paul's house and well, where a small part of the Roman city has been excavated. The only Christian church is a museum today, due to the dominance of Islam, though crosses and doves of peace can be seen carved in stones around the city.

Ten miles north, you can see a mile-and-a-half segment of the old **Roman Road** near Sağlıklı.

Scripture:

Acts 6:9, 9:1–30, 11:25, 21:39, 22:3

Galatians 1:21

definingmomentsbook.com/resources

THYATIRA (AKHISAR)

Historical Significance:

Thyatira was originally known as Pelopia, founded by Seleucus I Nicator, a Macedonian, as a military outpost in a valley in what is now western Turkey, thirty miles from the Aegean, fifty miles northeast of Izmir (formerly Smyrna) on highway 565.

Its well-known trade guilds included makers of linen, wool, pottery, bread, leathers, and bronze. Guild memberships included immoral pagan rituals. Thyatira had tolerated Jezebel's works.

Thyatira was famed for its purple cloth exports, made from a scarlet dye from shellfish (though some think it was from a madder fish, which made a less expensive, red dye). Paul's first European convert at Philippi was Lydia, *"a dealer in purple cloth from Thyatira,"* a member of one of the city's guilds. As Thyatira was in the province of Lydia, it is possible that may not even be her actual name.

In John's vision, the risen Christ condemned Thyatira, one of the Seven Churches addressed in Revelation, for accepting a false prophet's ("Jezebel") teachings promoting immoral, idolatrous practices. Jezebel in the Old Testament was king Ahab's wife who worshipped Baal and persecuted prophets of Israel. To those who overcame, Christ would give them authority to rule the world.

What to See:

The modern city (Akhisar) was built over the ancient city (Thyatira), so little has been excavated except an ancient roadway and period columns in the Tepe Mezari area downtown.

Today, with a population of over 100,000, the modern city of Akhisar is known for agriculture: tobacco, cotton, grapes/raisins, olives, and wheat.

Scripture:

Acts 16:14

Revelation 1:11, 2:18–29

definingmomentsbook.com/resources

GREECE

___

Greek History:

Around 1600 BC, the Mycenaean kingdom conquered the highly developed Minoan civilization on Crete. The Minoans were similar to the Egyptians, a seafaring people, weak militarily. The Mycenaeans were warriors who mostly lived in fortified hilltop cities, and were the inspiration for Homer's Trojan War myths. After 1200 BC, they were conquered by intruders. By 1000 BC, in the middle of the Greek Dark Ages, they were using the Phoenician alphabet (Linear B had been forgotten), relearning to read and write. Only two centuries later, Homer wrote his epic poems (*The Iliad* and *The Odyssey*) based in Greek mythology.

Due to the rocky, mountainous terrain, crops were difficult to grow, resulting in many seafaring conflicts with Italy to the west and Asia Minor to the east.

Persia's invasion (490 BC) was stopped at the long Battle of Marathon by the Athenians. This led to the Classical Period (480–430 BC), also known as the Golden Age of Pericles, a time of peace and prosperity when many monuments were erected in Athens.

Philip II of Macedonia conquered and "united" Greece by force over the southern city-states. He was assassinated in 336 BC at the instigation of his twenty-year-old son (the future military genius Alexander the Great), his first wife (Olympias) or both. Greek influence spread 11,000 miles into Asia Minor, Persia, Syria, Egypt, Palestine, Rome, and India. Alexander was educated by the philosopher Aristotle. He never suffered a defeat, founded over seventy cities, and created an empire stretching across three continents (two million square miles), united by a common Greek language and culture.

Alexander the Great's generals divided the kingdom in 323 BC, after his death at age thirty-three of a fever in Babylon. Ptolemy I ruled over Egypt, Seleucus I Nicator over Syria and Asia Minor, and Antigonus over Macedonia, launching the Hellenistic Age (330–42 BC), a time of universalism.

Corinth was destroyed (146 BC) and rebuilt by Roman emperor Julius Caesar a century later. In between, Athens also fell, but Caesar created an academy there where Roman leaders studied for centuries. The Pax Romana had spread Latin and Greek along with good highways from Rome, through Greece and Asia Minor, to Asia and Egypt.

The Roman empire lasted from 42 BC to 476 AD (when Rome fell). After Julius Caesar was assassinated, civil war erupted until Octavian and Marc Antony defeated Brutus and Cassius in battle on the plains of Philippi. After the division of the Roman empire, Greece was in the Eastern empire, Byzantium her capital. Greece's prior religions gradually disappeared, the temples replaced by churches. The Byzantine empire (a.k.a. the New Roman empire) lasted from 325–1453 AD when Constantinople fell.

Greece got her independence from the Ottoman (Islamic) empire in 1821–1830, and Bavarian king Otto I was made monarch. Greece periodically added Greek-speaking neighboring territories and islands (over 1,400 islands today) to its territory, and was occupied by the Germans from 1941–1944.

Greece was fully united after World War II when the Italian-controlled Aegean islands were ceded to Greece. There was a massive citizen exchange—one and a half million Greeks in Turkey returned to Greece, while 800,000 Turks in Greece returned to Turkey. After a civil war, the communist rebels were defeated in 1949. Greece had installed king Paul (1947–64) and joined NATO in 1952. In 1967, military dictators exiled the king, Constantine II, and Greece finally became a parliamentary republic in 1974 with two major political parties by referendum, and joined the European Community in 1981.

In 2004, Greece hosted the Summer Olympics. Greece is about the size of Alabama. It is developed, stable and has a modern economy. They are not happy that the former Yugoslavia is now known as Macedonia. The official name of the country is The Hellenic Republic.

The Old Testament barely mentions Greece and does not cover the period during which Israel was controlled by the Hellenists (approximately 300–180 BC). Hellenism was all about "me," similar to Adam and Eve's succumbing to the temptation to see themselves as the ultimate authority.

The battle was fierce when God sent Paul into this foreign, secular, pagan land.

Hellenists were comprised of Platonists, Aristotelians, Stoics, and Epicureans, each with different philosophies yet united in the focus on the rational mind, on accomplishment, and on the notion that humans are the ultimate source of truth and authority. This resulted in early Christian converts also emphasizing knowledge over obedience. Greek was considered the language of the educated. While Greeks had many gods created in their own image, they truly worshipped *themselves* as god creators. Christianity was illogical and revolutionary, as it is based on an objective point of reference, reverence, and authority, the one true God.

Judea conqueror Alexander the Great introduced Hellenism to Israel in 330 BC. Rather than compromise their Jewish beliefs, the Maccabees led their revolt in 167 BC, yet later adopted Hellenistic lifestyles, as did the Sadducees, which resulted in a bitter split with the Pharisees and the Zealots. Today Hellenism is known as Humanism, with its focus on *self,* comfort, pleasure, and sexuality. Our world is really not that much different than Paul's world 2,000 years ago, is it?

The **agora** (or marketplace) was a focal point in Greek cities, the main public area, often with elaborate sculptures, colonnades, paved walkways, and a **bema** (speaker's platform) for court cases before the city's magistrates. **Stoas** were covered, colonnaded buildings of various sizes for meetings, courts, shops, offices, or storerooms. A **theater** was half-moon shaped, while an **amphitheater** was circular (like two theaters put together).

Greece Today

The best times to visit are late spring and early fall, when temperatures are in the mid-sixties to the low eighties. Summers are hot, with cool nights, and air conditioning is rare. Electric current is 220 volts, requiring a converter and adapter plugs. Many cities are located on hills with many steps. Local guides know more about archaeology than about Paul and Christianity. Most sites are "A" sites.

Cultural Tips

- Greeks are more expressive than Americans with their voices and hand gestures.
- Their standard of living is lower than ours.
- Driving is hectic, but life is much slower.
- Crime is low, but be cautious.
- Greeks eat lunch and dinner much later than we do.
- Greeks are more hospitable, so enjoy their friendship.

Aside: It was Shakespeare in *Julius Caesar* who had Cicero first say, "It was Greek to me."

Greek Traditions

Greeks are both religious (Greek Orthodox) and superstitious (paranormal). While most festivals and customs are religious, some have pagan roots.

Name Days: As most Greeks are named after a Saint (and usually a grandparent), each has a given day annually when friends and family drop by without invitation to offer their blessings along with a small gift, and to enjoy appetizers, pastries and desserts. A baby is not called by its name until baptized.

Smashing Plates: There are many theories as to the origins of breaking plates on the ground, but it seems mostly connected to showing appreciation for a dancer or musician expressing *kefi*—emotion and joy. It also could represent abundance; noise being used to drive away evil; or "killing" the plate at feasts for the dead; and the breaking of and moving on from unresolved conflict. Sadly for us, the custom is frowned upon today and requires a license for a taverna to practice it. (By the way, you will be charged 1–2 Euros for each plate you break). More common today would be to applaud, shout "Opa!" or throw flowers instead. This certainly beats what preceded plate smashing—throwing knives into the floor at the performer's feet! Me, I will stick to using my plate to hold my moussaka.

Greek Easter: This celebration lasts an entire week. Greek Easter is on a different date than ours, as it is based on the Julian (not Gregorian) calendar, is after Passover and is on the first Sunday after the first full moon after the March 21 Spring Equinox.

On Holy Thursday, they prepare bright, dyed-red eggs for the Sunday Resurrection Table.

On Good Friday (or Great Friday), flags fly at half-mast and all join in a procession carrying a "tomb" (kouvouklion) with flowers and an icon of Jesus Christ entombed (epitaphios) through the streets, chanting the Lamentations (ritual lament).

On Holy Saturday, church services begin at 11 p.m. with all carrying large white candles (*lampada*). At midnight, amidst fireworks and church bells, priests announce "Christ is Risen" (*"Christos Anesti"*). The people respond, "Truly He is Risen" (*"Alithos Anesti"*). They then begin a Divine Liturgy that lasts until 2 to 3 a.m. Then, they go home, burning the candles all night long (symbolizing The Light of Christ returning to the world), break the eggs (symbolizing Christ breaking from the Tomb), and dine on smoked salted pork (*hiromari*) or lamb sausage, Greek Easter bread (*koulouri or tsoureki*), cheeses, a creamy, lemony soup (*magiritsa*), along with retsina or other wine, and ouzo.

On Easter Sunday, either lamb or kid goat is served (symbolizing the Lamb of God), spiced and roasted whole over charcoal, at yet another feast.

Greek Customs

- Greek men love to carry komboloi (worry beads, which have no religious significance), or komboskini (Orthodox prayer ropes) and to meet for a short time for conversation in cafes (*kafenion*) to kill time or play backgammon.
- Greeks generally pay cash when dining out, and always ensure they have enough to pay for their company also.
- They try to never use a public toilet, so tourists have to often endure low standards.
- It is considered rude to enter a church with uncovered knees or shoulders.
- Tipping at ten percent is appropriate, even if it says that tips are included.

- Greece is on GMT (Greenwich Mean Time), also known as "Greek Maybe Time"—a lot like in Africa. Siesta time is sacred, between 3 p.m. and 5 p.m. Dinner rarely starts before 9 p.m.

Greek Orthodoxy:

The Greek, Russian, Serbian, and (insert nationality here) Orthodox Churches are bound together by liturgy, using similar worship, yet the same dogmas. They believe the Church is the Bride of Christ, the Body of Christ, not merely the building where God's people come together to worship and then go forth to seekers out in the world.

They consider theirs to be the oldest church, that Catholics are schismatic or outside the true Body of Christ. They also consider the Reformation (i.e. Protestantism) to be another abomination, as they do not see the Protestant sacraments as a means of dispensing grace. The Orthodox are more Trinitarian; the Protestants focus more exclusively on Jesus.

"Ortho" means correct, "dox" means belief. Their focus is not on a suffering Savior on the Cross, but on Christ's victory ("Nike") over death. Their celebration bread (prosphoron) is stamped "Jesus Christ, Nika." which means "Jesus Christ Conquers." To reflect the Trinity, they cross themselves three times (in the name of the Father, Son, and Holy Spirit) with the thumb and first two fingers touching to represent the Trinity; the last two fingers represent the two natures of Jesus as fully man and fully divine. Those fingers touch the palm to represent Christ descending from Heaven to Earth to dwell among us.

The seven Ecumenical Councils (between 325 and 787 AD) defined what it means to be a Christian. Jesus did not write any books. All we have about Him is tradition, so tradition (Gospels, church councils) are important to the Orthodox Church. The western Church increasingly distanced itself from the Councils, since the Bishop of Rome moved from primacy, "first among equals" to superiority (i.e. papal infallibility) and the Roman Catholic Church was born.

The Orthodox churches prefer consensus. Icons describe the incarnation of God. In the west, we see statues; in the east (Turkey), we see two-dimensional icons (paintings). They consider it prideful to say, "Jesus is my

Savior." These are the holy mysteries, which they believe God initiates on our behalf:

1. Baptism (literal, not symbolic)
2. Chrismation (the oil is the seal of the Holy Spirit)
3. Holy Eucharist (again, literal, not symbolic)
4. Confession (individually before Christ, with a priest as witness, rarely, "general confession with a body of believers")
5. Marriage (God lets us get married to be holy, not happy; divorce takes two years in Greece);
6. Holy Orders (ordination to the priesthood or the diaconate, men only)
7. Holy Unction (healing oil, accompanied by prayers for physical and spiritual healing, as the Lord wills [James 5:14]. Orthodox do not do "last rites" in the way that the Catholic Church does.)

*Note, the additional Roman Catholic sacrament of Confirmation is included in the Orthodox sacrament of Baptism. For Roman Catholics, this confirms full membership in the Roman Catholic Church, and was historically part of their baptism service. Orthodox Christians believe that once baptized, a person, regardless of age, has received the Holy Spirit and is already a full member of the Church.

The Greek Orthodox Christians represent ninety-eight percent of the population, with about one percent Muslim along the eastern border with Turkey and only 15,000 Evangelicals out of a population of eleven million.

The year 600 AD marked the rise of Islam and the captivity of the eastern church under Islam's dominance in north Africa, the Middle East, Turkey, and Spain.

By 800 AD, western Christianity had spread throughout Europe. In a slight to Constantinople, the pope crowned Charlemagne head of the holy Roman empire.

By 1053 AD, the eastern Church and the western Church had each excommunicated the other over, among other things, the filioque controversy. The eastern Church believed that the Holy Spirit "proceeds from the Father," as Jesus said in the Bible. The western church began to evolve a theology that had the Holy Spirit proceed from the Father *and* the Son (filioque means "and the son").

By 1200 AD, the eastern Church had asked the western Church for help against the threat of Islam. Byzantine church attacked by Catholic Crusaders in 1204.

In 1453 AD, the Muslims sacked Constantinople.

In 1683 AD, the Muslims were stopped from spreading to Europe at the Battle of Venice.

definingmomentsbook.com/resources

GREEK MAINLAND

ATHENS

Historical Significance:

Athens was known for its culture, not for its political or religious distinction. Education, arts, philosophers (Plato and Aristotle), and public works projects (temples, statues, and monuments) flourished, making Athens the cradle of western civilization as we know it today. While the west was politically and militarily dominated by the Romans, its culture most reflected that of the Greeks. Today, only Rome surpasses it in the richness of antiquities.

The Corinthians were viewed as immoral drunkards and the Spartans as militaristic barbarians. These rival city-states saw the Athenians as past their glory and irrelevant.

Between 340–260 BC, Stoicism (emphasizing rationality) and Epicureanism (emphasizing pleasure instead) were developed by Zeno and Epicurus, respectively. Zeno was an ascetic from Cyprus, at that time a Hellenistic culture teaching logos (or reason) as directing the universe. Epicurus was a wealthy Greek teaching nationalism and individualism.

Philip II of Macedonia had conquered northern Greece, then central Greece, and then Athens, effortlessly. Rome conquered Greece in 168 BC, but exempted Greece from taxation, let them keep judicial autonomy, and sent Roman children to be educated in Athens.

Paul visited Athens alone on his second missionary journey, sailing without Silas and Timothy, who remained in Berea. He likely landed at the port of Piraeus, where cruises and ferries depart from today. He would have traveled north on foot to Athens entering the agora (the civic and cultural center) via the Dipylon (Double Gate) on the northwest side.

The Epicurean and Stoic philosophers from the two leading schools, along with most Athenians, enjoyed a good debate. While its supreme glory days were past, it was still the greatest town for academics and philosophical learning. It was said there were more statues of gods than there were in all the rest of Greece, more than there were citizens in Athens. After hearing Paul speak daily in the agora, the snobbish philosophers invited him up to the Areopagus (Athens) Council on Mars Hill, where he gave his famous (though unfruitful) "*To the Unknown God*" sermon. While *some* believed, *most* did not respond to the absurd message of a man raised from the dead. Ironically, Paul's sermon is similar to the first one he heard years prior by Stephen—that you cannot box God inside a temple made by human hands.

The Council consisted of about thirty members (philosophers and magistrates) and dealt with matters of morals, culture, education, and religion, inviting speakers to share new ideas. Today, the Areopagus Council is the name of the Greek Supreme Court. In one of the few usages in the Bible, Paul called Athenians "religious," which was not a compliment. They were all about talk and not action—yet God's Word *demands* action to change our lives. It is no different today with "intellectuals," is it?

Though Timothy had not returned from being sent to Thessaloniki, Paul did not wait for the Council to approve his license to teach, but instead left alone for Corinth without planting a church and never returned. Athens (population less than 25,000 then; four million today) had been passed over in significance by Corinth, Ephesus, Antioch, Alexandria, and Rome. (There are hundreds of Christian churches in Athens today, though).

The emperor Justinian later closed the schools of philosophy. The Parthenon, at one time the largest temple in the world, was originally the House of the Maiden/Virgin. Dedicated to Athena, it was built to commemorate victory over the Persians in 447 BC. The Parthenon became the Church of the Virgin Mother of God in the sixth century. In the 1687 war between the Athenian Turks and the Venetians, a cannon blew up a Turkish ammunition dump in the prized Parthenon, then being used as a mosque. Today the Parthenon is in the midst of a long-term preservation project. As four million of Greece's eleven million populace reside in Athens, which sits in a bowl and is often smoggy, the pollution is affecting the monuments such as the Parthenon.

What to See:

The **Parthenon**, meaning "virgin's chamber," was already 500 years old and a tourist attraction in Paul's time. It was originally built as a temple to honor Athena, the goddess and patroness of Athens. The temple was built upon three huge twenty-inch-high platforms—eight Doric columns on each end, seventeen on each side, each thirty-four feet high, tapering to the top and leaning inward. Your first view after entering through the Propylaea (a monumental gate building with two reception halls) is not straight on, but at an angle. It represents the "harmony between matter and spirit," the monument that "puts order in the mind."

The Parthenon is located on the world-renowned **Acropolis** (meaning "upper city"), 500 feet above the city at the intersection of Apostolou Pavlou (Paul) and Dionysiou Areopagitou streets, with steep slopes on three sides (open 6 a.m. to 10 p.m. and lighted beautifully at night). Its rock has dominated the city's panorama for 2,500 years. Women and children were sheltered there during war. Athena, the city's patron goddess, considered it sacred. The roof was lost in 1687 (the wooden beams covered in marble burned for a week) when Venetian mortars blew up the gunpowder the Turks had stored inside. Destruction is part of its history. To replace it would be to take away part of that history. The buildings represent some of the most architecturally perfect ever constructed.

The **Acropolis Museum** has been moved down the mountain to a much larger facility on the south side.

Roman Forum (320 feet by 370 feet) is below the northern cliff, next to Polygnotou Street;

The **Temple of Olympian Zeus**, made from 15,000 tons of marble, with only sixteen fifty-five-foot-tall Corinthian columns remaining of the original 103 columns. The temple was started in the sixth century BC and was still unfinished in Paul's day.

The **Theatre of Dionysus,** the god of the theater, at the foot of the Acropolis on the south base, was the birthplace of Greek tragedies and comedies in the fifth century BC; the oldest theater in Greece from the sixth century BC, before the Parthenon had even been built.

The **Temple of Hephaestus** (Vulcan), the god of fire, is the best preserved at this site because it was later converted to a Christian church;

The **Odeon of Herodes Atticus**, also on the south base, seats 5,000 today for concerts with great acoustics. Descending from the Acropolis to the northwest, you will find on the right the gray limestone rocky rise called the **Hill of the Areopagus** in Greek, **Mars Hill** in Latin, where the Athens Council met. To the right, below the slippery, smooth steps, is a bronze sign with the text of Paul's sermon about "*the unknown God*" on it in Greek. There is a modern staircase to the left now. It functioned as Athens's homicide court in classical times and later held the Council of Elders. The rockiness reminds you of the image of the first soil (in the parable of the sower), representing hard hearts. Paul debated unsuccessfully with the intellectual community of his day here.

Continuing down, you will then pass the meeting place of the senators, the Tholos; the **Temple of Hephaestus** with a great view above the **agora**, the ancient marketplace and center of Athenian public life (later a Christian church), the **Stoa Basileios** (Royal Stoa, where Socrates may have drunk the hemlock in 399 BC); the **Stoa Poikile** (Painted Porch, where Zeno spoke of Stoicism); and the **Stoa of Attalos** (rebuilt in the 1950s, with a cool, shaded colonnade to rest under). The Museum of the Ancient Agora displays scenes of everyday life: jury selection, coins, grills, a child's potty-training chair, etc. Paul likely preached to the skeptical Athenians in the agora, the political heart of Athens since 600 BC, before he spoke at the synagogue.

Off to nearby **Plaka** with its quaint shops and narrow streets for some food and drink!

Also worth seeing:

The current **Olympic stadium** is east down Leoforos Vasilissas Olgas, carved into the hill at the site of the original Panathenaic Stadium (335 BC). This was the site of the first modern Olympic games in 1896, seating 50,000. The original stadium's track was 600 feet long (185 meters, which equals one *stadion*).

Olympics trivia:

- The first Olympic contest was held in Olympia (at the foot of Mount Olympus) in 776 BC as a tribute to the Greek Pantheon of gods that were believed to reside on Mount Olympus. A festival to Zeus, it recurred for nearly 1,200 years until Rome ended it due to its pagan roots in 393 AD, after Christianity was the official religion of the empire. There were eighteen events originally, only one of which (the 600-meter run) resembles an event today.
- In 1896, there were forty-three events in nine sports. Today there are 339 events in 33 sports.
- The marathon was created for the 1896 Olympics, and remains the only event ever created specifically for the Olympics. It is still the very last event, ending in the stadium at the beginning of the closing ceremonies. It was a tribute to the runner from 470 BC who ran non-stop from Marathon to Athens with news of the victory over the Persians. He pronounced "Nike" ("victory"), and dropped dead. Only nine of twenty-five runners finished the first marathon. Some Americans at those games then came home and started the Boston Marathon in 1897.

Paul always spoke of living the Christian experience as either fighting a battle or running a race. There are 26 miles, 385 yards in modern marathons. How are *you* going to finish that last 385 yards of *your* Christian race?

The **National Archaeological Museum** is one of the best in the world. We suggest you buy their helpful keepsake guide to enhance your experience. Also: The **Temple of Athena Nike**, the goddess of victory, to the right of the west entrance before the **Propylaea**; the **Erechtheion**, with its peerless porch on the heads of six maidens; the **Hellenic Parliament** on Syntagma Square; the **Tomb of the Unknown Soldier**; the **Presidential Mansion** (with its soldiers in picturesque uniforms performing the Changing of the Guard throughout the day); the **Arch of Hadrian**; **Constitution Square** (Syntagma); **National Library of Greece**; National and Kapodistrian University of Athens; Academy of Athens.

Scripture:
> Acts 17:14–18:1
> 1 Thessalonians 3:1–2
> definingmomentsbook.com/resources

Defining Moment . . . Mars Hill

The citizens of Athens were great orators and thinkers. They were skilled philosophers who could debate with consummate arguments. Unfortunately, faith in Jesus Christ is about much more than debating skills. When Paul taught them about Jesus, the truth fell on deaf ears, and Paul left Athens without having started a church. A few men did believe, but for the most part the Athenians were more intrigued with the idea of debating *about* Jesus rather than relating *to* Him.

Our current culture is much the same. So many of the lost are so entrapped in their arguments *about* Jesus that they do not consider getting to *know* Him first. They make their judgment strictly on esoteric rhetoric instead of considering a relationship with the God of the universe. When the Holy Spirit taps us on the shoulder to invite these folks into the truth, many times we leave the conversation with little or no fruit realized, just like Paul did on Mars Hill.

Journal Time:

Spend a few moments thinking about your personal "Most Wanted List." Who are the friends and family that do not know the Lord, who are just great debaters?

Share Time:

Share with your group a time that you had conversation with a friend or family member that cared more about seeing proof that there was a God than they did about having a relationship with Him. Talk about any success stories and share how God brought them into a place of relationship instead of debate about Him. Use this time to pray for the person that God is putting on your heart, and ask God to give you the words that they can hear to invite them into relationship with Him.

Prayer:

During this prayer, we will have a time to call out the names of family and friends that do not know the Lord whom we want to lift up before Him.

Lord,

We all have people that we know and love that we are so excited about inviting into Your Kingdom and having them belong to our family of believers. Father, these are people we love and we long for them to spend Eternity with You and us. We have debated, discussed, and reasoned with them. Alas, without the power of the Holy Spirit, and without their hearts softening toward You, they stay in their stance. Father, please use us in any way You can to bring them to a saving faith in You. We want to sow truth into their lives in a way that they can hear, but we can only do it in Your power as You reveal it. Also, please keep us from doing the Holy Spirit's job. Let us speak truth, but leave room for You to move into inviting them into relationship with You in a supernatural way that can only come from You.

Father, today we specifically pray for (I invite you to call out the names of your unsaved loved ones). Father, You know the hearts of each of these people that we have called out. Please, Lord, give each one an invitation to a saving faith in You with a relationship that they just cannot walk away from. We are depending on You, Lord, and thanking You ahead of time for all that You are going to do in these lives we have lifted up to You.

In Jesus' name,

Amen

Worship:

"Jesus, You Are the Answer"

"Turn Your Eyes Upon Jesus"

Defining Moment . . . The Agora

In Paul's time, the Greeks worshipped many different gods. They were such an integral part of the culture that they would be seen everywhere, from city public works buildings to the agora. Think of the agora as the Walmart of the day: a flea market, grocery store, public square, and meeting place all rolled into one. You would see all of your neighbors there, and, if you wanted to thrive in that culture, you had to be there. It was the center of commerce; you even had to get water there from the public fountains.

If you were an early Christian in Greece, you had to pass by the shrines to the Greek gods throughout the agora. The merchants would honor these gods by dedicating their goods to them. The meat one bought in the agora had usually been offered or sacrificed in the gods' temples before it came to market. As Christians, not honoring these gods resulted in serious economic consequences. The believers in ancient Greece had to answer complicated questions about what was right and wrong for them, given the cultural demands.

In our lives today, the way a Christian lives and what we expose ourselves to is very different than the way the world lives. Television and movies that promote immoral ideas or visuals, video games that promote needless violence, and even participating in our culture's version of Halloween are topics Christians have to wrestle with. The world paints these things as having an innocuous effect on people, but that is a *lie*. Whatever a person allows into his life and his family's life has consequences, even if it is in the unseen world.

Journal Time:
Spend a few moments alone with God, and ask Him if there is anything from your culture that is affecting you in ways that are not positive. Ask Him to give you strength to let go of whatever you are getting from this "thing" and to give you the strength and courage to let go of any cultural effects that could be creating strongholds in your life.

Share Time:
Share with the group any cultural issues that conflict with your Christian beliefs and how you are dealing with them.

Prayer:

Lord,

There are so many things in this world that affect us in ways that we cannot understand. Thank You for Your Word and for the way it guides and protects us from the unprofitable effects our culture can have on us. Please give us wisdom and discernment in making important decisions about what we allow into our lives, from the media we view to the songs we listen to. Let us choose those things that edify You and Your ways, and bring us into deeper relationship and intimacy with You. Give us the courage and conviction to make right decisions.

In Jesus' name,

Amen

Worship:

"Lord, Reign in Me"

"I Surrender All"

BEREA (BEROEA)

Historical Significance:

The peach capital of Greece, forty-two miles west of Thessaloniki and nine miles northwest of Vergina, is today known as Veroia, in ancient times was a beautiful city between the ocean and Mount Olympus, the mythological home of Greek gods and goddesses. Today little remains of what was once the number two city in Macedonia (after Philippi).

Paul fled to Berea with Silas one night after a riot in Thessaloniki in 54 AD, while on his second missionary journey. Initially, Paul found the Bereans receptive to his teachings in the synagogue and eager to hear the Truth: both Jews and Gentiles were converting. The vindictive Thessalonians followed them, to incite the people against them, so the new brothers escorted Paul to the coast and on to Athens, probably by sea. Silas and Timothy remained for a short while before joining him in Athens. One of Paul's traveling companions, Sopater, was a Berean.

What to See:

Unlike Philippi, modern Veroia is still a bustling town of nearly 50,000 people. The most impressive monument in all of Greece to Paul is in the **bema** (or rostrum), which is in the southern section of the town. The monument was rebuilt in 1961, and tradition says that it includes the steps from the original synagogue Paul preached in. Mosaics of his journey include one of him holding the Word and a double-edged sword: Paul ironically was beheaded. Reminding us that we also face resistance today, there is graffiti on the back of the monument.

There is a small park just up the street that has a mighty, old tree with deep roots. It is a great reminder for us to have deep roots in the Word to handle life, based on Psalm 1:2–3 *"who meditates on His law day and night. That person is like a tree planted by streams of water, which yields its fruit in season."* There are little peeks here and there of remains from the ancient city's Jewish Quarter: public baths in Pindou Street, near Agiou Antoniou Square in the city center; streets with curbs/drainage (Elia Street); and shops in Parodos Edessis Street. Also, you can view parts of the Via Egnatia, the Roman Road.

Scripture:

Acts 17:10–15, 20:4
1 Thessalonians 3:1–2
definingmomentsbook.com/resources

Defining Moment . . . The Bema Monument

Charles Spurgeon used to say that "the devil never kicks a dead horse." When Paul was in Berea, his ministry was enjoying great success: many Jews as well as Greeks were believing in Jesus. Imagine having so many people convert to a real relationship with the Lord because of your ministry, only to find yourself being chased out by the enemy—folks from Thessaloniki, in this case. Where in your life have you reached, or are you reaching, opposition that is overwhelming when you look at it from an earthly perspective? Is it in your ministry, finances, job, or family? What are the questions you are asking yourself about the decisions you are making? And, most importantly, what is God saying to you about the situation? We consider it a *compliment* when the enemy attacks us- it means we are dangerous through our service; otherwise, if were impotent, he would just leave us alone.

Journal Time:

Spend some quiet time with God, asking the question, "Should I stand my ground, as Paul did in Corinth, or should I move to a different place where God can use me to a greater measure in His Kingdom?" Ask Him to reveal His will to you for any ministry conflicts you are experiencing.

Share Time:

Share a time when you faced difficult opposition when you were working on something that was benefiting the Kingdom. How did God show up for you? What is going on in your life right now that you are challenged by, and that you need God to show up for?

Prayer:

Lord,

How we praise You for Your power and might. Thank You so much that greater is He that lives in us than he that lives in the world. Lord, we submit to You and Your power to help us overcome any obstacle that comes against our ministries, our families, our businesses—anything in our lives, Lord. We surrender to Your protection and we move forward confidently, believing that You will be our strength and fortress. "Let us not become weary in doing good, for at the proper time we will reap a harvest if we do not give up" (Galatians 6:9).

In Jesus' precious name,

Amen

Worship:

"All Things are Possible"

"Stand Up, Stand Up for Jesus"

CORINTH

Historical Significance:

Ancient Corinth, probably named for Corinthus, son of Zeus, is about one and a half hours (fifty miles) southwest of Athens, a beautiful drive today known as the "Sacred Way." The modern four-mile-long Corinth Canal was started by Nero in 66 AD, abandoned, begun again in 1881, and not finished until the modern era in 1893. The canal is three and a half miles long and sixty-five to seventy-five feet wide, separating the three-and-a-half-mile-wide Peloponnese from the Greek mainland and connecting the Ionian and Aegean seas. Land traffic was controlled north–south, and sea traffic east–west. The canal connects the Adriatic and Italy to the west, with the Aegean and Asia Minor to the east, along what was once a vital trade route between Athens in the north and Sparta in the south of Greece. Corinth was first inhabited in the Neolithic period (5000–3000 BC). On the Peloponnese Peninsula, there were two harbors, Lechaeum on the Gulf of Corinth, and Cenchreae (modern Kenchreae) on the Saronic Gulf (from which Paul landed and sailed). Corinth's strategic trade route was vital to the spread of the Gospel in all four directions.

The Acrocorinth is the 2,000-foot-tall mountain to the southeast, which was topped by the temple of Aphrodite (Venus), the Greek goddess of love and sex. One thousand prostitutes "served" the "faithful" (*Korinthia Kor* means "prostitute"). Paul's reference to gongs and cymbals (1 Corinthians 13:1) is about the pagan worship at the temples of Demeter and Cybele.

Corinthian bronze, favored by Augustus Caesar, was considered the world's finest. It was even used in the gate called "Beautiful" outside the Temple in Jerusalem and was worth more than the other nine Temple gates combined. Raisins were first developed here: currant is a medieval adaptation of Corinth. It was a leading center of commerce and industry, particularly pottery and ceramics.

Philip of Macedon, Alexander the Great's father, made conquered Corinth the headquarters of the Hellenic League in 338 BC. Rome destroyed it, except for the Doric Temple of Apollo, in 146 BC, after Corinth refused an order to disband the league and sheltered the leaders of the Greek opposition to the Roman conquest.

In 46 BC, Julius Caesar began rebuilding Corinth, but then died. It was completed by Augustus to be a Roman colony: one-third each freemen, slaves, and freedmen (emancipated slaves). The Romans made it the capital of Achaia, a Roman province of western Greece, in a time when Corinth outshined Athens. To this day, it is blessed by an unlimited underground water supply. There were 300,000 residents, 500,000 slaves, and 1,000 prostitutes here in Paul's day.

Paul visited cosmopolitan Corinth, the capital of Roman Greece and ancient center of luxury and sin, three times. First in 50 AD, coming from Athens on his second missionary journey with Timothy and Silas, when he planted the church with Aquila and Priscilla, who had been expelled from Rome in 49 AD. Paul stayed for a significant eighteen months, working with them making leather tents (remember the commercials about "*rich Corinthian leather*?"). At that time, all Jewish teachers had a trade six days a week, rabbis as we know them not evolving until early in the second century. During Paul's third missionary journey, he sent Timothy and Erastus here from Ephesus. Then he sent the first letter to the Corinthians via Stephanas in the spring.

The Jews brought Paul to the agora for a trial before the bema (judgment seat) of Lucius Julius Gallio, the proconsul of Achaia (Rome's name for western Greece), and rejected the accusations of treason. Paul said that from then on, he would go to the Gentiles (here in Corinth, not elsewhere). After hearing Paul preach, Gallio's favorable verdict on the Christian faith essentially permitted Christianity to be preached by imperial policy 300 years before Constantine made it the official religion! This made the trial the second most important trial in history after Jesus'! Paul likely wrote 1 and 2 Thessalonians, which were among the earliest epistles, from Corinth.

The synagogue leader, Sosthenes, was then beaten without objection by Gallio. Could it be this Sosthenes who converted and was addressed as "*brother*" in 1 Corinthians 1:1? Paul's second, brief, "*painful*," emergency visit was in response to conflicts within the church and questioning of his authority. The Corinthians had miraculous leadership, vision, and teaching gifts (what we *do*), but lacked fruit (who we *are*).

He wrote 1 Corinthians from Ephesus on his third missionary journey to correct a few more problems. His use of athletic metaphors (boxing, wrestling, and running in 1 Corinthians 9:24–28) could mean he attended the Isthmian Games there in 49 and 51 AD. The "perishable crown" refers to the wreaths made of pine or wilted celery.

His third visit was delayed until he had heard from Titus about their repentance and reconciliation, and still further until after he wrote 2 Corinthians from Macedonia (possibly Philippi). Paul and Timothy spent three months in Corinth. Paul wrote the book of Romans and collected an offering for the suffering Christians in Jerusalem in 55–56 AD. After this journey, Paul never revisited Greece.

The population of Corinth in Paul's time was under 200,000; today it is about 20,000.

Corinth was held through the centuries by the Byzantines, Turks, knights of Malta, Venetians, and Turks again before coming into Greek hands in 1822.

What to See:

The **Archaeological Museum of Ancient Corinth** is in the northwest corner of the primary ancient site, a short drive from the modern city. There is an inscription to Theophilus ("lover of God"), the name of the person that Luke addressed the Gospel of Luke and the book of Acts to. The museum consists of two chambers and a courtyard. There is a sun god image: a bust of Nero; synagogue stones; and a statue of Julius Caesar.

From there, you can walk through the extensively excavated ruins, which are mostly Roman, and not Greek. The ruins include a race course, the bema of Gallio, the Odeon (built into the hill of natural stone), a theater, temples, first century shops, water fountains (including Fountain of Peirene), public buildings, and the biggest forum (agora) in the ancient world—at 300 feet by 600 feet. There is the prominent bema (rostrum) where Paul was acquitted in 52 AD by the Roman governor Gallio, a trial which effectively made Christianity a legal religion in the eyes of Rome. They have also uncovered inscriptions of Erastus, the director of public works mentioned in Romans 16:23; a meat market; a synagogue; and cult dining rooms in the Asclepius and Demeter temples. The springs of the Acrocorinth that once filled the Fountain of Peirene still bubble under the ruins.

The **Temple of Apollo** has seven monolithic columns (each made from a single stone) remaining from the sixth century BC.

You can drive up to the gates of the **Acrocorinth** fortress on the mountain behind Corinth and then climb up within and see the Byzantine fortifications, temples, fountains, shops, and public buildings.

You can also view the canal across the Isthmus of Corinth, including the sixth century Diolkos which means "haul across," an adjacent portage or roadway to move cargo and small boats across. The **Corinth Canal** was built at the end of the nineteenth century over the remains of Nero's attempt at building a canal in 64 AD. Shipping crosses east to west through the canal, and trucking travels north to south via the bridges above.

Lechaion Road winds from the harbor up to the agora, with its vaulted shops with arched doors, showcasing goods from all over the world.

Scripture:
>   Acts 18:1–18; 19:1
>   Romans 16:23
>   1 and 2 Corinthians
>   2 Timothy 4:20
>   definingmomentsbook.com/resources

Defining Moment . . . The Ruins of Corinth
"In all things love"—the theme of 1 Corinthians 13's famous "love chapter"—seems like a sweet group of verses we hear at weddings, as we read these words out of context. However, study what was really happening in the church at Corinth, and a much bolder picture of a broken, self-absorbed body appears. This church was an absolute mess. It was made up of warring factions. There was elitism and conflict over spiritual gifts. Sexual immorality

was being allowed. Heresy about the Resurrection was infiltrating teachings. Aberrant practices were occurring during the very worship services. People were justifying behaviors they had no right to justify, but that did not stop them. Jealousy, gossip, arrogance, debauchery, quarrels, outbursts of anger, and slander were the order of the day—*inside* the church!

This laundry list of sins could be placed in our same church bodies today. Churches are made up of people that are broken. We hurt each other without intending to, but the wounds are still deep and bloody. The only salve for these wounds is love; love that bears all things. The Greek translation for "*bears all things*" is that of putting a roof and covering over something to protect it—if you demonstrate the love that is being taught here, you will protect and cover that person who agitates you *always*. Not just when they deserve it, not when you feel like it, not when they are right. The verse says *always*.

The only time a church looks perfect is when you are standing on the outside of it, because on the inside it is made up of the same imperfect human beings that inhabited the Corinthian church. We are all broken, or we would not be here.

Journal Time:
Take a few moments to ponder the following: Where have you had disagreements and hurts in ministry that you are still aching over? Where have you been wronged, and where have you kept forgiveness at bay by holding onto your "rightness" instead of letting God give you His righteousness?

Share Time:
Share with the group, without using names and creating gossip, a time that you have been offended in your church and whether you are willing to let go of it and leave it in Corinth, covered with love.

Prayer:
Father God,

Thank You that You invented love and that You teach us how to use it on a daily basis. Lord, we confess that we have all been unloving at times. No matter how great our performances and intentions are to build Your Kingdom, if they are not covered in love, they are absolutely meaningless. Lord, that boggles our minds, that no matter how good and perfect our ministries and works appear, if they are not covered by love, they are actually nothing; they are empty and appear as if they were never even accomplished. Lord, we repent of the part that each of us has played in our churches where we have acted outside of love, no matter what our motivations were. Your Word is clear. When it comes to Your body, it is never OK for us to act outside of love, no matter what has been done to us.

Lord, thank You for forgiving us of these trespasses, as we forgive the trespasses of those who have sinned against us. Please keep us away from situations in our churches that are unloving, and give us Your abundant love that will overflow onto everything we do for Your Kingdom. Yours is the kingdom, and the power, and the glory.

In Jesus' name,
Amen

Worship:
"Hungry"
"Change My Heart Oh God"
"What a Friend We Have in Jesus"

Defining Moment . . . The Bema

Judges had their place in Corinth: it was at the bema. Literally, it was a raised platform where citizens stood to appear before officials. Bema is the Greek word for 'judgment seat,' and it appears several times in the New Testament:

- Jesus was tried by Pilate at Jerusalem's bema (Matthew 27:19).
- Paul was tried at Corinth's bema (Acts 18:12–17).
- Paul appeared before Procurator Porcias Festus at Caesarea's bema (Acts 25:1–12).

As believers, we, too, will appear at Heaven's Bema seat for believers. Paul tells us in Romans 14:10 that *"We will all stand before God's judgment seat."* However, since Romans 8:1 also tells us that *"there is now no condemnation for those who are in Christ Jesus,"* we will not be appearing at the bema to pay for sins. Christ has already done that for us. We will be judged and rewarded on what we have done with what God gave us *after* we received His free gift of Salvation, by our works. (Nonbelievers will be judged at a different bema.)

Each one of us has been given time, treasure, and talents that are intended to build up the Kingdom of God. They are meant to edify the Church and the people in the Church. How often we innocently use what God has given us for *His* Glory, but instead, use His gifts for *our* comfort, pride, or image. You name it, we have misused it.

Journal Time:

What has God given you that He wants you now to use specifically for *His* purposes? Take a few moments and let God reveal to you those things that He wants you to begin using for Kingdom purposes.

Share Time:

Share with the group the things that God whispered to you, asking you to invest them for *His* Kingdom purposes. What are they? What does He want you to do with them? What have you already experienced as an outcome of being faithful to Him in this area?

Prayer:

Father God,

Thank You so much for all the gifts You have given us. We confess that we have used them at times for our own glory instead of for Your purposes. Right here, right now, we ask You to help us commit to purposing the things You have given us to build Your Kingdom to be used as You intended, Lord. While Your will is for us to have an abundant life and enjoy what You have given us, You also ask us to use those things as You intended: to build Your church and Your people. Thank You, ahead of time, for how You are going to help us change our ways and act on what You have revealed to us today. We cannot wait to see what You are going to do in us and through us as we are cheerfully obedient to Your direction in this area. We love You, and want to love others for You.

In Jesus' name,

Amen

Worship:
  "Father, I Adore You"
  "Take My Life"

DELPHI

Historical Significance:

Ancient Greeks considered Delphi on the slopes of Mount Parnassus, a landscape of unparalleled and majestic beauty, to be the sacred center ("Omphalos," meaning navel) of the world. This place, where heaven and earth met, was where man was closest to god. In Greek mythology, it was the place where the two eagles Zeus sent in opposite directions eventually met, and the center of worship of Zeus's son, Apollo. ("Med" from the word "Mediterranean" also means middle of the earth).

Delphi is the home of the Sanctuary of Apollo and the world-renowned "Delphic oracle." The oracle was a spiritual experience where Apollo's spirit would be asked for advice. "Oracle" refers to both the pronouncement and the person. The oracle was controlled by the priests who did the interpreting. They were generally politically conservative and favorable to the powerful Persians when responding to questions from the city-states. The oracle did not usually take questions from individuals. The answers were often ambiguous, requiring the petitioner to know themselves.

There were no residents in Delphi, as it was not a city but the center of Greco-Roman religion. Greco-Roman religion was about the *holiness of beauty* (represented by harmony with the gods, world, community, and self) versus the Judeo-Christian religion's focus on the *beauty of holiness* (represented by living distinctively different lives through holy law).

Each city-state had a treasury building, trying to one-up the others with their treasures inside. After decision-making shifted to the Roman Senate in the late second century BC, the treasuries were stripped and sent to Rome. There is an unexcavated hippodrome in the valley, covered by olive trees.

What to See:

Delphi is a day trip, 120 miles northwest of Athens; Greece's most popular **archaeological site** after the Athens Acropolis. Leaving the shops and cafes, make your way along the Sacred Way to the ancient site where you can see the well-preserved, 5,000 seat, fourth century theater. The theater is behind the **Temple or Sanctuary of Apollo,** with the world-renowned Delphic oracle. Notice how the entire base of the Athenian Treasury is covered with inscriptions mostly made by ex-slaves witnessing their freedom. The 7,000-seat hippodrome/stadium up above is the best preserved in all of Greece. See also the gymnasium and the stoas.

The recently renovated **Delphi Archaeological Museum** includes a rare, fifth century, life-size bronze charioteer from the Temple of Apollo, and an inscription placing governor Gallio in Corinth 51–52 AD, proving Claudius's letter referred to in Acts. Apollo has a feminine look, while Athena has a masculine look. No flash photography or posing with statues is allowed. Delphi is quite a beautiful site, overlooking the Gulf of Corinth and a valley of olive and cypress trees.

The first (Doric) stone temple was the home of Pythia, who pronounced prophesies to be translated for the people by the priests. It was destroyed by fire in 548 BC and rebuilt.

Defining Moment . . . The Theater in Delphi

The ancient Greeks believed that Delphi was a holy, set apart place where they could hear the gods. They sought prophecy over their lives from the different spiritual entities that they believed existed and had power. Two thousand years later, little remains of the "gods" that they went to for guidance. Only the immutable Word of God has lasted throughout the centuries.

We can think of the ancient Greek ways as unsophisticated and see ourselves as so much wiser than they were. We would never put our trust in some invisible god that was not the real deal. We know the Lord. The enemy, however, is constantly attempting to deceive us to get us to put our trust in things of *this* world instead of in our Lord. We get tempted to put too much of our trust in things by gratification through relationships, by secure finances, by shopping excessively, or by overeating. We should trust none of these things to bring us what we *really* need, but we unwisely turn to them all the time, trusting in them to give us what, in reality, only God can deliver. Only our one true God is to be trusted to guide us and bless us with what is real, true, and lasting.

Make a decision to invest and trust in those things with eternal value, that are not fleeting. Imagine being alive in the South right before the Civil War and having hundreds of thousands of Confederate Notes, the currency of the time. You are extremely wealthy. Now imagine you have a crystal ball and can see that, in a matter of a few years, those notes will be completely worthless after the South loses the war. They were not even as valuable as the paper they were printed on. How will you invest your Notes, knowing that they will be worth nothing? The same can be asked for what we invest in and trust in as believers in God today. Indeed, when we pass on, we will have "Notes" that are valuable today, but will be worthless in Eternity—unless we invest them in something that lasts.

Delphi is a reminder that we also can get caught up in ritual, repetitive, religious performance today.

Journal Time:

Take a few moments and ask God to reveal to you anything that you are putting your trust in that is unworthy. Ask Him for the gift of repentance to completely let go of that "thing" and leave it here for good.

Share Time:

Share with the group a time when you put your trust in something that was not lasting, and the consequences that resulted from that. Is there anything in your life that you want to leave here in Delphi that has become a thing you have trusted in, instead of trusting in your God? Leave it here with the rest of the gods that have no power.

Prayer:

Lord Jesus,

Thank You for being eternal. Thank You for pointing the way to what is lasting, and revealing to us those things that will disappear over time, that really have no power. Please, Lord, open our eyes and show us the things in our lives that we are trusting in, like money, possessions, relationships, or addictions, and make a way for us to leave those things right here, in Delphi, and to look to You for our every need instead. We are surrendering to You and Your power to give us wisdom and discernment to follow You and Your everlasting ways, and to renounce those things that are not of You. We praise You and worship You for the one, true, eternal God that You are.

In Jesus' name,

Amen

Worship:

"I Lift My Eyes Up"

"I Am Trusting Thee Lord Jesus"

METEORA

Historical Significance:

Southwest of Berea in western Thessaloniki, on the drive south to Delphi, you will see a remarkable rock forest—huge, iron-gray, impregnable towers—with tranquil Byzantine monasteries on their tops. These Cenobitic monasteries date from the eleventh century and sit precariously on the top of cliffs, 1,300 feet above the Peneios River Valley floor. Hermits began living alone in caves in the cliffs, and later formed communities living in wooden shelters here in the ninth century. Meteora means "suspended in air." A windlass was used to haul supplies and people up and down the steep sides in nets made of rope. Today they use a cable car.

What to See:

Six of the original twenty-four monasteries remain, each with about a dozen monks or nuns who work for eight hours, pray and meditate for eight hours, and sleep for eight hours. You can visit the **Holy Monastery of Great Meteoron** (a.k.a. the Monastery of the Transfiguration) with its kitchen, church (with icons of the apostles and scenes such as Pentecost), workshop, ossuary (a collection of the skulls of the brothers), Independence Museum, and Martyr's Hall, dedicated to John the Baptist, featuring numerous Byzantine icons depicting various means of martyrdom (a reminder that our faith comes to us through the blood of the martyrs.) Martyr means "witness"—we are all called to be His witnesses, His ambassadors.

There are hundreds of steps, first down and then up, to get in and out. (Side note: a scene from the James Bond film "*For Your Eyes Only*" was shot here). Women visitors must wear long skirts (which they will lend you to wear over slacks or shorts) and cover their shoulders.

Defining Moment . . . The Holy Monastery of Great Meteoron

Because the Turkish invasion drove monks further and further away, they sought refuge in the inaccessible rock cliffs of Meteora. They built a way to set themselves apart to worship and focus on God.

In the fast-paced lives we live, we, too, need a refuge to get away to: a safe, quiet place to sit still before God and listen to His voice. Where is the safe haven in your life that you use to get away and have alone time with God, free from the demands of your everyday life?

Journal Time:

Take a few moments and be still before God. Ask Him to help you remember times when you could hear His voice through your heart. If you have never heard His voice, ask Him for that gift and to show you how to be still and listen.

Share Time:

Share with the group your experience in getting to a quiet place before the Lord where you can "be still" before Him. Has anything remarkable happened in any of your quiet times with Him that you would like to share? Is He saying anything to you now?

Prayer:

Father God,

Thank You for the blessed lives that we have and all of the opportunities that are presented to us while we live in this world. Father, please give us the tenacity and commitment to get away to a quiet place, just like Jesus did, and hear Your voice often. We long to set ourselves apart from this world in a safe, quiet haven and just be still before You. We want two-way communication with You, both to hear and be heard. Please, Lord, help us to commit to those sweet times of devoting all of our attention to You and all the wonder and awe we feel toward You. Give us rich times of worship where we remember who You are on a daily basis. Most of all, whisper to us in that gentle way of Yours, guiding us to practice Your will in this world. We want Your will more than anything else, Lord. Thank You.

In Jesus' name,
Amen

Worship:
"He Knows My Name"
"I Need Thee Every Hour"

PHILIPPI

Historical Significance:

Today, all that remains of the once leading city of Macedonia is an archaeological site along both sides of Highway 12, nine miles northwest of Kavala, next to Krenides. Philippi was located at the eastern end of the Via Egnatia, an important Roman trade route due to the neighboring gold mines in the mountains to its west, and a strategic military route between the Adriatic and the Aegean. Its wealth was reflected in many monuments for a relatively small urban area. The population was about 40,000 in Paul's time.

Alexander the Great's father, the ruthless militarist Philip II of Macedon, rebuilt it after capturing it in 360 BC, and renamed it after himself. The Romans captured it in 168 BC, but its importance waned when its gold ran out.

In 42 BC, another ruthless militarist, Octavius (or Octavian), later known as Augustus Caesar, and another Roman general, Mark Antony, overcame Julius Caesar's assassins, Brutus and Cassius, in the Battle of Philippi, on the plains outside its western wall. Philippi became the center of a large, prosperous Roman colony with many veterans of the battle given land. It includes the port of Neapolis; Kavala today. Roman colonists tried to live like they were in Rome, just as Christians try to live like we are in Heaven, our true home.

On his second missionary journey after receiving the vision to come to Macedonia, Paul sailed to Neapolis, twenty years after the Resurrection, with Timothy, Silas, and Luke (who had joined them at Troas). With favorable winds, they made the 150-mile crossing in just two days, versus five days on their return. After walking the ten miles inland from the port, Paul would have normally headed straight to the synagogue to preach, but there was none, as a minyan (required ten-man quorum) was lacking. On the Sabbath, women prayed down by the river to the west.

Around 50–49 BC, Philippi was the first European city where Paul preached. He stayed for several weeks after landing in Neapolis. Philippi also had the first European converts, Lydia, a half Gentile, half Jewish merchant from Thyatira in Asia Minor, and her household. They were baptized a mile outside the city gate down by the Gangites River. As Thyatira was in the province of Lydia, it is possible that may not even be her actual name. Lydia sold cloth treated with an expensive purple dye that would not fade in the sun; the color of royalty. She invited them to stay in her home, which is most likely where the new church met as well.

When Paul healed a possessed slave girl who foretold the future, her greedy owners had Silas and him arrested and tore their clothes; they then beat them with rods and imprisoned them. Singing praise hymns, and choosing not to escape after a midnight earthquake opened the doors and freed their chains, their behavior touched the jailer so profoundly that he and his household converted. After they were freed the next morning, Paul refused to leave until the magistrates came to apologize for arresting and flogging a Roman citizen without a trial.

They moved on to Thessaloniki, leaving behind Luke, Lydia, the jailer, and the slave girl, but Paul returned a number of times and sent an epistle (Philippians) to them from his imprisonment in Rome. It is deeply affectionate and appreciative, dealing with some problems there, encouraging them to stay faithful, thanking them for sending Epaphroditus to him. He wrote 2 Corinthians from here. Note that he chose not to declare himself a citizen *before* the flogging—they likely remembered this when years later, again amidst prison suffering, he wrote in his letter "Rejoice in the Lord always." The church at Philippi was a strong supporter of Paul's ministry.

The town never fully recovered from the total destruction of a huge earthquake in the early seventh century. There was a strong Byzantine fortress in the hill above Philippi that was manned from the tenth through fifteenth centuries. It was later abandoned due to the many earthquakes in the area.

What to See:
This is the most important archaeological site of what was eastern Macedonia. The site is on both sides of Highway 12. Begin to the south, across from the

ticket booth, on to a parallel piece of the Via Egnatia, the main east–west road built by the Romans. You can also see crosses, two major basilicas, the forum, dating from after Paul's time, the agora, the Greek theater, the Acropolis, and the Basilica of St. Paul, the oldest church dedicated to him. Dating from 343 AD, it has a mosaic floor inscription "Pavlos" in yellow, dedicated to Paul's Macedonian call. As in Ephesus, there are carvings in the pavement of a circle with lines through it like pizza slices, in which you can spell out "ΙΧΘΥΣ" which means "Jesus Christ, God's Son, Savior."

They also have uncovered a **bema** where Paul and Silas would have been flogged before the rulers. There is a motocross track over the unexcavated area today. Seventy percent of the inscriptions discovered are in Latin, since the Philippians had sided with the Romans and received colony status. There is also a **cemetery**, since tradition held that Lydia was buried here and people wanted to be buried near the saints.

On the north side of the highway, on a rocky ledge above the town's main road, is a very small Byzantine structure called **St. Paul's Prison**, but it is actually just a cistern transformed into a Christian basilica. In the ancient city, a crypt exists that is possibly the actual prison where Silas and Paul were held. There is a restored fourth century theater which hosts plays each August.

The **Baptistery of Lydia**, an Orthodox chapel (with great acoustics) is a two-minute drive further, commemorating Lydia's baptism. It is a quiet, riverside, open-air baptistery ideal for baptism renewals and singing today. It is upriver (therefore, it is clean) on the Gangites. The chapel's ceiling depicts Jesus' baptism with the Holy Spirit and heavenly hosts. There is a stained glass behind the altar of Paul and Lydia.

Nearby, through the Macedonian Plain, is **Kavala (ancient Neapolis),** Greece's most picturesque port on the mainland where Paul landed with Timothy and Silas, on the coast of Thrace. There is a modern mosaic just up from the waterfront behind a Greek Orthodox church depicting Paul's vision in Troas and arrival (with Acts 16:9–12 translated into four languages on it); the Roman aqueduct (that carried water up to the citadel on the hill); and the ruins of the Acropolis. There is a small monastery right off the highway dedicated to Silas, Paul's companion.

Scripture:
>   Acts 16:11–40; 19:22, 20:2–6
>   2 Corinthians 2:13, 7:5
>   Philippians
>   1 Thessalonians 2:2
>   definingmomentsbook.com/resources

Defining Moment . . . The Baptistery of Lydia

> *On the Sabbath we went outside the city gate to the river, where we expected to find a place of prayer. We sat down and began to speak to the women who had gathered there. One of those listening was a woman from the city of Thyatira named Lydia, a dealer in purple cloth. She was a worshiper of God. The Lord opened her heart to respond to Paul's message. When she and the members of her household were baptized, she invited us to her home. "If you consider me a believer in the Lord," she said, "come and stay at my house." And she persuaded us*
> (Acts 16:13–15).

Lydia was a woman of great influence. She was wealthy and well connected through her business dealings. Imagine being in her social position and coming to know Jesus as her Savior. She must not have been able to contain herself, since her entire household chose Him as Lord also. Lydia was quick to use the spiritual gift of hospitality that the Lord had given her. She invited Paul to stay in her home, and it is speculated the Church also met there. When Paul got out of jail, it was Lydia that took him in.

Journal Time:
Spend some quiet time with God reflecting on the spiritual gifts that God has given *you*. Do you know what they are? What would it look like to pour them out on others as Lydia did? How have others responded to having your gifts poured out on them? How do you respond when another's gift is poured out onto you?

Share Time:

Share with the group one of the spiritual gifts you have identified in your life, and how God is calling you to use it now.

Prayer:

Lord,

Thank You for pouring Your spiritual gifts out on us so that we may pour out onto others. Thank You for sending Your Holy Spirit that manifests Your gifts of wisdom, extraordinary faith, teaching, helping, and encouraging giving and mercy in us, along with so many other gifts like hospitality and discernment. We have been given these gifts to build up and strengthen Your people, Your church, just as Lydia did. Lord, please show each one of us how You want us to use the gifts we have been given to Your Glory.

Please keep us from being prideful about the fruit that we experience from these gifts, and keep our eyes on You, knowing that all good things come from You. Help us to be good stewards of the precious combination of gifts that are unique to each one of us. Let us each encourage each other to use these gifts to their fullest.

In Jesus' name,

Amen

Worship:

"The Potter's Hand"

"I Need Thee Every Hour"

Defining Moment . . . St. Paul's Prison

The crowd joined in the attack against Paul and Silas, and the magistrates ordered them to be stripped and beaten with rods. After they had been severely flogged, they were thrown into prison, and the jailer was commanded to guard them carefully. When he received these orders, he put them in the inner cell and fastened their feet in the stocks. About midnight, Paul and Silas were praying and singing hymns to God, and the other prisoners were listening to them. Suddenly there was such a violent earthquake that the foundations of the prison were shaken. At once, all the prison doors flew open, and everyone's chains came loose.

> *The jailer woke up, and when he saw the prison doors open, he drew his sword and was about to kill himself because he thought the prisoners had escaped. But Paul shouted, "Don't harm yourself! We are all here!"*
>
> *The jailer called for lights, rushed in, and fell trembling before Paul and Silas. He then brought them out and asked, 'Sirs, what must I do to be saved?'*
>
> *They replied, "Believe in the Lord Jesus, and you will be saved—you and your household." Then they spoke the word of the Lord to him and to all the others in his house.*
>
> *At that hour of the night, the jailer took them and washed their wounds; then immediately he and all his household were baptized. The jailer brought them into his house and set a meal before them; he was filled with joy because he had come to believe in God—he and his whole household*
>
> (Acts 16:22–34).

Journal Time:

Spend some time remembering when you have had a similar experience in your life where you could have gotten away with something, but you chose to "do the right thing" instead. How do you think others were impacted? Ask God to reveal any situations to you that currently need to be addressed where you need to correct your course to reflect who God is in your life.

Share Time:

Share with your group an experience where others observed how you live your life (or how you have handled a situation with grace) and wanted to know more about your decision and/or God? Or, share how someone *else's* choice to "do the right thing" affected *your* walk with God in a positive way. Are there any changes you would like to make to the way you are handling current situations?

Prayer:

Holy Spirit,

How our souls yearn for You to give us direction on a constant basis. There are so many times that our circumstances seem to suggest we go a certain way, but only when You reveal the will of the Father to us can we make the decision that honors the Kingdom. Please help us to practice Your presence in a way that enables us to know God's Will in the heat of the moment, as Paul did when he chose not to escape prison.

Give us the courage and conviction to lead our lives as living testimonies to our Lord and Savior, no matter what the cost. Finally, we pray for the people around us that see Your Spirit at work in our lives. We pray that they would respond as the jailer and his family did, inviting You into their lives and becoming integral parts of Your Kingdom.

In Jesus' name we pray,

Amen

Worship:

"Lord, I Give You My Heart"
"Blessed Assurance"

PORT OF NEOPOLIS (MODERN-DAY KAVALA)

Defining Moment . . . The Port of Neapolis (modern-day Kavala)

Paul and his companions traveled throughout the region of Phrygia and Galatia, having been kept by the Holy Spirit from preaching the word in the province of Asia. When they came to the border of Mysia, they tried to enter Bithynia, but the Spirit of Jesus would not allow them to. So they passed by Mysia and went down to Troas. During the night Paul had a vision of a man of Macedonia standing and begging him, 'Come over to Macedonia and help us.' After Paul had seen the vision, we got ready at once to leave for Macedonia, concluding that God had called us to preach the Gospel to them. From Troas we put out to sea and sailed straight for Samothrace, and the next day we went on to Neapolis
(Acts 16:6–11).

God used many different ways to guide Paul during his journeys. From direct visitation on the road to Damascus (Acts 9:1–9), to visions given to others (Ananias in Acts 9:10–16), to visions he gave directly to Paul (see above), the Holy Spirit was constantly keeping him on the right path. How does God guide *you*? How does he invite you to hear His voice? Henry Blackaby, in *"Experiencing God,"* says that there are four ways to hear God's will for your life:
- God speaks through the Bible.
- God speaks through prayer.
- God speaks through circumstances.
- God speaks through other believers.

Journal Time:
Ask God to speak to you right now. Then be still, do not speak to Him, just wait for *His* thoughts to come into your heart. It will not be an audible voice.

Whenever we hear from God, it always should be tested against Scripture and confirmed. God never contradicts His Word.

Share Time:
Share with your group how you hear God guiding you. What is it that He is whispering to you, be it encouragement, direction, or discernment?

Prayer:
Lord God,

We thank You that we are not left in this world alone to make our decisions, but that You have given us several ways to hear Your guidance. We trust Your ways over our ways, Lord, and ask that You would impart to us, just as You did to Paul, Your divine will for our lives. Please conform our will to Your will. Please give us ears to hear and eyes to see when You use Your Word, prayer, circumstances, or the counsel of other believers to confirm Your direction to us.

We trust You alone, Lord. Thank You for never letting us down and for always loving us.

In Jesus' name,

Amen

Worship:
"Be the Center"

"My Faith Looks Up to Thee"

THESSALONIKI (THESSALONICA)

———

Historical Significance:

Thessaloniki was founded in 315 BC by the king of Macedonia, Cassander of Macedon (Kassandros), one of Alexander the Great's four general successors. He named it in honor of his wife, Thessalonike, half-sister of Alexander the Great. It was built in the form of an amphitheater at the head of the Thermaic Gulf. It was a crossroad between east and west (Italy), the Balkans (Danube) and the Aegean. Thessaloniki prospered as the key capital city of northern Greece (Macedonia) under Hellenistic, then Roman (the capital of the Roman province of Macedonia), then Greek rule—though always under threat from conquerors. Cicero, the exiled Roman orator, lived there 58–57 BC. Pompey's army was quartered there in 49 BC, hiding from Julius Caesar.

On his second missionary journey in 49–50 AD, after he was beaten and jailed in Philippi, Paul traveled with Timothy and Silas, leaving Luke behind in Philippi, 100 miles over several days to get here and stayed for at least three weeks. Again, he had great fruit preaching to Jews in the synagogues and to the Gentiles. Again, just like with Jesus, the Jewish authorities resented his popularity and feared the Roman authorities' response to the people's reverence for another "king."

The Jewish rioters could not find Paul and Silas, so they dragged their host, Jason, from his home, accusing them all of defying the emperor by speaking of another king, one greater than the emperor. Again, Paul's friends helped them leave town quickly for Berea, which was thought to be safer. The Gospel was then spread east and west along the Via Egnatia. There are 365 churches in Thessaloniki today, one for every day of the year. The earliest books written of the New Testament are thought to be 1 and 2 Thessalonians, penned by Paul shortly after departing during the second missionary journey, encouraging them to serve as a model Christian community.

Demetrios was a Roman military officer around 300 AD, who was arrested at the age of twenty for his faith by the emperor Galerius. Galerius promised him freedom if Demetrios's champion (Nestor) killed the emperor's champion. Nester won, but Galerius martyred them both, trying to eradicate the growing church. Instead, Constantine embraced the faith after a vision. It is said that Demetrios was speared in the Roman bath and a spring came forth.

Thessaloniki flourished under the Byzantine empire. Repeatedly invaded, it was returned to the Greeks in 1913 after occupations by Slavs, Saracens, Crusaders and Ottoman Turks. The White Tower (1535–36) was known as the "Tower of Blood" during the Ottoman reign due to the many executions there: it was later painted white to cleanse it. A major fire in 1917 wiped much of the city out. The Nazis occupied it during World War II. Today it has 900,000 residents, a major university, great nightlife, and tree-lined streets with piazzas, cafes, and shops.

What to See:
Modern Thessaloniki, over 2,300 years old, the second largest city and port in Greece, is served by frequent, less-than-an-hour flights from Athens. It features sea views, tree-lined streets, Turkish-influenced food, and is an excellent base for side trip explorations. Most of the ancient sites are near the city center within walking distance of each other, including the old city **ramparts**, the triumphal **Arch of Galerius** (303 AD), the landmark, round **White Tower** on the waterfront to the side of the **monument of Alexander the Great,** and the **Archaeological Museum of Thessaloniki.** Behind the **Byzantine Museum**, baths, theater, the Roman Market, city walls, Chain Tower, Citadel and Byzantine churches.

The Arch of Galerius, which started the Via Egnatia (a strategic artery of the Roman empire), has a Rotunda (resting place) that was a church, then a mosque and now a museum (and church on holidays). Follow the massive Byzantine wall to the citadel for a panoramic view back to the city.

A street today called Egnatia Street is built on top of the ancient road, as is the entire city, so there are limited archaeological excavations to view. However, they are rebuilding the ruins of the Roman forum (225–150 BC).

There is also a vibrant open marketplace nearby the forum, offering goods similar to those of Paul's day. There were shops in use here until the middle of the fourteenth century. You can walk directly down to Aristotle Square on the waterfront where there are many cafes with outdoor sofas—they let you linger as long as you want over a beverage, day or night.

Also: See the **House of Jason**; the **Roman Agora** where Paul preached; **Aristotle's Square**; statue of Alexander the Great; fabulous view from upper town. The site where **Monastery of Vlatadon** was built is considered where Jason's house was and where Paul stayed.

(Hagia, "holy") **Sophia and Agios Demetrios** (a.k.a, Dimitrios), dating from the fifth century AD, is the largest and one of the most beautiful basilicas (meaning "royal") in Greece. It has the actual tomb downstairs of the patron saint of Thessaloniki, St. Demetrios. The site began as a small shrine and curative spring but kept getting larger. The 1917 fire burned the wooden beams and collapsed the roof. Today the beams are concrete painted to look like wood. There is a silver casket under plexiglass where people insert prayer notes. Valuable mosaics and frescoes are found here as well.

Admission to all churches is free and usually best in the mornings due to irregular afternoon closures.

Not too far outside the city are the (three) **Royal Tombs of Macedonia at Vergina**, the original capital of the ancient Macedonian empire, featuring the fully intact 338 BC burial tomb (with a sunburst on top, the Macedonian flag) of king Philip II, Alexander the Great's father. The tomb was discovered in 1977 and opened to the public in 1996. Displaying the family's riches, it is one of Greece's highlights, comparable to the king Tut treasures in Cairo. No pictures are allowed inside the museum.

They marked their burial sites with tumuli, mounds of earth or stones. This mound is 120 yards wide by 40 feet high. The key tomb was discovered in 1997 through its roof and is not open to viewing. The massive temple-like façade, featuring mighty Doric (straight, unadorned) columns, a fresco of Alexander the Great and Philip II hunting lion and wild boar, and unopened marble doors, is all that can be viewed of this tomb. There is a second major tomb, Tomb of Persephone, possibly that of Cleopatra Eurydice, Philip II's last wife. The burial place of Alexander the Great is unknown, as he died en route home from his battles. There are also three other smaller tombs including the small prince's tomb.

Philip II's first wife, Olympias, was threatened by his second wife, Audata, a Macedonian. He was killed in 336 BC in the theater at Amphipolis at the instigation of either Olympias, Alexander, or both. His bones would have been washed in wine after partial cremation on a massive funeral pyre ("purifying" the mortal flesh). They were then laid on an ivory and gold funeral bed and placed inside a marble sarcophagus, covered with a gold oak leaf wreath and sunburst.

The museum also contains elaborate artifacts, royal purple and gold cloth and Macedonian art (showing perspective, movement, and emotion) whose style was then lost through the Byzantine era until the Renaissance.

Scripture:
Acts 17:1–19; 20:4; 27:2
Philippians 4:16
1 and 2 Thessalonians
2 Timothy 4:10
definingmomentsbook.com/resources

Defining Moment . . . The Roman Forum (Ancient Agora) of Thessaloniki

Thessaloniki was "life in the fast lane" in Biblical times. It was a big commercial and military city on the Via Egnatia, a major Roman road that connected Asia Minor (Turkey) with the Adriatic Sea. With the number of different value systems that a major crossroads like Thessaloniki experienced, we can only imagine what positive and negative effects were imported and exported. Paul talks about the community in Thessaloniki becoming a "model to all believers." Greeks and Romans had vastly different moral standards than Jews and Christians, so they regarded chastity as an unreasonable restriction. What a culture clash. Wait. It sounds like the world we live in today. As believers, we know and hopefully choose the ways of God, but we live among a majority of people that choose the ways of the world.

Journal Time:

Spend a few moments alone and ask God what His plan is for you to keep you set apart from the world and reflecting God's ways to those around you. How can you protect yourself and your family from the world, but still live in the world as His ambassadors?

Share Time:

Share with the group ways that you reflect God's values to the world that have glorified Him. How does your life reflect God's holiness now? Tell the group about any changes you want to make in the future.

Prayer:

Lord,

Thank You that greater is He that lives in us than he that lives in the world. Please use the Holy Spirit in our lives to gently warn us when we are veering off into worldly ways that seem innocent to our world. Encourage us when we are reflecting the light of Christ into our surroundings. Help us to be lights in this world, that men may see our good deeds and praise our Father in Heaven.

Help us to influence the world instead of being influenced by the world. Give us ways to live our lives set apart and holy for Your name's sake. We can only do this with Your help and power, and we are depending on Your guidance so that we can do Your will and glorify Your name.

In Jesus' name,

Amen

Worship:

"Here I Am to Worship"

"Holy, Holy, Holy"

GREEK AND MEDITTERANEAN ISLANDS

CRETE

Historical Significance:

Crete, the largest and most southerly of the Greek isles (fifty miles southeast), and fifth largest in the Mediterranean on the southern border of the Aegean Sea, is 156 miles long with 8,000-foot mountain peaks. Crete's history dates back to the 7th millennium BC. The advanced Minoan civilization (Bronze Age, 2000–1200 BC) was the first civilization in Europe. Crete was part of the Roman empire, Byzantine empire, Venetian republic and the Ottoman empire, then an autonomous state and now part of Greece. In the Old Testament, it is referred to as Caphtor.

In the New Testament, Crete is known as where Paul stopped in 59–60 AD for several days as a prisoner en route to Rome prior to the storm and his shipwreck on Malta, after the ship's owner and captain concluded the port of Phoenix to the northwest would offer better shelter for the winter. The harbor of Kaloi Limenes (Good Harbor; Fair Havens in the New Testament) is beautiful, but offers little beyond a small, white chapel on a hill overlooking the bay dedicated to Paul, which is built over the ruins of an older church. Before the chapel to the west is a cave traditionally viewed as where Paul stayed.

Paul sent Titus (perhaps his longest companion) here from Rome to be Crete's first bishop.

What to See:

The impressive reconstruction of the **Palace of Knossos**, three miles south of the port capital of Heraklion, is not a Biblical site. In 1900, Sir Arthur Evans discovered the site and spent thirty-five years working on the oft-criticized project. The Minoans inhabited Greece between 3000–1400 BC. Their civilization was based on sea power and sea trade. The Palace was built in 2000 BC, destroyed 300 years later by an earthquake, rebuilt immediately, and destroyed again around 1500 BC. There are ruins of Europe's first amphitheater, the earliest known drainage system, and the first flush toilet.

In mythology, king Minos was the ruler of Knossos, born from Zeus and Europa. His son was the Minotaur—half bull and half man.

Heraklion (population over 100,000) has a great archaeological museum and the Church of St. Titus, a church turned mosque restored to a church, where you can view a crown with Titus's skull inside, and icons of scenes from Paul's life. Nearly three miles of Venetian walls and seven ramparts still stand today as the most important fortifications in Greece.

The largest site is **Gortyna** (also Gortyn or Gortya), a major Roman city with city walks six miles long back then. Thirty miles southwest of Heraklion, it features the ruins of the sixth century Basilica of St. Titus, a Greek convert who stayed to minister after Paul left on another visit here; another is **Phaistos.**

Scripture:

Genesis 10:14
Deuteronomy 2:23
1 Chronicles 1:12
Acts 2:11, 27:7–21
Galatians 12:3
Titus 1:5, 12
definingmomentsbook.com/resources

Defining Moment . . . Fair Havens Coast (Kaloi Limenes)

Integrity and the lack of it is as old as humanity. Cretans during Paul's time had a reputation for being liars. The island was rumored to be a base for pirates. A Cretan poet named Epimenides supposedly labeled his fellow Cretans "liars." Paul refers to this poet in a letter he wrote to Titus, his colleague who was in Crete, to get the churches organized both structurally and doctrinally. After Paul mentions *"talkers and deceivers,"* he says in Titus 1:12, *"One of Crete's own prophets has said it: 'Cretans are always liars, evil brutes, lazy gluttons.'"* It is not surprising that, at the beginning of this letter, Paul talks about *"God, who does not lie,"* as if that was something that had to be explicitly stated. Thank goodness we have a God who does not lie. Humanity, however, is a different story.

The first lie in the Bible occurs when Satan tells Eve she will be like God if she eats the forbidden fruit. We can expect lies from Satan. God's Word tells us Satan is *"the father of lies."* The problems begin when we start believing these lies and then start authoring our own deceit. The second recorded lie comes in Genesis 4:9. Cain has just killed Abel over jealousy, and when God asks Cain, *"Where is your brother, Abel?"* Cain replies, *"I do not know."* Cain knew that God was all-knowing—how could he possibly try to trick God with a lie? But do not *we* do the same thing at times?

Journal Time:

Ask God to reveal to you a time, either currently or in the past, where you lied to yourself about a situation, and also lied to God about it. Have you asked for the gift of repentance from God, to choose His direction for that part of your life?

Share Time:

Share with the group a time that you were not truthful with God, or even yourself, how you came into the truth and acknowledged this truth to God. What difference did it make in your life? Is there any part of your life in which you are struggling with truth now that you would like to change?

Prayer:

Father God,

We know how much You hate lying. It is detestable to You. We confess and repent of the lies that we have told others, ourselves and, most importantly, You. We ask You to work in us to keep us from exaggerating, stretching the truth, and also hiding the truth from others for any reason. Lord, we renounce lies and we cling fast to Your truth, instead. Please bless us abundantly with Your precious truth, and use Your Holy Spirit to encounter us when we are walking in untruth. Thank You for sending Your Son to take away all of our sins—even lying—and keep us walking in Your light.

In Jesus' holy name,

Amen

Worship:
   "Be the Strength of My Life"
   "Just As I Am"

CYPRUS

Historical Significance:

Cyprus has always been a target for invasions as a prime naval stepping stone in the Mediterranean, 250 miles from Egypt, 60 miles from Syria and only 40 miles from Turkey. Today, the island is split between the Turkish Muslim north (only considered an independent country by Turkey) and the Greek Christian south, with United Nations created Nicosia and Lefkosia in between, making it the sole divided capital city in the world after the Berlin wall fell. Unification is in the works though.

Northern Cyprus: Jews were not allowed after their revolt in 116 AD. **Salamis** was made the capital and called Constantia by the Byzantines. It was mostly destroyed by earthquakes in the fourth century and abandoned after Arab raids in the seventh century.

Salamis was the first stop for Barnabas (a native), his cousin, John Mark, and Paul on their first missionary journey, where there presumably were already some Christians. The site today is rather large and requires walking and driving around. A guide is needed due to few helpful markers.

Southern Cyprus: In the Old Testament (Numbers 24:24, Daniel 11:30; Ezekiel 27:6), Kittim refers to Kition. Kourion rests on top of a dramatic cliff with a great view of the sea.

Paphos, where Paul met with the Roman governor, Sergius Paulus, and recorded his first convert, is picturesque and popular, with a number of sites and ancient mosaics. This is where Paul blinded Paulus's sorcerer, Elymas the Magus, also called Bar-Jesus, in his first recorded miracle. An ancient inscription has been found in Rome of naming Paulus.

Some believe the missionaries crossed from Salamis to Paphos by land, others by sea. Paul never returned, but Barnabas (traditionally thought to be the first bishop) and John Mark did.

Scripture:
Isaiah 23:1
Ezekiel 27:6–7
Acts 4:36. 9:27, 11:19, 13:1, 4–12, 15:39, 21:3, 16, 27:4
definingmomentsbook.com/resources

Defining Moment . . . Any Port in Cyprus
Imagine ship travel in those days. It was a rough proposition to travel on a ship, between food and sanitary practices, let alone the safety of the vessels at that time. Yet Paul boarded ship after ship, tirelessly sailing—all for the sake of the Cross. There must have been times he was exhausted and wanted to just give up, but he kept doing what he might not have really wanted to do because he was led by the Holy Spirit. Paul was driven, but he was human. We sometimes venerate Paul to such an extent we forget he was just as sinful as you and me. He must have complained at times, must have been overwhelmed, and we know he even lost his temper at times. He was very blunt when he said in Romans 7:19 *"For I do not do the good I want to do, but the evil I do not want to do—this I keep on doing."*

Journal Time:
Ask God to reveal *one thing* to you that you keep doing that you really do not want to do anymore, that you *know* is outside God's will for you. Ask God to give you the gift of true repentance, so you can finish strong in that particular race.

Share Time:
Share with the group that one thing that you want to give up doing, because you know God has a better way for you. What is that better way?

Prayer:
Lord Jesus,
How we long to live in Your holiness! Lord, we confess that on a daily basis we do the very things that we do not want to do. On our own, we are powerless. But through You, Lord God, we can overcome anything. You have promised in

Your Word that there is no temptation that You will not give us a way out of. So, Lord, we lean into You, right now, depending on Your redemption, Your mercy, Your forgiveness, Your guidance, Your love and Your power to keep us from doing the things we do not want to do. Give us Your strength, Your truth, Your discernment and Your grace to do the things that we want to do for Your sake, no matter how overwhelming they seem.

In Jesus' name,
Amen

Worship:

"Here I am to Worship"
"Rock of Ages"

MALTA

Historical Significance:

Paul (the "spiritual father of Malta") was miraculously shipwrecked on the shores of Malta in 60 AD, pulled ashore by the natives. They thought he was a god when he did not die from the bite of a poisonous viper. After wintering here for three months, they sailed on the ten days to Rome.

Suleiman the Magnificent failed, despite intense battles by his great army, to conquer Malta and the Knights of the Hospital Order of St. John of Jerusalem in 1565. While some wished to relinquish the then vulnerable island, Jean Parisot de La Valette convinced the knights Hospitaller to stay and build a beautiful new city, indestructible by the infidels, Valetta. Aided by generous Christian European kings and princes, along with contributions by the knights and taxation on imported wheat and wine, "a city built by gentlemen for gentlemen" was born.

What to See:

St. John's Co-Cathedral in Valletta: this convent church, which looks more like a fort, was completed in 1573 for the Knights of the Hospital Order of St. John of Jerusalem. One had to trace nobility of all grandparents for four generations back to join the Knights, essentially a religious order established in Malta in 1530 that took vows of poverty, chastity, and obedience. The façade is more like a fort, but it has a beautiful Baroque interior.

The main altar was originally gilded in silver, and a silver monstrance was later stolen by Napoleon. There is a statue depicting John baptizing Jesus behind the altar, carved from a single massive block of marble. Each of the six sections of the vault has three paintings (directly on prepared stone) representing parts of John's life.

There are 375 marble graves of the knights and grandmasters, nine rich chapels, and the Oratorium, featuring the *Beheading of St. John* by Caravaggio.

The original flag was a white Cross on a red background—the Cross of peace on the blood-stained fields of battle. The eight-pointed Maltese cross (representing either the eight lands the knights came from, or the eight Beatitudes) came years later.

St. Paul's Shipwreck Church in Valetta: this church in the shape of a patriarchal cross was built in 1639 with a Baroque façade added circa 1885. Under the two belfries are statues of Peter and Paul. There are seven bells, eight small, domed chapels, silver altar façades, candlesticks, lamps, a seventeenth century organ, and forty marble and mosaic graves. Paintings depicting Paul's life cover the vault.

There is a statue atop the island overlooking **St. Paul's Bay** on the north shore.

Scripture:

Acts 27:41–28:11
definingmomentsbook.com/resources

Defining Moment . . . St. Paul's Shipwreck Church

Think about what it must have been like to be the Apostle Paul. People around you wanted healing in a time that there was no modern medical care, and people had little hope. When you came into town, people went into a frenzy. They were taking your handkerchief to lay on their sick friends, and people were actually getting healed. That is pretty heady stuff for a mere mortal. Paul knew it was not his own power that was healing people, but even so, it must have been pretty impressive. To get bitten by a venomous snake with no physical consequences must have blown Paul's mind.

Imagine that you were Paul in today's world. You could go to hospitals and heal the sick just by touching them. That would indeed impress upon you the glory of God. But Paul was *more* impressed by something else: God's Word. Throughout his letters, he referred to it again and again. He knew that God's Word was the real healing power that we have in this world, and nothing else is more powerful. He exhorted believers to preach it, know it, and defend it.

2 Timothy 3:16–4:2 tells us:

All Scripture is God-breathed and is useful for teaching, rebuking, correcting and training in righteousness, so that the servant of God may be thoroughly equipped for every good work. In the presence of God and of Christ Jesus, who will judge the living and the dead, and in view of His appearing and His Kingdom, I give you this charge: Preach the Word; be prepared in season and out of season; correct, rebuke and encourage—with great patience and careful instruction.

Often, in this world, we get so caught up in "doing" that we forget to immerse ourselves in God's Word. We become more impressed with God's provision and favor, and we forget that the way to get as close as possible to our Lord, on a daily basis, is through His Word. We are told in Hebrews 4:12, *"the Word of God is alive and active. Sharper than any double-edged sword, it penetrates even to dividing soul and spirit, joints and marrow; it judges the thoughts and attitudes of the heart."*

We have been given a powerful weapon in the Word of God. If we were totally conscious of its power, we would probably never put it down. Imagine if someone gave you a sword to carry around in this world, and you were assured it would protect you in *any* situation—physical, emotional, or spiritual. You would carry it everywhere. Well, we *have* been given that powerful weapon. It is amazing that God has entrusted to man something of such amazing power. But we also know that only those who know our Lord know how to understand this weapon, and, to unbelievers, it appears as foolishness. We read in 1 Corinthians 2:14 that *"the person without the Spirit does not accept the things that come from the Spirit of God but considers them foolishness, and cannot understand them because they are discerned only through the Spirit."*

Journal Time:

Think about how you interact with the Word of God. Reading it just to check it off your list for the day feels like drudgery, and does not impress God either. But depend on the Holy Spirit to reveal the meaning of God's Word specifically for your life, and His Word becomes more precious to us than anything in life.

Share Time:

Share with the group a time when you had an experience with God's Word that helped you through a situation. What was the verse, and what did God do in your life at the time? Is there a verse that God is giving you for any of the current challenges in your life?

Prayer:

Dear Lord God Almighty,

The mystery and wonder of Your Word is amazing to us! We are so grateful that You made a way for Your Word to overcome all odds and be available to us. Thank You, Lord, for Your generous and lavish love that You pour into us through Your Word. Thank You for the safety, protection, discernment, enlightenment and intimacy with Your Spirit that comes through the Bible. And thank You for sending Your Word in bodily form, through Jesus Christ. How we treasure our Jesus! Lord, please keep us in awe of Your Word and its power in our lives.

We confess that we become more caught up in the seen world than we do in the unseen power of Your Word at times, and we ask You for the gift of repentance. Set us right, dear One, and give us a righteous hunger for Your Word, revealed through Your Spirit. Keep the evil one far away from us, so that we do not fall into the trap of studying the Bible for the sake of knowledge alone. That attitude comes from legalism and the law, and we renounce it. Use Your Word to give us a greater knowing of who You are, that we will fall more deeply in love with You than ever.

In Jesus' name,

Amen

Worship:

"Thy Word is a Lamp Unto My Feet"

"Break Thou the Bread of Life"

PATMOS

Historical Significance:

Patmos is rocky and barren, the northwestern most island of the Dodecanese Islands (in the southern Sporades chain) in the Aegean Sea, forty miles from Turkey. It is part of Greece, only seven miles long by three miles wide, with two narrow isthmuses dividing the island into three sections. The port and commercial center is at Skala, with medieval Chora and small rural Kampos and Grikou being the other villages, a total population of only 2,500. While Patmos is one of a number of places to which Romans banished political prisoners, its charm and sacred feel are quite lovely.

Around 93–95 AD, the apostle John, son of Zebedee and Salome, was exiled from Ephesus at the age of eighty-three to this Roman penal colony for his faith. The exile was to last for one to three years under the realm of the Roman emperor Domitian (Domitianus), who emulated Nero by persecuting Christians throughout the empire with death or enslavement for not publicly recognizing his "divinity" through public sacrifices to his statues.

It is here that John the Divine dictated the book of Revelation (Apocalypse) after hearing the voice of God and likely had copied the other three Gospels, Acts, and the Epistles for Timothy to distribute to the Seven Churches. It is thought he first worked cutting stone in the state-owned marble quarry and then was put in a cave after he converted other inmates and guards. He was not killed, as the Ephesian Procurator feared riots if anything happened to this "Christian sorcerer." He returned to Ephesus, where he later died, after being released upon Domitian's death in 96 AD, when Trajan declared a general amnesty.

He had first encountered Jesus at his baptism by John the Baptist, who then told Andrew and him to now follow Jesus. He had been with Simon Peter's brother at Cana and in the Garden of Gethsemane and had run with Peter to the empty Tomb.

John spent his last months in Ephesus with Timothy and died as the last living disciple, the only one to die a natural death, though previously during the persecution of Domitian in Rome, they had tried to boil him in oil. Luke was still alive but had not been with Jesus. He was later crucified by the Romans in Achaia.

Imagine the Romans attending John's funeral (to make sure he was there!) and hearing *praises* to God!

The Gospel of John was the last of the four, the "essence Gospel," the shortest on Jesus' public ministry and the longest on Passion Week, the only one written from a Roman and Greek point of view, best known for John 3:16 ("*that whoever believes in Him*" i.e. , not just the Jews). It was written to Turkey, from Turkey.

Patmos was virtually abandoned for the seventh through the eleventh centuries.

What to See:

The majestic Byzantine **Monastery of St. John the Theologian** (aka the Divine) in the village of Chora was built in the style of a medieval fortress in 1092 by a Nicaean (İznik, Turkey) monk on one of the highest hills in the central part of the island, in the village of Chora, with an amazing view. It is run by the Greek Orthodox Church today.

The monastery consists of interconnecting courtyards, chapels, stairways, arcades, galleries, and roof terraces. It is on the site of an ancient temple of Artemis destroyed in the eleventh century. The main chapel is adjacent to the Chapel of the Theotokos, with priceless icons, manuscripts, and twelfth century frescoes.

A fifteen-minute walk downhill on cobblestones leads to the **Cave (Grotto) of the Apocalypse**, the traditional site where John penned Revelation, now located inside the Orthodox Monastery of the Apocalypse, a great place to sing worship songs. Today it is under statutory protection as a historical monument. There are silver niches in the wall believed to mark the pillow and ledge used as his desk along with a three-fold crack believed to be made by the voice of God to emphasize the honor of the Trinity. Go early or late to avoid tour groups.

Scripture:
> Revelation 1:9
> definingmomentsbook.com/resources

Defining Moment . . . The Cave (Grotto) of the Apocalypse

What John must have been thinking as our Lord revealed to him such overwhelming ideas. Who could John share these thoughts with? Who would understand them? It is all so rich and amazing, but how does he share this treasure with the body of believers? The thought may have gone through his head, *What if people think I have dreamed all of this*, but, when this "revelation" was compared with the ancient Scriptures, many parallels appeared. The book of Daniel supported much of what was revealed to John, lest anyone need to approve what John was sharing.

The same process can occur for believers today, even if it is not as intense as the scenes from the book of Revelation. God reveals thoughts and ideas to us to guide us, and if we test them against Scripture to validate them, we can be assured that the guidance is His.

Journal Time:

Think about a time where the Lord has revealed something to you that you had a hard time believing others in your life would understand, let alone believe. What Scripture supported the direction you were given? How did it all turn out?

Share Time:

Share with the group your experience of hearing God's voice. What did He say, and how did He say it? How did you confirm that it was His voice? Is He speaking anything to you right now that you would like to share?

Prayer:

Lord,

We submit ourselves to You today, with quiet and ready spirits, to sit at Your feet and listen. We do not want to miss a thing of what You have for us to guide us in this life. Please reveal to each of us the direction You have for us in each of our lives right now. Please confirm through Your Word that it is indeed Your guidance and Your will for us to move forward in great wonder and courage because You have revealed Yourself to us. We await Your direction with great anticipation and give You the glory for what will happen ahead of time.

In Jesus' holy name,

Amen

Meditation Verse:

Proverbs 3:5–7

Worship:

"The Potter's Hand"

"Thy Word is a Lamp Unto My Feet"

"Come Holy Ghost, Our Hearts Inspire"

CHAPTER FOUR:

———

The Reformation

England, France, Germany, Scotland, Switzerland

This righteousness is given through faith in Jesus Christ to all who believe. There is no difference between Jew and Gentile, for all have sinned and fall short of the glory of God, and all are justified freely by His grace through the redemption that came by Christ Jesus (Romans 3:22–24).

Introduction to The Reformation

See ***Appendix***: The Reformation
- Key Figures of the Reformation
- Key Timeline of the Reformation
- Bible Translation Timeline

- Church Branches and Denominations Timeline
- Arminianism versus Calvinism
- Five Solas of the Reformation
- Luther's 95 Theses
- Suggested Resources: The Reformation

Most of us naturally think of Martin Luther when we think of the Reformation. We will, indeed, explore his life and impact in great detail. There were, however, multiple Reformations in the sixteenth century:

- in Germany, with Martin Luther and Philip Melanchthon
- in Switzerland, with John Calvin and Ulrich Zwingli (and precursor John Hus)
- in England, with William Tyndale and Myles Coverdale (and precursor John Wycliffe)
- in Scotland, with John Knox
- in France, with Jacques Lefèvre d'Étaples

The Church had stood as the sole authority in the life of believers for 1,500 years, with few challenges. The Reformation was spawned because great church followers like the men above saw that Jesus' Bride, the Church, was way off course. They were willing to face persecution and death to bring her back to the Biblical path. Luther gave the Church back the Gospel and its singular identity. Denominations since the 1960s have been losing it again. As the Church today has *also* drifted off course, let *us* learn from *their* faithfulness to also help bring Her back to that Biblical path.

The Reformation was a call to Biblical faithfulness. It was developed within a perfect storm of intellectual, social, and political reforms, though it was primarily a spiritual movement led by imperfect, committed, Christian scholars who wanted the Church to return to emphasizing the Gospel and to move away from its secular, corrupt practices.

The Catholic Church's reputation was damaged by its many immoral acts, including popes having illegitimate children, greed (including selling positions in the Church and government and selling indulgences), and abuse of power. Meanwhile, common folk had been revitalized by education and wealth throughout the Renaissance. In 1517, a monk in Saxony (now Germany) nailed his 95 Theses to a church door, appealing to the pope and unwittingly launching Protestantism and major reforms throughout Europe to the present day.

Luther was preceded by John Wycliffe at Oxford, and Jan Hus at the University of Prague, and soon followed by Ulrich Zwingli and John Calvin. The Roman Catholic Church thought that they had ended the earlier debate at the Council of Constance (1414–1418), when they condemned and executed Hus, and posthumously burned Wycliffe as a heretic. The Reformation is said to have ended either in 1562–1563 with the Heidelberg Catechism—the most important statement of Protestant doctrine, or in 1648 with the Peace of Westphalia at the end of the Thirty Years' War.

In addition to attempting to reform the Roman Catholic Church's immoral acts, greed, and abuse of power, Reformers also attacked Catholic doctrine. Among the doctrines attacked were the doctrine of purgatory, Marian devotion, intercession by and devotion to the saints, most sacraments, mandatory celibacy of the clergy, and the authority of the pope. They believed that these were all created by man and not in the Bible, which is why they also pushed for publication of the Bible in the common languages of the people.

The Protestant Reformation is also called the German Reformation, Protestant Revolution, Protestant Revolt and Lutheran Reformation.

An outgrowth of the Renaissance, when many local rulers wanted independence from emperor Charles V and many peasants wanted more rights from their local rulers, the Reformation had roots in those who saw the Church as favoring their oppressors.

As Luther was starting in Wittenberg, Germany, Ulrich Zwingli was starting in Zürich, Switzerland, although they never resolved their theological disagreements. Luther and John Calvin had similar theological philosophies, though Calvin cut ties with Rome even more stringently. The Church of England separated politically from the Church of Rome under king Henry VIII between 1529–1536. Riots occurred in many European cities between 1523–1559, including Zürich, Geneva, Augsburg, and Scotland.

Luther stood for grace and faith alone (not to include good works), Scripture alone (not to include manmade traditions) and the priesthood of all believers (not the authority of priests). He did, though, embrace two of the Roman church's sacraments: baptism and the eucharist, while rejecting the other five.

The gravity of the Reformation did not fall on the first two popes affected: Leo (1513–1521) and Clement VII (1523–1534). Pope Paul III (1534–1549) led the Counter-Reformation. In 1541, Luther and the pope rejected the Regensburg Compromise offer by Protestant Martin Bucer and Catholic Johanne Grappa, claiming *Imputation* is what God does solely by Himself and *Importation* is what God does in us with our permission.

In 1545, the same offer of double justification was made at Trent and again failed. Four hundred years later, the Catholic Church adopted Vatican II reforms (1963–1966), and not one Protestant attendee encouraged those reforms.

The English Reformation was driven initially by Henry VIII's desire to annul his marriage to Catherine of Aragon (for only bearing him a daughter) in order to marry his mistress, Anne Boleyn. The pope refused this petition. A prior unapologetic Catholic who had strongly criticized Luther, Henry VIII now broke from Rome due to *political* reasons (wanting a male heir for succession), not due to *religious* differences. He named himself Supreme Head of the Church of England in 1534.

The Scottish Reformation, led by John Knox, shaped the Church of Scotland and ultimately all Presbyterian churches worldwide. In 1560, Parliament denied the pope's authority, outlawed mass, and approved a new Protestant Confession of Faith.

European states adopted either Catholicism or Protestantism as the state religion based on the ruler's preferences. Then the courts and police investigated and penalized dissenters. Expulsion, imprisonment, torture, death, and mass executions were the tools of religious repression by *both* sides.

Once rebuked for trying to *reform* the Catholic Church, the Protestant movement shifted to *replace* it. It took 200 years for both sides to accept a wary coexistence, with Catholics prevailing in Spain, France, Portugal, Ireland, and southern and eastern Europe; and Protestants in England, Scotland, Scandinavia, and central and northern Germany.

After 200 years of religious strife in Europe, the United States launched in 1775 with free expression of religion. The framers of our Constitution were convinced that government dominated by religion is incompatible with a free society—for both the individual and the churches. Alexis de Tocqueville, a Frenchman visiting the U.S. in 1831, wrote: "Religion here takes no direct part in government, but it must be regarded as the *first* of their political institutions."

The four original American colonies in New England (1620–1682) were founded, mostly by Puritan separatists (or Pilgrims), for religious motives, escaping persecution and the worldly excesses of England. For example, the Massachusetts Bay Colony was formed in 1630 as a Godly Commonwealth, when nearly 1,000 Puritans sailed in seventeen ships after religious conformity restrictions in Europe became intolerable. A dissenting minister, John Harvard (1607–1638), was among them and gave half his small estate and library to a new school: Harvard University.

Will we ever learn and be reconciled to the Biblical Church Body, not the many manmade church denominations? In 2007, then pope Benedict XVI agreed with pope Leo X, who condemned Luther's views in 1520, saying, "Christ established here on earth only one church, the other communities cannot be called churches in the proper sense, because they do not have apostolic succession." So, after all these years, he said that unless the church you attend is Catholic, it is defective.

As the Reformation is obviously part of our post-Biblical Christian heritage, little Scripture will be included in this section, similar to *Mission Trips* and contrary to *Holy Land* and *Paul's Journeys* sections. This was a rich period of discovery in many of the best traditions in art, architecture, literature, and music, reflecting the huge and continuing contributions by Christians to western civilization.

These giants of faith sacrificially brought us back to the true Gospel message.

Geographically, the Reformation is much more spread out than are the Holy Land and Paul's Journeys sites. You may choose to focus individual trips to just Germany or Switzerland and France, or to England and Scotland. There will be more hotels and more driving time between sites. We are intentionally not covering Italy, as it has been covered so well and extensively elsewhere.

Luther wanted simply initially to *reform* the Church (i.e., *Reform*ation), but ended up splitting the Church into Catholics and Protestants.

Martin Luther
Born November 10, 1483. Died February 18, 1546

Martin Luther was a Saxon (German) monk, theologian, Church reformer, hymn writer, loyal husband, father of six children, the founder of Protestantism, and translator of the German New Testament.

Luther was born when Saxony was at the height of its power: the most powerful country in the holy Roman empire. Two years later, Elector Ernst and his brother Albert made the huge mistake of splitting the region into two separate groups of small duchies, Ernestine duchies and Albertine duchies.

Luther challenged the authority of Rome and the pope with his *Five Solas* (see *Appendix: The Reformation*), basically stating that the Bible is the sole authority and that all believers are priests. He translated the Bible into the common German language and inspired congregational worship through his hymns. He modeled clerical marriage. Sadly, he did also write in his later years that Jews' homes and synagogues should be destroyed and funds expropriated, writings that were used extensively 400 years later for Nazi propaganda. He advocated kindness to Jews to convert them but became bitter when those efforts did not succeed, arguing they were no longer God's chosen people.

His parents were Hans and Margarethe Ludher (later Luther). He was born in Eisleben and moved a year later to Mansfield, where Hans leased a copper mine. He was the eldest of many siblings. Luther was sent to Latin schools, as his father wanted him to be a lawyer. He quickly dropped out of law school due to his interest in theology and philosophy.

On July 2, 1505, when lightning struck near him during a fierce storm as he was returning to school, his fear of divine judgment led him to vow to St. Anna that he would become a monk. He left university, sold his books, and entered a closed Augustinian monastery in Erfurt fifteen days later, saying to his friends, "This day you see me, and then, not ever again." He fasted, did penance, was whipped, held vigils, confessed, and took pilgrimages to please God but only realized even more his own sinfulness. The more he *worked*, the more distant God seemed to him.

He was ordained as a priest in 1507, and he began teaching theology at the University in 1508, lecturing on Psalms, Hebrews, Romans, and Galatians for ten years. He was convinced that the Church had lost track of key Biblical truths, particularly justification by faith alone, a gift from God. As Professor of Biblical studies, in a great spiritual crisis, he had encountered the phrase the "righteousness of God" in Psalms and Romans. He knew that he could never attain to such a standard. Luther then understood that God's righteousness was not an impossible standard that he could never reach, but was God's free gift in Christ, received by faith alone.

He visited Rome in 1510, and he was shocked to see its unholiness and the massive St. Peter's Basilica under construction and began to realize Christians come to God by faith alone, not though pious acts like his pilgrimage. The early Christians did not take pilgrimages, and he knew even from the Old Testament that God does not reside only in the temple. He realized it was more about the journey than the destination.

Around 60 AD, the Apostle Paul had prophesied a great apostasy from true Christianity, through corrupting of the Gospel by a wolf in sheep's clothing who would sit in God's Temple and call himself God. Luther felt this had been fulfilled for centuries by the papacy. Also, the Latin Vulgate (Jerome) version of the Bible was corrupted.

A Dominican friar was sent to Germany in 1516 by Rome to raise funds to build St. Peter's Basilica by selling indulgences—the remission of temporal punishment for a forgiven sin. Based on a collection of good deeds by past saints, referred to as the treasury of merit, the practice of plenary indulgences was started in 1095 by pope Urban II and over four centuries later was used as the primary funding source for the construction of St. Peter's Basilica. You could even buy forgiveness for *future* sins. Luther knew the Bible said forgiveness was *God's* alone to give.

Luther's *Five Solas* (See *Appendix: The Reformation*) came from Paul's adaptation of Abraham's faith in God's promise—*"Abraham believed God"* (Romans 4:1–2), *"we are justified by faith"* (Rom. 5:1), and *"by grace you have been saved by faith"* (Ephesians 2:8). As Paul used it for *Jews* who did not understand the Gospel, Luther used it for *Christians* who did not understand the Gospel.

Luther nailed his 95 Theses (see *Appendix: The Reformation)* in Latin to the bronze door of the Castle Church in Wittenberg on October 31, 1517, as church doors were the community's bulletin board. They were quickly translated into German, printed (by Gutenberg's press, developed thirty years before Luther's birth), and distributed within two weeks throughout Germany and within two months throughout Europe. Pope Leo only responded over a three-year period, finally warning Luther in 1520 with a papal bull (edict) that he would be excommunicated unless he recanted within two months. Luther publicly burned it outside Wittenberg's Elster Gate on December 10, 1520, and was excommunicated on January 3, 1521.

Three months later, he was promised safe passage and ordered to attend the Diet of Worms with emperor Charles V presiding. He held to his writings and was declared an outlaw, a heretic who was subject to arrest, and his literature forbidden. No one could give him food or shelter; anyone could legally kill him.

Elector of Saxony Frederick the Wise, founder of the University of Wittenberg, "kidnapped" him on his way home and hid him at Wartburg Castle in Eisenach, disguised as knight Junker George for eleven months (with long hair, a beard, and wearing secular clothes again for the first time since he went into the monastery), where he translated the New Testament from Greek into German. When under intense demonic attack, he threw his inkwell at Satan; the mark is still on the wall of his small study there! He secretly returned to Wittenberg in March 1522, and preached the Invocavit Sermons for nine days of Lent.

Pastor and author Mark Driscoll in *Real Marriage* writes of the beautiful, unlikely love story of Luther and Katherine von Bora. She was one of twelve nuns he helped escape from a convent in 1523. Thinking they would become brides of Christ escaping a corrupt world, they discovered they were required to become priests' lovers and bear their children instead. He found husbands for eleven of the nuns. In 1525, when he was forty-two and she was twenty-six years old, they married and later had six children. Clergy had not been allowed to marry, so this was bold, and they were a great example. Frederick III gave them a former monastery to live in, where she farmed the land and took in boarders.

Luther spent three hours most mornings on his face before his Lord, saying, "If I do not give God daily my first fruits, Satan will get the rest of them."

He understood the peasants' grievances but did not support attacking the upper classes or burning bishops' palaces, convents, and monasteries. He discouraged the destruction of religious images because of their great educational value to the illiterate majority of people. The most widely read author of his generation, Luther drafted the *Small Catechism* for the people, and the *Large Catechism* for the pastors, as well as much instructional and devotional literature (on the Ten Commandments, the Apostles' Creed, the Lord's Prayer, the Lord's Supper, Baptism, Confession, and Absolution). His New Testament translation was published in 1522 with illustrations by Lucas Cranach the Elder, and his complete Bible in 1534, which influenced Englishman William Tyndale's translation, a precursor of the King James Bible.

In 1520, he wrote *The Babylonian Captivity of the Congregation*, comparing the previous 1,000 years of the Church of Rome's domination to the seventy years of Babylonian captivity of the Jews. Copies were confiscated and burned by soldiers. His sermons alone total over 100 volumes.

Luther, nicknamed the "Wittenberg Nightingale," had a gifted singing voice, played the flute, and was in a boys' choir. Among many hymns he wrote, "A Mighty Fortress is Our God" is the most beloved, the national hymn of German Protestantism, and the first line on his tomb (from Psalm 46). In rediscovering congregational singing in the German language, he said, "The devil flees from the sound of music almost as much as from the Word of God." He also said: "Next to the Word of God, the noble art of music is the greatest treasure in the world. It controls our hearts, minds, and spirits." His first hymnal was published in 1524.

Martin and Katherine's Marriage

Easter morning 1523, Martin Luther smuggled twelve runaway nuns in fish barrels from Marienthron Convent after they had begged him to rescue them after they had read his *On Monastic Vows*, condemning much of monastic lifestyle. He found husbands for the other eleven, but Katherine, whose family did not want her back, only wanted *him* as her mate. He actually twice tried to act as matchmaker for her.

Born in 1499, she was sent at age six to a Benedictine cloister upon her mother's death, then at age ten to a convent, becoming a nun at age sixteen. Luther did not want to marry, knowing he might be killed at any time as a heretic, but they were wed on June 13, 1525. It caused a public scandal—an ex-priest and an ex-nun, perhaps the most significant and least romantic marriage ever outside the Bible. A folk tale then claimed the antichrist's parents would be a priest and a nun.

Their marriage was not due to physical attraction or to compatibility, as she was quite unattractive, and their temperaments were always in conflict. Even his friends disliked her.

Katherine birthed three sons and three daughters in nine years, two dying in childhood. Frederick the Wise had given them a forty-room former monastery as their home. She sold linens, farmed the land, brewed beer, took in up to twenty-five boarders at a time, cooked for over 100 people at times, improved Martin's diet, and nursed him (due to his poor health, depression, and notorious flatulence), took in eleven orphans, and sat with him as he wrote. He studied, wrote, published, traveled, and in the evening played music for his children and taught them the Bible.

They were very honest and regularly joked with each other as great friends do. He called her affectionately "Lord Katie," "my dear rib" and "a gift from God" and even called his favorite Bible book, Galatians, "my Katherine von Bora." She was such a diligent worker that he would offer to pay her to sit and read the Bible. She was able to debate theology with Luther and their visitors.

In 1540, he bought her the manor of Zollsdorf near Borna, two days' ride by horse and carriage, where she would often spend several weeks.

He said of her: "The greatest gift of grace a man can have is a pious, God-fearing, home-loving wife, whom he can trust with all his goods, body, and life itself, as well as having her as the mother of his children."

Luther died while traveling, in a house above Eisleben marketplace, on February 18, 1546 at age sixty-two. Naming her as sole heir contradicted the "Sachenspiegel" (law book) that needed to be overridden by decree of Saxon Elector John Frederick the Magnanimous.

Katherine died in 1552, at age fifty-three, in a house in the center of Torgau after breaking her pelvis in an accident three weeks earlier.

ENGLAND

Introduction to England

Many prominent Christian figures (including clergy, royalty, writers, and Bible translators), historical events, and denominational movements make England a key part of the Reformation and more.

St. Augustine of Canterbury in the sixth century introduced Christianity into England. The official state religion is Christianity through the (Anglican) Church of England.

The English Reformation was driven initially by king Henry VIII's desire to annul his marriage to his brother Arthur's widow, Catherine of Aragon, whom he had married incestuously, for only bearing him a daughter. He wanted to marry his mistress, Anne Boleyn. The request was refused by the pope. A prior unapologetic Catholic who had strongly criticized Luther, he now broke from Rome due to *political* reasons—wanting a male heir for his succession—not due to *religious* differences. He named himself Supreme Head of the Church of England in 1534, not intending to create a Protestant church along the lines evolving on the Continent.

William Tyndale, a parish priest, translated the entire New Testament and portions of the Old Testament into English in 1526. He was condemned as a heretic, fled to Europe for its printing, was arrested in Brussels, imprisoned for sixteen months, and then in October 1536 was strangled and burned as a martyr for his conviction.

Henry arrested Cardinal Wolsey, Lord Chancellor, for failing to get him an annulment and replaced him with Thomas Cromwell and Thomas Cranmer. Attorney Thomas Cromwell (1485–1540), who was influenced by Luther, was a Member of Parliament and close friends with soon-to-be Archbishop of Canterbury Thomas Cranmer (1489–1556). In 1532, Cromwell brought nine grievances against the Church of Rome before Parliament and became Henry's chief minister, replacing Thomas More, who was beheaded for his silence about the annulment. Cranmer was willing to grant Henry his annulment, but could not convince the pope, who excommunicated both Henry and Cranmer. Cranmer was part author and editor of the first two books of *Common Prayer*.

In 1534, Cromwell visited the monasteries to value their assets for expropriation, which he did after claiming the visits revealed sexual immorality and financial impropriety. He could bind the gentry and nobility to Royal Supremacy by selling them Church lands (The Church owned twenty to thirty percent of all land in England). He began dissolving the smaller monasteries and then four years later the larger ones, facing a series of violent uprisings by Catholics in northern England. Henry executed Cromwell in 1540 after discovering his longtime advisor had hidden the revolts from him. In 1553, Henry restricted reading of the Bible to men and women of noble birth.

In 1553, Henry's Roman Catholic daughter, Mary I, repealed the Reformation legislation, tried to reunite with Rome, and tried Cranmer for heresy (not treason), but he withdrew his recantations and was burned at the stake. To get an heir, she married the holy Roman emperor's son, Phillip II of Spain, to prevent her Protestant half-sister Elizabeth from inheriting the crown. She never became pregnant but got stomach cancer. Then pope Julius died, and his successor, Paul IV, declared war on Phillip. Mary I became known as "Bloody Mary" after 283 Protestants were burned at the stake for heresy. John Foxe's *Book of Martyrs* recorded the executions in brutal detail. Mary died in 1558 after only five years on the throne. Elizabeth inherited the throne after all, severing ties again with Rome, and reigning for over forty years. Her reign saw the emergence of Puritanism.

Calvinists who objected to the enforcement of uniformity in the dress of the clergy and who wished to do away with all ranks above parish priest were called "Puritans." King Charles I reigned from 1625–1649 and confronted the Puritan-controlled Parliament in 1640. Oliver Cromwell, a devout Puritan, led the Parliament's army (called Roundheads due to their close haircuts) in the civil war, defeated the royalist followers, and beheaded Charles I in 1649 after his ouster and trial. Ultimately, the people and the army became disillusioned with puritanical restrictions and Cromwell's dictatorship (despite his calling it a Republic). The monarchy, the Church of England, and the Parliament were restored in 1660, two years after his death.

Charles's son, Charles II, was proclaimed king, and both government and religion were restored to their status as of 1640. Charles II, an Anglican with Catholic leanings, was replaced in 1685 by his Catholic brother, James II. When James had a son, the political leaders replaced him with his Protestant daughter, Mary, who assumed the throne jointly with her Dutch husband, William III, in 1689 *after* they gave in to Parliament's demand for a Bill of Rights that assured Parliament's preeminence over the king in government, including a provision that no Roman Catholic would wear the crown.

Religious conflict spawned the Quaker movement and the desire to escape religious repression, leading to the founding of six of the original thirteen English colonies in North America.

John Wesley (1703–1791) and brother Charles (1707–1788) borrowed from Anglicans, Catholics, Calvinists, Lutherans, and Orthodox Christians. For Luther, conversion is the *goal* of Christian life; for Wesley, conversion is the *beginning*. The Wesleyans joined with George Whitfield (1714–1770) and with Jonathan Edwards (1703–1758) for the First Great Religious Awakening in America, though Whitfield and Edwards, ("Sinners in the Hand of an Angry God"), embraced Calvinism while the Wesleyans did not.

Two American churches came from Anglicanism, the Episcopal and the United Methodist. Catholicism only resurfaced in England from its underground existence in the nineteenth century.

Dating back to sinful, wife-killing king Henry VIII, for whom the title was ludicrous, the reigning monarch of England is the titular head of the Anglican Church of England, the Defender of the Faith. Few have truly either deserved the title or taken it seriously. Prince Charles even in 1994 said he would call it Defender of Faith, not *the* Faith, so as to not elevate Christianity over Islam, Hinduism, or Wicca. Ironically, Henry was given the title in 1521 by pope Leo X after Henry wrote his lengthy denunciation of Luther's 95 Theses! He was neither a friend to Protestants nor Catholics, being just an ungodly political opportunist.

CAMBRIDGE

Historical Significance:

Cambridge has been a university city since 1209, and was considered a city even though it had no cathedral. It was founded by students fleeing riot-torn Oxford. Tour highlights would be King's College Chapel (fifteenth century, containing Ruben's Adoration of the Magi); Emmanuel College, and Corpus Christi College.

Thomas Bilney secretly, in violation of Cambridge University rules, bought and read the Greek New Testament and was converted by 1 Timothy 1:15, where Paul stated that Christ Jesus came into the world to save sinners of whom he was chief. It was extremely rare for someone to find Christ through direct reading of Scripture, so he realized it was imperative to get an English translation for his people. In the 1520s, Bilney then led a group of scholars, including Thomas Cranmer (the eventual archbishop of Canterbury), Hugh Latimer, Miles Coverdale and William Tyndale, in discussions of Luther's teachings, Erasmus's recently completed Greek translation, and the need for Reformation in England. Bilney converted Cranmer, one of the most important men of the English Reformation, who was later martyred for his faith. Tyndale (New Testament) and Coverdale (Old Testament) did key Bible translations into English. Tyndale, after sixteen months' imprisonment in Belgium, was burned to death by order of the holy Roman emperor in 1536, praying for king Henry VIII's conversion. Coverdale, after imprisonment by Mary Tudor, fled to Geneva, where he contributed to the Geneva Bible.

Many Reformers were educated at Cambridge University, including Erasmus, Bilney and Tyndale. Queen Victoria's consort, Prince Albert, served as the Chancellor of the University between 1847–1861.

What to See:

St. Edward King and Martyr Church, "Cradle of the Reformation," on Peas Hill, was dedicated to the martyred king Edward (reigned 975–978 AD). It is believed the first sermon of the English Reformation occurred here at Christmas Eve Midnight Mass in 1525, accusing the Roman Catholic Church of heresy.

White Horse Tavern (Inn) was where Reformers met from 1521 on to discuss Protestant ideas. The tavern was located on King's Lane, and was later demolished when the King's College Scott's Building was constructed in 1870. A blue plaque commemorates this in Chetwynd Court, at the corner facing where King's Parade becomes Trumpington Street. The White Horse was referred to as "Little Germany" due to the extensive conversations about Luther and the German Reformation there.

If you are driving to Cambridge, be aware that there is very little parking within the city. Park in one of the many parking areas outside the central city, with low-cost shuttles into the city itself.

Defining Moment . . . The Former Site of the White Horse Inn in King's College, Cambridge

The blue plaque commemorates the White Horse Inn as the birthplace of the English Reformation. There was a student at Trinity College in Cambridge that experienced similar struggles with his faith as Martin Luther did. Thomas Bilney feared that it was up to him to earn his own Salvation, and knew he fell woefully short. He was without spiritual peace and was willing to break the rules of his university to find it. The Greek New Testament was banned: no scholar was allowed to have one at Trinity College. Bilney defied the rules and secretly bought a copy, and when he got to 1 Timothy 1:15, he realized that it was Christ's work in him, and not his own, that granted him Salvation: *"Here is a trustworthy saying that deserves full acceptance: Christ Jesus came into the world to save sinners—of whom I am the worst."*

"I see it all," said Bilney, "my vigils, my fasts, my pilgrimages, my purchase of masses and indulgences were destroying instead of saving me. All these efforts were, as St. Augustine says, 'a hasty running out of the right way.'"

That verse changed his life, and he could not keep from sharing it. He went to "confession" under Hugh Latimer, considered the foremost conservative preacher in all of England and an early opponent of Luther. Bilney confessed his new beliefs in great detail. Latimer thought he would save a student from going down a heretical path, but Bilney ended up converting Latimer, who would later be killed for the very beliefs that he initially opposed. Latimer joined the small group that began meeting at the White Horse Inn to discuss Reformation ideas.

This group of men would meet over pints of ale in the White Horse Inn to discuss these newfound truths, but ended up offering their lives so that the actual truths of the Gospel would be spread. These meetings helped them forge their beliefs in the knowledge that God wanted to share with His beloved, the Church. While there is little except a plaque to physically remember these men, their sacrifices and commitment to stand for what God called them into is evidenced by the Bibles that each of us owns. God used the spiritual struggle of a single man, Thomas Bilney, to spark freedom and truth for English-speaking peoples throughout Eternity. Bilney's struggle sparked a uniting of these men in truth. They took the Word of God out of the hands of a corrupt church that forbade the Bible to be published, and then put it into the hands of all believers.

Journal Time:

Often, we see our spiritual struggles as painful burdens that we would rather not have. Our God sees them as opportunities to reveal Himself to us and set us free. Bilney's struggle not only ended up setting him free, but also gave freedom to countless others who would eventually own their own Bibles.

Journal about a spiritual struggle that you have had, either past or present. Has God used it yet to help set others free? Sit and ask Him what His truth is about your struggle. What is He wanting to show you?

Share Time:

Talk about your spiritual struggles. How has God used them? Are there any that you would like to ask God to answer, as he did for Bilney, in this very place?

Prayer:

Pray together as a group, asking God to reveal the truth about the spiritual struggles that you are carrying. Just as God used Bilney's struggles for good, thank Him for how He will use your struggles in the same way.

Worship:
   "Thou Art the Way"
   "Awakening" (Chris Tomlin)

Defining Moment . . . St. Edward King and Martyr Church

Imagine walking into your church and hearing a sermon that commanded you to give money to your church or face an Eternity in hell. That is what was happening in churches in the 1500s. The church used fear as a motivator to extort money out of people who had very little to give. There were no Bibles available to the common people, so they could not read the truth for themselves. They were completely dependent on the church to teach them about God.

Then, imagine one man, Robert Barnes, a member of the White Horse Inn group, finding out about God's truth about Salvation through their meetings. Imagine him exposing the Church's lies publicly for the first time ever. That is exactly what happened at the church you are visiting right now. In 1525, Barnes preached at the Christmas Eve Midnight Mass. Instead of the usual fear and condemnation that the people heard, Barnes shared the first openly evangelical sermon they had ever witnessed about God, not the Church, being the supplier of their Salvation.

He then openly accused the Catholic Church of heresy. Because of this sermon, St. Edward King and Martyr Church has been deemed "The Cradle of the Reformation." As a result of that evening, Barnes was brought before the vice-chancellor and condemned to abjure (renounce his rights to freedom) or be burned. He chose to abjure, eventually escaped confinement, moved to Germany, and went on to preach more truth throughout his life until he was burned at the stake for heresy in 1540.

Journal Time:

Truth can be a hard "gift" to share with those who do *not* want to hear it. Think of a time that you shared truth and the price you paid. Journal about your heart's journey through that time. Was there pain involved? Elation? Freedom? Joy? Resolution? Here is an example from Susan's life: Rick and I had close friends who were bitterly facing an impending divorce. Because both of them were confessed believers, somewhat active in their church, I asked the wife if she was listening to God for His direction to divorce or if she was deciding to move forward out of her own feelings. She angrily chastised me for asking the question, and never spoke to me again. The price I paid was her friendship. I never told her divorce was wrong; I simply asked what she was hearing from God about it.

Contrast this to a time when I was coaching a young woman who was struggling through her relationship with Christ and her commitment to physical purity. I shared the truth about what God was calling her to. She listened and tearfully recanted her ways, accepted God's forgiveness and restoration, and is now an amazing, Godly wife and mother, leading other women to the place she is in now. The gift of watching God's Glory rule her life is priceless to me.

Journal about *your* experiences in sharing Truth.

Share Time:

Process together your experiences of sharing truth, both the joys and the sorrows. Give yourselves the gift of encouragement, support, and a safe place to discuss healing for those of you who have been wounded in the process. Give each other hope by talking about the times you have shared truth and seen the fruit of your labors.

Prayer:

Lord,

Thank You for truth. Thank You for the divine appointments You give us to reveal who You really are both to ourselves and to others. Please forgive us when we cower from the truth. Give us Your immutable strength and power to stand in as we share truth in love, without condemnation, but in its full power. We trust You with Your work in us to stand for Your truth.

In Jesus' name,

Amen

Worship:

"O God of Truth"

"Our God is Mighty to Save"

CANTERBURY

Historical Significance:

Canterbury in Kent, in southeastern England, is the ecclesiastical capital of England, the most important ancient city in England. It became the Christian king Ethelbert and queen Berta's kingdom in AD 560. In AD 597, pope St. Gregory sent St. Augustine and his missionaries, for whom the king provided a monastery and church where Ethelbert was later baptized. It became the burial place of kings and archbishops and a pilgrimage center after St. Thomas Becket was martyred in 1170 by king Henry II's knights.

What to See:

Canterbury Cathedral is the mother Church of England and the global Anglican faith, built in Romanesque/Perpendicular Gothic style. A pivotal moment in the history of the Cathedral was the murder (also known as the martyrdom) of the archbishop, Thomas Becket, in the northwest transept on December 29, 1170 by four knights of king Henry II. The king had frequent conflicts with the strong-willed Becket and is said to have exclaimed in frustration, "Who will rid me of this turbulent priest?" The knights took it literally, and murdered Becket in his own cathedral. Becket was the second of four Archbishops of Canterbury who were murdered. The posthumous veneration of Becket made the Cathedral a place of pilgrimage. This brought both the need to expand the cathedral, and the wealth that made it possible. The cathedral is now a UNESCO World Heritage Site.

St. Augustine's Abbey was a Benedictine monastery, founded by St. Augustine in 598 AD marking the rebirth of Christianity in southern England, and functioned as a monastery until its dissolution in 1538 during the English Reformation. It is a UNESCO World Heritage Site.

St. Martin's Church, situated slightly beyond the city center, is the first church founded in the nascent proto-English civilization, specifically in the Jutish kingdom. Within about a century, its faith spread into an Anglo-

Saxon cultural wave, restoring Christianity in the majority areas of the island where the Romano-British church had either long ceased or never existed. St. Martin's has practiced continuous service since its founding, thus making it also the oldest parish church in constant use in England and thus the oldest church in the English-speaking world throughout the globe. Since 1668, the church has been part of the benefice of St. Martin and **St. Paul** Canterbury. Both St. Martin's and nearby St. Paul's churches are used for weekly services. It is a UNESCO World Heritage Site.

Defining Moment . . . Canterbury Cathedral
(This Defining Moment teaching may also be used at *any* cathedral.)

It is staggering to look at the intricate details and design of the Canterbury Cathedral. Most of the hundreds of craftsmen who built this cathedral never saw its completion. Structures like this take generations to build. Imagine spending your entire life working on something knowing that you would *never* see its completion. There is a great story about a worker who spent an inordinate amount of time carving a small statue that would be placed high on one of the spires of a cathedral. It was good but not perfect yet. This worker's apprentice asked why he spent so much time on this piece when no one would be able to see it up close. The worker replied that God would be able to see it up close. He was working as if working for the Lord, literally. The legacy he was leaving was for *God's* Kingdom, not his own.

The outcome for the builders of the Canterbury Cathedral is that it is the longest continuously running worship center in England. This place of worship has had prayers offered to God daily for over 1,400 years.

The great Reformers did the same for the Christian faith. Reformer upon reformer made the specific contribution that God was calling him to make. Whether it was William Tyndale, who was strangled and burned for translating and printing the New Testament, or Martin Luther, whose life was threatened because he called out the Catholic Church for selling indulgences (telling people that they could buy their way into Heaven), each reformer played his part. The Church is what it is today because of the courageous stance these men took.

There is a drama put out by Campus Crusade called *The Bema Seat*. In this fictional account of what Heaven might be like, a believer is waiting for his turn on the Bema (judgment) Seat for believers, where he will be awarded his crowns. Jesus explains that the award given to each person had to wait until the end of time, because the only way to look at the entire effect of a life's work is to look at the repercussions that work had throughout history. As an individual sat on the Bema Seat, Jesus asked all individuals to stand up that had been affected directly or indirectly, perhaps generations later, by the Kingdom work of that individual. Some only had a couple people stand. For others, millions arose as generation after generation had been affected by *their* Kingdom work.

Daydream with me for a moment. What is God's call on your life? What is His purpose for you? If you choose to live out that purpose, what kind of ramifications will it have on the Kingdom? Who will get to know who Jesus really is through your work? Who will then go on to have children who know Jesus through their parents, and who will grow to be Kingdom workers themselves and affect millions down their family line? What are the possibilities of building part of the great cathedral that is the Church, the Body of Christ, even though you will not see the effects of your work until the end of time?

Journal Time:
Ask the Holy Spirit to remind you of God's purpose for you. How has He uniquely gifted you? What is His call on your life? Should you accept this call, envision the Bema Seat possibilities. Who might stand up with a story about how *your* Kingdom work affected them, and their children, and their children's children, and so on?

Share Time:
Share with each other the purpose and calling that you think God might have on your life. Daydream aloud about the ramifications that taking up that call might have for the Kingdom.

Prayer:

Lord,

Thank You for the unique way you have made each person here. Thank You for giving each of us a purpose and a call that only we can fill. Thank You for the privilege it is to work with You, Lord, and know that while we might not see the effects of our service on earth, You will use our sacrifices of work to build Your Kingdom. Help us, Lord, when we grow weary because we do not see how we are making a difference. Keep us focused on You, and give us hearts to work as if we are working for You, and not to satisfy ourselves. For those that have not yet heard Your purpose, please give them the gift of seeking and then hearing Your whisper of revelation over them, waking them up to the joy of living in their purpose.

In Jesus' name,

Amen

Worship:

"Cast Thy Bread Upon the Water"

"You Give Me Joy"

GLASTONBURY

Historical Significance:
Formerly the Isle of Avalon, an ancient market town, Glastonbury is considered the birthplace of Christianity in England.

Legend has it that Joseph of Arimathea, who gave Jesus his tomb, not knowing he would only need it for three days, brought the Holy Grail—the cup used by Jesus at His Last Supper—to settle here. Legend says also that Joseph of Arimathea stuck his staff into the ground, and the staff rooted and grew into a thorn tree known today as the Holy Thorn, which is said to bloom each Christmas Eve. He is said to have buried the Holy Grail there, and the quest for the Grail is what the legendary king Arthur and his knights of the Round Table undertook. It is believed that a miraculous spring, today called Chalice Well, is also a part of the Holy Grail legend. Joseph built the first Christian sanctuary in England at Glastonbury, which thrived until king Henry VIII dissolved it along with hundreds of other convents and monasteries.

What to See:
Glastonbury Tor is a sacred hill and pilgrimage site with St. Michael's Tower on top.

Glastonbury Abbey and its peaceful ruins include beautiful grounds and an impressive museum.

Wearyall Hill, located just below the Tor, is the traditional resting place of Joseph of Arimathea and the site of the Holy Thorn.

Scripture:
Matthew 27:57–61
definingmomentsbook.com/resources

LONDON

Historical Significance:

The Westminster Confession of Faith was written at Westminster Abbey. The first third of the Old Testament, along with the first half of the New Testament, were translated as part of the King James Version by seventeen men in the Jerusalem Chamber of Westminster Abbey.

John Wesley, the most influential Protestant leader of the English-speaking world, and the Founder of Methodism, fifteenth of nineteen children, lived in London, and worshipped at St. Paul's Cathedral on the day of his conversion.

John Bunyan (1628–1668), a tinker, began to preach the Gospel in 1655. He was imprisoned by the Church for twelve years and refused to stop preaching in return for his freedom. He wrote sixty books, including *Grace Abounding to the Chief of Sinners,* which went through six editions during his lifetime—a first edition copy is in the British Museum—and *Pilgrim's Progress,* an allegory of the life of a believer which was required reading in the U.S. until the 1950s.

What to See:

Westminster Abbey, founded in 1065, is the national church of Britain, a UNESCO World Heritage Site. It is a Royal Peculiar, meaning that it is under the direct jurisdiction of the sovereign and exempt from the jurisdiction of the diocese to which it belongs. Westminster Abbey, a former gothic monastery, has been host since 1066 to many coronations and notable burials of English monarchs, including queens Elizabeth I and Mary II, heroes, scientists, warriors, and poets.

St. Paul's Cathedral and Churchyard, recently renovated, was designed by Christopher Wren. It is the largest cathedral in the city, seat of the Bishop of London, parish church of the British Commonwealth, the Mother Church of Methodism since the eighteenth century. St. Paul's is the spiritual home for the British people, seat of the Anglican Bishop, host to Churchill's funeral and Lady Diana's wedding. John Wesley worshipped in the chancel in May 1738. A statue of Wesley was erected in 1988 in the churchyard, a bronze cast of a nineteenth century statue at Methodist Central Hall, Westminster.

Wesley Chapel and House was built by John Wesley in 1778 on City Road to replace the Foundry Chapel. The site includes John Wesley's home, chapel, and his tomb. Wesley's tomb and the tombs of his sister and six of his preachers are in the back garden, along with some late eighteenth and nineteenth century busts of Wesley. The memorial Foundry Chapel, to the right, includes Wesley's organ. The Museum of Methodism is below the chapel in the crypt.

John Wesley, a scholar, poet, and evangelist, is the best known of the founders of the Methodist movement. John was part of Oxford's "The Holy Club," and his brother, Charles, who was known as the "Sweet Singer of Methodism," also preached here. Their "method" of study led to a taunt of being called "Methodists" which stuck as the name of the movement they started. Wesley's last words were "The best of all—God is with us." He encouraged people to go back to the basics of loving God and our fellow man (the First and Second Commandments), and often said, "The world is my parish," which is ironic as Wesley was banned from so many traditional churches.

The property has a great guided tour, and robust grounds to explore, so make sure to plan at least one to two hours for your visit. The guides are well-versed in their history and it is the highlight of all of the faith-related sites in London. It is the first Methodist church built specifically for celebrating Holy Communion as well as preaching, and is considered one of the finest Georgian buildings in London today.

The home he moved into on October 9, 1779 was owned by the church and is a beautifully preserved, modest Georgian townhouse, and includes, on the ground floor, his dining room and an early "chamber horse" exercise machine. On the first floor was his bedroom (in which Wesley died on March 2, 1791), his prayer room, and his study where he wrote many letters and entertained many guests (though without serving tea, which he considered to be too expensive). On the second floor were the rooms where visiting preachers stayed. There was no oven, so his kitchen help would have to take roasts to the baker to be cooked. Wesley used this home intermittently due to his extensive evangelistic travels. He traveled mostly by horse, even into his eighties.

The chapel, renovated by the global Methodist Society, has many stained-glass windows in the vestibule, main chapel, and the upper galleries that were added after 1891, including *The Adoration of the Magi*. The baptismal in the front right features a carved stone from Antigua (the beginning of Methodism in the Caribbean) depicting a Cross breaking the chains of slavery. The front communion rail was donated by former Prime Minister Margaret Thatcher, who was married here and had both her children christened here.

The museum, funded by South Korean Methodists representing the worldwide movement, includes original Wesley letters written to his missionary friends in his last years; a model nineteenth century missionary ship, 'John Wesley'; and a model Fijian boat, representing the Methodist faith being spread in the Pacific.

This site is within walking distance of both St Paul's Cathedral and the Museum of London.

Methodist Flame is a memorial plaque honoring where John Wesley had his "Aldersgate Flame" evangelical conversion revelation (just days after Charles's) on May 24, 1738 when his heart was "strangely warmed." The memorial is located on the high walkway directly outside the entrance of the Museum of London. The Museum also houses memorabilia connected with Wesley.

Bunhill Fields Cemetery, across the street from **Wesley Chapel**, hosts the graves of several Puritan dissenters, unable to be buried in consecrated church graveyards, such as John Bunyan, author of *Pilgrim's Progress*, (1678), the most popular book of his time after the Bible. A pilgrim carrying his burden while leaning on a staff can be seen on the side of Bunyan's tomb. Isaac Watts, hymn writer, ("When I Survey the Wondrous Cross"); John Milton, author of *Paradise Lost*; Daniel Defoe, author of *Robinson Crusoe*. Susanna Wesley is buried here. John and Charles were among the youngest of her nineteen children; her white marble gravestone is to the left of the central path. Also buried here are descendants of Oliver Cromwell. The burial site was known in early Saxon times as "Bonehill" Fields and included 123,000 burials through the last burial in 1860.

The **British Museum** features Bible artifacts.

Southwark Cathedral, burial place of Lancelot of Andrews, King James Version translator. Puritan clergyman John Harvard was baptized here. A chapel is named in his honor, as is the famous New England University.

Metropolitan Tabernacle, a Reformed Baptist church, one of the first mega churches, which has a thriving congregation today, is where Charles Spurgeon held great revivals in the late nineteenth century, with 6,000 people in attendance daily—20,000 on Sundays. He is estimated to have preached to ten million people.

Other places to visit include **St. Bartholomew the Great Parish Church**, the last Anglican pulpit where Wesley was welcomed long after he had been disbarred from other London churches. **Lambeth Palace**, home of the archbishop of Canterbury; **Charter House**, the school John Wesley attended from 1714–1720, featuring a commemorative plaque in the cloisters. The school relocated in 1872 to Surrey; **St. Luke's**, Wesley's parish church; **Spital Yard** where Susanna Wesley, youngest of twenty-nine, was raised; **Mayflower Pub jetty**, the home berth of the Pilgrim's ship.

Defining Moment . . . John Wesley

As you visit the **Wesley Chapel and House**, you will be standing in the home of a man who cared more about men's souls than he cared about what the establishment thought of him. John Wesley was ordained as an Anglican priest and decided to follow the steps of George Whitefield—preaching in the fields to folks who would not ever enter a church. At one time, even Wesley had thought that preaching outside of church walls was sinful, but he quickly got over that once he witnessed the winning of souls outside the structure of a church building. The result was that his ministry grew into the Methodist Church.

The problem was that the organized church of that day began to feel threatened. Wesley's ministry was growing so large that he chose to place itinerant preachers in the field to keep up with demand. Because these preachers were not ordained by the Anglicans, the Anglicans began to feel threatened. His movement was seen as a social threat that completely disregarded the current institution. They preached wherever they saw need, ignoring the preaching boundaries set by the Anglican Church. Wesley and his followers were slandered as "blind fanatics" in print and were physically attacked by mobs. They continued to minister to the neglected, needy, and imprisoned, sometimes purchasing freedom for inmates from debtor's prison. They continued to work to abolish slavery while being severely attacked. However, Wesley knew that God had put a call on his life for revival, and he refused to give up. For the next fifty years, he continued to minister to the broken wherever they were.

As we read the Church's reaction to Wesley's God-ordained work, we can feel rather self-righteous—*my* church would never do that. We feed the homeless and have a great prison ministry, but there are many times when a church member has a great idea for a new way to do ministry, and it falls on deaf ears at their own church. When the Church does not embrace their idea or implement it with their vision, there can be hurt and disillusionment, and sometimes a yearning to leave that church. Wesley chose a different path. He chose to *stay* connected to his church while he moved his ministry forward outside of it, with great blessings from God.

He showed no feelings of entitlement for his church to come and help him. Even when his own church attacked him, he never gave up. He just kept on serving the neglected at all costs. He reached many souls that would have been lost forever outside the church's boundaries of care. Throughout all the attacks, he never left the Anglican Church. They banned him from preaching in their churches for a time, but he chose not to formally announce separation from them, believing that "With all her blemishes, she is nearer the Scriptural plans than any other in Europe."

Instead of Wesley feeling disillusioned and hurt, he remained focused completely on saving as many souls as he could and following God's call on his life. The evidence of his lack of bitterness is even seen passed down to the next generation. His nephew, whose father also worked tirelessly for the ministry with Wesley, wrote the hymn, "The Church's One Foundation." It is a beautiful homage to the Church standing unified through all the tribulations meant to separate it.

As I write this, I have been remembering a woman who had a call on her life to start a ministry. She jumped into the deep end of the pool by quitting her job, and her ministry started out beautifully—except that her own church did not come alongside her and even at times competed with her in that space. There were times of disappointment and frustration but, to her credit, she stayed a member of her church. She avoided conversations where she could have badmouthed the church, even though most would have thought her comments justified. Meanwhile, other churches in the community heard about the work that she was doing and asked if they could join her. God used her ministry to knit together many large churches into the same fabric of serving a specific and needy population. Her church, after several years, caught the vision and is now one of her most faithful partners.

The bottom line is that when God is calling *you* into an assignment, it might not include *your church* being called into the same place. Stand in grace as John Wesley did.

"Religion that God our Father accepts as pure and faultless is this: to look after orphans and widows in their distress and to keep oneself from being polluted by the world" (James 1:27).

Journal Time:
Have you ever felt let down by your church? Write about it and ask God to show you the part of Himself that He wants to reveal to you through that trial.

Share Time:
Share one or two words that represent any hurts you recorded in your Journal Time. Have the leader of your group stand in the gap and represent the Church. Have him ask for forgiveness from you and from God for the hurts that have been done.

Prayer:
Father God,
Thank You, that as our Father, You cover every one of us with Your love and grace. Please help each of us when we are facing hurts, especially from our

church, not to return evil for evil. Help us to give our offenses over to You, and to trust You with those who hurt us—that You, not us, would convict them, heal them and restore them to Your ways. We ask that You heal hearts right now that are still carrying bitterness and unforgiveness. Please give all of us the gift of forgiving not just from our heads, but from our hearts, that we can be set free of the effects of unforgiveness that we cannot see with our earthly eyes. Lord, we do forgive those that we have carried bitterness for. We release them to You. Thank You that our callings and ministries depend on You alone. Please guide and bless our work in the Kingdom, and keep us focused on You as our audience, and no other.

In Jesus' name,
Amen

Worship:
"The Church's One Foundation" (written by Wesley's nephew)
"This is Amazing Grace"

OXFORD

Historical Significance:

Oxford is home to thirty-nine of the world's most respected universities and colleges, and many famous students and citizens, including C.S. Lewis, John and Charles Wesley, John Wycliffe, William Tyndale, Lewis Carroll, J.R.R. Tolkien, William Penn, Albert Einstein, and John Locke. John Wesley graduated from Christ Church College in 1724.

What to See:

Christ Church College and Cathedral: The College was founded by Cardinal Wolsey as Cardinal's College in 1524. The Cathedral is one of the oldest (twelfth century) buildings in Oxford, originally a Catholic priory, now one of the smallest Anglican Cathedrals in England. This is the only church in the world to both be a cathedral and a college chapel. The prior monastery was part of the early settlement in the ninth century. Among the most famous of Oxford's many chorales are their men's and boy's choirs. Great Tom, the 18,000-pound tower bell, is rung 101 times nightly at 9 p.m. to honor the 101 original scholars, to signal the closing of the college gates.

St. Michael at the Northgate Church in Cornmarket Street is the oldest building in Oxford, dating from the early eleventh century, and restored in 1986. Archbishop of Canterbury Thomas Cranmer—along with Hugh Latimer, the bishop of Worcester before the Reformation and later the chaplain to king Edward VI; and Nicholas Ridley, bishop of London and Westminster—was held in Bocardo Prison before being burned at the stake. Cranmer was burned alive on March 21, 1556, in Oxford Yard on Broad Street. Latimer and Ridley were burned on October 16, 1955. All three were educated at Oxford. John Wesley preached here in 1726.

University Church of St. Mary the Virgin, the official church of the University of Oxford, was the site of trials for Anglican bishops, including

Archbishop Cranmer's for not believing in transubstantiation. John Wesley preached his famous "Almost Christian" sermon here in 1741.

Martyr's Memorial, a Victorian spire-like hexagon with statues of Cranmer, Latimer and Ridley, at the intersection of St. Giles, Magdalen and Beaumont Street, was restored and dedicated to martyred Reformer bishops and archbishops.

Defining Moment . . . Martyrs of Oxford

Around the corner from Martyr's Memorial, a small area covered in granite setts (paving block) forms a Cross in the center of the road on Broad Street in front of the Information Center. This, and a plaque on the wall nearby, marks the execution spot of the three martyrs of Oxford. Hugh Latimer, Nicholas Ridley, and Thomas Cranmer, archbishop of Canterbury, were burned at the stake here after being found guilty of heresy. Cranmer played a major role in the English Reformation, so when Mary I, a devout Catholic, came into power, Cranmer was brutally persecuted. During the abuse, his mind began to grow feeble, and he signed a renouncement of his Reformation beliefs. That was not enough for Bloody Mary, so she sentenced him to death. As Cranmer was being led to the execution stake, he was walking so fast that his captors could barely keep up. He then renounced the Catholic Church and his previous recantations of the English Reformation that he had made to save his life. Once fastened into place, he placed his right hand near the hottest part of the fire, purposely burning it first because it had signed those previous recantations.

John Foxe describes the scene in his *Book of Martyrs*:

"Then were the glorious sentiments of the martyr made manifest—then it was, that stretching out his right hand, he held it unshrinkingly in the fire till it was burned to a cinder, even before his body was injured, frequently exclaiming, "This unworthy right hand!" Apparently insensible of pain, with a countenance of venerable resignation, and eyes directed to Him for whose cause he suffered, he continued, like St. Stephen, to say, "Lord Jesus, receive my spirit!" till the fury of the flames terminated his powers of utterance and existence. He closed a life of high

sublunary elevation, of constant uneasiness, and of glorious martyrdom,
on March 21, 1556"
(John Foxe, The Unabridged Acts and Monuments
Online or TAMO, 1576 edition).

Mary I's intentions to squelch the flames of Reformation actually fanned them. Cranmer and his work on the Reformation not only survived his execution, but were magnified because of it. 2 Thessalonians 1:4 played out before her eyes: *"Therefore, among God's churches we boast about your perseverance and faith in all the persecutions and trials you are enduring."*

As we read this account, we cannot help but think about the thousands of brothers and sisters in Christ who are being persecuted for their Christian beliefs around the world today. Would we, like Cranmer, renounce what we believe or stand strong like he did at the end? As we see the persecutions of Christians worldwide increase, even in America, will *we* be asked to take a stand in our lifetime?

In America, while persecution against Christians is more subtle than being burned at the stake, it is still progressing. Have you ever heard of the boiling frog experiment? If you boil a pot of water and throw a frog into it, he will jump right out. If you put a frog into room temperature water, then slowly turn up the heat degree by degree, he will allow himself to cook to death.

In America, while we are not being killed, we are suffering persecutions in mainstream media, in educational institutions, and even in our homes. When a couple from San Juan, Capistrano, held weekly Bible studies in their home, they were issued citations for breaking public assembly laws. The Pacific Justice Institute took their case to court, and the city reversed their position and refunded all the fines that the couple had paid. In another case, Rick Warren was named as a defendant in a lawsuit for praying at the Presidential Inauguration. PJI represented him, also, and eventually won after a long legal battle.

Knowing that Ephesians 6:12 says, *"For our struggle is not against flesh and blood, but against the rulers, against the authorities, against the powers of this dark world and against the spiritual forces of evil in the heavenly realms,"* how do we fight this battle? Pray unceasingly!

Journal Time:
What are the Christian ideals that you hold that are being most "persecuted" in your culture right now? Write down the areas of concern in your community and country.

Share Time:
Discuss the areas of persecution you are seeing in your country and also what you are hearing about in other parts of the world. Do you see any commonalities to those that Cranmer was facing?

Prayer:
Pray now, in community, over the areas that were just discussed. Pray for the persecuted church worldwide, for the persecutions in your own country and for the protection of all saints during persecutions that are to come.

Worship:
  "I Will Follow Thee"
  "By Your Blood"

OTHER SITES IN ENGLAND

Austerfield
The birthplace of William Bradford (Governor of Plymouth Plantation).

Babworth
Where you'll find **All Saints' Church** (home of Richard Clyfton and the Pilgrim movement), and St Helena's Church.

Bedford and Surroundings
Bedford is home to the John Bunyan statue. Olney, Buckinghamshire, was where John Newton lived and ministered as rector before moving to London, and where he wrote hymns with William Cowper, eighteenth century hymn writer; it is home to the Cowper and Newton Museum and grave site. Near Madingley, you can visit the Cambridge American Cemetery and Memorial. In nearby Elstow, you will find John Bunyan's early childhood church, and the John Bunyan Meeting House and Museum.

Boston
A must-see is Boston's Guildhall Museum, with the courtroom and cells where the Pilgrim Fathers were tried. Boston was also the home of John Cotton while he was pastor of St. Botolph's Church before leaving for New England.

Bristol
The location of John Wesley's Chapel and home.

Epworth
John and Charles Wesley's home and birthplace; Old Rectory; Dad's Tomb at St. Andrew's (parish) Church; Wesley Memorial Church

Gainsborough
Visit Old Hall, where John Smyth and the Mayflower Pilgrims worshipped.

Gloucester

This is an inland port on the River Severn. Small Church of St. Mary de Crypt, where Robert Raikes launched the "Sunday School Movement" was also the birthplace of an early women's missionary movement. George Whitefield was baptized here and delivered his first sermon, "Great Awakening" here. Whitefield was the most outstanding preacher of his generation's literary evangelical revival. Here also is Gloucester Cathedral, founded in 1089 as a monastic church with exquisite stained-glass windows, considered to be the sixth most beautiful building in Europe.

Lutterworth

The location of St. Mary's Church, where Wycliffe translated the English Bible and trained "Lollard Preachers."

Olney

Where John Newton was a rector. He is buried at the church here.

Plymouth

Learn about the Pilgrims' last night at **Island House on the Barbican**; the memorial "Mayflower Steps" at the Barbican is where the Mayflower sailed.

Scrooby

St. Wilfred's Church from which the Pilgrims separated

Southampton

Mayflower sailed in 1620; birthplace of hymn writer Isaac Watts; Mayflower Memorial

Winchester

Along with London, considered Alfred the Great's proto-capital of England from 829 AD for almost 250 years until the Norman Conquest, it features Winchester Cathedral, the longest overall length medieval church in Europe, begun in 1079.

FRANCE

Avignon

The Palace of the Popes (Palais des Papes), was both an austere-looking fortress and a lavishly decorated palace. It was the seat of the Catholic Christian world in the fourteenth century, the home to nine successive popes from 1325–1417 when the Church temporarily shifted its base from Rome because the French pope Clement V refused to go to Rome. The most famous of the Avignon popes were Benedict XII and Clement VI. Here, visit twenty-four areas including ceremonial rooms, frescoes, chapels, private apartments, and cloisters. There are audio guides in eleven languages. It is a UNESCO World Heritage Site.

Avignon Bridge (Pont d'Avignon, properly the Pont Saint-Bénézet) *was originally built in the twelfth century; often damaged by the Rhone River's raging floods, wars, and then rebuilt, it was abandoned in the seventeenth century. The bridge was made famous by a fifteenth century French song and dance, "On the Bridge of Avignon" ("Sur le Pont d'Avignon"). See the 3D technological recreation of the bridge and surrounding landscape as it was during the Middle Ages. This is a UNESCO World Heritage Site.*

Noyon

Birthplace of John Calvin; Cathedral of Notre Dame de Noyon, on the site where emperor Charlemagne was crowned.

Paris

Cathedral of Notre Dame de Paris (Notre Dame)

Reims

Champagne region. Cathedral of Notre Dame de Reims

Strasbourg

Principal city of the Alsace region in northern France; nicknamed the City of Hope, seat of the Council of Europe and the European Union (EU) Parliament.

St. Thomas' Church is the principal Protestant church since 1549, where native Reformation leader Martin Bucer served as pastor.

Peter Waldo and the Waldensians were excommunicated by pope Lucius III in 1184, and later over eighty were burned for heresy in 1211 under pope Innocent III, beginning several centuries of persecution.

Calvin settled here as a scholar and author before being used mightily in Geneva; L'église réformée du Bouclier is a direct descendant of his parish church.

Also: Nightly illumination of the Gothic-style **Strasbourg Cathedral**. The cathedral contains the **Strasbourg Astronomical Clock**. The Strasbourg press formed a strong base for Protestant reformer Martin Luther. See also **Place Gutenberg**, with statue of the inventor of the printing press. Strasbourg was an original center of the Germanic holy Roman empire. There is a statue of the Reformers at the University of Strasbourg, and lovely area called **La Petite Strasbourg** (also known as La Petite France) **quarter**.

GERMANY

Introduction to Germany:

Germany is home to Martin Luther and the Reformation, the town of Oberammergau's once-a-decade *Passion Play*, and the famed December Christmas markets. About two-thirds of Germans are Christians, half of them Protestant, mostly in the north and east, and half Catholic, mostly in the south and west.

It has been said without exaggeration that the Reformation is Saxony's most significant contribution to world history. The strong, rapid wind that circulated Luther's writings turned smoldering discontent toward the Roman Catholic Church into raging flames of religious rebellion. The Reformation set the stage for the Modern Age, because the freedom in choice of religion led to a focus on one's own regional interests.

The Thirty Years' War, one of Europe's most destructive, raged in central Europe from 1618–1648. It began over *religious* differences between Protestants and Catholics, then grew to encompass differences between *political* powers. Nearly one-third of Germany's population died due to famine and war.

Philipp Melanchthon, Luther's colleague at the University of Wittenberg, became the chief theologian of the German Reformation.

The word *Protestant* was first used formally in 1529. The Lutheran faith mostly spread through northern Germany to Scandinavia.

ALTENBURG

Historical Significance:

In 1522, Altenburg asked Luther to send them a German pastor. Luther sent Wenzeslaus Linck, whose marriage he officiated at in 1523, in what was one of the early clerical marriages. Luther traveled to Altenburg sixteen times. In 1518, he met the pope's envoy, who tried without success to convince Luther to be silent. Luther bought Katharina an estate in nearby Zulsdorf, a two-day horse and carriage ride from home. She would regularly spend a few weeks at a time there.

George Spalatin also went to Altenburg at Luther's request to establish Reformation ideas throughout the region. These ideas affected both clerical and secular life.

What to See:

Red Spires, the town's landmark, is the only remnant of the mighty Romanesque-style monastery Church of St. Mary's, funded by the Hohenstaufen emperor Frederick Barbarossa, who attended its inauguration in 1184. Their Augustinian monks were a challenge to Spalatin's reforms for twenty years.

Church of the Brethren, built on the grounds of a former Franciscan monastery in 1905, has opulent Art Nouveau mosaics, a Sauer organ, and large statues of Luther and his friend Spalatin on the façade.

St. Bartholomew's Church, where Luther preached on several occasions. Spalatin is buried here. The church is a gothic hall church with a Romanesque crypt, a Ladegast organ and a Baroque tower with a great view.

Castle Church, along with former St. George Collegiate Church, where Spalatin was canon, has carved choir stalls, murals by an Italian master and a large Trost organ. Organ concerts can be experienced periodically in each of these churches. Church services can be enjoyed at the Church of the Brethren and St. Bartholomew's.

AUGSBURG

Historical Significance:
The most important doctrinal statement of the Lutheran faith, the Augsburg Confession, was drafted and presented by Philipp Melanchthon, Luther's close friend, on behalf of Luther who was in hiding at Wartburg Castle. In 1530 the holy Roman emperor Charles V had asked the German princes to gather and state their religious beliefs at the Fronhof Augsburg at the Diet of Augsburg, also attended by Luther's lord, the Duke of Saxony. The Augsburg Confession was adopted here over Charles' objections.

What to See:
Protestant **St. Ulrich Church,** named after a tenth century bishop; a former monastery assembly hall; and Catholic **St. Afra Church,** the more elaborate, with a beautiful altar. Both built on the site of a Roman temple in the late 1400s, symbolically sit side by side on the Maximilianstrasse, which is known as the most beautiful street in southern Germany.

    St. Anne's Church is the oldest Renaissance building in Germany, where Luther was welcomed as a hero in 1518 when he met with cardinal Cajetan (Thomas de Vio), the papal legate. It has the Luther staircase, and was originally a Carmelite abbey—Protestant since 1525; the small Luther courtyard; and the Fugger chapel.

    Town Hall (Fronhof or Bishop's Palace), on the site of where the Peace of Augsburg was signed in 1555, ending for a time the wars between German Catholics and Protestants (until the Thirty Years' War beginning in 1618). The Renaissance building (built 1615–1620) was destroyed by a 1944 air raid. The "Golden Hall" was reopened in 1985 to celebrate the town's 2,000-year jubilee.

    Also: **St. Mary's Cathedral** (Dom St. Maria), a Gothic cathedral whose restoration begun in 923 AD after damage from invading Magyars. St. Mary's has Europe's oldest stained-glass windows dating from the twelfth century: Old Testament prophets Jonah, Daniel, Hosea, Moses, and David. **Church of the Holy Cross**, where Luther lodged in 1511 after his trip to Rome, impressive **Augustus fountain; Perlach Tower**, adjacent to the Town Hall, with a 210-foot tower offering great views, if you brave the staircase; **Mozart House**, where Wolfgang Amadeus Mozart's father, Leopold, was born, with a museum including an original piano.

Augsburg, a former Roman city, is less than an hour by train northwest of Munich. It has Bavarian hospitality, cuckoo clocks, elaborate Renaissance buildings, ancient canals and medieval buildings.

BERLIN

Historical Significance:

Originally the capital of Prussia, then of East Germany and now of unified Germany, Berlin's faith history started shortly before the Reformation. Later, Lutheran pastor and theology professor Dietrich Bonhoeffer (1906–1945) was arrested with his brother-in-law in 1943, and martyred by Hitler at Flossenburg Concentration Camp for his role in helping Jews escape to Switzerland, and for assassination attempts in this Third Reich capital, shortly before the American liberation. Bonhoeffer opposed the victimizing of religious, ethnic, and social minorities. The Berlin wall went up on August 13, 1961, dividing the city, families, and friends. The 100-mile-long, 13-foot high wall finally came down on November 9, 1988, over twenty-eight years later. The reunified Berlin is one of Europe's largest cities.

What to See:

Three centers today: west (Kurfuerstendamm Boulevard and Memorial Church); east (Unter den linden, Brandenburg Gate and Alexanderplatz); new (Potsdamer Square).

Kaiser Wilhelm Memorial Church, built 1891–1895 in memory of emperor Wilhelm I; old church ruins next to new church (1959–1961).

Pergamon Museum is world famous for its archaeological holdings. It has Islamic and Near East art and antiquities, including the Ishtar Gate of Babylon (sixth century BC), the Pergamon Altar (second century BC) and the façade of the throne hall of king Nebuchadnezzar.

Dietrich Bonhoeffer House Museum, built in 1935 as his parent's retirement home, where his manuscript *After Ten Years* (detailing his analysis of the Germany resistance) was hidden until after the war.

Berlin Cathedral, the former court cathedral of Prussia's royal family, designed as a Protestant response to St. Peter's in Rome.

Also: **Olympic Stadium** (Hitler's 1936 Games); **Brandenburg Gate; Checkpoint Charlie** museum at former Berlin Wall; the **Reichstag**; lively boulevards.

Defining Moment . . . The Berlin Cathedral

Standing on the steps of the **Berlin Cathedral** (the short name for the Evangelical Supreme Parish and Collegiate Church) in formerly communist East Berlin, you would have no idea that the land you are standing on is representative of the course that the Reformation of the Church took. On what is now "Museum Island" where the cathedral is located, Frederick II built a Catholic Chapel which eventually included a convent and then became a Catholic collegiate church. In 1555, Joachim II Hector officially converted from Catholicism to Lutheranism, as many of his subjects had already done, and the collegiate church became Lutheran.

In 1608, prince-Elector John Sigmund took the throne and renamed the cathedral into Supreme Parish Church of Holy Trinity in Cölln. In 1613, he publicly confessed his Calvinist faith and did not demand that his subjects convert, but he did convert the building to a Calvinist church. In 1747, the church was completely demolished to clear space for the Berlin Palace, and in 1750, a new Calvinist church was erected north of the palace. In 1817, the Lutheran and Calvinist congregations joined an umbrella organization called the Evangelical Church in Prussia. In 1893, yet another demolition and rebuilding occurred, resulting in the inauguration of the present building in 1905, under the Evangelical Church of the Union, and was viewed as the Protestant counter to St. Peter's Basilica.

Sometimes we wonder what God thinks as He watches us building up and tearing down, over and over, whether it be the physical buildings we have church in or the religious denominations themselves. It must look like a bunch of children playing in a sandbox, intently building with sand what will only be reformed in a matter of time.

The one, lasting thing that will not be torn down, though, is the very Bride of Christ, the Church with a capital C. Through all of its highs and lows, Jesus is washing His Bride to prepare her ultimately for the Marriage Feast of the Lamb. In the meantime, how do we come together as the one

Bride, ready for our Groom? A gospel preacher once said, "We have got to unite ourselves as one body. Because Jesus is coming back, and He is coming back for a Bride, not a harem." How well that picture illustrates our current status and where we need to be heading—seeing ourselves as a unified body of believers getting ready for our Lord to return. The early Church that Acts describes feels like the ultimate in unity. How do we get back to where we started?

"Just as Christ loved the Church and gave Himself up for her to make her holy, cleansing her by the washing with water through the word and to present her to Himself as a radiant church, without stain or wrinkle or any other blemish, but holy and blameless" (Ephesians 5:25–27).

Journal Time:

What ideas do you have to move our Church (with a capital C) toward the unified Bride that Jesus is coming back for? How have you seen examples of different churches in unity in your community?

Share Time:

Share your ideas for Church unity with each other. Are there any projects coming up in your church that you could invite other churches to join you in?

Prayer:

Lord,

How we long to be the pure, blameless Bride that Jesus is returning for. Keep us from being divided. We repent of being more of a harem than a bride. Show us the path to being the unified Bride that You long for. Help us to remember that in essential beliefs we must remain steadfast as one Church, without wavering or compromising on those Scriptural mandates. In those areas that are non-essential to agree on, let us operate in grace and harmony. Show us how we can be agents of unity in our communities without compromising essential beliefs. We gladly and willingly submit ourselves to Your cleansing through the Word that we will be that radiant Church for You.

In Jesus' name,

Amen

Worship:
"Blessed Be the Tie That Binds"
"With One Voice"

Defining Moment . . . Dietrich Bonhoeffer House Museum

"Silence in the face of evil is itself evil: God will not hold us guiltless. Not to speak is to speak. Not to act is to act."—Dietrich Bonhoeffer.

The Jews have had a long, progressive history of persecution in Germany. Jewish settlers came in the fifth to tenth centuries and, during the Crusades beginning in 1095, saw their persecution begin in Germany with entire communities murdered. They were accused of poisoning wells during the Black Death period (1346–1353), and massive numbers were then slaughtered. At the end of the fifteenth century, many evils were ascribed to the Jews, which resulted in severe religious hatred.

After the fall of Napoleon in 1815, nationalism resulted in further repression with many states stripping Jews of their civil rights. With the founding of the Nazi party in 1920, the persecution began increasing again, and, in 1933, Jews were banned from all professional jobs. In 1933, the *London Daily Mirror* showed a picture of a graveyard plot insinuating that Hitler's grandfather was Jewish.

Enter **Dietrich Bonhoeffer,** a German Lutheran pastor, theologian, and author who publicly took a stand against the Nazis and their treatment of Jews. Two days after Hitler became Chancellor, Bonhoeffer delivered a radio address attacking Hitler and warning Germany to beware of slipping into an idolatrous cult following this *Führer* (leader), who really may be *Verführer* (misleader, or seducer). Bonhoeffer was cut off in the middle of his broadcast. He raised a public voice for Church resistance to Hitler's persecution of Jews, declaring that the Church must not simply "bandage the victims under the wheel, but jam the spoke in the wheel itself." The home that you are standing in was the place he did some of his writing and theology work, as well as the place for many conspiratorial conversations for resistance to the Nazi regime. As did Martin Luther, he spoke out loudly and confidently when he saw wrongs that needed to be righted.

In addition to becoming known for his staunch resistance to the Nazis, he voiced opposition to Hitler's euthanasia program and genocidal persecution of the Jews. Arrested by the Gestapo in April 1943 in this home, and imprisoned for one and a half years, he was then transferred to a Nazi concentration camp. After being allegedly associated with the plot to assassinate Adolf Hitler, he was briefly tried and then executed by hanging in April 1945, just two weeks before Allied forces liberated some of the nearby camps in Europe, and *three weeks* before Hitler's suicide.

A witness at the execution said, "I saw Pastor Bonhoeffer . . . kneeling on the floor praying fervently to God. I was most deeply moved by the way this lovable man prayed, so devout and so certain that God heard his prayer. At the place of execution, he again said a short prayer and then climbed the few steps to the gallows, brave and composed. His death ensued after a few seconds. In the almost fifty years that I worked as a doctor; I have hardly ever seen a man die so entirely submissive to the will of God."

Even though he took a stand early and loudly, he could not convince the majority of Germans to do the same. However, his books and theology have led many to deeper places with God and have even had an impact on ecumenical work in the political and church arenas as far away as South Africa and South Korea.

"I have been crucified with Christ and I no longer live, but Christ lives in me. The life I now live in the body, I live by faith in the Son of God, who loved me and gave Himself for me" (Galatians 2:20).

Journal Time:

Do you ever find yourself wanting to speak out against something that you *know* is wrong, but you do not want to upset the people around you? How have you handled it? How have you witnessed others handling those situations? Is there any difference between how you *have* handled that specific conversation and how you *wished* you had handled it? What inspired you? What were you afraid of? How do you want to handle these situations in the future?

Share Time:

Talk about what it must have been like to take a stand like Bonhoeffer's, standing in the truth while the majority of those around you, even in your church, chose to ignore the situation. What role could the Church have played? What can we learn from the blind consent that most Germans showed, and its repercussions? How do *we* take a stand in our culture for those things that are being blindly endorsed, but that we *know* are wrong? Share examples of times that you have witnessed people handling these types of conversations like Bonhoeffer did—in truth.

Prayer:

   Lord,

   We confess right now that there have been times that we have wanted to speak out on things that we knew were wrong, but we shrunk back, afraid of the consequences. We repent, and we want to be a people that are unafraid to speak out in truth and love no matter what the cost. We cannot do that on our own. Only by Your supernatural power infused in us can we take a stand when You call us into these conversations. We are depending on You to use the Holy Spirit to speak through us and embolden us under Your strength and might. We are committed to standing for You, walking in Your Truth and Love, and trusting You to use us to speak Your light into the world with great love.

   In Jesus' name we pray,
   Amen

Worship:

   "Be Thou My Vision"
   "Give us Your Courage" by Tim Hughes

EISENACH

Historical Significance:

Eisenach, thirty miles west of Erfurt, is where Luther was raised and where he preached in 1521 at St. George's Church on the way to and from the Diet of Worms (Imperial Parliament). Nearby Wartburg Castle, a UNESCO World Heritage Site, is where he hid in refuge for a year under the protection of Frederick the Wise of Saxony in 1521, disguised as "knight George" (Junker Jörg) after a faked kidnapping. He translated the New Testament from Erasmus's Greek language *Textus Receptus* into German during that year. He called Eisenach "my dear town" and visited again in 1529 en route to the religious rallies in Marburg, and for three weeks in 1540. The town sits in the Thuringian Forest, northeast of Frankfurt/Mainz, west of Leipzig and Dresden.

Johann Sebastian Bach was born here in 1685 and attended St. George's Latin School as did Luther (1498–1501).

What to See:

An entire quarter is transformed into a series of lovingly detailed scenes from the late Middle Ages. Artisans, entertainers, and people in historical costumes recreate a medieval market atmosphere. Luther's life story is staged in three parts at open-air venues.

Luther House Museum (Lutherhaus) is a childhood home where he lived with the councilman Cotta's family (relatives) from 1498–1501. One of the oldest half-timbered homes in town, it now houses a modern exhibition.

Bach House (Bachhaus) is a museum with a statue dedicated to Johann Sebastian Bach, the great composer (you might hear a curator playing period instruments impromptu). While Bach likely never lived here, it is a good example of an early eighteenth century, middle income home, with original furnishings. The museum includes an extensive collection of sixteenth to nineteenth century musical instruments, with hands-on features.

St. George's Church (Georgenkirche) is where Luther was baptized, served as a choir boy, and preached in 1521 on his way to and from the Diet of Worms; Bach was baptized at St. George's Church in 1685 and several members of his family were organists here (his baptismal font is still here); see the large painting on the north wall of Luther and Martin Hus at the Augsburg Conference. The Bach statue is at the entrance hall. Organ concerts can be enjoyed July through September.

Wartburg Castle, occasionally called "Lutherburg," is just up the hill on a rocky spur looking north and south. Built in 1067 by Louis the Springer, it includes the room in which Luther took refuge in 1521–1522 and translated the New Testament. It retains original sections from the feudal period and was reconstructed in the nineteenth century by the Grand Duke of Saxony. Richard Wagner's "Tannhauser" was inspired by the Castle. Guided tour and museum; concerts in the Great Hall from May to October; organ concerts in the Chapel. This is a UNESCO World Heritage Site.

Reuter-Wagner Museum has the world's second largest collection of Wagner's works.

Luther Festival (August) tells the story of Luther's life in three parts.

Defining Moment . . . Wartburg Castle

With his 95 Theses, Luther had taken a stand against the Church for selling indulgences for the forgiveness of sin. Since this was a major revenue source for the building of St. Peter's Basilica in Rome, the Church leaders were incensed. On May 25, 1521, the holy Roman emperor Charles V declared Luther an outlaw, banned all of the books he had written, branded him a heretic, excommunicated him from the Catholic Church, and made it a crime for anyone to give him food or shelter. He also legally allowed anyone to capture Luther and be rewarded for bringing him to the courts to be sentenced by a court of law and executed. Talk about a bad day! But God had other plans.

Frederick the Wise did not have much interaction with Luther and stayed a Catholic until his death, but was gradually inclined toward the Reformation doctrines. Frederick planned a fake highway attack on Luther's route to Wittenberg, "kidnapping" him and then hiding him in Wartburg

Castle. From May 1521 to March 1522, Martin Luther was hidden in this castle under the name "knight George." Hidden away for this extended period, he could have been depressed and questioned God about what He was doing. Luther chose a different route. He got busy and translated the New Testament from Greek into German. It was not the first translation in German, but it was in a vernacular that the people could understand, and it quickly became the most circulated translation of the Bible.

Luther referred to Wartburg as "his Patmos," comparing his time there with John, who wrote the book of Revelation when *he* was imprisoned in a cave in Patmos, Greece. What Satan meant for harm, God turned into a blessing for the Kingdom that was like rocket fuel for the Reformation. Just as Joseph said to his brothers who had sold him into slavery and eventual imprisonment: "*You intended to harm me, but God intended it for good to accomplish what is now being done, the saving of many lives*" (Genesis 50:20). In hindsight, Luther can now say the same thing to the Catholic Church.

With the Bible in the hands of the people, written so they could understand it, the power of the Word of God was about to reveal itself in a whole new way.

Journal Time:

Consider this Scripture.

> *In the same way, the Spirit helps us in our weakness. We do not know what we ought to pray for, but the Spirit himself intercedes for us through wordless groans. And he who searches our hearts knows the mind of the Spirit, because the Spirit intercedes for God's people in accordance with the will of God.* ***And we know that in all things God works for the good of those who love Him, who have been called according to His purpose***
>
> (Romans 8:26–28).

Ask the Holy Spirit to remind you of a time of difficulty that He eventually turned into a blessing. Are you going through a difficult time right now? Ask God to help you remember His promise above, and that He is faithful, just like He was last time. Write down the thoughts and feelings He is putting in your heart about this subject.

Share Time:

Share with each other testimonies of how you or others went through a difficult situation and watched God show up and turn it into good. How can we encourage one another to remember God's faithfulness? Are you going through a situation right now that you can ask this group to encourage you through, to remind you of how God will work this situation out for the good?

Prayer:

Lord,

Thank You for Your promise that in all things You work for the good of those who love You, who have been called according to Your purpose. Please infuse those of us going through difficult times right now with trust. Help us to remember the times You turned seemingly impossible situations into good, right before our eyes. We confess our fear. Please help us turn around and stand in Your strength and love, keeping our eyes on You, and not the problem. Help us to be more impressed with Your power than we are with the circumstances around us.

In Jesus' name,
Amen

Worship:

"Great is Thy Faithfulness"
"I Walk By Faith"

Defining Moment . . . Bach House

The "Defining Moment" teaching from Leipzig's St. Thomas Church can also be used at the Bach House.

EISLEBEN

Historical Significance:

Martin Luther was born and baptized here in 1483, gave his last sermon and died here in 1546, while mediating a dispute between the Count of Mansfield and his family over copper mining. The official name of the city is Lutherstat Eisleben ("City of Luther"). Luther's father, Hans, owned copper mines here, and he encouraged his son to be an attorney. Luther lived seven miles away in Mansfield for most of his youth. Eisleben was first mentioned in 997 AD, and recognized as a town since the twelfth century. The town was the economic and cultural center of once powerful Mansfield county, at the crossroads of two major trading routes. Eisleben was referred to as "the Reformer's Bethlehem and Jerusalem."

What to See:

Near Wittenburg; a two-hour drive from Berlin; in the hilly countryside at the eastern foot of the Harz mountains. Eisleben is one of the oldest towns between the Elbe and the Harz, a medieval market, town hall, and residences. It is home to 25,000 people.

Martin Luther's Birth House (Geburtshaus, reconstructed after the town fire in 1689) in the Langen Gasse (Long Alley) neighborhood, has been a museum since 1693 and features an original baptismal font dating back to 1517. **Martin Luther's Death House** (Sterbehaus), on St. Andrew's Church Square, built in 1498, has replicas of his death mask and hands, as well as the original pall that decorated his coffin. In this place where he died, you can see a copy of the first translated German Bible. These are UNESCO World Heritage Sites.

St. Peter and Paul Church/Baptistery is where Luther was baptized the day after his birth. It was renovated in 1983 to commemorate the 500th anniversary of his birth. It has three bells from the Reformation period.

St. Andreas' Church (Andreaskirche) is where Luther preached his last four sermons in 1546, and where he laid in state before burial in Wittenberg. It is in excellent shape and features the original pulpit and a late Gothic altar. It is directly across from Luther's Death House. Organ concerts from May through September.

Luther Monument (Lutherdenkmal) is in the center of town, in Market Square, created in 1883 and consecrated on the 400th anniversary of his birth. In his hands are the papal bull and his Bible.

St. Anne's Church is an old miner's church with unique Biblical scenes cast in stone, visited by Luther as the curate of his Order, along with the adjacent Augustinian Hermit Cloister.

Sunday services are held in each of these three churches.

Defining Moment . . . Luther's Death House

"Therefore, since we are surrounded by such a great cloud of witnesses, let us throw off everything that hinders and the sin that so easily entangles. And let us run with perseverance the race marked out for us" (Hebrews 12:1).

Luther ran an amazing race. God used him to sanctify a Church that was veering scarily off course. While other Reformation giants took part in this same amazing process, Luther was one of the standouts. His unwavering faith and trust in God was formidable. He stood for God's truth, putting his own life in mortal danger. We stand in awe of what God achieved through him in this process—and then we see the end of his life.

As we think about Luther's death in Eisleben, we are confronted with a haunting reality. It is an end that evades resolution when viewed from the beginning. Luther did not "finish well." He ended poorly. His vehement destructive directives toward the Jews would have repercussions for centuries, as outlined earlier in this book's biography of Luther:

"He sadly did in his later years, however, also write that Jews' homes and synagogues should be destroyed and funds expropriated, writings that were used extensively 400 years later for Nazi propaganda. He advocated kindness to Jews to convert them, but became bitter when those efforts did not succeed, arguing they were no longer God's chosen people."

The result of his cultural blindness was disastrous. His diatribes against the Jews were used to fuel the fire of one of the largest atrocities in world history through the Nazi concentration camps.

This conflicting view of Luther led me to discuss my lament with a friend, who reminded me that many other heroes of the faith had the same propensity to sin: David killed his adulterous lover's husband, and Saul went from being chosen by God as Israel's first king to going on a murderous rampage, intending to kill his replacement. My friend also reminded me that not even Luther was exempt from cultural standards that are built in sin, brick by brick. In Luther's time, there was immense hatred and prejudice against Jews. They were thought of in dehumanizing terms. Think of the way black slaves were viewed in the first half of the 1800s. Instead of questioning the status quo, like he did when he nailed up those 95 Theses, he "drank the Kool-Aid" of his culture. He did not see himself as sinning.

Pythagoras had a brilliant parable of how this plays out. If you are on a large ship and the tables are set for dining with the room filled with people laughing and chatting in elegance and luxury, everyone is comfortable—even though they may be heading the wrong direction, toward disaster. If one person takes a stand and becomes a fixed point that does not move with the rest of the room, he creates utter havoc. Tea cups shatter, tables implode into each other and chaos ensues—all because the entire room keeps on moving to that same destination, regardless of the person who took a stand. Luther was willing to take a stand for the Reformation of the Church and the ensuing chaos. But even he was duped when it came to taking a stand for the rights of Jews.

How can we learn from his mistakes? There are still pastors in the United States that see blacks as inferior, even in this enlightened age. There are Blacks that hate Whites because of slavery that happened over 150 years ago. How do we look through God's lens, like Luther did for the Reformation, and not through culture's lens, like Luther did with the Jews?

Journal Time:
Ask the Holy Spirit to reveal to you any ways that you, or the culture around you, are headed in the wrong direction with your thinking. It could be

about race, sexuality, marriage, church leadership—the list is long. Ask God how *He* wants to change your thinking on this issue. Also think about changes that you see, or culture that shows that we are heading in the right direction. Where are we listening to the Holy Spirit, as a nation, and making breakthroughs?

Share Time:

Use this time to repent, either for yourself, or your culture, on issues that we have wrong thinking about. How can you be an advocate for change in the culture you live in? Also share with each other about the ways that you see God showing up in our culture, steering us in the right direction.

Prayer:

Dear Lord,

Thank You for Your truth that inspires us and sets us free. Thank You for Your Holy Spirit that we can depend on to reveal those areas to us that we and our culture are heading in the wrong direction on. Lord, at this time, we stand in the gap and repent on behalf of our culture for _____ (use what was discussed in share time). We want to finish strong for You. We claim Your words in Hebrews over this lament: "since we are surrounded by such a great cloud of witnesses, let us throw off everything that hinders and the sin that so easily entangles. And let us run with perseverance the race marked out for us."

In Jesus' name,

Amen

Worship:

"Awakening"—Chris Tomlin

"O God of Truth"

ERFURT

Historical Significance:

Erfurt, founded in 742 AD by English missionary Boniface, was Luther's spiritual home. He attended the leading university in Germany, the University of Erfurt, the equivalent of Harvard or Oxford, founded in 1392 by wealthy merchants. He received his liberal arts degree in 1502 and a Master's of Philosophy in 1505. Luther then served as a monk from 1505–1511 at the former Augustinian church—he dedicated himself as a monk on its floor—and monastery. While a student, he made a vow during a terrifying lightning storm to enter the monastery. Originally built at a major trade crossroads, Erfurt is still the capital of Thuringia.

What to See:

Erfurt is one of the better-preserved medieval city centers with Renaissance buildings in Germany, eighty miles southwest of Leipzig, thirty miles east of Eisenach. Half-timbered buildings are dwarfed by the towering spires of St. Mary's Cathedral and the Church of St. Severus. Pope Benedict XVI visited in 2011.

Luther's Augustinian Church and Monastery (Augustinerkirche), founded by hermits in the mid-thirteenth century, a Protestant monastery today. The former Augustinian monastery, with a cloister, church, and courtyards, was built in 1277. Here Luther studied the "seven ancient sciences." Luther hesitated a long time before celebrating his first mass (Primiz) here—feeling so unworthy, he sat on a stone bench to the side of the altar, which is still there. It was badly damaged in 1945 in World War II but later rebuilt in authentic historic style.

The church is now used for international Protestant conferences, and it houses exhibitions on the history of the Bible and the monastery. Luther was inspired to create the "Lutheran Rose" here. You can stay at the monastery today with the Sisters of the Casteller Ring. As Luther first entered to become

342 | DEFINING MOMENTS

a monk in 1505, he closed the doors on his friends, saying "You can see me today, but never again." There is a window depicting the lives of Jesus and St. Augustine, and a permanent Luther exhibition.

Known as the Merchant's Bridge, or Tradesman's Bridge, unique **Kramer Bridge** (Krämerbrücke), with thirty-two timber-framed, restored homes, plus shops and cafes on its 400-foot length, is the largest inhabited bridge in northern Europe. It was built of stone after repeated fires, and originally had a church at each end.

Buchenwald Concentration camp from World War II is nearby.

The **University of Erfurt** was closed by the Prussians in 1816, nearly completely destroyed in World War II in 1945, and recently restored. A Defining Moment for Luther was discovering a rare copy of a complete Bible in 1503 in the university library that opened his eyes to the depth of the Word far beyond the few Scriptures used in church services.

Also: **Luther Monument**; the **Church of St. Aegidius**; the **Predigerkirche,** where you can attend organ concerts from May through September; **St. Andrew's Quarter**; **St. Michael's Church** where Luther preached; and two churches high on a hill: **St. Severus's Church** and late Gothic **St. Mary's Cathedral**, where he was ordained in 1507; Erfurt also has the third-oldest university building in Germany (1392), the renovated **Imperial Hall**.

Nearby in Stottenheim is the **Luther Stone** where Luther made his vow during the storm.

Lutherkeller Restaurant at Kaisersaal, (emperor's hall) recreates meals based on authentic medieval recipes with period music.

St. Martin's Festival each November celebrates both Luther and their patron saint, St. Martin of Tours.

The largest Christmas Market in Thuringia has been held for over 150 years, set against St. Severus's and St. Mary's.

Defining Moment . . . Luther's Augustinian Church and Monastery
As we stand inside **Luther's Augustinian Church and Monastery,** we can imagine the peaceful life of monks who served God, but if this is how we imagine Luther's early life as a monk, we would be wrong. The twisted

ideas Luther experienced all started back in his childhood home. His father, Hans, was harsh, demanding, unforgiving, and impossible to please, and his mother was not much better. Luther grew up in great fear of his father. When he made a vow to God to become a monk if He protected him during a severe thunderstorm, Hans's reaction was as judgmental and rejecting of Martin as they come. He wanted Martin to be a lawyer.

When Martin finished his vows and was ordained, Hans attended the mass intending to forgive his son's disobedience. When Martin was nervous and did poorly performing the mass, Hans is reported to have said, "God give that it was not a devil's spook." He was implying that Martin's vow made during that storm on the way to Erfurt was satanically inspired.

It is no wonder that the harsh, unforgiving, performance-based upbringing Martin had resulted in him projecting that same image onto Father God. When Martin was at this monastery, he was tormented by the thought that no one could be good enough for God to accept. He fasted and lay out in the snow until other monks dragged him back in half dead, all because he thought that was what would make him *enough* to be accepted by God. Luther described this period of his life as one of deep spiritual despair. He said, "I lost touch with Christ the Savior and Comforter, and made of Him the jailer and hangman of my poor soul."

Had not his mentor, Johannes von Staupitz, provided one of the cornerstones of Luther's faith, he might have literally killed himself by mistakenly trying to gain God's acceptance through self-punishment. Staupitz urged him to trust in the goodness and mercy of God instead of relying on his own effort to earn Salvation. He pointed Luther's mind away from continual reflection upon his sins toward the grace and love of Christ. He taught that true repentance does not involve self-inflicted penances and punishments but rather a change of heart. These ideas laid the groundwork for Martin to discover a few years later that the grace of God *alone* saves.

As we think about the needless torment that Martin Luther went through because of his mistaken image of God, we still see that same wrong projection appear in people's thoughts of Him today. The ideas that are embedded into us by our authority figures at an early age can have a great effect on how we see *God* as our authority figure in later years.

I grew up with perfectionistic parents who did more punishing than comforting. It is no surprise that I viewed God that way, and it took years for me to see him as the loving, fair, gracious, merciful, forgiving God that He really is. For years, I thought that my Salvation was in my own hands, and that if I was not perfect, I would not be going to Heaven. But God later showed me that those were lies from my childhood, and that He had never set those conditions for me.

God did the same for Luther, and was not about to let him continue down the painful, condemning path he was on. In fact, God was about to use his pain and torment to turn a wayward church from darkness to light. Only someone with Luther's history could understand how vital the truth was about God. After discovering it himself, he knew that it needed to be shared with the world, so that the darkness that the Church was propagating about God could be stopped.

Psalm 124:1–8
If the LORD had not been on our side—
let Israel say—
if the LORD had not been on our side
when people attacked us,
they would have swallowed us alive
when their anger flared against us;
the flood would have engulfed us,
the torrent would have swept over us,
the raging waters
would have swept us away.
Praise be to the LORD,
who has not let us be torn by their teeth.
We have escaped like a bird
from the fowler's snare;
the snare has been broken,
and we have escaped.
Our help is in the name of the LORD,
the Maker of Heaven and earth.

Journal Time:

The good news about authority figures is that they also can be wonderful influences who can reflect true and right images of God to us. Think about the authority figures in your childhood. What did you learn from them that showed you parts of God's character that have built up your relationship with Him? On the other hand, are there any negative things that you learned from authority figures that you have falsely projected onto God? Write them down and leave them here, in Erfurt, like Luther did.

Share Time:

Share from your Journal Time the good things that you learned from those in authority over you in childhood, and also the wrong things that have been projected onto God. When you speak about the wrong things, begin by declaring in front of the group: "In the past, I thought that God was _____. I know that is a lie, and I renounce that thought and leave it here in Erfurt. The truth is that God is _____."

Prayer:

Dear Father in Heaven,

Our hearts break as we think of the needless torment Your sons and daughters have gone through by believing lies about who You really are. Forgive us, Lord. Give us the gift of Your true repentance. Show us when these lies come up in us and others. Give us all the revelation and discernment to see the lies when they appear, renounce them, and then to walk in the freedom, liberty, and abundant life that You died to give us. Lord, we pray for all those whom we love, that we can be examples to them and set them free of this same trap.

Help us to do for others what Staupitz did for Luther. Show us, also, the deeply hidden lies that are hidden in the cracks of our own souls that we need to have revealed so that we can renounce them and declare the truth of who You really are. We trust You to do this work in us. Thank you for what You have already done while we are here in Erfurt. Thank You for what you did in Martin Luther. Let the re-formation happening in each one of us spread like yeast in each of our churches and communities. We praise You for what is to come.

We praise you with the words Martin Luther eventually wrote as a hymn:

"Dear Christians, One and All, Rejoice" (Lutheran Service Book #556)

Dear Christians, one and all, rejoice,
With exultation springing,
And with united heart and voice
And holy rapture singing,
Proclaim the wonders God has done,
How His right arm the victory won,
What price our ransom cost Him!
Fast bound in Satan's chains I lay;
Death brooded darkly o'er me.
Sin was my torment night and day;
In sin my mother bore me.
But daily deeper still I fell;
My life became a living hell,
So firmly sin possessed me.
My own good works all came to naught,
No grace or merit gaining;
Free will against God's judgment fought,
Dead to all good remaining.
My fears increased till sheer despair
Left only death to be my share;
The pangs of hell I suffered.
But God had seen my wretched state
Before the world's foundation,
And mindful of His mercies great,
He planned for my Salvation.
He turned to me a father's heart;
He did not choose the easy part
But gave His dearest treasure.
God said to His beloved Son:
"It's time to have compassion.
Then go, bright jewel of My crown,
And bring to all Salvation.
From sin and sorrow set them free;

Slay bitter death for them that they
May live with You forever."
The Son obeyed His Father's will,
Was born of virgin mother;
And God's good pleasure to fulfill,
He came to be my brother.
His royal power disguised He bore;
A servant's form, like mine, He wore
To lead the devil captive.
To me He said: "Stay close to Me,
I am your rock and castle.
Your ransom I Myself will be;
For you I strive and wrestle.
For I am yours, and you are Mine,
And where I am you may remain;
The foe shall not divide us.
Though he will shed My precious blood,
Me of My life bereaving,
All this I suffer for your good;
Be steadfast and believing.
Life will from death the victory win;
My innocence shall bear your sin,
And you are blest forever.
"Now to My Father I depart,
From earth to heaven ascending,
And, heavenly wisdom to impart,
The Holy Spirit sending;
In trouble He will comfort you
And teach you always to be true
And into truth shall guide you.
What I on earth have done and taught
Guide all your life and teaching;
So shall the kingdom's work be wrought
And honored in your preaching.

But watch lest foes with base alloy
The heavenly treasure should destroy;
This final word I leave you.
In Jesus' name,
Amen

Worship:

"Dear Christians, One and All, Rejoice" by Martin Luther
"Here I am to Worship"

LEIPZIG

Historical Significance:
City of the Disputation, Leipzig has been a flourishing trading city since the Bronze Age, and became a Protestant city in 1539 upon the death of Elector George the Bearded. Luther visited here seven times, including for the consecration of St. Paul's Church as the first Protestant church at a German university. It survived multiple wars, but was demolished in 1968 by the Communists. Their rule could not stop the Reformers, though. The prayers for peace led to the Monday Demonstrations that led to the downfall of the East German regime, resulting in German reunification.

What to See:
The Town Hall is on the site of Pleissenburg Castle, where Luther debated Johann Eck during the Leipzig Disputation. The tower dates back to the original castle building.

St. Nicholas's Church (Nicholaskirche), where the "Pray for Peace" Christians held peace prayer services until the Berlin Wall fell in 1989.

St. Thomas's Church, where Luther preached and Johann Sebastian Bach directed the boys' choir (then 54 boys, today 100), and served as cantor and organist for 27 years, and is buried in front of the altar. St. Thomas's Church was built on the site of a thirteenth century monastery, and heavily restored after World War II damage. The choir still performs twice weekly with the Gewandhaus orchestra when they are not traveling. Mozart and Mendelssohn also performed here. Richard Wagner was christened here in 1813. Schiller wrote "Ode to Joy" here; the poem that became the principal theme of Beethoven's Ninth Symphony. Bach's statue and tomb are here; afternoon and evening Bach concerts are held here.

The Old City Hall History Museum (Stadtgeschichtliches) in the city center has Luther's chalice, a goblet that was a gift from the king of Sweden;

Luther's writings, and Katherine von Bora's wedding ring (engraved with their wedding date).

Bach Monument, Johann was in in charge of music for the city, the churches, and the university.

Also: **Lutherkirche**; **Auerbachs Keller**; a restaurant made famous by Goethe in his play *Faust*; **Bach Museum**; **Thuringer Hof**, the oldest restaurant in Leipzig which was frequented by Luther; **Museum of Fine Arts** with its extensive collection of Lucas Cranach workshop pieces.

Defining Moment . . . St. Thomas's Church

Surprisingly, Bach's twenty-seven-year appointment at **St. Thomas's Church** was far from happy. During his time as musical director, the community saw his compositions as obsolete, and thus paid him at near poverty levels. They were far from impressed while Bach was creating what are today considered some of his finest pieces. He wrote, for a time, a cantata a week. Many composers today take a year to write a cantata. When he died, much of his music was sold, and reportedly, some of it used to wrap garbage. He was largely forgotten by the public until Felix Mendelssohn performed *The Passion of St. Matthew in 1829 and began a revival of his work. This revival had an impact on God's Kingdom that Bach most likely never imagined in his wildest dreams.*

Bach was a musician and composer, but he was also a theologian. At the age of forty-eight, Johann Sebastian Bach obtained his own copy of Luther's three-volume translation of the Bible. For him, it was like finding a gold mine. His margin notes show how closely Scripture and music were intertwined for him. Near 1 Chronicles 25 he wrote, "This chapter is the true foundation of all God-pleasing music." At 2 Chronicles 5:13, where Temple musicians are praising God, he wrote, "At a reverent performance of music, God is always at hand with His gracious presence."

The trumpeters and musicians joined in unison to give praise and thanks to the LORD. Accompanied by trumpets, cymbals and other instruments, the singers raised their voices in praise to the LORD and sang: "He is good; His love endures forever." Then the temple of the LORD was filled with the cloud.

(2 Chronicles 5:13).

Bach is known for being able to write the musical equivalents of verbal ideas. Since most of his music was based on Biblical texts, he used music to express his theology in ways that are bringing people to Christ even today. He wrote 1,000 compositions. Almost seventy-five percent of them are written for worship. Through this amazing gift that God gave him, he was able to communicate Scripture through music, without using words. People actually hear Scripture coming through his pieces long after he died. The repercussions of this gift still occur centuries later.

An article from *Christianity Today* reported that Yuko Maruyama, a Japanese organist working in Minneapolis, was once a devout Buddhist. Now she is a Christian thanks to the music of J.S. Bach. "Bach introduced me to God, Jesus, and Christianity," she told *Metro Lutheran*, a Twin Cities monthly. "When I play a fugue, I can feel Bach talking to God." Masashi Masuda, a Jesuit priest, came to faith in almost the same way: "Listening to Bach's *Goldberg Variations* first aroused my interest in Christianity." Today, Masuda teaches theology at Tokyo's Sophia University.

Additionally, current-day Hungarian composer György Kurtág gave this quote: "Consciously, I am certainly an atheist, but I do not say it out loud, because if I look at Bach, I cannot be an atheist. Then I have to accept the way he believed. His music never stops praying. And how can I get closer if I look at him from the outside? I do not believe in the Gospels in a literal fashion, but a Bach fugue has the Crucifixion in it—as the nails are being driven in. In music, I am always looking for the hammering in of the nails."

Because of Bach's musical genius, his love of Christ, and the effect that his musical arrangements have of sharing the Gospel, he is known in many circles as the Fifth Evangelist. Someday, in Eternity, Luther will get to see that his three-volume German translation of the Bible fell into the hands of a man who then translated it into music. That man, Johann Bach, will be able to see how his translation of Scripture into music brought people into God's Kingdom beyond his wildest imagination.

> *And to know this love that surpasses knowledge—that you may be filled to the measure of all the fullness of God. Now to Him who is able to do immeasurably more than all we ask or imagine, according to His power that is at work within us, to Him be glory in the church and in Christ Jesus throughout all generations, for ever and ever! Amen*
> (Ephesians 3:19–21).

Journal Time:

In his lifetime, Bach saw little appreciation for his musical work, yet God is using it years later for His Glory. Are there times you have put a lot of effort into serving God, while not seeing the outcome you anticipated? Journal about your experiences. Can you think of ways that God might use your work years from now?

Share Time:

Sometimes God lets us see the direct fruits of our work, and sometimes it is hidden from us until Eternity comes. Talk about your experiences in serving God without seeing the outcome. Encourage each other and bless each other with stories—your story or the stories of others having found out how God used something for His purposes.

Prayer:

Lord,

We have to admit that we really do desire to see the effect of our work for You. We do long for that immediate gratification. But in Your wisdom, You have chosen that we get to see the fruits of our labors only sometimes. We know that You have great reasons for what You are doing, and acknowledge that You might even be protecting us from our own pride. Please keep us humble when we do get to see the glimpses of Your Glory through the work You allow us to help with. Please keep speaking encouragement over us when we know that we are working in the calling You have assigned us, even when we do not see it making a difference.

Thank You for the example of Bach and how he gave his all in his work for You, despite disapproval from his community and a complete lack of appreciation for his effort. Keep us working for an audience of One, which is You, our Lord.

In Jesus' name,

Amen

Worship:

"Jesu, Joy of Man's Desiring" arranged by J.S. Bach

NUREMBERG

Historical Significance:

Nuremberg played a key role in the Reformation, as its citizens readily accepted the new ideas to the point that Luther called it the eyes and ears of Germany. It was the first German city to become Protestant. It was also known as a major media center, as it had up to twenty-one print shops where Reformation pamphlets were distributed to the masses. Luther's Bible was printed here from 1613–1792. Because Nuremberg's print skills were so advanced, Saxon dukes had their ceremonial Bibles printed here, not in their homelands. The Reformation took such a strong hold of the city that, until 1806, Catholics were unable to become citizens.

What to See:

Kaiserburg Castle, also known as the Imperial Castle of Nuremberg, was built in the Middle Ages, and is mentioned as royal property as early as 1050. With its towers and gardens, it is one of the prime tourist attractions in the area. Tours are available of the Double Chapel, tower, gardens, and museum.

Albrecht Dürer's House is the four-story home of the artist who lived here from 1471–1528. Dürer was an artist whose media included engraving, watercolors, and woodcut prints, mostly of religious themes. It is not known if he ever left the Catholic Church, but he had contact with the most outspoken Reformers of his time: Zwingli, Melanchthon, and Erasmus. He drew a picture of Luther in his private diary and said, "God help me that I may go to Martin Luther; thus I intend to make a portrait of him with great care and engrave him on a copper plate to create a lasting memorial of the Christian man who helped me overcome so many difficulties." Tours of the home are available through a headset with "Agnes Dürer" explaining what it is like to live in an artistic household.

St. Lawrence Church was begun in 1250 and became a three-aisled, late Gothic church. Severely damaged during World War II, it has been reconstructed to its former beauty.

St. Sebaldus Church is one of the oldest and most important churches in the city. It is located at Albrecht- Dürer -Platz. Named after a missionary, it has been a Lutheran church since Reformation times.

Defining Moment . . . Nuremberg

Pieces of land hold significance emotionally and symbolically in our world, and Nuremberg is no exception. Nuremberg is symbolic in Reformation history because in 1525 it officially accepted the Protestant Reformation, and in 1532 the Peace of Nuremberg was signed here. This document entitled the followers of Luther to important concessions.

This city is also the site of other symbolic events. The Nazis chose to use Nuremberg as their primary location for party conventions and propaganda rallies because of its relevance to the holy Roman empire at one time. It was the place where empire leaders met and made agreements, and also the location of the courts. Hitler chose it as if it would add legitimacy to his party. It became the center of Nazi activity. Hitler even arranged for the Nuremberg Laws to be passed here, stripping Jews of their rights as German citizens.

But here is what Hitler did *not* see coming: after the Nazi defeat in World War II, the Trials at Nuremberg also took place here. The Russians wanted these military tribunals to take place in Berlin, but because Nuremberg was the city where Jews were stripped of their citizenship, there was great symbolism in justice being brought here. The leaders were sentenced to prison or death for their roles in Nazi crimes during the war. Justice was served in Nuremberg.

There is a pattern in these events. Wrongs have been committed, yet justice prevails, and it is Nuremberg where it is served. This pattern is but a whisper of what we as believers encounter with our Lord. In Jerusalem, our Christ was wrongly accused and hung on a Cross—the greatest injustice that ever occurred on our planet. Yet, Jerusalem is the city that will be redeemed, where Christ will reign forever, and where we will experience paradise with our Lord. Our God turns our mourning into dancing, our sorrow into joy—on the same land where we experienced our hurt.

When it comes to His Bride, His beloved, the Church, the same pattern appears. There has been much trauma that has happened in the name of the Church. In Luther's time, authority was abused by the Catholic Church and people were lied to. In England, men were burned at the stake for making Bibles available to the masses. The Crusades were responsible for killing thousands of innocents.

The Church, the Bride of Christ, has been disloyal, deceitful, prideful, irresponsible, and even murderous. Yet it is this very Church that our Lord promises to wash clean for Himself, to redeem and to love for Eternity. Just as Jerusalem will be redeemed from the land where our Savior was crucified, to the land that He will rule eternally, the Church will experience that same redemption. The same place where mourning and sorrow came from will hold dancing and joy, under the power and sanctification of our Lord.

"Christ loved the Church and gave Himself up for Her to make Her Holy, cleansing Her by the washing with water through the word, and to present Her to Himself as a radiant Church, without stain or wrinkle or any other blemish, but Holy and blameless" (Ephesians 5:25–27).

The Reformation is a great example of this verse: Christ washing the Bride "with water through the word." It was His Word that enabled Luther to be the first individual to Scripturally hold the Catholic Church accountable for the heretical sale of indulgences. It is through the Reformation era that the Word was made available to the masses, again to "wash" the Bride. There are countless ways that our Lord continues to sanctify us, His Bride, His Church, to make us holy and blameless so that we can be presented to Him as his Eternal beloved.

Journal Time:

As Christ cleanses the Church and makes Her Holy for Himself, He does the same for each one of us. Think of a time that you were mired in a sin issue in your life, and remember how God rescued you and made you Holy for His Glory. Write God a prayer of thanks for His work in your life. If you have not had an encounter like this with God, ask Him to cleanse you through the Word and to take you through the gift of sanctification.

Share Time:

Share with each other the victories of how God has rescued you, washed you and then used you in the very place you used to be enslaved by sin. Talk about how you also see Him washing and restoring the Church today.

Prayer:

Dear Lord,

We are beyond grateful for Your sanctifying work in us and in the Church. Thank You for never giving up on us. Thank You for washing us in the Word, and for the Word itself. Please let us hold Your cleansing for what it really is—a gift to us. Thank You for using this cleansing as the way out of misery and all the consequences of sin. Thank You that it is You who does the washing. We trust You to wash us and make us a "radiant Church, without stain or wrinkle or any other blemish, but holy and blameless."

In Jesus' name,

Amen

Worship:

"Nothing But the Blood" (Hillsong version)

"Nothing But the Blood" (Traditional version)

WITTENBERG

Historical Significance:

Known as the Birthplace of the Reformation, this is the prime spot, sixty miles southwest of Berlin, on the trail of Martin Luther, where he lived for more than thirty-five years, raised his family, posted his *95 Theses* to the door of All Saints Castle Church in 1517, and is buried. The door was used as the University's bulletin board at the time. Luther lived here from 1508 until his death. The text of the *95 Theses* is now cast in bronze on the door. The 500th anniversary of Luther's bold act was in 2017. Wittenberg's official name today is Lutherstadt-Wittenberg ("city of Luther"). This small town on the Elbe became the center of Europe's spiritual life.

Wittenberg was also the home of Frederick the Wise's princely residence. Luther's benefactor, Frederick the Wise, a very large man who had never met Luther, ruled the Electorate of Saxony from 1486–1525. He made Wittenberg his primary home, building a residential castle in lieu of a military fortress. Today only the castle church in the northeast wing is standing. He protected Luther for political, not spiritual, reasons, as he sought to weaken the power of the pope and the holy Roman emperor. He earned the moniker, The Wise, for his success in avoiding military conflict. On his deathbed, he received sacraments, a late commitment to the Reformation he had contributed to.

What to See:

Luther House Museum (Lutherhalle), built by Frederick the Wise, is where Luther lived and worked for thirty-five years, beginning his career as an Augustinian monk. Luther House Museum is the largest and greatest Reformation museum in the world. Exhibits include his teaching robe, desk, pulpit Bible, first edition writings, manuscripts, pamphlets, and monk's habit. It had been the three-story Augustinian monastery he lived in as a monk, and later as co-owner with wife Katherine von Bora and their six children, after Frederick the Wise purchased it for him. This is a UNECSO World Heritage Site.

(All Saints) Castle Church (Schlosskirche) to the west has a bronze replica door that replaced the original wooden door that Luther nailed his protest to. The tombs of Luther and Melanchthon are here. Castle Church was built by Frederick the Wise between 1490–1511, burned down during the Seven Years' War in 1760 (which is when the original door was lost), and rebuilt as a monument to the Reformation in 1892. It lost its original character when used as a barracks in the nineteenth century. The painting over the door features Luther with Philipp Melanchthon and the Augsburg Confession on the left and the German Bible on the right. Organ concerts from May to October and Saturday church services. UNECSO World Heritage Site.

St. Mary's Church (Stadtkirche St. Marien), near the marketplace, is the oldest building in town. It has two massive towers and was built in late Gothic style. Here, Luther baptized his six children and preached. The church features Cranach's famous detailed Last Supper depiction with Christ serving Luther communion. This is a UNECSO World Heritage Site.

Melanchthon's House Museum (Melanchthonhaus), a narrow, three-story home built in 1536 in Renaissance style, was the home from 1539 of Philipp Melanchthon, a strong advocate for education, second only to Luther in the German Reformation, the presenter on his behalf of the Augsburg Confession of Faith. Rooms largely preserved, unchanged for centuries. This is a UNECSO World Heritage Site.

Lucas Cranach's House (Cranachhaus) is the home of the famous painter and his son. The house contains multiple portraits of Luther. They illustrated Luther's teachings, making the Bible accessible even to illiterates.

Luther Monument and Memorial is in the town center's market square, unveiled in 1821, featuring Luther preaching from the Bible, and stands on a tall, granite pedestal.

Luther's Oak is where it is said Luther publicly burned the papal bull which threatened him with excommunication if he refused to recant his beliefs.

Also: Renaissance **Town Hall**

Defining Moment . . . Castle Church

In order to understand the 95 Theses that Luther posted, let us try to put ourselves in his shoes. As a monk who had for years thought that his Salvation depended on him and not God, he battled tormented thinking that he could never perform enough to get into Heaven. As his mentor guided him to focus more on Christ's love and mercy over his own sin, he began his journey to the truth. He received his Doctorate of Theology in 1512 and joined the faculty at the University of Wittenberg. He had a spiritual awakening when he read for the first time that he was *"saved by grace through faith"* alone (Ephesians 2:8), and it completely set him free from the torments that he had been dealing with about God's rejection of him.

In 1514, he began to serve as priest for this very church, preaching that only God's grace would get people into Heaven, not their works. People were flocking in to hear his sermons in record numbers. This is the first time they had ever heard this. At the same time, there had been a habit of the Catholic Church of selling indulgences, guaranteeing that people could buy their way into Heaven if they just paid the Church.

As Luther learned more about God, that His grace alone saved, he began to be bothered about this practice. He decided to take a stand when pope Leo X created jubilee indulgences, where fifty percent of the profits went to building St. Peter's Basilica in Rome, and the other fifty percent went to the archbishop of Mainz to pay off the loan he took out when he bought his archbishop position.

On October 31, 1517, Luther posted his 95 Theses on the church door which served as a bulletin board for the University. Copies of the Theses spread like wildfire, as Luther was not the first to complain about the indulgences. He was, however, the first to Scripturally build a case against them. He never meant to divide the Church, merely to keep it true to the Word of God. These Theses were copied over and over and made Luther famous internationally, in places where the Holy Spirit was stirring up very similar truths as far as Cambridge, England. (See the "Defining Moment . . ." teaching from Cambridge for more details.)

Frederick the Wise had already forbidden the sale of these jubilee indulgences in his territory, and became a friend to Luther from afar. While the Church rejected and eventually excommunicated Luther, he was heralded as a hero among the people.

Journal Time:

Luther was taught by his mentor to test everything against Scripture, but the complete Scripture of the Bible was not as available as it is now—even to Bible scholars. Once Luther got his hands on it, everything changed. His is a great example of Hebrews 4:12: *"For the Word of God is alive and active. Sharper than any double-edged sword, it penetrates even to dividing soul and spirit, joints and marrow; it judges the thoughts and attitudes of the heart."*

Think about a time when Scripture has shown its power in your life. Did it show you something precious that touched the depths of your heart? Did it bring you out of deep fear during a challenging time? Journal that memory, and take time to thank God for His Word and its power in your life.

Share Time:

Share with each other about times that Scripture has shown you a truth, and talk about the effect that it had on the situation you were going through.

Prayer:

Lord,

How precious Your Word is to us. Thanks for its power. Thank You for giving it to us in such great abundance, in our own language. Lord, many of us own several Bibles and we are so grateful to You for that privilege. Please help us to hold Your Word dearly in our lives. Please help us to study it, to listen to it with open hearts, and to draw on Your power through it. Keep us in a constant state of readiness to use it as a sword by helping us to learn it and memorize those Scriptures that You long to use in our lives. Thank you, Lord for your goodness.

In Jesus' Name,

Amen

Worship:

"A Mighty Fortress is Our God," written here by Luther

Defining Moment . . . Melanchthon's House Museum

God has given us the example of several beautiful working relationships in the Bible that were filled with great affection and friendship. From Elijah and Elisha, to Paul and Timothy, we see great examples of people working together on Kingdom assignments with their joy all the more increased because they loved *who* they were working with. We see yet another example of this in Martin Luther and Philipp Melanchthon. These two men had extremely different gifts and dispositions. Luther was more forceful and opinionated, while Melanchthon was more passive and peace-loving. Together, they made a great team. God had given them opposite gifts, and their full spectrum together was needed for the work that God was about to accomplish.

Luther said about Melanchthon: "I prefer the books of Master Philippus [Melanchthon] to my own. I am rough, boisterous, stormy, and altogether warlike. I am born to fight against innumerable monsters and devils. I must remove stumps and stones, cut away thistles and thorns, and clear the wild forests, but Master Philippus comes along softly and gently, sowing and watering with joy, according to the gifts which God has abundantly bestowed upon him."

It was, indeed, Luther that brought the idea of Reformation into the public view and gave the common man an opportunity to participate. However, it was Melanchthon that organized Luther's ideas, put them in logical formation, and presented them to scholars who eventually carried them out academically. For example, during the Diet of Augsburg, the emperor Charles V refused to hear Luther's ideas. However, when he requested an orderly presentation of Luther's position, it was Melanchthon who wrote the Augsburg Confession, which even today is the basis for the doctrine of the Lutheran church.

Luther and Melanchthon both were working toward the same end. Neither man intended to break from the Catholic Church, but, instead, to bring it back to the Gospel. Even twenty-five years after the 95 Theses were posted, Melanchthon met with Cardinal Contarini to heal the breach between Lutherans and Rome, but it was eventually rejected by the powers above them.

Melanchthon had said at one time that he would rather be dead than without Luther. Sadly, Luther died fourteen years before Melanchthon, who was his obvious successor. The more passive Melanchthon did not have Luther's power, and struggled in his last years as the theological leader of the Reformation. Even on his deathbed, he was consumed with the state of the Church instead of his own situation. The Scripture that seemed to influence him most is:

"He came to that which was His own, but His own did not receive Him. Yet to all who did receive Him, to those who believed in His name, He gave the right to become children of God" (John 1:11–12).

He is buried next to Luther in the Castle Church.

Journal Time:

Have you ever worked with someone in God's Kingdom who was your opposite but whom clearly God intended for you to partner with? Do you have a friend who is different from you but is dear to you because God uses them to influence you in areas where you are not as strong as they are, and vice versa? Take some time to think about which of your friendships might be similar to Luther's and Melanchthon's. Write a prayer to God, thanking Him for your friends and the unique way they bless your life. Consider sending this prayer to your friends.

Share Time:

Read some of your prayers aloud and share examples of friendships that are like Luther's and Melanchthon's.

Prayer:

Lord,

Thank You for the gift of friendship. Thank You for the unique way You have made each one of us, and the way that we are called to work together with people who are opposite of our giftings, yet vital to the mission You give us. Please give us patience and understanding in our friendship. Let us keep focused on the purpose that You have us working on together. Please help us finish well. Thank

You for being the ultimate partner in our ministry work. All that we accomplish
we give You the glory for.
    In Jesus' name,
    Amen

Worship:
    "Blest Be the Tie that Binds"
    "Make Us One"—Phil Driscoll

OTHER SITES IN GERMANY

Christmas Markets

Dresden and Nuremberg are home to the two biggest Christmas Markets that are held across Germany during Advent season. More than 2,500 Christmas Markets appear in the town squares of small villages and large cities each year. Enjoy homemade crafts, Christmas programs, concerts, crèches, decorations, drinks, and food (gingerbread, roasted nuts, dried fruits).

Coburg

Coburg Fortress (Veste Coburg, the Franconian Crown), high above Coburg, the best-preserved large medieval German fortress with three protective rings of walls, is where John the Steadfast hid Luther for five and a half months during the 1530 Diet of Augsburg (because Nuremberg refused to host him). It is where Luther continued translating the Bible. Visit the Luther Room (Furstenbau or Lutherstube) where he worked and had Psalms 1:6, 74:21, and 118:17 painted for encouragement as well as the chapel where he spoke and worshipped. Nearby in Goetz is the Hummel Factory.

Dresden

This city was the center of the Baroque movement and once known as the Florence of the North. Luther visited the city in 1516 and 1518. Located on the Elbe River and formerly part of the former East Germany, Dresden was destroyed by fire bombing at the end of World War II. It is still being ambitiously rebuilt since the reunification of the two Germanys.

Frauenkirche (Church of Our Lady), 1743, largest pre-war Protestant church in Germany, reconstructed between 1994–2005.

Trinity Lutheran Church, where founders of Lutheran Church Missouri Synod (LCMS) worshipped before eight hundred of them emigrated to Missouri in 1841 after their services had been banned in Dresden.

Church of the Holy Cross, home of the famous Dresden Boys' Choir, formed during a revival in 1245.

Saxon State Archive has a preserved document announcing the papal bull that was burned in Wittenberg by Luther in 1520.

Dresden Old Master's Gallery hosts the world's largest collection of Lucas Cranach workshop pieces.

Also: Court Church; Zwingler Gallery; Christmas Markets.

Fulda

Fulda was a center of religion and scholarship in the Franconian empire. **Fulda Cathedral**, built in 1704 and modeled after St. Peter's in Rome, was dedicated to St. Boniface, apostle to the Germans. Boniface was martyred by pagans in 754 AD, and Fulda was his home. Boniface's crypt is behind the high altar. There are occasional sacred music organ concerts. The cathedral's museum has artwork featuring Boniface.

Also: **Town Castle, St. Michael's Church**.

Halle (Saale)

Known as The Cradle of the Reformation. Cardinal Albrecht and Luther argued here over the sale of indulgences. Luther preached three times at the Market Church of St. Mary in 1545–1546. Today, it houses his original death mask, a plaster cast of his hands taken on his deathbed, and a pulpit he used. It is a magnificent piece in Central German Renaissance style.

Composer George Frideric Handel was born in this city, which is now known as the Handel City. It is home to the **Handel House Museum** and the annual Handel Festival. Market Church, where he was baptized, the cathedral organ he played, and the Handel Memorial.

The Marionbibliothek (Library of Our Lady), founded in 1552, part of the Market Church parish, has one of the most extensive church library collections in Germany.

Heidelberg

Located at the confluence of the Rhine and Neckar Rivers and populated since Celtic times, Heidelberg was an ancient Electorate of the Palatinate and stronghold of German Reformation in 1560. Originally Lutheran, then Calvinist, it was sacked in the Thirty Years' War by Catholics in 1622. The city was made famous by the 1954 film *The Student Prince*.

Ruins of Heidelberg Castle, overlooking the Neckar River, where one of the most important Calvinist statements of faith, the Heidelberg Confession (or Catechism), was written in 1563 by a young professor, Zacharias Ursinus, and a young preacher, Caspar Olevianus.

Also: Germany's oldest University, founded in 1386, where Luther was honored and defended his *95 Theses;* Old Bridge (said to be Germany's most beautiful); Red Ox Inn (*Student Prince* fame).

Konstanz

On the Rhine River, close to the Swiss border, this is the largest town on Lake Constance. Here, the Council of Constance of 1414–1418 ended the papal schism and declared Bohemian reformer, Jan Hus, a heretic. He was burned at the stake in 1415 and his ashes were scattered on the Rhine. See **site of Hus's Burning, Hus House**, and the eleventh century Cathedral.

Magdeburg

An important trading center on the River Elbe where Luther attended school at age thirteen.

St. John's Church, the Augustinian monastery church where, in 1524, Luther gave such a historic sermon on true and false righteousness to an overflowing congregation that a month later, nearly every church had converted to Protestantism. It is a triple-nave cruciform basilica, built in 1131, destroyed by many fires and always rebuilt. Luther Memorial in bronze from 1886 stands outside at the northwest corner and is inscribed with his words, "God's word with us for Eternity." Also see Magdeburg Cathedral, resting place of emperor Otto the Great.

Mainz

This city has been an ecclesiastical center since 746 AD, when Boniface was made its first archbishop.

Cathedral of St. Martin, built in 975 AD in the Romanesque style and host to seven coronations, was largely destroyed by a fire.

Johann Gutenberg Museum, first movable-type printing and first German Bible printed here. Be sure to view original copies of the Bible.

Take a Rhine River wine cruise from Rudesheim to Koblenz.

Old university town in which Phillip I, Landgrave of Hesse, was a local leader of the Reformation.

Luther and Zwingli met at Colloquy to attempt to unite (unsuccessfully) in 1529; St. Elizabeth's Church, 1283 (with fourteenth century frescoes); Landgrave Castle; Town Hall (Rathaus) with its ancient mechanical clock's hourly animated figures.

Oberammergau

At the turn of each decade (i.e., 2030, 2040), more than 2,000 residents of this small town continue to honor a vow the village made to God in 1633, for sparing them from the deadly plague, by performing a **Passion Play**. The play is an eight-hour spectacle (including a three-hour meal and intermission) for 5,000 spectators, at the Passionspielhaus open stage. There are also woodcarver shops and a museum featuring Christmas crèches (Heimatmuseum). It is about one and one-half hours southwest of Munich, almost to the Austrian border, and has many beautiful painted houses.

Nearby is the beautiful **Wieskirche**, the "Church in the Meadow," with gilded stucco, carvings, and bright frescoes.

Oberursel

Lutheran Theological Seminary (Lutherische Theoligische Hochschule).

Rothenburg

The most picturesque and well-preserved medieval town along the Romantic Road, it is the only walled city (you can walk the entire one and a half miles) in Germany with no modern buildings (most were built prior to the fifteenth century). It has beautiful gateways and towers, imposing town walls, and cobblestone streets.

World famous for Christmas Shop and Museum, Kathe Wohlfahrt's **Christ Kindl Markt,** with ornaments, nutcrackers, and Father Christmas figures from many eras.

The Ratstrinkstube featuring the **Market Square Clock**, where the Meistertrunk legend is reenacted on the hour. The story is that Rothenburg was attacked by Imperial troops in 1631 and the mayor offered the count a welcoming drink of local wine. The count then offered to spare the town if someone could drink a six-pint tankard in one drink, which the mayor then accomplished to save the town.

Also: (Renaissance) Town Hall.

Schmalkalden

Formerly part of Hesse, the Schmalkaldic League was formed here in 1530 by Landgrave Philip I of Hesse, one of the first Protestant princes and an opponent of Charles V. He believed that only a united alliance of all Protestants could be protection against the emperor. Seven diets were held here.

It is in the historical old quarter and has medieval architecture, half-timbered buildings, and stone towers. Concerts are held from May through September on the Renaissance organ built in 1590, one of the oldest of its kind in Europe, with 252 wooden pipes and 6 registers in **Schmalkalden Castle Church**.

Speyer

Located in southwestern Germany, Speyer is home to **Speyer Cathedral**, a basilica with four towers and two domes. The Cathedral was founded by Conrad II in 1030 and remodeled at the end of the eleventh century. It is one of the most important Romanesque monuments from the time of the holy Roman empire and was the burial place of the German emperors for almost 300 years. This is a UNESCO World Heritage Site.

Torgau

Torgau is known as the Wet Nurse of the Reformation and located on the River Elbe near Wittenberg. Its imposing sixteenth century town center is miraculously preserved, nearly intact with 500 Renaissance and late Gothic-style monuments. The magnificent town hall dominates the market square. The town council closed all cloisters in 1523. Luther visited the town more than forty times, and Luther's benefactor, Frederick the Wise, was born here at Hartenfels Castle.

Upon Frederick the Wise's death in 1525, his brother, John the Steadfast, became Elector, and was friendly with the Reformers. He led Torgau to become the Reformation's political center. In 1526, the League of Torgau was founded. John the Steadfast was followed in 1532 by his eldest son, John Frederick the Magnanimous, who completed Hartenfels Castle with its incredible staircase, soaring more than two stories like a spindle without support. While a supporter of the Reformation, his poor political skills led to the Schmalkaldic War.

St. Nicholas' Church hosted the first German-language baptism in 1519, the first Protestant sermon in 1520, and welcomed Luther to preach in 1522. It was secularized a few years later and is now part of the inner courtyard of the Town Hall.

Castle Church and **Hartenfels Palace** are where Luther consecrated the first Protestant church building in the world in 1544. This is the best-preserved early-Renaissance palace in Germany.

St. Mary's Church is where Katharina von Bora was buried in 1552. There is a small museum here. Luther's musical advisor and close friend, Johann Walter, helped compile a new liturgy and composed many Lutheran hymns while serving in Torgau.

Trier

A Roman colony from the first century AD, Trier became a trading center in the second century, and was known as the Second Rome in the third century. It is located on the Moselle River in western Germany

The **Cathedral of St Peter**, one of the oldest church buildings in the Western world, is a UNESCO World Heritage Site.

The **Church of Our Lady**, the earliest French High Gothic-style church built outside of France, was constructed over the course of thirty years and is also a UNESCO World Heritage Site.

Weimar

Luther repeatedly preached in the Palace Church and the Town Church, St. Peter and Paul (now called the **Herder Church**). Look for Lucas Cranach the Elder's painted triptych altar (1552–1553). The building was severely damaged in World War II, and reconsecrated in 1953. Guided tours are available at this UNESCO World Heritage Site.

Composers Johann Sebastian Bach and Franz Liszt both lived here, and Liszt, who was court musical director, is remembered at the Liszt School of Music and Liszt House.

Weimar is home to three UNESCO World Heritage sites and the entire city was declared a UNESCO World Cultural Heritage Site in 1998. It is the location of the **Duchess Anna Amalia Library** (one of Germany's most famous) with its beautiful Rococo Hall and a Luther Bible from 1534, the Goethe Residence, Schiller's home, and lovely parks.

Worms

One of Germany's oldest cities; surrounded by lush vineyards.

Worms **St. Peter's Cathedral** (Dom St. Peter), built 1181–1230 with its Baroque high altar, is where Luther came in fear and trembling to defend his beliefs at the Diet of Worms (the most famous of more than 100 Diets or Summit meetings here) after being summoned in 1530 (there is a commemorative plaque at the Heylshof Garden). He was subsequently declared an outlaw by newly elected holy Roman emperor Charles V. The Bishop's Palace no longer stands. The Cathedral is still Catholic today, though the citizens are mostly Protestant. During the Thirty Years' War, the city was heavily damaged.

Also: Jewish Cemetery; Church of the Holy Trinity.

Fifty miles southwest of Frankfurt, Worms (pronounced "Vorms") also features Trinity Church (evangelical) and Magnuskirche (a very early Protestant church dating from the seventh century).

An impressive **Reformation Monument** near the town square was unveiled in 1868, this is the world's largest Reformation statue. Luther is depicted as surrounded by his precursors, John Wycliffe and Jan Hus, and his peers, Philipp Melanchthon and Frederick the Wise.

In what is now a park, Charles V convoked the first Imperial Diet of Worms in 1521, inviting Luther to defend or recant his beliefs (which he refused to do). William Tyndale finished printing the first English New Testament Bible from Greek here after fleeing English persecution in 1525.

Famous Liebfrauenmilch white wines are named after Worms' Church of Our Lady (Liebfrauenkirche), first produced by the convent in the 1400s.

Wurzburg

This city is located on the Main River in northern Bavaria and sites to see include Hofkirche; Cathedral of St. Kilian fortress of Marienberg, and Old Main Bridge (Mainbrucke).

SCOTLAND

Introduction to Scotland

Known as the Land of Knox, Scotland learned of the Christian faith thanks to Ninian, who brought it to Scotland in 397 AD. Columba started the monastery on the Isle of Ionia 200 years later.

John Knox (1505–1572) founded the Protestant faith in the 1550s in Scotland, shaping the Church of Scotland and ultimately all Presbyterian churches worldwide. In 1560, Parliament denied the pope's authority, outlawed mass, and approved a new Protestant Confession of Faith.

Nearly seventy-five percent of its residents are Christian, about half are Presbyterians.

EDINBURGH

Historical Significance:

John Knox, the Martin Luther of Scotland, led the Reformation in Scotland in the sixteenth century, teaching John Calvin's principles, and founding Presbyterianism. Edinburgh is the birthplace of the Scottish Reformation.

What to See:

Edinburgh, the capital of Scotland, is second only to London in U.K. tourism. It is one hour east of Glasgow, on the southeast coast, south of St. Andrews.

John Knox ministered and did most of his preaching in Thistle Chapel at **St. Giles Cathedral** (also known as the High Kirk of Edinburgh). Today it is the spiritual cathedral of Scotland, the mother church of Presbyterianism.

Knox lived and possibly died (in 1572) at the medieval fifteenth century **John Knox House**, owned by the Church of Scotland.

Edinburgh Castle, Scotland's best known and most visited building, is a fortress atop an extinct volcano, with tiny St. Margret's Chapel (Edinburgh's oldest building). Here you can see the Crown jewels and the famous siege gun, Mons Meg.

Stirling Castle, Scotland's grandest castle, sits atop a tall crag and was a strategic military post during the thirteenth and fourteenth century Wars of Independence. It was here that Mary Queen of Scots was crowned in the Chapel Royal in 1543 at less than a month old. She was raised here as well.

Also: **Duddingston Kirk** (Greyfriars Kirk); **Magdalen Chapel**; **Grassmarke**t (associated with the Covenanters and John Knox); **Royal Mile** (walking tour); and **Walter Scott Monument.**

Defining Moment . . . St. Giles Cathedral

John Knox is considered to be the founder of the Presbyterian Church, and he did most of his preaching at this church. While there are many individuals who banded together to win freedom for reform in the church, Knox stands out as one in Scotland who spoke out for reform the loudest, which put him in difficult situations much of the time. When he died, it was spoken over him at his graveside: "Here lies one who never feared any flesh."

While we read about these key Reformation figures and think of their great heroism and courage in the faith, we can make the mistake of thinking they are super-human. We do not think about the times they forged ahead, even though they were frightened and tired. Early in Knox's career, he was called to pastor the parish church in St. Andrews as chaplain of the castle garrison—a dangerous post because of the unstable government. According to his own words, he burst into tears and fled to his room, rejecting the call.

However, within the week, he accepted the post and was preaching his first sermon there. That post did not last long as the castle was put under siege and captured within months of his appointment. He was sent to the galleys as a slave for nineteen months before being released. Government and church politics were closely intertwined *and* corrupt, and thus began Knox's long journey of standing for truth when he was opposed on many sides.

At that time, people were furious with the Catholic Church, which owned more than half of all of the real estate in Scotland, and was paid an annual income from the government eighteen times that of the crown. The church leaders led immoral lives and did not bother to hide them. For example, the archbishop of St. Andrews, cardinal Beaton, openly cavorted with a concubine and fathered eight children with her despite the Catholic Church's insistence on celibacy for church leaders.

Yet, this cardinal was more than willing to execute anyone who called out grievances against the Catholic Church. Patrick Hamilton, at age twenty-four, was the first Scotsman sentenced to death by Beaton and burned at the stake for bringing the ideas of Luther to Scotland and distributing them in a tract that he had printed. Beaton labeled the ideas heretical, even though they were completely supported by Scripture. Many other men were ordered executed under Beaton for similar acts.

It is ironic that Beaton and the Catholic Church's accusation against Protestantism (or Reformation) was that it was heretical, when it was actually they who were the heretics of their day.

So how did these church leaders get so far away from God? They stopped listening. C.S. Lewis said: *"Heaven is when man says to God, Thy will be done. Hell is when God says to man, thy will be done."*

The church was more interested in its will than God's will, and many innocents paid for that mistake with their lives. At one time, the Church was guided by the Holy Spirit, but degree by degree it had fallen away. It did not happen overnight. Have you ever heard of the anecdote of the Boiling Frog? If you throw a live frog into a boiling pot of water, it will jump out immediately. If you put the frog in a pot of cool water on a stove and turn the heat up one degree at a time, it will allow itself to be cooked to death. While God promises us that the Church will never die, degree by degree the church at the time had stopped being guided by the Spirit. Sadly, that seems to be repeating today.

We can read the above with judgment and disdain for those who have, and still do, fall into the trap of moving forward in church and ministry without listening for God's guidance, until we realize that there is a good chance that *we* do the same thing—even if to a lesser degree.

I have been involved in two types of ministries. My first encounter in serving was coming alongside a group that did outreach to the unchurched. We spent more time stressing about the food and flyers than we ever did praying and listening. The net result of our efforts: a nice afternoon of food and not one unchurched person even came to this very low turnout event.

However, once I tasted what it was like to be part of serving in a ministry where God was sought constantly and given free rein, it changed how I thought about ministry forever. Friends of ours were longing to return to their native Democratic Republic of Congo as missionaries. Out of nowhere, a friend introduced them to a friend who wanted to leave his inheritance to start a ministry in eastern DRC. The day after my friends officially accepted the post he offered to them, the benefactor died, and they began a wild ride with God that is still going. This is where I first saw that going to God for guidance *first* changed the game. However, I confess that after working with this ministry for years, I can still fall into the trap of forging ahead with ideas that I am excited about instead of listening for God's guidance.

It is ironic that the very move of God that excites and invites us into ministry is the one we forget about once we are entrenched in the work. It is much less risky for us to take a stand to follow God's will than it was in John Knox's day. The real risk is when we forget to do just that.

Journal Time:

Are there areas in your ministry, church, or family life where you are spending more time on seeking your *own* ideas than on spending time with God and asking for *His* guidance? Spend time with God, right now, and ask Him to show you where you are doing well in this arena, and where you could learn how to do better. Record what God puts on your heart.

Share Time:

Talk with each other about the areas where you are actively seeking God's guidance. How do your experiences differ when compared to those areas where you are choosing your own way, instead of coming to God, even in the small things?

Prayer:

Lord,

You are so precious to us. We long to be guided by You in all things. Please forgive us for when we have forged ahead on our own without bringing things to You first. Please let us be living tributes to Proverbs 3:5–6, that we would trust in You, Lord, with all our hearts and not depend on our own understanding; that we would seek Your will in all that we do, and then You will show us which path to take, and that we would not be impressed with our own wisdom.

We choose to be impressed with Your wisdom alone, Lord. Please use us for the Kingdom. Take away any fear of man that we have, just as You did for John Knox. Help us to walk away from those things that are not from You and to run toward those things that are Yours. We adore You alone and bless your Holy name.

In Jesus' name,
Amen

Worship:
  "God's Way is Best"
  "Show Me Your Ways"—Hillsong

Defining Moment . . . Greyfriars Kirk and the Covenanters

The Greyfriars Churchyard is a welcoming place to freely worship Jesus now, but the Scottish Reformation has a long and bloody history that began here in 1638. Politics and religion were too closely intertwined for the tastes of the masses in Scotland. King Charles I pursued his belief in the divine right of kings. He believed that it was God who appointed him king, so he had the ultimate say in all matters, including placing himself as head of the church.

A group, calling themselves the Covenanters, believed instead that Jesus was the head of the Church, and they refused to let the government claim itself as the intermediary between them and Jesus. In 1638, the Covenanters posted an agreement, a covenant, for believers to sign in the Greyfriars Churchyard. Sixty thousand individuals signed the covenant in just two days, stating that they had the freedom to worship under the Biblical beliefs they upheld, and that Jesus was the head of the Church. Thus began a fifty year battle between the Scottish government and the Covenanters, but the upside is that a massive revival took place within Scotland immediately after that signing, bringing many to Christ.

The government went after the Covenanters as an enemy of the state and killed and tortured many of them. Daniel Defoe, a prominent author of *Robinson Crusoe* fame, estimated that as many as 18,000 were killed while upholding the covenant. Members would be captured and hung publicly, with their bodies dismembered and displayed as a lesson to the rest of the population. The government used torment and grisly methods of punishment as a means to get Covenanters to renounce their commitment to the covenant.

Because Covenanters could not meet in churches, they gathered in open fields in the country at services called Conventicles. Thousands attended these services with only a few hours' notice. They had to post guards and be highly selective of those who were invited because, if they were caught, executions occurred. The Covenanters were attacked until 1690 when politics changed as a result of the Glorious Revolution. Parliament then voted to recognize Presbyterianism as a religion with all the freedoms that the Covenanters stood for and the Church of Scotland remains Presbyterian today.

Journal Time:

As we hear about the commitment and sacrifices made by the Covenanters so that they could freely worship under the banner of Christianity, we are tempted to think that history could not repeat itself. With the internet and the media, how could such a thing happen again? Yet, there are Christians in North Korea, Somalia, Syria, Iraq, Afghanistan, and dozens of other countries who are being treated in the exact same way as the Covenanters.

Think about how God is calling us to come alongside the persecuted Christians of today. Ask God if He is calling you to help them in any way. Specifically, ask Him how you can help.

Share Time:

Talk about stories, especially uplifting testimonies, that you have heard about today's persecuted church. Talk about ways that we as a Church can come alongside them.

Prayer:

Lord,

How our hearts ache for the martyrs who are being persecuted in Your name today. Lord, what would You have us do? We feel helpless and hopeless at times for them, yet we know that Your power and might are bigger than anything that is attacking the Church. Please show us, Lord, how to pray for them. Show us how we can support them financially, physically, emotionally, and spiritually. Give us ways to connect with our persecuted brothers and sisters to show them that they are not alone. We are asking You to rescue them from torment and pain and give them Your miraculous protection and joy in the midst of their circumstances. Thank You for coming alongside them in the miraculous ways that we are hearing about. Forgive us for forgetting about them. Keep nudging us into action, dear Savior, especially when we return to our homes.

In Jesus' name,
Amen

Worship:
"The Church's One Foundation"
"By Your Blood"

IONA ABBEY

Historical Significance:

Celtic St. Columbia, who was from Ireland, founded an abbey and monastery in 563 AD, which launched faith throughout Scotland and continues to be its most sacred site. It shifted from Celtic Rule of Columba to the Benedictine Catholic Rule and was closed along with many others throughout what is now the United Kingdom, during the Reformation. It was revived in the nineteenth century by the Church of Scotland, and, since 1938, has been led by the ecumenical Iona Community. It has been a historic, peaceful place for Christian scholars and pilgrims for many centuries.

What to See:

Iona Abbey is off the western coast of Scotland, accessible by ferry to the Isle of Mull, bus to Craignure, and another ferry to Iona. Fifty people can spend a retreat week here and be immersed in the daily life of worship, teachings, and prayer.

View the eleventh century abbey's church, cloisters, museum, and cemetery, St. Columba's writing cell and burial shrine, the twelfth century Benedictine convent, chapels (St. Mary's, St. Oran's, St. Roman's) and many crosses (MacLean's, St. Matthew's, St. John's, St. Martin's).

OTHER SITES IN SCOTLAND

Glasgow

Glasgow Cathedral, although no longer a bishop's seat, is also known as the High Kirk (Church) of Scotland. It was originally Catholic, but today is under the Church of Scotland. You can take a guided tour of this oldest building in Glasgow in the spring and summer.

Haddington

Knox was born and raised here. You can see the gardens only of Haddington House.

Perth

Knox preached against idols in 1559 at St. John's Kirk. Unintentionally, he started a Protestant uprising in which statues, which were thought of as idols, were destroyed in churches, monasteries, and convents.

St. Andrews

St. Andrew's relics were brought here in the eighth century. You can visit the preserved ruins of **St. Andrews Cathedral**, which was ransacked in 1559 during the uprising against idols, and the ruins of St. Andrews Castle, the seaside home to archbishops and bishops and then the Church of Scotland. In 1546, reformer George Wishart was executed here for heresy. Later, Knox preached in the castle and then parish church, which later became a cathedral.

Golf was invented at the historic Old Course at St. Andrews, rotating home of the (British) Open Championship.

Stirling

Church of the Holy Rude (where in 1567, Knox preached at James VI's coronation). Stirling Castle is where James VI was educated by reformer George Buchanan.

SWITZERLAND

___

Introduction to Switzerland:

Switzerland's contribution to Christianity centers around John Calvin in Geneva, Ulrich Zwingli in Zürich, and the Benedictine Monastery in Einsiedeln near Zürich.

Calvin, Father of the Reformed Faith, stopped in Geneva en route to Strasbourg, saying, "I am staying only one night," and he never left (except for a three-year eviction). His famous book, *Institutes of a Christian Religion*, was written for the many who thirsted after God and who had little real knowledge of Him.

Zwingli, greatly influenced by Luther, took on Zürich's city council in 1523, arguing his sixty-seven-point thesis, which began with, "Christ is the only mediator between God and ourselves." He secretly married in 1522.

Switzerland has no official state religion, but approximately forty percent each are affiliated with either Protestant or Catholic traditions.

Calvin's theology is summarized under the acronym of *TULIP*:

T: Total depravity: with no image of God remaining in the sinner.
U: Unconditional surrender: we bring nothing to the table.
L: Limited atonement: not all will know Eternity.
I: Irresistible grace: those in His grace cannot but remain in it.
P: Predestination: some are saved by advance decision, some not.

John Wesley (1703–1791) later revised Calvin's *TULIP*, feeling the *T* went too far, approving the *U*, accepting the *L*, saying the *I* could be resisted and refusing the *P*.

GENEVA

Historical Significance:

Geneva, the Protestant Rome, was most influenced by John Calvin, who was second only to Martin Luther in the Reformation, a minister and theological professor in the sixteenth century. The first church was built here in 350 AD. The city council eventually evicted Calvin from 1538–1541 for trying to integrate Christianity too much into law and government. His desire was to establish a "City of God"—essentially a theocracy. He supported capitalism and progress, while demanding conservatism in every aspect of living. He died here in 1564.

Geneva became a refugee center for Reformers persecuted in their own countries, including France, England, Italy, and Spain. Calvin published his first edition of *Institutes of the Christian Religion* here in 1536. The Geneva New Testament was published in 1557, and the complete Bible in 1560.

What to See:

Today, Geneva is better known as a global political power center than a Protestant center, with many organizations such as the United Nations and the International Red Cross headquartered here. It sits on the French border in the southwest. French is the most commonly heard spoken language.

International Monument to the Reformation (Wall) features John Calvin, John Knox, and other Reformers in a 300-foot-long monument that was erected between 1909–1917 to commemorate Calvin's 400th birthday.

St. Peter's Cathedral (Cathédra le St. Pierre), where Calvin preached biweekly between 1536–1564, includes an underground archaeological find (a fourth century basilica and a sixth century church). In the north aisle are Calvin's chair and many of his teachings. It dominates the town center with Romanesque/Gothic style. Walk up 157 steps for a great view from the North Tower.

International Museum of the Reformation (or Reformed Tradition) is adjacent and includes many books, artwork, artifacts, and manuscripts. It was opened in 2005 at the Maison Mallet, on the very site where the Reformation was proclaimed.

La Fusterie Church (New Church), built between 1713–1715 to handle the flood of arriving Christian refugees, it was modeled after the French Protestant church in Charenton, near Paris. The Lutheran World Federation, the World Communion of Reformed Churches, and the World Council of Churches all have their administrative headquarters here.

Also: **Knox Chapel**; **Auditoire de Calvin** (Calvin's Academy), the "Protestant Lecture Hall" where he taught. John Knox also taught here for three years.

Defining Moment . . . International Monument to the Reformation (Wall)

John Calvin was a French lawyer turned theologian and scholar who fled France because of the religious uprisings against Protestants. Calvin decided to escape to Strasbourg, Germany, and live a quiet, scholarly existence. Because of a war going on between the holy Roman empire and France, he could not take the direct route. In 1536, he traveled through Geneva, Switzerland, intending to stay for only one night, but he ended up staying twenty-five years. Geneva only legally approved of the Reformation one month before Calvin arrived, but a man by the name of William Farel recruited him to help with the Reformation of the church there. Calvin initially refused, but Farel scared him into staying by saying that God's curse would be upon him if he did not stay to help where he was needed. Calvin was so terrified that he stayed.

He was made a pastor and helped to create one of the most fertile grounds for the Reformation in all of Europe. Pastors came from countries near and far to learn about the Reformation and return to their own countries with it. Even John Knox journeyed from Scotland to Geneva to learn what God was doing. He reported it to be "the most perfect school of Christ, since the apostles." Calvin and Farel had battles for their faith in Geneva and were exiled at one time. They were accused of requiring believers to live out morality as an evidence of their faith. This way of living had never been required, and the people of the city were outraged that a Frenchman would come to their city and make this demand.

However, three and a half years later, residents of the city asked them to come back and serve as their religious leaders. Calvin replied that, "Whenever I call to mind the wretchedness of my life there, my very soul must shudder at any proposal for my return! I would rather die a hundred deaths than take up that Cross." However, Farel reminded him that God had called him to Geneva, and he returned in a triumphant welcome as the spiritual leader of the city, where he served twenty-three more years.

Today, Geneva is the home to the World Communion of Reformed Churches, representing 50 million people in 110 countries. These are the spiritual descendants of Calvin.

Calvin's motto was, "I offer you my heart, O Lord, promptly and sincerely." He certainly lived out that motto, even when it railed against his own plans.

Journal Time:

Calvin's motto served him well and kept him on the path that God had called him to. Ask God to reveal *His* motto for *your* life. What is the Holy Spirit sharing with you about what your motto is? Your purpose is what you are called to *do*, but your motto is who you are called to *be*. What is your motto?

Share Time:

Share your mottos with each other.

Prayer:

Lord,

Thank you for Calvin and all the others who You called into the truth during the Reformation. Thank You for Your church and the ways that You keep refining it. Lord, thank You for mottos for our lives. Please keep us mindful of our mottos so that they will keep us on the pathway of our call. Please help us to hear Your calls even when we do not want to go a certain direction. We trust You to keep us on Your right path.

    In Jesus' name,

    Amen

Worship:

    "Take My Life and Let It Be"

    "Freedom is Here" by Hillsong

ZÜRICH

Historical Significance:

Prior to John Calvin in Geneva, centered in Zürich, Ulrich Zwingli had great impact on the Swiss Reformation. He was instrumental in convincing the city's residents to be freed from Rome's control and convert to Protestantism in 1520. The mass, with its focus on transubstantiation, was abolished and replaced with a simple service that included the Lord's Supper. His motto was "Pray and Work."

In 1525, the Swiss Brethren Anabaptist movement started here in Felix Manz's home. Manz was later martyred for his faith. Many hid in caves near Rapperswil.

The plague struck Zürich in 1519, killing one-third of its population. Afterwards, Catholics were tolerated, but restricted. In 1531, a Catholic army of 8,000 men attacked 1,500 defenders, killing 500—including Zwingli, 25 town council members, and 24 pastors. The resulting peace treaty prevented any further Protestant expansion in Switzerland.

What to See:

With origins dating back to 15 BC, the modern commercial and financial center of Switzerland, Zürich is close to Germany in the north and is Switzerland's largest city. The most commonly heard spoken language is Swiss German.

Grossmünster Church (Cathedral), Mother Church of the Swiss Reformation, with Zwingli as its first pastor in 1519. Its twin towers, the most recognizable symbols in town, face the Limmat River. Endowed by Charlemagne, the church dates back to the eleventh century. Zwingli's small study is preserved in the deacon's home.

Also: **Helferei** (where Zwingli lived and worked); the **Guild Hall and Museum** (of Reformation art); the **Limmat River** (where Anabaptists were drowned for their beliefs); **Zwingli Statue and Monument**; **St.**

Peter's Church (with the largest clock face in Europe and free concerts); **Zolliken** (first Anabaptist meeting remembered with a plaque at 23–25 Gstadtstrasse); Fraumünster (ninth century Catholic cathedral, originally a Benedictine abbey, with Chagall stained-glass choir windows, endowed by Charlemagne's grandson, German King Ludwig, in 853); **Swiss National Museum** (Landesmuseum Zürich) is a castle-like museum with religious art as well as Zwingli's helmet and sword used at the Battle of Kappel.

Wildhaus, sixty miles east, hosts the Zwinglihaus, a small museum and garden at the farmhouse where he was born in 1484 and raised.

Zug, twenty miles south, features the monument where Zwingli died of a sword wound in 1531 at the Battle of Kappel, while attempting to force the remaining cantons (states) to accept Protestants.

Defining Moment . . . Grossmünster Church and Ulrich Zwingli

Zwingli was a Swiss parish priest who served amidst a background of war. He was called to minister on the battlefield early in his career and watched as 6,000 of his countrymen died around him. Young Swiss men were often hired by other countries or by the pope to serve as soldiers. Zwingli was outraged by the losses and accused his country of choosing gold over life. Because he spoke out, he lost his parish and was removed from his post.

Zwingli moved to another parish and met Erasmus, who had just published a Greek New Testament. He taught himself Greek and devoured this New Testament. He had heard of Luther and, after reading the Bible for himself, had the same doubts about the Catholic Church that Luther had. In 1519, Zwingli moved to Zürich to serve as a priest for this very church, Grossmünster, and started preaching straight from the book of Matthew. This was a bold move for 1519. At the same time the plague swept through Zürich, killing one out of every three people. Zwingli learned a lot about pastoral compassion during this time and was never the same.

Zwingli was supported by a yearly payment from the pope, and now refused that along with Catholic teachings that he saw as not Biblical. Zwingli eventually presented his sixty-seven articles in front of the city council. In Zürich, he decided "to preach nothing but what can be proved by the Holy Gospel and the pure Holy Scriptures." Drastic changes ensued.

The government rejected monastic vows and took over the monasteries, turning them into places to serve the poor and needy.

Because the cities were turning Protestant and the villages in the countryside were still Catholic, nearly a hundred years of civil war ensued, and Zwingli died as a casualty of war in 1531. His last words were, "They may kill the body, but they cannot kill the soul."

His enemies were trying to kill his work, but they could not. Zwingli's work set the stage for all the other Reformation leaders in Switzerland to build on.

Journal Time:

As we watch the Reformation unfold, we see that it is not just one individual who led the reforms. God raised up an army of collaborators to purify His Church. Men like Zwingli built the foundation, but God planned for a massive number of believers to build on Luther's and Zwingli's initial work. Is not that just like God? He could have reformed His Church with a wave of His right hand, but instead He chose to use His children to His Glory. It was a lot messier this way, but God was up to something.

Think about the churches and ministries you work with. It gets messy because imperfect human beings are invited by God to do His work.

Can you think of a time when you collaborated with God and others on a project that was messy, but it was worth every sticky minute? Journal about that time, and how you felt looking at it from beginning to end.

Share Time:

Have a conversation in your group about an experience (ministry, church, work, or family) that looked messy at the beginning, but God later revealed His Glory and purposes once you saw the end results. Encourage each other in your faith and hope in God and not the current circumstances you see around you.

Prayer:

Lord,

Thank You for showing up in the middle of our messy lives. Thank You for inviting us into Your work and giving us the opportunity to experience working in Your Glory when You could finish the project perfectly and efficiently on Your own. Thank You that You are a God of relationship and up through our experiences with You. We adore You and with open hearts, invite You to rule in our mess and show us Your Glory.

In Jesus' name,

Amen

Worship:

"Holy, Holy, Holy"

"Show Us Your Glory"

OTHER SITES IN SWITZERLAND

Basel

Switzerland's third largest city is at the crossroads of Switzerland, France, and Germany. The University Library contains rare volumes by Luther, Erasmus, and Zwingli. Basel is the hometown of Johannes Oecolampadius (1482–1531), who was a Reformer of Basel after time with Melanchthon, Erasmus, and Luther.

Bern (Berne)

Berne is the Swiss capital and a preserved medieval town. This was one of earliest cantons to embrace the Protestant Reformation.

Constance (see Konstanz, Germany)

Constance is known thanks to the Council of Constance, 1414–18, when the papal schism ended. Bohemian reformer, Jan Hus, was declared a heretic and burned at stake in 1415, and his ashes were disposed of outside of town in the Rhine River. Be sure to see the **site of Hus's Burning, the Hus House**, an eleventh century cathedral, Council Hall (reconstructed), and Schaffhausen Waterfalls (Europe's highest).

Lucerne

One of the few Swiss towns that began as a monastery.

Kapellbrücke (Chapel Bridge, fourteenth century); Spreurerbrücke (Spreuer Bridge, 1408).

CHAPTER FIVE:

———

Mission Trips

But you will receive power when the Holy Spirit comes on you; and you will be My witnesses in Jerusalem, and in all Judea and Samaria, and to the ends of the earth

(Acts 1:8).

Introduction to Mission Trips

OK, now *it is no longer about you*. The rest of this book up to this point focuses on the blessings to you of walking in the footsteps of great Christian leaders and drawing closer to God in a life-changing way. One of the clear ways to see evidence of a life change is with a renewed heart toward being of service to others. This section on short-term mission trips means it is no longer about *you:* it is about serving *others*. It is time for you to go out into the world, to baptize and make disciples, and to help others find the blessings of a personal relationship with our Lord.

Ready to go? OK, not quite yet. This section will detail *how* to serve both the full-time ministry worker as well as their people. It will also show how *not* to go about that. Just like with the other trips in this book, we want you to experience more than an interesting, observational, learning experience. The beauty is that by focusing on effectively serving them, you *will* be blessed beyond your expectations. The saying, "You get more out of it than you put into it" is not a cliché, it is a powerful truth.

But, to be clear, the motivation to move forward is not about what you get out of it, because God has made you for this: for witnessing to the unsaved. Acts 1:8 tells us, "*But you will receive power when the Holy Spirit comes on you.*" As a believer, you are blessed by having the power of the Holy Spirit whether you ever witness or not. It is not a conditional, earned blessing. It is your inheritance.

So, what will you do with that inheritance? The second part of the verse goes on to say, "*…and you will be My witnesses in Jerusalem, and in all Judea and Samaria, and to the ends of the earth.*" That is why we go on mission—to respond to God because He already equipped us to do this. Our prayer is that by responding to God's call, what you encounter will spiritually transform you to experience God's Glory in an even greater way.

For the last two centuries, the church in America has commissioned missionaries to third-world countries, giving money and resources but rarely giving of the members' own personal time. Nowadays, it is normal to hear of short-term trips where Christians serve in foreign lands. Teams build houses, feed the poor, teach vacation Bible school, and administer medical services. The need is great in third-world countries, and they are eager for "rich Americans who have it all" to give them a hand.

What is *God's* purpose for the church at this point in time? God is great about turning *our* efforts into *His* Glory, but, as good stewards, we are called to maximize the investments we make in the Kingdom. We long to hear from our Master, "*Well done, good and faithful servant! You have been faithful with a few things; I will put you in charge of many things. Come and share your Master's happiness!*" (Matthew 25:23).

Our heart's focus in writing this section of the book is similar to the rest of the book. We want to give you the tools to experience a trip that is led by the Holy Spirit—to maximize your investment in God's Kingdom. There is a big difference between going on a mission trip that is task-focused and going on a trip that is focused on God and His purposes. In the mission field, there is the possibility to be blessed by an intimacy with God that surpasses anything you have ever imagined. We are sharing our experience and pointers on how to stay under God's power and covering during these trips and how to experience the fullness of all that is possible from Him.

There is a simple way to make sure that you get on the right track and stay there: *Keep your eyes on Jesus!*

What is Your Agenda?

There are many points of view on the purpose of mission trips for Americans. Even more confusing is that the very nations that Americans have been sending missionaries to for decades now see *America* as lost; *they* are sending missionaries of their *own* back here. Africans now actually send people *here* to save Americans! Given the disunity in American churches over gay clergy, pluralism, inerrancy of Scripture, and so on, who can blame them? The student may have become the master at this point. Given the cost of airfare, time, precious resources, and the busyness these trips create, why go at all? Because our Lord told us to:

> *"Therefore go and make disciples of all nations, baptizing them in the name of the Father and of the Son and of the Holy Spirit, and teaching them to obey everything I have commanded you. And surely I am with you always, to the very end of the age"*
> (Matthew 28:19–20).

If we have any other driving focus, other than keeping our eyes on our Lord and obeying Him, we will miss the mark. Not only will we not accomplish our spiritual goals if we make these trips about anything other than God, but we can even impede what God is *already* doing in the very places we are trying to help. If there is any other primary purpose beyond serving God, there is a real danger of disunity entering the group because of individual agendas overriding the group purpose.

Two Ends of the Same Spectrum

If people are not primarily driven by their love of God to go on these short-term mission trips, there is usually one of two polarizing forces driving them: to solve the problems of the poor *or* to experience life change for themselves or their team. While either of these two outcomes are admirable, neither of them should be the primary driver for a mission trip.

Rescuing the World, or Playing God?

The need is great in these foreign lands. *We* have so much materially, and *they* have so little. The physical needs of the people are like a bottomless pit. It is heart-wrenching to see people starving, in need of medical help, without shelter, and without hope. Their needs can have a huge pull on our hearts. But God is not moved by our *needs* alone. If He was, the entire lot of starving people in the world would be immediately fed by Him. He is moved by our interaction with Him. He is moved by our arms reaching up to Him and crying out for His help, like a toddler cries up to his Daddy. He is moved by our prayers to help these people, by our willingness to go in His power and tell them of His love and saving power.

Because God is our Father, and we have hearts shaped like His, we should be moved by things in the same manner He is. Our *primary* motivation for going on these trips should be Him. While our hearts are affected by the needs of the poor, just like our Father's, we are *moved* into action by being in a relationship with God and making Him the focal point of our trip. If we try to solve the problems of these countries by our own power, we could really be getting in God's way and trying to do His job. We might even be leading these folks out of a pit that God was going to use to bring about His power and deepen His relationship in their lives.

Another reason our primary motivation should not be the needs of the people: *we really do not know what we are doing.* There are churches that make the mistake of trying to solve the problems of these foreign nations when they have no idea of the cultural influences and societal pressures that hugely affect the problem. They arrive with a can-do attitude as if they know better than the wisest spiritual and political leaders of these poor countries. Americans sometimes confuse the extravagant blessing they have in their lives with the idea that they earned what they have through their own brilliance. Some people want to share what they assume to be brilliance on mission trips. In reality, even though we make the most of our opportunities, God has allowed and sourced every blessing that comes our way. It was not *our* brilliance alone that garnered our success, or the luck of where we were born. We would do much better to speak less and learn more on these trips instead of thinking that we are superior to our hosts.

Michael J. Nyenhuis, President of MAP International, tells a compelling story about being on a trip to an African village, and asking them what their needs were. MAP is a Christian medical organization, so the expectation is that they would insist on building clinics and bringing medicines to third-world countries. But, instead, Michael tells the story of sitting with the people of a certain village, asking them what *they* think would improve the health of the community and have the greatest impact. Their answer was a soccer field. At first blush, the average medical mission visitor would shoot this idea down. How could that be the best thing for the community? They need a hospital! They need doctors!

They need Americans to tell them what could really get them out of the jam they are in! But, as Michael listened to the village leaders, they shared that what they really needed was a place for their children to focus on something constructive, like soccer. They needed a place for their kids to exercise, to build team unity, to learn new skills, and to focus on learning something they loved instead of getting into trouble. They needed a community goal to focus on.

That is exactly what MAP did—they built a soccer field. They respected the community by listening instead of forcing an agenda on them. Humility is the lesson here. Is your team humble enough to respect the needs of the people they are serving, even though they may be poorer and less sophisticated? Are you willing to come alongside to help them get where *they* want to be, or are you only compelled to help them *your* way? Check your heart before you leave to make sure it is pliable enough for the Lord to lead, because He is the only one that will be able to navigate you through these waters.

Trips are for Life Change, or for Playing God

At the other end of the spectrum are the churches who organize short-term mission trips with the primary goal of transforming the hearts of the people who are going. Instead of entrusting life change to the Holy Spirit, they think they are "helping" God by planning trips with the primary motivation that when travelers return, they will have changed lives. It is God's job to transform hearts, not ours. While these are noble and worthwhile goals for any church, the Scriptural directive for mission trips is just the opposite of this thinking.

"But you will receive power when the Holy Spirit comes on you; and you will be My witnesses in Jerusalem, and in all Judea and Samaria, and to the ends of the earth" (Acts 1:8).

This Scripture tells us that power is received by believers through transformation by the Holy Spirit. That information comes *first* in the verse, which is important in understanding Scripture. It is the event that happens first, therefore it appears in the verse first. *Then*, you are to go to the ends of the earth to be witnesses for the Lord. I have heard this Scripture interpreted backward by a well-meaning pastor speaking about mission trips. His point of view was that when you go to the ends of the earth to serve God, the Holy Spirit will give you power.

His primary motivation for supporting these trips was life change, but the effect that it had was to separate and disunify his flock. He confessed that, in thirty years of ministry, he only had one global ministry leader in his church who agreed with him wholeheartedly. The rest of the leaders eventually broke away because they were motivated by the needs of the people they were to serve. They did not feel aligned with the head pastor's point of view.

Neither of these groups was fully on target—neither the pastor nor his global ministry leaders. The *only* valid primary driver for short-term mission trips is that God is asking you to go where He is *already* working! Serve Him by doing specifically what He is asking of you. The outcome of your service may be life change *or* a reduction in poverty—maybe both. However, these are results and not appropriate primary motivators for the trip. *Our* focus should be on *obedience* and then trusting *God* with the *results*.

God sent His Son to be His hands and Heart in this world. When Jesus ascended, He handed that job over to the faithful. We do not serve a God who uses a magic wand as a great cosmic magician to solve the problems of the world. Our God is all about face-to-face relationships and loving others interactively. The mission field enables believers to "be Jesus" for others in ways that they may never encounter in their own community.

One Vision Under God

I will never forget my first international mission trip. As I was praying about what God wanted me to do on the trip, since I did not speak the language and knew little about the healthcare aspect we would be working on, He directed me to Psalm 133. When I looked up that Scripture, it was clear what His primary motivator for that trip was:

"How good and pleasant it is when God's people live together in unity!
It is like precious oil poured on the head, running down on the beard,
running down on Aaron's beard, down on the collar of his robe. It is as
if the dew of Hermon were falling on Mount Zion. For there the LORD
bestows His blessing, even life forevermore"
(Psalm 133:1–3).

The word bestows is *tsiwaah* in the original Hebrew and means literally *to command*. So, this Scripture says that when we live in the precious unity that God finds so pleasant, He COMMANDS blessing on us. This is the only place in Scripture where God tells us that when we obey Him, He COMMANDS a blessing. There is nothing that can separate us from the promises of God.

Though there were tense moments on that trip over which we prayed for unity, God did bless the trip abundantly. We were able to get medicine, supplies, and help to the indigent who so badly needed assistance. We overcame political and corrupt hindrances, notorious for fleecing well-meaning humanitarian organizations and taking the aid for themselves. We had huge success, because God was giving us our purpose and primary motivation. We were not going *mainly* to change the hearts of our mission team. Nor were we *mainly* trying to solve the problems of the world. We felt a call by God and were united to go for His purposes, more than any other motivation.

I tell this story to invite anyone considering a mission trip to inquire of God about what it is that he wants to get done on the mission. Until you have two or more people hearing in their heart a similar directive from God, I would be leery about putting much effort behind the adventure. Being called by God to serve Him in the mission field is an amazing experience filled with awe and wonder. Deciding to go save the world under your own power because you want an exciting vacation is an entirely different, and usually unpleasant, experience.

The point is that you and your team must lean into God to be given the vision and purpose for the trip. Shared purpose will unify you and enable you to get those things done that God is putting onto your heart.

Should My Children Come Along?
Allowing children to experience the mission field has risks and it is the parent's role to weigh them against the tremendous rewards that are possible through Spirit-led ministry travel.

Risks:
- Illness
- Spiritual warfare and manifestations of evil that are magnified in third-world countries
- Dangerous road and travel conditions

Rewards:
- Seeing firsthand the poverty and non-material lifestyles that millions lead in our world humbles us to be grateful for exactly what God has blessed us with
- Strengthening of their own faith as it is shared with others
- Understanding that Jesus really is the only answer to the world's biggest problems. Man's solutions are not enough
- Life change—your child will never be the same, as they experience serving God in this way

Signs that show that your child is ready to serve on a mission trip:
- They are interested in helping those less fortunate than themselves.
- They are excited about sharing God with others, even if they do not know how.
- They are willing to let God lead the trip and will set down their own expectations.
- They are willing to make the sacrifices involved without being pressured (giving up sports, spending time preparing, sacrificing to raise support, etc.).

Raising Support Funds

Sometimes we are mission goers and sometimes we are senders. When David and his warriors returned from one of their many victories from which God allowed them to bring home the spoils, some of the men complained that they should not have to share with the men who just guarded and supplied the camp. David disagreed and insisted that everyone involved share in the victory and the spoils.

There is something to be learned from David when it comes to mission trip funding. It was the guys who were taking care of the camp that enabled the battle to be engaged in the first place. Because of their hard work and support, soldiers could be sent to the front lines and ultimate victory. When believers at home are planning on going to the front lines of the Kingdom battle in these foreign lands, it is a *privilege* to be involved in supporting them. Not everyone can go every time, but everyone can be involved in the battle and the victory.

Writing letters and soliciting help can come from a few different intentions. I must confess that before I understood God's intentions for involving others, I was embarrassed to ask for funds, pridefully paying my own way. I felt that I would be pressuring people and embarrassing them simply by asking. Then I heard a sermon reminding me that *where my treasure goes, my heart will follow,* and the light bulb went on.

When support is requested and given, it allows others to become interested in the population you will be serving. Their hearts will follow the treasure and support they give you. They may begin regularly praying for the group you visit, as their heart follows the financial treasure they have invested. God will use the investment that supporters give in ways that you may never see, including dynamic spiritual and heart changes that would have never occurred outside of these folks being included in your specific mission.

Support Guidelines
Ask God to identify those individuals who will receive support requests:
- Church friends
- Coworkers
- Neighbors
- Family and friends of family

Send an email or letter with the following outline:
- Tell them what you will be doing.
- Tell them why you are doing it.
- Tell them you would like them to join you in this work, even if they cannot go with you.
- Identify the ways for them to join with you in your endeavor: consistent prayers, financial support, spreading the word to family and friends about the trip, etc.
- Ask them to ask God if He has a part for them to play in this adventure.
- Thank them for their consideration of support.
- Identify the contact information for the organization to whom they can send support (church, missionary organization, etc.) for your trip, preferably in such a way that you know *who* gave, but *not* how much.

Team Bonding Before the Trip
You are about to go through some very intimate experiences with your faith on this adventure. It is beneficial to get together with the people you are going with to get to know them before you travel. Get together twice a month for the following:

- Fellowship with your team where you can share with each other your concerns and your expectations.
- Invite each other to discuss the reading materials that you have chosen to read and share what each person is getting from them.
- Get a speaker who has been on a mission trip to the same country you are going to and learn about the culture.
- Get advice on local customs. For example, to my surprise, I learned that in Congo, our hand gesture waving goodbye actually means "Come here quickly!"
- Learn a few phrases to delight your hosts such as hello, goodbye, thank you, please, etc.
- Invite a guest speaker to speak on spiritual warfare. The darkness you encounter in third-world countries is unlike anything in America due to the high occurrence of witchcraft and the occult.

Much of the rest of this chapter is very similar to the directives outlined in the Introduction of this book. However, because mission trips have *specific* differences, we have edited these steps accordingly.

Preparation for the Journey
Many details will have been planned and prepared for the physical aspects of this trip. Your travel agent has coordinated flight schedules, hotels, airport transportation, payments, the list goes on. But these details account for only half of the preparation necessary for the transformational trip you are invited to participate in. The most important preparation will take place in your heart. The following steps to prepare your Spirit for all God has for you on this trip will bless you and others before, during, and after the experience.

Prayerful Mindset
Pray first! *Cultivating* a prayerful mindset is important. Begin to ask God to prepare you for the trip several weeks before you leave. Ask Him to reveal anything to you that needs to be exposed and dealt with, so you can enter this experience with a clean slate. Ask the Holy Spirit to do a mighty work. Ask to surrender to all that God has for you, because you do not want to

miss a thing. Get your team to pray together several times before you go. An example of a group prayer for these meetings is below:

Prayer for the Journey

Lord God,

Thank You for each person You have brought on this journey. Thank You for the amazing privilege of serving those less fortunate than ourselves. Set us apart for this journey. We repent of any uncleansed sin we are carrying with us. Set us apart in Your holiness for this journey. Please keep us focused on You. Reveal Your purposes for this trip.

Keep our entire group in unity, just as Jesus is in unity with You. Give us a love for each other, for those we serve and give us a new depth for our love for You. Give us the power and strength to love Your Son as You do. Please let us have an encounter with Jesus that glorifies You and Your Body of believers. We pray over each person on the trip, that they would have the revelation and transformation that You have planned for them alone. We pray for each person we serve, that they would know You more intimately through their interaction with us.

We invite the Holy Spirit to be in every conversation on this trip, to inspire every thought, to encourage us to deeds of love for each other, and to enable us to worship You in Spirit and in Truth as we journey together. And may we return home with enriched testimonies of whom You have shown Yourself to be, so that we can inspire others into deep relationship with You.

Amen

30 Days of Prepared Hearts

You will find a Prayer Countdown schedule below that enables your group to pray for the same things on the same days and includes specific Scriptures to pray over each day's subject. This 30-Day Countdown is meant to set apart hearts and minds, one day at a time, to ready spirits for the journey ahead. The Scripture verses are given to aid in the Prayer Focus for the day and can be used to pray the specific request based on the Word itself. When we pray God's promises back to Him over our lives, we are sure to be praying in His will!

Days Before Departure	Prayer Focus	Scripture Focus
30	Unity for our mission team	Psalm 133
29	God's guidance in all aspects of the trip	Psalm 32:8
28	That each person will hear God's voice during transforming opportunities, giving us direction for how we can be the Gospel to others	Isaiah 30:21
27	That the Word of God will give our minds further insight on this trip for the people we are serving	2 Timothy 3:16–17
26	That God's Word would dwell richly in our hearts during these travels, even when it is not right in front of our eyes, and that God would give us exactly the right Scripture to share with those to whom we are ministering	Proverbs 4:20–22
25	That God would protect our group and keep us safe during our time together	Deuteronomy 33:27
24	That God would keep us strong through Him, despite jet lag, hunger, fatigue, homesickness, and being emotionally overwhelmed	Ephesians 3:16–17
23	That no one on our trip would be fearful of the unknown experiences that come with serving in foreign places	Isaiah 41:10
22	Ask that our entire group will be praying for themselves and for each other	Philippians 4:6–7
21	Ask God to keep our group from stumbling, either physically on paths, or spiritually by being closed minded to what He has to give us on this journey	Jude 24–25
20	That our knowledge of God and who He is in our lives will increase as we serve Him on this trip	Colossians 1:10–12
19	That peace would rule among our travel family	Colossians 3:15
18	That every detail of this trip, travel, hotels, food—everything—would be blessed by God as part of His plan for us	Matthew 6:25–34
17	That each person on the trip experience dwelling in the secret place of the Most High during our travels	Psalm 91:1–2
16	That the hectic travel schedule will not weary our team	Isaiah 40:31

15	Pray against individuals comparing their experiences or how spiritual they appear to others in a way that distracts them from God's specific plan for them and others on this trip	Hebrews 13:5
14	As the Holy Spirit may allow some to encounter challenging personal truths, pray that God's love envelopes them	Romans 8:35–39
13	That the group would be bonded and sensitive to each other's needs	2 Corinthians 1:3–4
12	Pray for our group focus to be on the things God would have us focus on, not getting caught up in our own agendas	Philippians 4:8
11	That there would be a spirit of humility among our group, that enables us to experience all He has for us on this trip	1 Peter 5:5–6
10	That our group would hunger and thirst for God and be satisfied	Psalm 63:1–8
9	Ask that God keep our group from confusion, and that we would impart Godly wisdom to each other	James 3:16–8
8	That each of us would confess and repent of anything that is keeping us from being real with God	Hebrews 4:14–16
7	That each person in our group would pray on the whole armor of God to be spiritually protected from anything the enemy might use to distract us from all God has planned for us on this mission	Ephesians 6:10–18
6	Ask God that each person on the trip would be kind to each other and to those serving us, and that we might be a good witness	Ephesians 4:31–32
5	Pray that, through this trip, God sets each member of our group free from those things that have been keeping them from living His abundant life	Isaiah 61:1–3
4	That God's purposes, through His Word, would be accomplished for this trip	Isaiah 55:10–11
3	Pray that anyone who comes on this trip who is not yet a follower of Jesus would invite Him into their heart and become a disciple	2 Peter 3:9

| 2 | Pray for all the leaders of your group, that they would put God's love first in all aspects of the trip | 1 Corinthians 13:1–8 |
| 1 | That our entire group loves one another | John 15:12–14,17 |

Reading Materials

In the **Appendix** there is a Suggested Resources list of reading materials, websites, and videos. The books have been specially selected to help get you into the mindset of serving in the mission field. The recommended resources can greatly enrich your experience and are helpful in bonding your group and setting expectations.

Realistic Expectations

This trip is not about *you*. It is not about your comfort, your appetite, your likes and dislikes, your rest, your preferences, your shopping opportunities, your own pace or even what you think is best for the people you are serving. It is about submitting and surrendering completely to the Holy Spirit, so that you can experience all that God has for you on this mission. Grace will be required, as you are required to get up when you are tired, eat things you are not familiar with, travel in cramped spaces and experience climates out of your comfort zone. If you want the comforts of home, please stay home.

Be ready for new experiences of how things are done. From differences in bathroom practices to eating customs, you will most likely be unfamiliar with almost everything around you. Get ready to be flexible. More than once I have served on a mission trip and had almost no warm water for days at a time, resulting in many cold showers. I have stayed in huts only accessible by steep ladders, sleeping on mats side by side with a dozen people I really do not know, and had to crawl to a village latrine that consisted of a fixed platform standing over a deep hole.

But I have also bawled my eyes out when I have learned that a family who invited me to dinner saved their disposable income for three months so they could fix a meal that they thought I would enjoy. I cry as I write this, remembering how humbled I was by their generosity and how silly I have been in putting my needs above all. Be ready for your heart to be blown away by what God will show you. You will never be the same.

A Cloud of Witnesses

In some of the places you will be going, you are the closest thing to a Bible people will ever experience. You are ambassadors of Christ and witnesses to the joy of walking with Jesus, no matter what circumstance you are in. Be kind, love the unlovable (especially if they are in your group!), and be humble. You have an opportunity to advance the Kingdom in every kindness you exchange with strangers, be they bus drivers, airline ticket agents or those you are specifically serving. This is the platform on which you can practice the nine fruits of the Spirit from Ephesians 5: love, joy, peace, patience, kindness, goodness, faithfulness, gentleness, and self-control. Also, realize that your team is a divine society, not a utopia. In other words, no one on this trip is perfect, including you. Make allowances for each other, holding each other up in love.

Group Etiquette

A big blessing you can give the group is to be on time, always. Synchronize all watches with the leader's, and commit to being where you are expected to be at all times. If you are easily distracted, bring a watch with an alarm to remind you to get back to the group.

Though many places will have people who understand English, there is a charm that comes with learning a few phrases in the native tongue that will melt their hearts. Spend some time collecting these phrases before you leave and learning them as a group. Have small bills and change available for small needs.

Packing

Less is always more when traveling internationally. Since this trip is not about you, consider leaving behind anything that seems frivolous. Do not bring expensive luggage. Pack as lightly as possible, keeping valuables at home. Consider bringing clothes that you are planning to part with and leave them for the people you are serving. Coming home with empty suitcases can be a great blessing.

Now, you are ready to embark on your journey. Get ready for the time of your life!

Staffing Your Faith Adventure

The most important thing you can do to bring the hearts of the travelers together during the trip is to meet every night after dinner in a place that enables a private conversation for your group, and do two things:

Affirmation Times

So many times, we hear what other people are up to in their lives and feel admiration for what they are doing. Rarely do those thoughts make it to the spoken realm. During affirmation time, team members are invited to tell the group about things they have learned specifically about other individuals in the group who they admire or were encouraged by. There is no order and not every person needs to participate.

For the leader, this time may feel awkward or uncomfortable as your group is embarking into unknown territory. What if no one gives an affirmation? What if there is nothing but silence? Give it time. The ball may start rolling slowly, but once it gets going, people jump on the affirmation band wagon who you did not even know were listening.

You are encouraged to be vigilant about scheduling and keeping this time together. While this may sound like an innocuous exercise, the results in team building are astounding. I have witnessed the most reserved and introverted individuals gradually bloom before a group, as they witness the loving comments flowing through these gatherings.

You will encounter resistance to this committed time together, as there will be many times travelers, and even leaders, are tired and would rather skip this nightly gathering. People are often exhausted after a long day of ministry, or they want to take a nap due to jet lag. If it is at all possible, keep the commitment to this meeting. The investment is definitely worth the reward of the hearts of travelers drawing together. Many groups feel like family after doing this during a trip. This exercise will help God create a unity among the group. Additionally, sharing thoughts and feelings brings others closer to their own insights, and participants experience a domino effect while sharing their revelations for the day.

Sharing Aha! Moments

The other part of these nightly meetings is to share with each other the things that truly touched your own heart. Did you hear a testimony that touched you? Did someone come to know the Lord or get to know Him more deeply? Did God say something to you that touched you today? Was there a time when you discovered something wonderful about yourself or your relationship with God? What did you let go of during your day that you had been carrying around awhile? Start the discussion with the questions like, "*What did you see?*" and "*What did you learn?*".

Sharing these minor or major revelations with each other also results in a snowball effect. As each person hears what the others are discovering, they build it into their own experience and the team's *aha!* moments grow exponentially.

Again, unless you have experienced this dynamic, it may not seem like a big deal. However, once your team gets going on this task, the entire team goes deeper into what God has for them on the journey.

Select a Trip Teacher

Anyone from a pastor to a layperson can lead your group into transforming experiences. You may be blessed with a pastor who will take this on and completely customize the day's ministry experience with his gift for teaching. Or you may have a volunteer trip leader that chooses to use the devotionals outlined later in this chapter as the teaching for each day. It is the Holy Spirit who is in charge of taking you deeper into the heart of God. Know that you will be well cared for, either way.

It is important that the trip teacher takes the responsibility for setting aside a teaching time during the day as well as getting the group together each evening to facilitate sharing affirmations and *aha!* moments of the day.

Select a Trip Coordinator

This person is responsible for taking care of the logistical details of the trip. He or she is the liaison with the travel agent and ministry contacts. They are the go-to person for questions on schedules and travel situations that come up. They need to be flexible, calm, and gracious no matter what is going on around them.

I will never forget my first mission trip with an awesome pastor who was a gifted evangelist and teacher. He was not a person with the gift of being detail oriented, but insisted on handling the details of the trip on his own. There were forty of us traveling, each with two seventy-pound suitcases plus allowable carry-ons all filled with medical supplies. We had to overnight in Amsterdam. After eighteen hours of flights and layovers, we dragged our luggage on the train and into the center of the city where the hotel was located. We entered the hotel lobby en masse, only to find out that the pastor had led us to the wrong hotel. We were now exhausted and had to haul everything back to the airport hotel where the travel agent had wisely booked us, instead of the usual hotel the pastor used. See, we told you that there would be opportunities to exercise grace!

Humility is knowing exactly what your gifts are. Just as importantly, it is knowing what gifts you have not been given. Stand strongly in what you have been given. Make sure your trip coordinator has the gift of detailed administration.

Select a Team Shepherd

There will be many spiritual surprises revealed on your trip. Along with these experiences comes a need to have counsel with which to share these revelations and to process them. Make sure your group selects a shepherd for the journey. It can be a pastor, but it does not have to be. It should be a mature believer, gifted in shepherding people into the deeper places of their faith. It is suggested that this person be available for individual conversations in the evenings. I have personally experienced trips with and without these shepherds, and they make a huge difference.

Here is an example: Chris was in Israel for the first time, and God was revealing areas of her life that were broken. These were first time revelations for her. The transformational moments on the trip were precious, but they also left her with open wounds. She felt like falling apart, and one night in the hotel lobby she ran into Pastor Eric who chose to be available for shepherding conversations between 8 p.m. and 10 p.m. each night, while he worked on his computer in the lobby. An hour-long conversation ensued, and Chris's pain was transformed from torment to revelation. She floated through the rest of the trip in awe of what God was doing in her instead of running from the pain.

Compare that experience with the same Israel trip itinerary and a church that did not have a trip shepherd. It was the first time for Carrie to travel to Israel. She, too, was brushing up against her own woundedness and revelations of the brokenness inside of her. But since there was no shepherd to navigate these waters, Carrie began to isolate. She missed dinner and said she had a headache. She would pretend like everything was fine when the group was together, but then would go cry alone in her room, sinking into depression during free times. She came back from the trip with more questions than answers about what God was doing in her life. God could have used a team shepherd to take her through her pain to the healing on the other side.

Select a Team Worship Leader

Find someone in your group who is a gifted singer, or who will take responsibility for prerecording worship songs and bringing copies of lyrics and audio speakers large enough to serve your group. Worship will bring you into the heart of God in a way that allows deep intimacy while you are on this journey. Take the time to match the songs your group knows well and is used to singing with the themes of the location teachings. Even if your group chooses not to sing aloud, music can be used by God to prepare your hearts for what He is about to do in your group.

Daily Devotionals

Teachings for specific mission ministry sites (thirty minutes per day) can take place any time during the day. It is highly recommended that they are done when the group can focus and have silence around them. The devotionals are written to focus on topics that are commonly experienced during mission trips and can be done in any order. Multiple devotionals can be done each day. For example, at the beginning of a day that will be spent at a village hospital, the healing devotional would be an excellent start. During a break in the day, the devotional on suffering could be done with the group, or could even be customized to include those who are being served. The devotionals will have the following format:

Defining Moment:
These teachings align spiritual subject teachings with the current-day experiences of the travelers and should be read aloud to the group.

Journal Time:
After the teaching is read, the group should have at least ten to fifteen minutes to go off in silence and reflect on the questions that were proposed in light of their own lives. During this time, they should write down their thoughts and any ideas God is revealing to them. The leader should provide journal times for all travelers specifically for this purpose. These questions will enable the group to leap from just experiencing the trip on a surface level to learning about what God is revealing to them personally at each place. Encourage your group to also keep notes in these journals about what is working well on this trip and what they would change, so you can discuss their experiences in debrief sessions after the trip.

Share Time:
The group reconvenes and is invited to take another ten to fifteen minutes to share with each other what they learned about their own lives while reflecting on the specific questions for that day. Not everyone will have a chance to share. In every group there will be dependable sharers who enjoy consistently participating. There will also be quiet folks who need to be gently invited into the conversation. The more diverse and complete the sharing during this time, the richer the transformation will be for individuals. Not every person will connect with every teaching. There will be someone during each session with a great *aha!* moment, while others experiencing the same teaching will come away with little insight.

Do not judge these times by what is seen or heard. Do not be discouraged if the leader's expectations for sharing are not always met. The capacity for the Holy Spirit to transform according to the unique experience of each traveler is astounding, and much of the transformation comes afterwards, while people are mulling over what they have heard from others. That is why a wide range of experiences and teachings is necessary to fully serve the needs of the entire group.

It is also necessary to have consistency in the Journal Time and Share Time with each teaching. Even when the leader may feel uncomfortable with prolonged silences or pressured to get the group back on schedule, keeping committed to these times will affect the transformational moments for the group in a greater way than anything else done on the entire trip. Hearing God reveal a condition in a person's heart whom He wants to bless will become part of a testimony that may live on for decades. Do not be fooled into keeping the schedule if it means sacrificing the transformational moments that the Holy Spirit has for your group.

Prayer:

An optional group prayer is provided for each teaching, and even more powerful Spirit-led group prayers are encouraged.

Worship Song Recommendations:

While there are relevant songs suggested for each teaching, you are strongly encouraged to put together your own song book that will be familiar to your group. There is one traditional hymn and one contemporary song choice for each teaching, but your travelers will get far more out of the experience if they are able to worship with lyrics that are already familiar and meaningful to them. You will need to put together a song book of lyrics for either the suggested songs or those you choose.

DAILY DEVOTIONALS

Defining Moment . . . Poverty

You are Blessed.

When Jesus saw His ministry drawing huge crowds, He climbed a hillside. Those who were apprenticed to Him, the committed, climbed with Him. Arriving at a quiet place, He sat down and taught His climbing companions. This is what He said:

"You are blessed when you are at the end of your rope. With less of you there is more of God and His rule. You are blessed when you feel you have lost what is most dear to you. Only then can you be embraced by the One most dear to you. You are blessed when you are content with just who you are—no more, no less. That is the moment you find yourselves proud owners of everything that cannot be bought. You are blessed when you have worked up a good appetite for God. He is food and drink in the best meal you will ever eat. You are blessed when you care. At the moment of being careful, you find yourselves cared for.

"You are blessed when you get your inside world—your mind and heart—put right. Then you can see God in the outside world. You are blessed when you can show people how to cooperate instead of compete or fight. That is when you discover who you really are, and your place in God's family. You are blessed when your commitment to God provokes persecution. The persecution drives you even deeper into God's Kingdom. Not only that—count yourselves blessed every time people put you down or throw you out or speak lies about you to discredit Me. What it means is that the truth is too close for comfort, and they are uncomfortable. You can be glad when that happens—give a cheer, even!—for though they do not like it, I do! And all Heaven applauds. And know that you are in

good company. My prophets and witnesses have always gotten into this kind of trouble"

(Matthew 5:1–12 THE MESSAGE: The Bible in Contemporary Language © 2002 by Eugene H. Peterson. All rights reserved).

Who Has Greater Wealth?

America affords its citizens some of the most affluent living on the planet. Not only do we have enough to eat, but one of our biggest problems is obesity. Our education, literacy, infant survival, and life expectancy boast some of the highest rates in the world. In material ways, we are rich beyond measure. But are we really as rich as we think we are in the ways that really matter?

A conversation my sister had with my then-seven-year-old niece, Ciara, underscores the importance our culture puts on materialism. It was Christmas time, and my sister had brought home a gift request card from a needy family. A little boy's picture was on the card, smiling from ear to ear. He had requested simple toys and gifts for the holidays, and Ciara was asking her mom why she was going to buy presents for this kid. My sister replied that his mom and dad were poor, that while they could afford to feed him and have a place to live, they did not have money left over to buy anything else.

Ciara, astonished that this was even a possibility, said to my sister, "But, then why is he smiling? How could he ever be happy if he does not have anything?" Tears welled up in my sister's eyes as she told me this story. She was convicted about her daughter's distorted point of view of what causes little boys to smile. She turned it into a flashpoint as to how she taught her daughter about the real meaning of wealth from that point on.

While our physical needs have been met in America, we have been robbed of the blessing of depending on God and reveling in the glory of watching Him deliver our basic life necessities. There are stories of poor families in our country, and how God has intervened to bless them, but they are few and far between compared to our third-world counterparts. Think about your circle of family and friends. How often have they gone hungry?

How often have they worried about whether or not they would have food for the day?

The people you are serving on this mission trip have, most likely, had many seasons where they did not know if they would have food or shelter. Yet, those among them who know Christ have a richness and depth in their faith that far exceeds that of the average American. As I have traveled and witnessed relationship dynamics between God and His people in third-world countries, I am astounded at the wealthy, unshakable, vibrant, extravagant love relationship they enjoy. Their manifestations of worship and their testimonies are amazing. They will worship and pray for hours on end, soaking in the presence of their amazing, almighty God. Dreams, visions, and miraculous healings seem to happen with greater clarity and proportion. It is not that God loves them more than us, but I cannot help wondering if they love God more than we do.

I was in eastern Congo ministering to women at Heal Africa Hospital. Hundreds of women arrive there to heal from wounds inflicted during horrific gang rapes from tribal soldiers. It can take years for internal damage to be set right. As I was teaching them one night, I marveled at their extravagant worship for Jesus. I wondered how I would react if I had the same plight as these women. How would I react to God? Would I blame Him for not protecting me?

During worship, one of the women shared that she was amazed that God saved her from being killed during her attack, and she absolutely knew that He had special plans for her. She was rejoicing and praising Him with all she had within her, like the woman with the alabaster box. She just wanted to serve Him and carry out His will for her life. Her testimony convicted me. When do I pour out myself in corporate worship so abundantly and unabashedly? Do I not have astounding reasons to be that responsive and worshipful for my relationship with Jesus?

Journal Time:

Spend a few moments alone thinking and praying about the following:

- What is the difference in the worship attitude and expression in this country compared to my home church?

- What is my vision for how my attitude of worship will change as a result of my experiences here?

Share Time:

Read the Beatitudes from the beginning of this teaching aloud again. Is your team truly blessed? Are you as wealthy in the spiritual realm as the people you are serving? How will worshipping with them change you?

Prayer:

Lord,

We adore You, and all the truth You are revealing to us about spiritual poverty and material wealth. Reveal to our hearts what wealth looks like to You. Please show us those places in our lives where we are impoverished and do not even know it. Please grant us wealth in all the ways that matter eternally. As a response to the amazing spiritual wealth that You bestow on us, give us a longing to worship You in Spirit and in Truth. Thank You for worship. Thank You for giving us a way to express our overflowing praise to You. Please give us a way to extravagantly pour our love out on You. When we return home, please bless us with an ongoing spirit of extravagant worship that is unquenchable in our body.

In Jesus' name,

Amen

Worship:

"Heart of Worship"

"I'd Rather Have Jesus"

Defining Moment . . . Mercy and Compassion

The dictionary definition of mercy is:

1. Compassionate treatment, especially of those under one's power; clemency.

2. A disposition to be kind and forgiving: a heart full of mercy.

3. Alleviation of distress; relief: Taking in the refugees was an act of mercy.

Think for a moment about what mercy means to you. Is it a spiritual gift that you possess? Is it something you have experienced from God? What does mercy mean in God's eyes? While God's mercy can be seen in the Bible as all three of the above definitions, the expression we are going to concentrate on for today is the compassionate side of mercy as described in 2 Corinthians 1:3–7:

> *"Praise be to the God and Father of our Lord Jesus Christ, the Father of compassion and the God of all comfort, who comforts us in all our troubles, so that we can comfort those in any trouble with the comfort we ourselves receive from God. For just as we share abundantly in the sufferings of Christ, so also our comfort abounds through Christ. If we are distressed, it is for your comfort and salvation; if we are comforted, it is for your comfort, which produces in you patient endurance of the same sufferings we suffer. And our hope for You is firm, because we know that just as You share in our sufferings, so also You share in our comfort."*

Have you ever gone through a period of trial and wondered how God could ever make good on His promise in Romans 8:28, *"in all things God works for the good of those who love Him."* I remember a young woman whom I was counseling that was at the bottom of a spiritual pit. She kept slipping into depression, felt cut off from God, slipped on and off a path of sexual sin, and could never see how God could ever use the darkness she was living in to be worked out for good. Several years later, through many spiritual victories, this woman was an amazing, strong, redeemed, and pure woman of God.

She went on to counsel other women who were stuck in their own spiritual morass, trying to find their way out. She was able to speak to them in a way no one else could, because she had been there herself. She had experienced God's compassion, mercy, and restoration in a way few could understand. She is now purposed by God to be used as an instrument to speak truth and grace into these women's lives. Through her, God is delivering women from their own hopeless pits.

Another woman built an entire ministry because of the forgiveness she received many years after she had aborted her baby. God met her in her own guilt and condemnation and showed her a path to righteousness, forgiveness, and the freedom of living for Christ. On a daily basis, she helps other women onto that path. She has the authority and is equipped to speak the possibility of redemption over women struggling with abortion issues. God uses her to deliver hundreds of women into an eternal relationship with Him.

The Scripture above quotes, "...*the God of all comfort, who comforts us in all our troubles, so that we can comfort those in any trouble with the comfort we ourselves receive from God.*" If God has comforted you through depression, you have God's comfort to give others who are suffering from depression. The person sitting next to you does not have that comfort—*you* do. Has God delivered you from financial ruin? Again, by His sovereign power, you have been allowed to go through that challenge so that you could help others through the same circumstance with the same brand of comfort God gave to you. You are uniquely experienced and purposed to do God's work in the areas of victory you have experienced.

If you were a general making battle plans for war, who would you choose to call into duty—the guy who has actually won on this particular battlefield, or the guy who has never even visited that land? You *have* overcome evil on several battlegrounds. Now, go lead others into the same victory.

Journal Time:

Spend a few moments praying and thinking about the most challenging times of your life from which God delivered you. What was the theme that God brought to your mind? (i.e. deliverance from a sin issue, right thinking in a severe conflict, provision when all was lost, etc.) How has God used you to speak mercy, compassion, and recovery to those who have been in your same situation? How might He use you on this trip?

Share Time:

Invite a couple of people on your team to share their story of how God delivered them from a difficulty and then used them to deliver others from the same challenge.

Prayer:

> *Father God,*
>
> *Thank You, so very much for Your mercy and being the Father of compassion and the God of all comfort, who comforts us in all our troubles, so that we can comfort those in any trouble with the comfort we ourselves have received. Thank You that through Christ our comfort overflows. Thank You that just as You share in our sufferings, so also You share in our comfort. Lord, please use us as we serve the people of _____. Please use our past, the overcoming spirit You give us through the Holy Spirit and the undeniable victory we know is available through Christ Jesus. We surrender to You right now our hopes and dreams for these people and ask You to make manifest Your hopes and dreams for them. Lift them out of their pits and into the abundant life You sent Your Son to give them.*
>
> *In Jesus' name,*
>
> *Amen*

Worship:

> "I Lift My Eyes Up"
>
> "Great Is Thy Faithfulness"

Defining Moment . . . Stewardship

One of the biggest challenges one can face on a mission trip is that needs outpace resources. One comes face to face with severe poverty, sickness, and hunger. While your mission team will most likely have as much food, water, and shelter as they like, many of those you serve miss meals and water on a regular basis. It is heart-wrenching stuff and can even induce feelings of guilt. Many struggle with obtaining basic necessities while those around them cannot afford to feed their families.

It is easy, especially as products of the American culture, to take on the responsibility to fix everything. It is a gift from God that the need is so great that you will never have enough resources to fix it all. It is like throwing a fistful of dirt into the Grand Canyon to attempt to fill it up. It cannot be done. God does call us to supply the needs of the less fortunate, but he does not expect us to *be* God to the people we serve. That is a great danger when wealthy Americans begin dispensing their financial support oversees. We can be the focus of a distorted hero worship because we give much needed gifts. Remember when Paul healed a lame man and was mistaken for a god?

> *"In Lystra there sat a man who was lame. He had been that way from birth and had never walked. He listened to Paul as he was speaking. Paul looked directly at him, saw that he had faith to be healed and called out "Stand up on your feet!" At that, the man jumped up and began to walk. When the crowd saw what Paul had done, they shouted in the Lycaonian language, "The gods have come down to us in human form!" Barnabas they called Zeus, and Paul they called Hermes because he was the chief speaker. The priest of Zeus, whose temple was just outside the city, brought bulls and wreaths to the city gates because he and the crowd wanted to offer sacrifices to them. But when the apostles Barnabas and Paul heard of this, they tore their clothes and rushed out into the crowd, shouting: "Friends, why are you doing this? We too are only human, like you. We are bringing you good news, telling you to turn from these worthless things to the living God, who made the Heavens and the earth and the sea and everything in them"*
>
> (Acts 14:8–15).

Not to imply that people who have missed meals for weeks would call you a god if you fed them, but they may be tempted to make more of you than you really are—simply God's vessel. So, what is a short-term missionary to do?

I learned a great lesson from our friend Esther, a missionary in eastern Congo, who is faced with this challenge on a daily basis. One day as she was reading Acts 3:6, God spoke to her about this issue. In this chapter, Peter was approached by a crippled beggar for money. Peter's response was *"Silver or gold I do not have, but what I do have I give you. In the name of Jesus Christ of Nazareth, walk."* Peter gave this man healing, which he did not even ask for, instead of supplying Him with money. God directed Esther, through this passage, that she was not there for peoples' physical needs as much as she was there to give people Jesus. She could never supply all the needs of those around her, but she could give people Jesus, and *He* could supply their needs and more.

There's a famous saying, "Give a man a fish and he will eat for a day. Teach him to fish and he'll eat for life." Give a man Jesus, and he will eat for life *and* live for Eternity.

Journal Time:

How are you feeling about not being able to supply every need you see? Are you able to trust God to meet peoples' needs as they turn to Him? Write down your thoughts, your struggles, your emotions, and what God is putting on your heart about this teaching.

Share Time:

Spend time talking over the group's challenges in being faced with great need. Have a couple of people share their feelings about this struggle. Discuss as a group how you can give more of Jesus to the people you are serving. Jesus, who will never leave them or fail them and is the ultimate provider of all their needs.

Prayer:

Father God,

Thank You that You do not tempt us to be God by giving us the resources to fix everything and everyone. Thank You for being our God who hears us crying out on behalf of those whom we serve, and who provides for their needs. We trust You with the people we are serving, that You will give them exactly what they need when they need it. Please, Lord, continue to help us to give these people Jesus at every turn. Please let us remember our purpose on this trip, which is to give these people the means to turn to Jesus as their source and their eternal life, and to equip them to do the same for others once we leave.

In Jesus' name,

Amen

Worship:
   "Give Me Jesus"
   "Take My Life and Let It Be"

Defining Moment . . . Eternity

"Look, I am coming soon! My reward is with Me, and I will give to each person according to what they have done" (Revelation 22:12).

The repercussions of your work on this mission trip will probably be evident in your heart as the people you serve respond in gratitude to your visit. You will return home remembering the God moments where the Holy Spirit revealed Himself, and you will probably feel the satisfaction of transformation in your life. But those experiences equate to a fraction of the benefits that will come from the trip you are investing in. Just as a pebble dropped in the water sends ripples far beyond what we can see, so is the work you are doing in this place.

God takes our effort and multiplies it through generations if it is for Him. There is a dramatic production by Campus Crusade for Christ called the *Bema Seat* that illustrates this point poignantly. The play observes the judgment seat, or Bema, for believers right before the Marriage Feast of the Lamb. Believers each take a turn on the seat, where their entire life flashes on a screen before all of humanity. Jesus explains that it is necessary that this judgment occur at the end of all time, because the repercussions of our work ripple through generations and it takes all of history to see the true effect our work through the Holy Spirit. After the screening, Jesus asks everyone to stand who has been affected, directly or indirectly, in the Kingdom by the work of the person sitting on the Bema. For some folks, millions stand because of the generations who were affected.

The same multiplier effect is true of the work you are doing in this country. The people affected by the Kingdom work you are doing will tell others, who tell others, who will tell others for hundreds of years until Christ returns. One of the most fun moments in Eternity will be to meet up again with the folks you have affected on this trip and meet the people they affected. One of the reasons Eternity lasts forever is because it will take that long to hear all these stories.

The intent of sharing this information is not to lead us into a prideful, self-congratulatory sense of satisfaction. The intent of ruminating on this multiplier effect is to encourage you to make as much of a difference as possible for the Kingdom with the limited time you have on this trip. Encourage each other to take every opportunity to share the Good News. As believers from a developed country, you have a unique position of authority.

The word *encourage* literally means to fill another with courage. Give each other courage to go out on spiritual limbs to reach every person whom the Holy Spirit identifies to you as one He wants to reach. Thinking of the possibility of leading even one person into eternal life with Jesus is motivation enough to tell others about our Lord. But what if you could see into the ripples of time and know that by sharing your Lord with that one specific person the Lord is nudging you to minister to, there are hundreds, or even thousands who will be brought to eternal life in Christ? Compelling, is it not?

Journal Time:
What is the biggest obstacle you come up against in sharing the Good News with others? Ask God to show you His way of overcoming that obstacle and spend some time journaling about His point of view of your obstacle.

Share Time:
Discuss the risks and rewards of going out on a limb and sharing the Gospel with others. How can you fill each other with courage?

Prayer:
Dear Lord,

Thanks for the way You have set Eternity before us and the great rewards You are preparing for us. More than anything, thank You that we will be spending Eternity with You and that nothing can take us away from Your love, ever. Lord, please show us every opportunity to share Your love and Your Gospel to those whom You want to reach. Please prepare their hearts to receive the Good News. Give us the courage, the conviction, and the words that You want us to speak to them to invite them into Your Kingdom. We are Your willing servants, excited to be Your hands, feet, and voice to the lost on this trip. Please use us to Your greatest good.

    In Jesus' name,
    Amen

Worship:

    "How Great Thou Art"
    "How Great Is Our God"

Defining Moment . . . Perseverance

What does perseverance mean to God? What does it mean to us? Are the meanings anywhere near the same? We saw what perseverance meant to God when He sent His Son to die for us on the Cross, overcome death, and go prepare a place for us in Eternity. Despite years of sin and disobedience, even from God's chosen people, the Israelites, He persevered to restore our broken relationship while still maintaining who He is—a holy, perfect, sinless God. Hebrews 12:1–3 tells us:

> *Therefore since we are surrounded by such a great cloud of witnesses, let us throw off everything that hinders and the sin that so easily entangles, and let us run with perseverance the race marked out for us. Fixing our eyes on Jesus, the pioneer and perfecter of faith. For the joy set before Him endured the Cross, scorning its shame, and sat down at the right hand of the throne of God. Consider Him who endured such opposition from sinners, so that you will not grow weary and lose heart.*

How do we, as believers, persevere toward what God has set before us? God does not expect perfection from us. However, He does expect us to *run the race marked out for us*. It is no mistake that you are on this mission trip. You have prayerfully considered this adventure and God hand-picked you to be with this specific group. The part of the race you are in with these people does not end when you get back on the plane to go home. In fact, it is just beginning.

One of my missionary friends shared with me the impact that most mission groups have on the poor whom they are serving in their African country. These folks already know that Americans are wealthier by a stratospheric multiplier. These poor are conscious and embarrassed about the disparity between their financial standings and those serving them. The wealthy seem genuinely interested in their plight, so the poor share with vulnerably about what their lives are like, even though it feels humiliating to them.

Imagine if the worst financial experience a person ever had was tattooed on his or her forehead, so that every person who met them could read it. What if the words *walked away from a mortgage* were written across your face? How about *could not afford to go to college*? Or *bad investment wiped out retirement*? The feelings you would have from that tattoo are the exact feelings people living in poverty have when they interact with you. They are ashamed even though it probably is no fault of their own that they are poor.

The real kicker, according to my friend, is the number of people that interact with these families on mission trips, only to completely abandon the relationship upon their return home. The people you are serving do not understand why people come to interact with them in the first place if they do not plan to help. Relationships are held with greater esteem by most cultures than in the western world. Never hearing from the people who they have been so vulnerable with is a double whammy because relationships are valued over almost everything.

What is the solution? It is you. It is up to you to change *this* pattern on *this* mission trip and on future trips from your church. Share this point of view with others in your mission community, so that you can serve the poor and needy in the way that they are longing to relate to us.

Journal Time:

You are among a great cloud of witnesses on this trip. The above passage tells us to "…*throw off everything that hinders.*" What is hindering you from making an eternal difference in the lives of the people you meet here once you get back home? Journal about what may hinder you and about ideas God gives you to stay connected to the race run in the country you are visiting.

Share Time:

Share your ideas to continue running the race upon reentry into your everyday life. In what ways can you continue to be a *cloud of witnesses* to encourage each other to keep investing spiritually and emotionally into the people you are affecting on this trip?

Prayer:

Father God,

Thank You so much for the cloud of witnesses whom You have selected to be on this trip. Thank You for choosing each one of us and for the specific gifts and calling that each person brings to help the poor and needy in this country. Lord, please give us a way to encourage each other once we get back home to be the witnesses for this country that will continue to make a difference for them both spiritually and physically. Guard us from being distracted with our own lives when we get back home. Show us the steps to keep ourselves and each other engaged in the work that You have revealed to us here. Keep us from hurting the hearts of people we are visiting by dropping the ball on their needs once we are home. Help us to pray over them, send them encouragement, and continue building them up in the Kingdom as long as it glorifies You, our Lord.

In Your precious name,

Amen

Worship:

"Complete"

"Onward Christian Soldiers"

Defining Moment . . . Healing

When Jesus sent out the seventy-two in pairs ahead of Him, part of the directive He gave was, *"When you enter a town and are welcomed, eat what is offered to you. Heal the sick who are there and tell them, 'The Kingdom of God has come near to you'"* (Luke 10:8–9).

While we know that Jesus did not heal *everyone*, He did heal many and the aftermath of those healings was varied. Sometimes He would tell the healed to share their story with others, and other times He would direct them *not* to tell a soul, depending on whether He was in Gentile or Jewish areas. Some wanted to give up their lives and follow Him around, to which He *sometimes* said, "No, stay put and tell others about Me."

The hemorrhaging woman's healing displayed such great faith that Jesus felt power surge out of Him and asked, "Who touched me?" Being the God of the universe, it is likely that Jesus *knew* who had touched Him, so why did he expose the woman? What was His purpose in sharing with us all of these varied responses to His great healing power? The mind of God is so great we can never know His exact reasons, but, in all of these instances, we are allowed to get a glimpse of God's Glory and His Kingdom.

Our God is performing healing miracles in many parts of the world for His Glory to be revealed. The faith of His people is being strengthened and sometimes birthed through these miracle healings. How can we pray over the sick, so that God can use us to display His Glory on mission trips?

First, we remember that it is all about God and not about us. It is the presence of Jesus that heals, and we are to invite it into the situation in all of its power. That takes the pressure off of us and puts it all on Him. I heard a story from a woman, Lynn, who was on a mission trip and was asked to pray for healing over a woman who had a sickness in the side of her belly. Lynn had never done healing prayer work before, but in faith she started praying over this woman in English, even though the woman could not understand a word she was saying. As Lynn prayed, she touched the woman's side where she was sick and felt a lump under her hands start shifting around completely on its own. She could feel it changing and the woman thanked her with great joy as she felt the same thing—healing! Now this woman is sharing her testimony of how God healed her, and Lynn is sharing her story of how God used her without any previous experience or training in healing prayer—God's Kingdom is bigger because of it.

Know that, if God is inviting you into a similar situation, He will provide everything you need to pray His healing into those you are serving. You are the pipeline, and God is the living water flowing through you to heal others.

Journal Time:

Do you have any fears about being asked to pray for healing over others during your trip? What wells up inside you? What expectations do you have? Spend some time with God chatting with Him about your expectations. Be honest with Him. Share your apprehension, performance anxiety, joy, expectation—whatever it is that is coming up for you when you think about praying for healing over others.

Share Time:

Share with your group stories you have heard about present day healings. Talk about the fears you have regarding praying over people for healing—be real with each other. Most likely many of you are facing the same issues. Once they are shared and out in the light, these fears lose their power.

Prayer:

Jesus,

You are the ultimate Healer. We recognize that it is Your presence that heals. Lord, help us confess our sins to You now so that we can be clean vessels for You to pour Your healing power through. (Pause in silence for a couple of minutes). Holy Spirit, please guide our prayers. Please show us how to pray that Jesus' presence is magnified in the sick so that healing can occur. Use us as agents to overcome disease, sickness, and unbelief. Lord, You tell us in James 5:15 that "The prayer offered in faith will make the sick person well. The Lord will raise them up."

Father, it is our joy to offer the prayer in faith. Please increase our faith so that we can be used by You to heal. We are depending on You to raise the sick up, not us. Thanks for taking the pressure off of us and for Your glorious power and presence that heals. We give You thanks and praise in this moment for the ways You are about to manifest Your Glory through healing.

In Jesus' name,
Amen.

Worship:

"Balm in Gilead"

"Healer" by Kari Jobe

Defining Moment . . . Grace

The definition of grace is *unmerited favor*. It is a blessing that you have no control over—that you did not earn through performance. It is simply given to you by God as a gift.

"For it is by grace you have been saved, through faith—and this not from yourselves, it is the gift of God—not by works, so that no one can boast" (Ephesians 2:8–9).

Knowing that grace is a gift, the only responsibility you have is to receive it. That sounds easy, but there are many professed Christians who are living outside of their inheritance of grace, the evidence of which is the lack of grace they extend to others. In order to *extend* God's grace to others, you must *receive* it first. Otherwise, you are giving away *human* grace which is counterfeit and does not have much staying power.

A great example is portrayed in the book, *Les Miserables*. Jean Valjean is a desperate man who has stolen a silver candlestick from a priest so he can buy food. He is caught by the police, and they bring him to confirm the theft with the priest. Instead of charging the thief, the priest says that he meant to give the candlestick as a gift, and he goes to find the other candlestick so that the thief has the pair. He did not charge him, though he had every right. He showed unearned and unreasonable generosity—grace.

On this trip, you will have many opportunities to show grace. Because you are building God's Kingdom, the enemy will attempt to disrupt your plans with disunity and despair, especially attempting to attack grace. Greater is the One who lives in you than lives in the world though. When your fellow travelers are getting on your last nerve, pour out grace, even if it is undeserved. If the people you are serving seem to ask more of you than you have to give, float in God's grace as your provision. It is in the moments when we are most tempted to deny grace that we have the most to learn about ourselves. I have a friend who calls unlovable people grace growers, because they really know how to challenge our grace muscle.

I was led on a mission trip by a pastor who had little awareness of the physical needs of the people he was in charge of. He would set up a schedule that gave people very few hours of sleep each night. Somedays, he would literally forget to set up meals for our large group so that we would not eat dinner until after 10 p.m. I was about at the end of my rope when the Lord woke me up at 2 a.m. with a verse I looked up. It was Romans 15:1, "*We who are strong ought to bear the failings of the weak and not to please ourselves.*"

He was telling me that, though I had the gift of being sensitive to the needs of others, this pastor was not given that gift. I also have been given the gift of being a good planner, but I was not to make this pastor out to be inept simply because he had not been given a gift that I had been blessed with. If someone gave me a coat as a gift, but did not give the pastor one, would I make him wrong because he was cold? I had been doing that very thing. Suddenly, I had a breakthrough, and I was able to move forward in grace with this pastor for the remainder of the trip. I was able to see his shortcomings as a lack of giftedness instead of as a judgment as to who he was as a person. God taught me grace in a way that I have never forgotten.

Journal Time:
When is the last time you were shown God's grace, either through Him or through a person? How did you feel?

Share Time:
Discuss your experiences with unmerited favor from God and others. How have you seen grace evidenced so far on this trip?

Prayer:
Lord,

Thank You for Your amazing grace. Thank You that we do not have to earn grace and that it is Your precious gift to us. Please help us to receive it and help us pour it on to others in great measure. We want to be Your vessels of grace who carry hope and forgiveness to others in a transformational way. We love You so and appreciate Your huge favor on us.

In Jesus' name,

Amen

Worship:

"Amazing Grace"

"Amazing Grace (My Chains Are Gone)" by Chris Tomlin

Defining Moment . . . Following the Holy Spirit

You will be entering into situations on your trip that can only be navigated by staying connected to the Holy Spirit and following Him. While it will be tempting to walk by your own sight, walking by faith is essential for your mission to be fulfilled on this trip. As believers, we are directed in 1 Thessalonians 5:16–19 to "*Rejoice always, pray continually, give thanks in all circumstances; for this is God's will for you in Christ Jesus. Do not quench the Spirit.*" Since the Bible does not randomly place ideas together, it is curious that immediately preceding the directive to not quench the Spirit, we are told to rejoice, pray, and thank. When thinking about not quenching the Spirit, we can interpret that to mean many things, but what does *God* mean?

There is a difference between *quenching* and *blaspheming*. We are not speaking here of rejecting the Holy Spirit, but merely *quenching*. We quench fires by spilling water on them. We also quench thirst by pouring water into our mouths. Is it possible that we quench the Holy Spirit by complaining, not talking to God, and by being ungrateful? Do those things throw water on the fire of the Holy Spirit? Those are the opposites of rejoice, pray, and thank.

We have God's invitation in this verse to stay connected to the Spirit by doing three things that seem so simple. However, in the midst of difficult circumstances (i.e. missed planes on your trip, going without meals for long periods, suffering through jet lag, etc.), how do we authentically stay in a spirit of rejoicing, praying, and thanking? We can fake it and pretend like everything is great when it is not, but that is not what God is saying here. We can be honest with our Father about what is happening around us and how we feel, but still stay in a state of:

Rejoicing—because He is God and will protect and provide even if we do not see when we are in the middle of a difficult situation. We can remember all the times He has come through for us when it looked like all hope was lost.

Praying—by lifting up our adoration and praise to Him in the middle of the battle, we undermine the enemy's plans. Also, by voicing to Him what we are really experiencing—even our lament—we can be real with God and ask Him for His help.

Being thankful—for all of the things that are going right so far on the trip. You will find there are truly more things to lift up to God than we can humanly think of.

The Holy Spirit's leadings are gentle. He is a gentleman who will never force His agenda or way onto you but will share it with you if you give Him the space. Rejoice, pray, and thank. Give Him the space.

Journal Time:
What are you rejoicing about today? What do you want to talk with God about? Be completely authentic with Him and listen for His response in your heart. What are you thankful for on this trip?

Share Time:
Think of times when you have felt led by the Holy Spirit in specific situations. Share those with each other. What happened? How did you experience the Holy Spirit? How was God glorified?

Prayer:
Spend time together praying out loud the Rejoice, Pray, and Thanks that each of you wrote during your journal time.

Worship:
"He Walks with Me"
"Holy, Holy, Holy"

Defining Moment . . . Suffering
Suffering is greatly misunderstood. So many people who do not know God well, and even some who think they do, place the blame for suffering on the Lord. They forget that sin and a fallen world created suffering. God made Adam and Eve in a perfect world where suffering was not possible. It was

the human fall into sin that opened the door on suffering, and we will not be able to close it until Jesus does so in Eternity.

Since God is all powerful, why does He *allow* suffering? Because He allows *free will*. If He took away our free will, He would be left with a world full of puppets whom He controlled, but they would not be real people. The only route to a person loving God authentically is if it is done out of free will. Imagine a dictator that imposes his will on everyone in his country and controls *everything*. He might have control, but he does not have love. People might *act* loving toward him out of fear and to get what they need from him, but it is not a *real*, loving relationship.

God wants a real relationship with us and will even bear the brunt of being falsely accused of inflicting suffering on humans to have that authentic friendship. Satan loves it when we ask the question: "Why would God *let* that person suffer?" The real question to be asked is: "What is God doing *during* the suffering?"

God mystically transposes what Satan means for pain into goodness for God's people. In Romans 8:28, it says: "*And we know that in all things God works for the good of those who love Him, who have been called according to His purpose.*" That explains why suffering is used for our good.

I am in Napa as I write this, learning that the best wine comes from vines that have been stressed and have to grow roots through rocky soil to survive. Some of the most expensive and rare wines in the world comes from those vines. I see a lot of the same fruit in my own life. My times of deepest pain have caused me to mature in ways that would have been unreachable to me had I had an easy life. As a child, I suffered through a period of physical abuse that has given me a driving resolve to protect innocents who cannot protect themselves. The result is that I work with a ministry that serves in eastern Congo where more innocent people have been killed through conflict than in any other place since World War II.

Would I be matured and driven with this passion *without* that suffering? It is highly unlikely.

Through our Lord, suffering ends up being a gift, but it is hard to watch those we love suffer. It takes maturity and discernment to know when to help, and when God is doing something deep and miraculous that we should not interrupt. There is a great story about a butterfly that was trying to escape its cocoon. A boy watched as the butterfly struggled for hours to make its way through the tiny hole it had made in the cocoon. Finally, he could take it no longer and tore the hole open to make it easier for the butterfly.

What he did not realize was that suffering to emerge through that tiny hole was part of God's design. All the fluids get pressed out of the body and into the wings during that process. The wings can then expand into their full splendor and enable the butterfly to take flight. This butterfly was doomed now to a short life with a bloated body of fluid and no expansion of his wings. He did not ask to be helped and what was intended as kindness kept him from growing into the full splendor for which he was made.

Journal Time:

Think of the times you have gone through the deepest valleys. What transformed in you? Think of times when you had hardly any opposition in your life. Did you grow more or less during that time?

Share Time:

Discuss the situations you are being exposed to on this trip where you see suffering. Are you discerning how God is inviting you to come alongside someone in their suffering? Is He asking you to be the solution, or is He asking you to stand alongside Him as He does something that you cannot see?

Prayer:

Oh Lord,

How we long to see the suffering we encounter on this trip through Your eyes. Keep us from trying to play Your role. We do not want to get in Your way, Father, and we do not want to leave any work undone that You are calling us to, either. The only answer is that You give us Your discernment so that we know when to move forward with a solution and when to be still and watch as You work. You are the ultimate Guide, Lord, and we are Your attendants. Help us not to get ahead of You or behind You on this journey but to stay in step where You are leading.

In Jesus' name,
Amen

Worship:
"He Loves Us"
"Be Still My Soul"

Defining Moment . . . Freedom

I was reading the autobiography of a woman named Hanzi. She was a teenager during World War II and truly believed that Hitler was god. She trained with the most elite Nazi groups and pledged her allegiance to that party. She was brainwashed and subjected not only to mind control, but almost all areas of her life were controlled, including what time she could go out in the morning, what food she could buy, what time she went to the store, what time she must be home by, etc.

Hanzi miraculously made it through the war alive, and upon being rescued by American soldiers, she learned the truth about Hitler. She was devastated that she could have been so duped and could have pledged her life to such evil. From that moment on, she had a strong conviction that she belonged in America. She wanted to be part of the freedom and liberty that reigned in the United States. She was able to immigrate to San Diego, California, and knew very little English.

She moved into a home and cautiously asked her new neighbor where she was allowed to shop, what time she was allowed go out in the morning, and what time she had to be inside by. Her neighbor looked at her dumbfounded and asked what she was talking about. Hanzi explained her questions again, to which the neighbor replied, "You are free to go anywhere you want, any time you want, and shop anywhere you want." Hanzi asked what that meant, to which the neighbor kept replying, "You are free. There is nothing else to explain. You are free."

Hanzi explained in her book that the concept of freedom was so foreign to her that she had to *learn* how to be free. She was even frightened a little by the complete lack of structure and control in her life. It took her years to truly grasp her freedom and be comfortable in it. Her experience is symbolic of the freedom believers experience once they really understand who Jesus, and what He has done for them. He came to set the captives free:

> *The Spirit of the Lord is on me,*
> *because He has anointed me*
> *to proclaim good news to the poor.*
> *He has sent me to proclaim freedom for the prisoners*
> *and recovery of sight for the blind,*
> *To set the oppressed free,*
> *to proclaim the year of the Lord's favor.*
> *(Luke 4:18–19).*

It takes us humans a while to grow into our freedom. Just like Hanzi, we are so used to being shackled that we do not quite understand what it is like to live out our complete freedom in Christ. We still believe the lies of the enemy at times and stay in the stress, guilt, shame, and anguish that go along with enslavement.

As you experience transformation on this mission trip, be conscious of the ways that the Lord is setting you free and run with that freedom for all it is worth. Notice when you are returning to old thought patterns that are attempting to take you back into bondage. You have a choice. You can choose freedom because you have Christ.

It is so important that you stand in your own freedom, because those you are helping on your trip will watch you and experience *their* own freedom in Him by how they see *you* living in liberty. They will affect others, who will affect others, and before you know it, your freedom will be used by God to set hundreds of captives free!

Journal Time:

In what areas of your life do you still experience enslavement? What are the lies that the enemy is trying to get you to believe so that you stay in bondage to anxiety and guilt instead of living the abundant life that Jesus died to give you?

Share Time:

When we share out loud with each other about our areas of bondage, the power of the enslavement is broken in mysterious ways. By getting those thoughts out into the light, their hold on us is loosened. Be courageous and share with each other what your areas of enslavement have been. You are in a safe place to be transparent and kind with each other, so take advantage of this gift God is giving you.

Prayer:

Lord,

We lift up these areas of bondage we have been sharing and lay them at Your feet. We thank You that Your Son's blood has set us free in miraculous ways. Lord, we are choosing to live in that liberty right now and forevermore. Please use us to show the people we are serving on this trip how to walk in the freedom that You died to give us. Show us how to stay strong and not return to thoughts of bondage.

We want to get out of the boat, just like Peter did, but we do not want to waver and sink. Please be our strength and truth and show us how to stay free in You.

In Jesus' name,
Amen

Worship:

"A Mighty Fortress Is Our God"
"Freedom is Here" by Hillsong

Defining Moment . . . Prayer

Prayer is one of those things that many people underestimate. If we really understood the power we bring down into situations when we pray, God probably could not get us to stop talking about it. That is all that prayer is—a two-way conversation.

There may be some people in your group who have never prayed out loud with others before. No one is going to force anyone into praying out loud. Let us invite the group to think of prayer from a new paradigm. It is simply having a conversation. Just like there is no right or wrong way to have a conversation with a person, there is no right or wrong way to have a conversation with God.

One mistake we make is that we pray through a filter of thinking that everyone, including God, is judging our conversation. Is that how *you* have conversations with people? When a friend introduces you to a new person, are you constantly worried about what your friend thinks about what you are saying? Of course not. You are interacting with them and getting to know the person. The same is true of God. He does not want flowery language any more than you would want that from someone you are talking to. That style is talking *at*, not talking *with*.

Another argument people try to make about prayer is that God is going to do what He is going to do, so why waste time praying? Because Philippians 4:6 says: *"Do not be anxious about anything, but in every situation, by prayer and petition, with thanksgiving, present your requests to God."*

Why would God want us to pray about *everything*? Why would He want us to talk everything over with Him? Think about parents and their kids. The parent is clearly in charge and has ultimate authority over their child. But do they want a life of dictating every move their kid makes with no interaction from the child? A healthy relationship between a parent and their child offers the child a place to express his or her dreams and needs. The parent keeps him in safety with all that the child needs to grow and live out their full potential. God is the most perfect parent you can ever imagine. He wants to interact with us, not call every shot. That is called prayer.

Journal Time:

Do you have any fears of praying out loud in groups? How does changing the word from praying to chatting change your viewpoint?

Share Time:

Share some of your concerns about praying out loud. If there are no concerns, ask everyone if they are comfortable praying over the people you will be serving on the trip. Discuss having a standard of praying over people whenever possible and what that looks like.

Prayer:
Pray out loud together!

Worship:
"What a Friend We Have in Jesus"
"Pray" by Sanctus Real

Defining Moment . . . Unity

How good and pleasant it is when God's people live together in unity! It is like precious oil poured on the head, running down on the beard, running down on Aaron's beard, down on the collar of his robe. It is as if the dew of Hermon were falling on Mount Zion. For there the Lord bestows His blessing, even life forevermore
(Psalm 133:1–3).

The word bestows is *tsiwaah* in the original Hebrew and means literally to command. So, this Scripture says that when we live in the precious unity that God finds so pleasant, He COMMANDS blessing on us. This is the only place in Scripture where God tells us that when we obey Him, he COMMANDS a blessing. There is nothing that can separate us from the promises of God.

On this trip, there can be many things that the enemy tries to use to throw discord into your group. The last thing Satan wants is blessings COMMANDED over everything your group attempts to accomplish. Keep your eyes on the prize. When disagreements arise, you may be fully convinced of *your* point of view, so take time to ask God what *He* thinks. If both you and the person you are working with get different answers, at least one of you is not hearing from God. Do not let pride and self-righteousness separate those on the trip from the full, commanded blessing that is available to you through unity.

James 3:17–18 tells us: "*But the wisdom that comes from Heaven is first of all pure; then peace-loving, considerate, submissive, full of mercy and good fruit, impartial and sincere. Peacemakers who sow in peace reap a harvest of righteousness."* Be the peacemaker who brings unity to your group.

Journal Time:
How is your group doing with unity? Where are you doing well? Where are you failing? Do you personally have any part in either?

Share Time:
Affirm people in your group who are acting as peacemakers and striving to create unity. If there are any issues among the group, confess your parts out loud to each other and ask for God's Spirit to unify you.

Prayer:
Lord,

When we read how pleasing it is to You when brothers and sisters dwell in unity, our hearts leap. We long to please You and we want to bless You by living out that unity. Please forgive us for any part that any of us have played in creating disunity. Lord, in the next couple minutes, please show us any areas that we are not aware of where we are dividing the group instead of unifying it. (Pause for a minute or two). Father, we confess these sins to You and ask for You to give us the power and strength through Your Son to make us peacemakers. We long for You to command Your blessing on this trip and we want to partner with You, in unity, to complete this mission in the fullness of the glory that You planned.

In Jesus' name,
Amen

Worship:
"Make Me A Channel of Your Peace"
"Let There Be Peace on Earth" by Harry Connick Jr.

Defining Moment . . . Patience

Wikiquote defines patience as the capacity for waiting: *"the ability to endure waiting, delay, or provocation without becoming annoyed or upset, or to persevere calmly when faced with difficulties."*

I am ashamed to admit how I sometimes behave when faced with difficulties. I persevere calmly much less often than I would like to admit. In Galatians 6:9, Paul tells us: *"Let us not become weary in doing good, for at the proper time we will reap a harvest if we do not give up."*

I do alright at the not giving up part, but I often become annoyed or upset when my expectations are not being met. I know that the Lord loves a cheerful giver, but when I am frustrated, while I continue to give, I am not cheerful. I sometimes think the lessons I am writing about in this book are more for me than for the reader, because I really do struggle in this area.

When I think about the people who are patient and persevere calmly, they all have one thing in common—it is not about them. They are able to leave outside the door their egos, their expectations, their insistence on being right, and their need to control. They are able to be like Jesus in a way that invites me to join them instead of condemns me for my shortcomings. By being selfless, they pull the rug right out from under the enemy. They are not tempted to be impatient, because they are not concentrating on themselves. They are focused on others with most of that concentration being on the Holy Spirit.

When Abraham was given promises by God in Genesis 17, he knew it was about his descendants. It was not about him. When Jesus died on the Cross, He was completely other-focused. When we take the focus from ourselves, it removes a lot of pressure from our expectations. It is counterintuitive, but the way God has made us actually creates a burden when we focus on ourselves versus on others.

You might even be experiencing that relief on this trip. As you focus on the plight of others, your joy is more complete, your sense of love is more profound, and your sense of fulfillment is more pronounced. Jesus himself said, *"It is more blessed to give than to receive"* (Acts 20:35).

It is tricky here, because you are on a mission trip to serve others, and your plans to do so seem selfless and other-focused on the surface. You are doing this for *them*! But how much of the program is being dictated by the way *you* want things to go? How upset do you get when *your* expectations of how you want to serve these people are not met? The patience we need God to gift us with includes our openness to the Holy Spirit. No matter how circumstances turn, we put our trust in God and not in our plans. If we will stand in that place, we will rarely be tempted to be impatient.

Journal Time:
What expectations are not being met on this trip (or at home, or with relationships) that are causing you to be impatient? How is God giving you patience?

Share Time:
Talk about times when you have seen great examples of patience on this trip. Does the culture you are serving practice patience exceptionally well?

Prayer:
Lord,

Thank You for the fruits of the Spirit You have given us. Thank You that patience is something You have already instilled in us. Please help us to use that gift and not just keep it in a box inside us. We long to use the gifts You give us to their full extent. Please, Holy Spirit, come alongside us when our needs are not being met and give us the gift of focusing on the needs of others instead of ourselves. Keep us mindful of Your work and how You want the situation to pan out. Keep us more excited about what You want to happen than what we want to happen. We trust You and are looking forward with great joy to the ways You will lead us in patience on this trip.

In Jesus' name,

Amen

Worship:
"Our God is Mighty to Save"
"My God, My Father, Make Me Strong"

Defining Moment . . . Faith

Physical exercise requires discipline, determination, and motivation. Without it, our muscles will not stay strong. It is only by stressing our bodies slightly that our muscle mass grows stronger, and we can lift more and do more. Faith works a lot like our muscles. It is a gift that we receive from God, just like our bodies, but *we* decide what we do with it. If all we do is feed our faith, such as going to church and Bible studies, but we do not exercise it, we become spiritually fat and unfit. By stepping into this mission trip, you are exercising your faith. You are putting your trust in God and depending on Him to complete the work He began in you. Expect that He is going to give you the gift that an exercise trainer would. Expect boot camp.

When the supplies do not show up for the VBS training you have worked on for a year, think of it as fifty push-ups. When only ten people show up for a program planned for a hundred, think twenty-five pull-ups. Your faith is being stressed, tested, and exercised. God will use what looks like failure to advance His Kingdom just because you showed up and were obedient. You might not get to *see* the glory, but it will be there, nonetheless.

Here is a great example. A group organizes the use of homes once a year in an effort to evangelize people in different neighborhoods. Christians open up their living rooms, and a believer volunteers to give his or her testimony about a specific life-changing encounter with God. The community is invited and anywhere from fifteen to fifty people show up without reservations for coffee and cookies. One year, a homeowner prepared for a big crowd, as they had invited many people. Only two people came. The testimony went on as planned, and one of the two accepted Christ as their Lord for the first time.

She was a neighbor and hated crowds. She was not planning on attending, but when she saw that no one was there, she ventured in. The hostess could have been exasperated because she went to all the trouble of preparing food for a big crowd, but imagine her joy as she saw her neighbor choose Jesus as her God. She had the gift of seeing why God allowed something different than *her* expectations. You may or may not have that same privilege of seeing the fruit of God's way versus your way, but know that it is there whether or not you get a glimpse of it. That is where your faith muscle comes in, and you have the gift of the God of the universe being your personal trainer.

Trust that He knows exactly what He is doing, and He will not ask you to do even one sit-up too many.

Journal Time:
Where has God allowed you to have your faith muscle exercised on this trip? How might that specific experience be strengthening you in a place where you are weak? What does it look like to have a strong faith muscle in that place that you have been exercising? How would you feel and think about that specific situation if your spiritual muscle became really built up in that area?

Share Time:
Share with each other about the faith challenges you have been experiencing on the trip. Give each other space to express fully your deepest joys, griefs, and revelations without trying to fix the situation. Be curious about how God is working, and what He is accomplishing.

Prayer:
Dear Lord,

Thank You for being our very own personal trainer in the things of faith. Forgive us when we complain because it feels like we are being asked to use a muscle that feels weak. We trust You to make us strong and not to give us more than our faith can carry. Thank You for giving us the gift of faith in the first place. Give us direction on how to exercise it so we do not become spiritually flabby. Our desire is to be fit and strong for Your purposes. Thank You for the specific faith-growing workout You are giving us on this trip. We trust You and praise You ahead of time for all the ways You are building the Kingdom through this trip, whether we see the fruit of it in this lifetime or not.

We love You, Lord!

Amen

Worship:
"I Walk By Faith"
"It Is Well With My Soul"

Defining Moment . . . The Body of Christ

There is a great quote from the south that Jesus is coming back for a bride, not a harem. The Body of Christ is to be one Bride, not bits and pieces of splinters operating completely independently because we have different theological understanding. Nor does it support competition between churches that brag about membership size or the number of salvations they have counted. We are to be one Body, each doing the part that we were made to do. Paul tells us in the following passage:

> *"Just as a body, though one, has many parts, but all its many parts form one body, so it is with Christ. For we were all baptized by one Spirit so as to form one body—whether Jews or Gentiles, slave or free—and we were all given the one Spirit to drink. Even so, the body is not made up of one part but of many."*

> *"Now if the foot should say, 'Because I am not a hand, I do not belong to the body,' it would not for that reason stop being part of the body. And if the ear should say, 'Because I am not an eye, I do not belong to the body,' it would not for that reason stop being part of the body. If the whole body were an eye, where would the sense of hearing be? If the whole body were an ear, where would the sense of smell be? But in fact, God has placed the parts in the body, every one of them, just as He wanted them to be. If they were all one part, where would the body be? As it is, there are many parts, but one body."*

> *"The eye cannot say to the hand, 'I don't need you!' And the head cannot say to the feet, 'I don't need you!' On the contrary, those parts of the body that seem to be weaker are indispensable, and the parts that we think are less honorable we treat with special honor. And the parts that are unpresentable are treated with special modesty, while our presentable parts need no special treatment. But God has put the body together, giving greater honor to the parts that lacked it, so that there should be no division in the body, but that its parts should have equal concern for*

each other. If one part suffers, every part suffers with it; if one part is
honored, every part rejoices with it"

(1 Corinthians 12:12–26).

The people you are serving in this foreign land, those who are in the Body of Christ already, have a specific function just as you do. You will learn from them just as they learn from you. You are equally important in the Body of Christ.

Journal Time:

What have you learned from those you are serving that you did not expect to learn?

Share Time:

What part of the body is the group you are serving in the Body of Christ? Are they a mouthpiece for Christ in their community? Are they the serving hands of Jesus to those in need? Discuss their role and how it relates to the part of the Body that your travel group represents.

Prayer:

Father God,

Thank you for making the Body of Christ just as you did: one Body to work together to glorify You and to become the Bride for Your Son. Please help us to move forward in unity. Keep up from pulling the Body apart by going in different directions. Let us look to Jesus always as our Head and get our direction from Him. Keep us also from trying to control or judge other parts of the Body that we are not. Keep us mindful of our own role and glorifying You.

In Jesus' name,

Amen

Worship:

"Be the Center"
"One in Christ"

Defining Moment . . . Evangelism

I had an interesting conversation with a family member about my eating habits. They had a strong conviction that my idea of healthy eating was incorrect, and that I needed an intervention conversation. While they really believed that they were having this conversation out of love, it ended up entrenching me in my own point of view even further. Afterwards, I found myself discounting this person's ideas, because the very thing they were so concerned about in my life was a struggle that *they* had been fighting unsuccessfully for years.

They did not have a victory that they had found and wanted to share. Instead, it felt as if they were working out their *own* pain with this issue through their focus on *my* eating habits. As a result of this conversation, I became curious as to what happens when I want to share Jesus with someone, and I choose not to tell my own story, and instead tell them about ideas I think will move them. I *do* have victories in my life that are from God that I want to share. When I do that, am I more deeply entrenching them in their point of view? Am I am forcing ideas on them instead of telling them about *my experience* with God and how He has transformed me?

The best thing about telling your story is that no one can take it away from you. Your story is what occurred and there is no debating its theology. My friend's dad was an orphan who had a pretty rough upbringing. He ended up knowing the Lord and becoming a missionary in Africa. No one can argue with him about the miraculous ways that God showed up in His life to protect him.

Revelation 12:11 tells us about a victory that takes place in the end times: "*They triumphed over him by the blood of the Lamb and by the word of their testimony.*" It was not just the blood of the Lamb by itself that delivered the victory. God required people to share their stories to achieve the victory. What is your story? They triumphed over him, "by the blood of the Lamb and by the word of their testimony."

Journal Time:
Ask God to help you write the story that He wants you to share on this trip. What is it that He wants to overcome in others that He has already overcome in your life?

Share Time:
Share a few of your stories.

Prayer:
   Lord,

   We praise You that You are the Overcomer in our life. We are humbled that You would use us as instruments to help others be overcomers by sharing our stories. Lord, please guide us in what we share with others. Please keep us from forcing ideas on them that will send them further away from You. Instead, Lord, please remind us of the victories that You have provided in our lives. Let them see Your Glory in these stories, Lord, and be forever changed by what they hear. We are trusting You to do this in Your power, Lord, and not ours.

   In Jesus' name,
   Amen

Worship:
   "I Love to Tell the Story"
   "More than Conquerors"

Defining Moment . . . Discipleship
The Great Commission in Matthew 28:19–20 is the best direction the Lord gives about discipleship: "*Therefore, go and make disciples of all nations, baptizing them in the name of the Father and of the Son and of the Holy Spirit, and teaching them to obey everything I have commanded you. And surely, I am with you always, to the very end of the age.*"

   For many years, every time I read this passage, I thought it was talking about evangelism. I pictured Jesus asking us to convert nonbelievers into followers. How mistaken I was. Conversion is the Holy Spirit's job. Discipleship is my job. Notice that the direction to disciple comes first in this verse. The Bible very specifically orders ideas in sequential order. It does not say to baptize and then make disciples. What is discipleship? It means, literally, to teach. My job is to teach anyone who wants to learn about Jesus. I am to tell them about my relationship with Him and how to build their own relationship with God. My job is not to wring my hands, hoping and praying that they will want to accept Jesus as their Lord.

As I am writing this, I am in a nail salon sitting next to a teacher. When I mentioned to him that I am writing about teaching in this section, we started talking. I told him that I am writing about the difference between teaching people who *want* to be taught (in our case, this represents believers who have accepted Christ and want to know Him more) and teaching people who *do not want* to be taught (nonbelievers who are not seeking).

He then told me that fifty percent of his class does not want to be taught. I asked him how he worked with those kids in particular. He said that it is a long process, three to five years, of building relationships with them. Once that is established, they want to listen, but it takes much time and many teachers with the same mindset. In his opinion, one teacher can ruin a kid.

He was teaching me about kids, but the Lord, through him, was teaching me about discipleship. On this mission trip, you will encounter both believers who want to learn more and nonbelievers that do not want to engage. Our job as teachers is to be one of those many people over the years who invite those nonbelievers into relationship. It will take many of us, so there is little chance you will see the fruit of your labors on this trip. Be one of those teachers who bring the people you serve closer to God's heart.

Journal Time:
What is your definition of discipleship? How do you see yourself being a teacher on this trip? What are you afraid of? What are you excited about?

Share Time:
Share examples of great disciples. Discuss what you have learned from them.

Prayer:

Lord,

How we long to fulfill Your Great Commission! Please make us great teachers who lead people deeper into Your heart. Help us not to take on the Holy Spirit's role of conviction, but instead to build relationships with people so that they are excited about learning about You.

Keep us from making our conversations about our expectations of how people relate to You, and instead point them to the Holy Spirit to manifest a real, eternal love relationship with You. We adore You, and we are so grateful to be Your children!

In Jesus' name,

Amen

Worship:

"The Potter's Hand"

"Brother, Sister, Let Me Serve You"

Defining Moment . . . Social Justice

Social justice can end up being an idol. People sometimes use the guilt and sadness they feel for those living in poverty and move ministries forward out of wrong motives. It is easy to see a person in need and want to fix their problems. We want to fix things so they will not encounter more pain, but is that what God is asking of us?

In Micah 6:8, God directs us to care for others: *"He has shown you, O mortal, what is good. And what does the LORD require of you? To act justly and to love mercy and to walk humbly with your God."*

God is not always moved to action by people's needs. Jesus told us that we *always* will have the poor among us. But we see examples throughout the Bible of God's hand being moved by people crying out to Him. God's directive for us is not to wipe out poverty in our generation. He uses the selfishness and greed that contribute to poverty to bring His beloved closer to Him. He uses believers to show the poor where their true riches lie—in Christ Jesus.

Our God cares much more about the eternal Salvation of the people that you work with rather than just giving them food for a year. Bob Shank of The Master's Program has a great line: "If you take care of people's needs—shelter, food, medicine, education, water—without teaching them about Salvation, you just make them more comfortable on the road to hell."

It is not that God does not want us to feed the hungry or minister to the sick, but it is all about doing it out of a right motive. Are our hearts moved by our own dread of seeing someone in pain, or by the amazing glory of the One True God that is calling us to minister to that person?

How does your team keep focused on *God's* view of social justice and not on the *world's* view? Keep your eyes on Jesus. Let Him guide you. Only He can see into each situation and what the condition is of the hearts of those you are serving.

I once heard a sermon from a pastor who had been a meth addict for twenty years. He stole and conned his way through that lifestyle. He had such a different perspective on social justice and how society responded to his addictive needs. He spoke with authority on where our culture is on social justice as opposed to where God is calling us to live.

When the Bible was written, people lived in tight community. You knew about your neighbor's life in great detail. You knew when they were truly burdened. You knew when they were being lazy and not wanting to work for food. When we have hearts that are moved by *need,* we give resources to people that sometimes keeps them on a path to hell. When we have hearts that are moved by the *Holy Spirit,* we minister to souls eternally.

Journal Time:

Why did you choose to come on this trip? What motivated you? How are you responding to God's call to come alongside those you are serving? Is it more out of the Spirit guiding you, or more out of their need?

Share Time:

What is occurring in your heart as you hear the line about making people more comfortable on their way to hell? Do you agree or disagree?

Prayer:

> Lord,
>
> We want to make this trip about You and Your Kingdom, not about our own brokenness. Lord, please help us serve on this trip out of an obedient heart to You. Not because we feel guilty about having more materially than the people we are serving. Keep our eyes on You and what You want us to share with these people. We do not want to fulfill their physical needs and make them more comfortable in their life apart from You. We want to feed them spiritually first and foremost and give them what they need physically out of Your leading. Father, this is confusing territory and we need Your vision. Please show us when to step into situations and when to get out of Your way. Please keep us from being an obstacle to the work that You are doing in these people, and use us to Your full glory.
>
> In Jesus' name,
> Amen

Worship:

> "There is a River" Gaither Vocal Band
> "I Am Trusting Thee Lord Jesus"

Defining Moment . . . Family

The people you are serving with and the people you are serving have one thing in common: they are your brothers and sisters in Christ.

> Then Jesus' mother and brothers arrived. Standing outside, they sent someone in to call Him. A crowd was sitting around Him, and they told Him, "Your mother and brothers are outside looking for you."
>
> "Who are my mother and my brothers?" He asked. Then He looked at those seated in a circle around Him and said, "Here are my mother and my brothers! Whoever does God's will is My brother and sister and mother"
> (Mark 3:31–35).

This passage tells us several things. While we may have grown up in a biological family with parents and siblings, our *real* family, our *eternal* family, are the believers around us who are doing God's will. Our earthly families are human. Unless they know the Lord intimately, they will disappoint us and fall short of loving us in the ways that we need. Jesus had it no differently than we do. He was the Son of God, yet members of His earthly family at times did not understand who He was.

But the Father, in His infinite wisdom, has given us a family in the Body of Christ that is going to be with us throughout Eternity. Look around at those you are serving who are His. You will be spending Eternity with them even if you never see them again before you die. Can you imagine all the catching up we will be doing in Heaven? All the rejoicing for an Eternity over being the brothers and sisters of Jesus Himself? This knowing that we will be family forever takes some of the sting out of leaving this land when the trip is over. Hearts will be woven together through the Holy Spirit that make it painful for us to leave the people we are serving. But the reassurance that we get to be together forever gives us hope and comfort.

Journal Time:
How has your own family wounded you out of their own human nature? How has God provided for you with His family?

Share Time:
In what ways have your brothers and sisters in Christ come through for you when you needed them? Who are the people you have served on this trip that you are looking forward to catching up with in Heaven?

Prayer:
Lord,

Thank You that You have given us a family in Your Kingdom who loves us through You. Thank You for the brothers and sisters around us who do Your will and are truly our real family. Lord, we adore and worship You as our Father forever and thank You because You will never fail us like humans do. You love us in such perfect ways. Help us to love each other with Your same perfect love. There are so many people we have grown to love on our visit here. Please keep them safe and in Your ways until we meet again in Eternity.

In Jesus' name,
Amen

Worship:
"Father, I Adore You"
"How Great Thou Art"

Defining Moment . . . Expectations

We begin by thinking about the subject of inconvenient love. Jesus explains it well:

> *If you love those who love you, what credit is that to you? Even sinners love those who love them. And if you do good to those who are good to you, what credit is that to you? Even sinners do that. And if you lend to those from whom you expect repayment, what credit is that to you? Even sinners lend to sinners, expecting to be repaid in full. But love your enemies, do good to them, and lend to them without expecting to get anything back. Then your reward will be great, and you will be sons of the Most High, because He is kind to the ungrateful and wicked. Be merciful, just as your Father is merciful*
> (Luke 6:32–36).

Being on this mission trip in this country is a great example of inconvenient love. It was not convenient to raise funds to get here. Nor was it convenient to fly several hours, be deprived of sleep, be hungry with no food, stay awake when you need rest, and minister to people when you are completely out of energy. But you are doing it voluntarily and gladly. You are choosing to do good without expecting anything back from them.

So here lies the tricky part in this passage: "*without expecting anything back.*" While you do not expect and would even be embarrassed to receive any payback from the people you are ministering to, there is a part of us that expects *results.* What if you do not see one person get saved on this trip? What if not one person is healed, has his lot in life improved, or reconciles with his brother? How will you feel?

The Holy Spirit called you on this trip to do His work, You may not see His results because you get information on a need-to-know basis. Pastor and author, Jack Hayford, tells a great story about his parents. They were led by the Lord to pray for the Campbell side of their family. They prayed over the Salvation of these mostly unsaved relatives every single day.

One day a traveling salesman came to their door. They invited the gentleman in, and during the conversation they learned that he had recently accepted his Salvation from God. Upon further inquiry, they realized that his last name was Campbell, and he was a relative of the Campbells that they had been praying over. They knew that God, out of grace, had allowed them to see the results of their labor in prayer. However, they were further encouraged to keep on praying for the other Campbells who would be saved that they would never meet.

That same learning can be applied to the trip you are on. You may never see the results of your labors, but know that they are there. This trip is about *serving God*, not about being gratified by the results you may or may not see. Keep on praying, ministering, teaching, and loving—all to the glory of God, no matter what you see. *Our* job is obedience, and *God's* job is results.

There is also a lesson in the Old Testament about taking account of one's power instead of relying on the Lord. In 1 Samuel 24, David decides to take a census of how many soldiers he has, despite knowing he is disobeying the Lord. He is choosing to audit his earthly power instead of trusting the Lord. He pays dearly in the end. While we are living under the new covenant, we can still learn from David's mistake. Trust in the Lord that the outcome of your obedience in taking this trip is in His hands, and the Holy Spirit will use all of the seed planting that your group is doing, whether you see it or not.

Journal Time:

How are you feeling about the trip so far? Do you have expectations that will burden you if they are not met? Are these expectations from you or from the Holy Spirit?

Share Time:

Talk about your expectations and whether they are from man or from God. Does your church or sponsorship have expectations you feel pressured to meet? How can you keep focused on what *God* wants from you on this trip instead of what *man* wants from you?

Prayer:

> *Lord,*
>
> *Thank You that the burden for the fruit of the work that our group is doing on this trip is on You, and not on us. Forgive us, Lord, when we are looking to build our own glory by judging our trip by our own standards. We know that Your ways are mysterious, and we may not see the fruit of our labor until we get to Heaven. We trust You with the seeds that we are planting and the life-giving water that is pouring through us on this trip. Our expectations are that You will use us to Your full glory even when we do not see the outcome. Thank You for Your leading. We love You.*
>
> *In Jesus' name,*
> *Amen*

Worship:

> "Be the Strength of My Life"
> "I Surrender All"

Debriefing

Your team has been through an amazing journey. There have been tremendous moments of both joy and heartache as the Holy Spirit has led your trip. Reentry into regular home life will not be the same, because you are no longer the same. Rick's prayer for people going on mission trips is that *God will ruin you*, meaning you will come back changed.

On this trip you may have seen greater need and loss than you have ever been aware of in your life. There may be feelings of guilt that bubble up as you return to your safe home with unending supplies of food and water. There may be sadness as you ruminate on the plight of those you have left behind and what they have suffered and will continue to suffer. Even though your time together was short, your heart may have grown so attached to the people you served that there is a real grieving process in leaving them. Emotions may come up that you did not know you had as you share details of your trip with others.

God will often protect you during your trip by allowing you to process only as much as you are able at the time, filtering out other sights, smells, and experiences until later. Sometimes it catches up with you upon your return home, and you find yourself crying for no apparent reason.

For example, Rick, after our first trip to the Democratic Republic of Congo, flew straight home and jumped immediately back into life. He had no debrief time and no idea that he needed that time to process what the Lord had just shown him. When people at church the day after his return began asking him about his trip, he found himself breaking down in tears. This went on for his first three days back in the United States.

For these reasons, it is important that your team plan a debrief meeting immediately after returning home to process your experience. If there is any opportunity to do so, book those meetings into the end of the trip itself. We recommend that your group spend a few days in a resort area to go through this debrief process *before* returning. However, if that is not possible, start this process as soon as possible upon return.

Here are the steps to a successful debrief:

- Schedule the session(s) before you leave for your mission trip and get consensus and commitment from each team member to show up.
- Meet as soon as possible after you return from your trip (within three days).
- Keep notes throughout the trip of things that worked and did not work as well as the best and worst ministry experiences you had.
- Give yourselves enough time to get through everyone's input. A group of ten may need a couple of hours. A group of thirty may need six or more hours.
- Meet in an area with privacy that is safe for emotional, intimate communication (not Starbucks!). There may be tears. Give your group a private place to process their feelings.

- Invite people to fill out an anonymous feedback form for issues they do not want to personalize.
- The leader should touch base with each person who attended the trip individually within the next week to discuss any additional ideas and feelings that have percolated upon reentry.

Debrief Discussions

Ideally, your group debrief time will have room for recreation, fellowship, and rest. It will not be overly programmed, giving each person freedom to experience the above with God's unique timing. Group worship and prayer times are essential to letting God minister to you after your adventure. Here are some group discussion ideas that may help get processing conversations going:

- What were the funniest moments of the trip?
- What were the most emotional experiences you had?
- What surprised you the most?
- What infuriated you the most?
- Is there a part you wish you could do over?
- Where did God show up for you?
- What was your favorite food experience?
- What is your biggest lament for these people?
- Are there specific areas where you see these people as more spiritually advanced than you?
- Who most inspired you on the trip?
- How can we stay connected with the people we served there?

Be aware of the *pulse* of the group. The team leader will know if more or less time spent in group conversations is needed. The trip shepherd also may be needed more than ever at this time as one-on-one processing needs may arise.

Once you have gone through the debriefing process, it is time to re-acclimate yourself to your life. You are not the same person you were before the trip. People who have not had a transformational mission trip experience probably will not have the slightest idea what you are feeling. Keep in touch with your group and get through reentry together. Here are some tips on living life after you return:

Practice giving thanks to God continuously. How do you look at life differently after what you have just experienced? Thank God for all of the abundant blessings you now see through a new lens.

Give yourself time to process feelings. It may take several days of journaling, quiet time, and conversations with mentors, leaders, or close friends to be able to speak aloud what is happening in your heart, but make sure you take care of your emotions.

Pray about your part versus God's part in these people's lives. It is tempting to think that we can be the solution, but that is a dangerous road. God is the solution. We are the tools He uses to bring glory to His Kingdom. Do not take responsibility for those things that only God can do. You are not God, but you are His.

Debriefing Supporters

It is important to realize that the average person you know, including many of those who contributed to your financial support and committed to praying for your trip, only have about thirty seconds of interest in hearing about your experiences. We suggest that you prepare a thirty second elevator speech to share when asked. Then let their response tell whether or not you can share deeper information.

If friends ask about your trip, you can also ask back, "What are you interested in hearing about?" If they were just being polite, the elevator speech will do. However, if they really want to know what miracles God provided on the trip, you will usually have an interested party who will be clear about the amount of information they want to receive.

Let God lead you as to how much to share with each person. Downloading too much, even if it is amazing stuff, can overwhelm some folks and disengage them. Give them stories and experiences that they can get excited about and share with others. Remember that your sharing is more about how God wants to use your stories to stir whatever He is already working on in the person you are conversing with. Once again, it is not about *you*.

Thank You Letter

When you write your thank you letter to your prayer and financial supporters, it is important to get it out soon after your return. Within the first week is preferred. While some of the thank you letters I have received that are hand-written touched me greatly, it is not usually feasible to do that for every supporter. Either emails or hard copies are fine for these communications, but what is most important is sharing the stories of what you experienced.

People will not remember the words you used to describe your trip as much as they will remember the emotion that was invoked when they read one of your stories that touched their heart. They do not have to be long missives, but succinctly share a few of the times that God showed up and how He touched hearts. You will find that those times can be magnified as people hear of them from you and then share them with others. It is like a holy multi-level marketing opportunity!

You Have Only Just Begun . . .

As we discussed earlier in this book, a mission trip is only the first step of a beautiful and amazing journey that God has in store for you. Take a minute to ask God about what He has begun doing in you through this trip. Take time to journal any *aha!* moments that arise as you reenter your routine.

How are you feeling? What were the highlights from the trip? What were the lowlights? What caused you to cry? Paying attention to those things that touched your heart will help you to see the unique way God made your heart and what it is crying out for. Writing down these treasures from your heart will help you to collaborate with God on the work He is doing with you and the revelations He has given you through this trip.

For example, Susan found herself crying as she heard stories of innocent people being attacked and hurt. By looking at the pattern of when she was emotional while hearing *these* types of stories, she got clearer on her heart's cry to overcome the effects of injustice. She found herself wanting to get even more involved in a ministry in the Democratic Republic of Congo where there was a great deal of atrocity against innocent villagers.

Not About You

I heard a story of a young boy in South America who became greatly attached to the mission team who had just built his family a shelter to live in. When it came time to say goodbye, he tearfully *begged* them to stay. The local missionary said that he was old enough to see many teams come and go, so he knew that he would most likely never see these new friends again and he was heartbroken.

What is the solution? God does not call all of us to permanently move to the country we just served in, but what is He asking of us? Know that He will lead you to that answer as you ask Him for His will.

As for the people you have just served, think about your relationship from *their* perspective. They have just had what they consider an extremely wealthy person come and visit their very humble lifestyle. They may have shared their deepest physical, spiritual, and emotional needs with you, and *now* what? What would you expect if someone came into your life and saw the very neediest parts of you? Would you expect them to respond? Do you think they would walk away and never contact you again?

Ask God what next steps He would like to lead you in as you think about ministering to the people whom you have just met. The important thing is to keep moving toward what God has for you in light of the trip you have just taken with Him. A missionary once said, "God cannot steer you if you are not moving." You must move forward for God's guidance to take effect. Every time we leave the Congo, Rick shakes the hand of, or hugs, each person, looks them in the eye, and says, "We will be back in two years." When we return and are greeted by them, he reminds them of this promise and of our love for the people of Congo.

These are some ways to keep moving:

- Begin a mentoring relationship with some of the people you served via technology. It is shocking how many Africans are on Facebook and love to keep connected with us. Our amazing technology makes it easy to stay in conversation with those you have just met.

- Hold weekly or monthly prayer meetings. Ask the people you have met to consistently send you prayer requests that you can lift up with others.
- Plan a fundraiser with the rest of your team to raise money for any specific projects that God is calling you to support.
- Consider going back to the same place on another mission trip. We visit eastern Congo for two weeks every two years, and cannot wait to get back there with the co-laborers and beneficiaries! It is amazing to see what God does with what He has invested through you over the years.
- Put together a clothing or book drive if you have the means to transport the goods. There are some places that this does not work. For example, in some countries, it could cost more to transport and pay import tariffs and bribes than the actual goods cost. Do your homework beforehand. Maybe you could send such supplies with others wo are headed there before you are again.
- Consider sponsoring a pastor or additional shepherd for the group. In many areas, pastors make nothing and must supplement their ministry with another job. Could your team commit to supporting a pastor's salary for the next year?
- Ask if there are any ways that the people you served are longing to contribute to *your* spiritual growth? Mariners Church in Newport Beach was given a transformational study called Rooted, by Mavuno, a church they serve in Nairobi. It became the seed for an amazing movement within the church. While they did not end up using the exact study due to cultural differences, it was a base that Mariners built on that changed the way they grew together.
- Create a micro-finance program. Rick was moved by the needs of a group just outside of Mexico City and in 2003 through The Barnabas Group, helped raise $100,000 to start a micro-finance project to set up ten $10,000 community banks mostly serving women in small businesses. Groups of ten began getting loans of $250 per person to start or grow their own business. They held each other accountable to repay the loan with substantial interest. The repaid money was

then available for others to go through the same process, and so on, and so on. Thousands of new small businesses have been launched through this one-time project. This is the gift that keeps on giving! Ten years later, over $100,000 was still available for loans.

- Sponsor a translation of the Bible into the mother tongue of the people you have just served.
- Consider whether God is calling you to return on a longer mission trip to this place. Six months . . . one year . . . five years . . .

We started this book by saying, "Our prayer for you is that this book will start you on new journeys, new possibilities and promises, new transformations. There is a vast difference between *knowing* Bible places and stories and *experiencing* ourselves in those stories. Imagine yourself in *that* time and place, and then listen to the Holy Spirit showing you where *you* are today in that story."

The whole objective of this book is that the Holy Spirit would be your tour guide on every faith journey that you take. While this book is a tool that can open up minds and hearts to what the Lord wants to uniquely reveal to you on your adventure, without the revelation and encouragement of the Holy Spirit, the book itself is useless.

As the Holy Spirit reveals your unique *aha!* moments, sharing them with one another will make them come alive. Travelers can keep excellent journals and track what they are hearing, but when they speak those same things out loud, in front of a loving community in Christ, hearts are changed. Not only does that individual traveler experience that moment in a new way in their heart, but the band of believers around them are led into deeper connection among themselves and the Lord. A sacred experience of trust and intimacy takes over between believers, which is just a taste of what we will all get to experience in Heaven.

Fostering this sacred sharing under the guidance of the Holy Spirit will turn your fellow travelers into even more of a family than they already are. Husbands and wives see hidden pieces of each other's hearts that they may have never known. Fellow passengers on tour buses now become family members in the Lord. Tender revelations of hurts and triumphs become treasures that are used by God to bring freedom to each other long after the trip ends. As the group returns home, there will be a lot of pondering over those meaningful times and how God will bring further revelation as each person processes what they have experienced. Stay connected in your new family by continuing to share how God is working in each of you once you return home.

To those *armchair travelers*, you are also called to share the revelations the Holy Spirit leads you into with the band of believers that *you* fellowship with. By sharing your interactive experiences with the Lord, God uses you to deepen other's experiences with Him.

We are asking you to get the word out on your experiences with this book. We never wrote this book to financially prosper off of it. We wrote it because we both experienced the awe and wonder of inviting the Holy Spirit to transform us as we went on our faith travels. Our hearts are broken that *every* believer on the planet that visits these sacred spots might come and go *without* that profound experience. We know what it is like to travel in the wonder of watching God go with us and what it is like to endure endless travel spots rich in history but poor in transformation. We want *every* saint that undertakes a faith journey to have *both*. Know that we will be praying for you to have soul-altering interactions with our Lord on your travels, which you can tell us about when we all meet up on the other side of Eternity. Be blessed in Him.

APPENDIX: GENERAL

General:
   Packing List
   Travel To-Do List
   30 Days of Prepared Hearts
   Christian History Timeline
   Glossary
   Suggested Resources: General

Israel: The Holy Land
   Major Archaeological Finds: New Testament
   Jesus' Teachings, in Biblical Order
   Jesus' Parables, in Biblical Order
   Jesus' Miracles, in Biblical Order
   Jesus' Disciples
   Resurrection Appearances
   Harmony of the Gospels by Region
   Jerusalem Occupiers, Old Testament and New Testament
   Suggested Resources: The Holy Land
   Map: First Century Israel
   Map: Modern Israel Today
   Map: Ancient Jerusalem

Paul's Journeys
   Letters Written by Paul, in Order of Writing Date
   Themes of Letters Written by Paul, in Biblical Order
   Paul's Traveling Companions
   Major Archaeological Finds: New Testament
   Roman Emperors During the Biblical Period
   Timeline of Paul's Life and Journeys

The Reformation

APPENDIX: GENERAL

Packing List
Travel To-Do List
30 Days of Prepared Hearts
Christian History Timeline
Glossary
Suggested Resources: General

Packing List:

Depending on where you travel, here is a comprehensive list to consider.

Passport that is valid at least six months from date of return with enough blank pages for the number of countries you are visiting

Visas or transit visas, as needed

Airline tickets with boarding passes printed out

Driver's license (for car rental, extra ID)

Luggage tags for every bag and carry-on

Neck pillow and sleeping mask

Books to read, including Kindle

Place your name and destination on a paper inside each suitcase in case tags tear off

Prescription medications in your carry-on

Eyeglasses, reading glasses, contact lenses, cleaning fluids, backup eyeglasses, prescription in your carry-on

Sunglasses in your carry-on

Hat or Visor

Moist towelettes to freshen up

Informal, comfortable clothing that is wrinkle-resistant

Blouses or shirts

Pants, shorts, skirts

Underwear

Socks

Comfortable shoes with non-skid soles, already worked in if new

Flip flops for the beach

A long wrap to cover knees and shoulders when visiting holy sites

One jacket or heavy sweater

Travel alarm clock (battery operated)

Toiletries:

- Shampoo
- Toothbrush and dental floss
- Comb or hairbrush
- Nail clippers
- Shaving equipment
- Diarrhea medicine
- Cold remedy
- Sleeping pills (consider taking first three arrival days to get on schedule there)
- Aspirin
- Motion sickness pills
- Laxative
- Antibiotic cream
- Copies of prescriptions (in case you need them filled)
- Sunscreen and insect repellent
- Earplugs
- Hand sanitizer
- Lip balm
- Toilet paper
- Petroleum jelly to stop potential foot blisters

Travel umbrella and raincoat

Electrical appliances (hair irons, dryers, etc., with converters and adapters)

Plastic bags (for wet bathing suits)

Laundry soap

Cell phone and charger

Camera and charger, plus backup battery and SD cards

Snacks

Scarf (planes gets cold)
Keys

Currency: $50 in $1 bills for those places that take U.S. currency but only give change in local currency. You can order foreign currency before you go.

Credit cards: bring cards that do not charge foreign transaction fees, if possible. Make sure your credit limit is sufficient for trip. Let your credit card company know when and where you are traveling.

Travel To-Do List:
- Adjust home thermostat.
- Set up lights on timers, so home is lit at night.
- Leave extra keys with a neighbor.
- Pay bills to be due.
- Lock doors and windows.
- Stop newspaper delivery.
- Understand your health care coverage overseas, and buy additional protection, if needed.
- Purchase travel insurance, if desired.
- Leave itinerary and contact info with family.
- Reconfirm flight forty-eight hours before departure.
- Check the web for tipping practices and etiquette in the country you are visiting.
- Make copies of passport and front and back of all credit cards you are taking, carried in a separate place.
- Empty refrigerator of perishables.
- Unplug hazardous appliances.
- Arrange with neighbor for mail pick up and plant watering.
- Consider turning water off to avoid internal flooding.

30 Days of Prepared Hearts:
The 30-Day Countdown: Setting apart our hearts and minds, one day at a time, to ready our spirits for the journey ahead. The Scripture verses

are given to aid in the Prayer Focus for the day, and can be used to pray the specific request in the Word itself. When we pray God's promises back to Him over our lives, we are sure to be praying in His will!

Days Before Departure	Prayer Focus	Scripture Focus
30	Unity for our travel group	Psalm 133
29	God's guidance in all aspects of the trip	Psalm 32:8
28	That each person will hear God's voice during transforming opportunities at the site visits, giving them direction for their walk with Him	Isaiah 30:21
27	That the Word of God will give our minds further insight on this trip	2 Timothy 3:16-17
26	That God's Word would dwell in our hearts richly during these travels, even when it is not right in front of our eyes	Proverbs 4:20-22
25	That God would protect our group and keep us safe during our time together	Deuteronomy 33:27
24	That God would keep us strong through Him, despite jet lag!	Ephesians 3:16-17
23	That no one on our trip would be fearful of the unknown experiences that come with travel to foreign lands	Isaiah 41:10
22	Ask that our entire group will be praying for themselves and for each other	Philippians 4:6-7
21	Ask God to keep our group from stumbling—either physically on paths or spiritually—by being closed minded to what He has to give us on this journey	Jude 24-25
20	That our knowledge of God and who He is in our lives will increase on this trip	Colossians 1:10-12
19	That peace would rule amongst our travel family	Colossians 3:15
18	That every detail of this trip—travel, hotels, food—everything—would be blessed by God as part of His plan for us	Matthew 6:25-34
17	That each person on the trip experience dwelling 'in the secret place of the Most High' during our travels	Psalm 91:1-2

Days Before Departure	Prayer Focus	Scripture Focus
16	That the sometimes hectic travel schedule will not weary our team	Isaiah 40:31
15	Pray against individuals comparing their experiences or 'how spiritual' they appear to others in a way that distracts them from God's specific plan for them on this trip	Hebrews 13:5
14	As the Holy Spirit may allow some to encounter challenging personal truths, pray that God's love envelopes them.	Romans 8:35-39
13	That the group would be bonded and sensitive to each other's needs	2 Corinthians 1:3-4
12	Pray for our group focus to be on the things God would have us focus on	Philippians 4:8
11	That there would be a spirit of humility amongst our group, that enables us to experience all He has for us on this trip	1 Peter 5:5-6
10	That our group would hunger and thirst for God—and be satisfied	Psalm 63:1-8
9	Ask that God keep our group from confusion, and that we would impart Godly wisdom to each other	James 3:16-18
8	That each of us would confess and repent of anything that's keeping us from being real with God.	Hebrews 4:14-16
7	That each person in our group would pray on the 'whole armor of God' to be spiritually protected from anything the enemy might use to distract us from all God has planned for us on this trip	Ephesians 6:10-18
6	Ask God that each person on the trip would be kind to each other, and to those serving us, that we might be a good witness	Ephesians 4:31-32
5	Pray that through this trip, God sets each member of our group free from those things that have been keeping them from living His abundant life	Isaiah 61:1-3
4	That God's purposes, through His Word, would be accomplished for this trip	Isaiah 55:10-11

Days Before Departure	Prayer Focus	Scripture Focus
3	Pray that any people that come on this trip that are not followers of Jesus would invite Him into their hearts and become disciples	2 Peter 3:9
2	Pray for all the leaders of your group, that they would put God's love first in all aspects of the trip	1 Corinthians 13:1-8
1	That our entire group loves one another	John 15:12-14,17

Christian History Timeline

6-4 BC Jesus is born in Bethlehem

29 AD Jesus begins his public ministry at thirty years of age. He teaches, performs miracles and proclaims that He is the Son of God.

30-33 Jesus dies on the Cross, rises from the dead, and appears to more than five hundred disciples. (1 Corinthians 15:6). He also gives us the Great Commission: "Go ye therefore and teach all nations…" (Matthew 28:19) He ascends into Heaven forty days later (Acts 1:3,9).

33 The Holy Spirit fills the disciples in Jerusalem and three thousand people become Christians. They spread the message through the Roman empire (Acts 2:8).

32-35 Stephen is stoned to death in Jerusalem, and believers scatter due to persecution.

35-37 Paul's conversion. He goes on three missionary journeys starting in 48 AD and writes thirteen letters to the new churches.

37-100 Josephus (Jewish historian)

41 Cornelius, the Roman Centurion, accepts Christ as his Savior. Peter is called to evangelize Gentiles, and Roman soldiers take the Good News to Italy. In Antioch, Christ followers are called "Christians" for the first time.

44 Christian persecution heats up under king Herod. James is killed, Peter is thrown in prison, Judea undergoes famine, and the Antioch Christians send support.

47-49 Paul's First Missionary Journey

49-100 The books of Matthew, Mark, Luke and John are written, as well as the rest of the New Testament.

49-51 Paul's Second Missionary Journey; Paul gets the Council of Jerusalem to agree that Gentile converts are not required to follow Jewish law (and circumcision).

52-57 Paul's Third Missionary Journey

49-53 Rome expels Jews (Priscilla and Aquilla included) and they meet Paul in Corinth on his second journey there.

62 James (Jesus' brother) is martyred.

64 Christians are blamed for a huge fire in Rome. Thousands of them are tortured and killed by Nero, an emperor.

67-68 Peter and Paul are extradited to Rome, where Paul continues to teach while under house arrest. Nero has both of them killed.

66-73 The Jews revolt against the Romans and the Temple is destroyed in Jerusalem. Both Jews and Christians scatter to all parts of their civilization, leaving Antioch as the Christian headquarters. John is exiled to Patmos (either in 68 or 70) and writes Revelation.

71-81 Romans build the Coliseum.

73 Masada falls to the Romans.

1-99 Christianity is taken to many foreign lands: Egypt (by Mark), Sudan (by the Ethiopian eunuch), Armenia (by Thaddaeus and Bartholomew), France, Italy, Germany, Britain, Iraq, Iran, India (by Thomas), Greece, Yugoslavia, Bosnia, Croatia (by Titus) Asia Minor (Turkey), Albania, Algeria, Libya and Tunisia (Africa).

100 John, Jesus beloved disciple, dies a natural death. He is the only one of the twelve disciples who is not killed for their faith.

132-135 The Jews revolt for a second time, and Jerusalem is destroyed. People either die or escape—none remain.

197 The Apostles Creed is written. The church will recognize twenty three New Testament books in their canon by 200 AD, but do not publish them together.

1-199 Christianity spreads to Morocco, Bulgaria, Portugal, Austria and North Africa.

200 Translation is completed on Scriptures into seven languages. Egyptian Christians are severely persecuted, and thousands are killed.

261 Christians begin meeting in churches (basilicas) instead of exclusively in homes. Egypt begins to produce monks and religious orders.

295 The word "catholic" refers to any church that agrees with whole apostolic teaching. Heretical groups are recognized as following "secret revelation" or information based on a single teaching.

200-299 Christianity spreads to Switzerland, Sahara, Belgium, Qatar, Bahrain, Hungary and Luxembourg.

312 Constantine wins a battle after seeing a vision of the Cross, credits Jesus and legalizes Christianity. Helena, his mother, visits Israel and builds many churches over sacred sites.

324 Church History is written by Eusebius.

325 Because of rampant heretical teaching, the Council of Nicaea is formed, which produces the Nicene Creed and clearly defines the Trinity.

330 Constantinople is established as the capital of the empire (formerly Byzantium).

337 Constantine is baptized only a few days before he dies.

367 New Testament Canon is confirmed and recognized by the Council of Carthage and the Bishop of Alexandria.

381 The Nicene Creed is finalized and condemns heresy under the authority of the Council of Constantinople.

300-399 Christianity spreads to Afghanistan and Ethiopia.

404 Jerome translates the Old and New Testaments into Latin. Taking twenty two years, The Vulgate, written in Bethlehem, is used as the Bible for one thousand years.

432 Patrick evangelizes Ireland, and, within 30 years, most of the country converts to Christianity.

400-499 Christianity reaches western north Africa, San Marino, Liechtenstein, Ireland and central Asia.

520 Experts in learning and training, Irish monasteries equip and send missionaries to the ends of the known world.

525 The Middle East receives Christianity (Saudi Arabia, Yemen and Oman.

590 The first of the medieval popes is chosen, after donating his wealth to church ministry and the poor. Gregory I send missionaries to England and promotes liturgical music and monasteries.

500-599 Christianity reaches Yemen, Ceylon, Nubia (Sudan) and Channel Islands.

610 (approximately) The Islam religion begins after Muhammad claims to have divine revelations and proclaims he is the prophet of God. His teachings are recorded in the Koran, and, by his death in 632, much of Arabia has received his message.

632 Palestine and Syria both receive Islam, and Jerusalem is conquered by Muslims. Islam spreads to Egypt and north Africa, and almost wipes Christianity out (previously there were over a million believers).

680-692 Eastern and Western churches are separated by different theologies, including clergy celibacy. The Western church discourages marriage among priests, and the Eastern church allows it as long it is done before ordination.

688-691 Islam builds the Dome of the Rock on the Temple Mount in Jerusalem to impress visitors. Some of the columns are decorated with Crosses taken from Christian churches.

600-699 Christianity reaches China, Netherlands, Indonesia, Niger and Mongolia but declines in North Africa.

711 Spain and Portugal are invaded by Muslim Moors—the first European conquest—and stay until they are overcome in the 1200's.

720 The Gospel of John is translated into English by Bede.

768-814 The empire of Charlemagne expands to France, Germany and Italy, forcing conversion of the German Saxons.

700-799 Christianity is received in Iceland, Pakistan and East Germany.

800 Charlemagne is made emperor of Rome. Monasteries are encouraged to teach reading and writing, schools are founded, and the Bible is copied by hand there. The Western Church begins to overpower the Eastern Church's influence.

846 Rome is attacked by Muslims.

800-899 Christianity enters Tibet, Burma, Denmark, Czechoslovakia, Norway and Sweden.

962 Otto I, the Great, is crowned pope and reigns through 1806.

999 Leif Erikson accepts Christ and takes it to Greenland the next year.

900-999 Christianity grows to Hungary, Kiev (Ukraine), Greenland and Poland.

1066 The Celts are evangelized by the French (Normans).

1096 The Pope asks for volunteers and Crusades begin to help Christians in Constantinople, to liberate holy sites in Jerusalem and to reopen Israel to Christian pilgrims.

1097-1099 Over seventy thousand who joined the First Crusades left for Israel. Their overzealous motivation led to killing Jews in Germany and vicious killing in Jerusalem.

1146 A Second Crusade is planned after the Muslims overtake Turkey—the capital of the crusades. Led by France and Germany, this Crusade fails.

1189-1192 The Third Crusade results in Christian access to Jerusalem for pilgrims.

1100-1199 Christianity reaches Finland.

1201 Pope Innocent III dictates authority over all political rulers.

1202 A Fourth Crusade, targeting Egypt, is planned by pope Innocent III. However, the Crusaders instead overtake Constantinople in a three day massacre which sets the eastern and western churches against each other.

1209 The Franciscan order is started by Francis of Assisi.

1217 Francis of Assisi preaches to the sultan of Egypt as the Fifth Crusade fails.

1229 Jerusalem is recovered during negotiations by the Crusaders.

1244 Muslims recapture Jerusalem by force.

1266 A Mongol leader asks the pope for one hundred Christians to bring Christianity to his country, but the pope only sends seven.

1295 Mongols begins converting to Islam.

1302 The pope commands rule over secular politicians.

1309 The Order of the Knights of Templar is ended and their wealth is given to France, where the pope rules from for the next 70 years.

1348-51 A third of Europe dies from the Bubonic plague (spread by fleas living on rats).

1371 English priest John Wycliffe challenges the power of the papacy, and suggests that Scripture be translated and made available to the masses.

1382 The Wycliffe Bible is translated into English from Latin.

1408 English law forbids reading the Bible unless the bishop approves it.

1431 Joan of Arc claims to hear God's voice leading her to save France. She leads them into military success, but is then tried for witchcraft and burned.

1456 Joan of Arc's verdict condemning her of witchcraft is reversed—oops, too late.

1453 Constantinople is overtaken by Ottoman Turks. Scholars run to the West with manuscripts of the Bible, which leads to a revival of classical learning in the Renaissance.

1456 The Gutenberg Bible is printed, and more people can finally afford copies, which previously cost one year's wages.

1479 The pope approves the Spanish Inquisition to punish heretics, leading to an abuse of power and cruel torture.

1493 Explorers colonize the Americas and Africa, which enables missionaries to spread the Gospel, and settlers to exploit the indigenous peoples.

1400-1499 Christianity spreads to Haiti, the Dominican Republic and Kenya.

1503-12 Michelangelo finishes painting the Sistine Chapel.

1516 Martin Luther challenges the Catholic Church and preaches that God's faith alone saves a Christian.

1517 Luther's Ninety-five Theses are posted on a church door in Wittenberg, demanding that the church stop selling indulgences (tickets to Heaven), beginning the Reformation.

1522 The New Testament is written in German by Luther.

1525 William Tyndale is burned at the stake in England for translating the New Testament from Greek in to English without permission, and smuggling copies into the country.

1529 Protestants confirm the Bible as the only source of God's Word, and that man is justified by faith alone (Ephesians 2:8-9).

1534 Henry VIII of England makes himself head of the English church and breaks away from Catholicism.

1545-63 Catholic Council of Trent condemns the selling of indulgences—and Protestantism.

1549 The majority of the Church of England is united around the Book of Common Prayer—a compromise between Protestantism and Catholicism.

1555 Protestants flee from England as queen Mary Tudor restores Catholicism.

1558 The new queen of England, Elizabeth I, tries to unite the Church of England and Catholics but is excommunicated by the pope and then persecutes Catholics.

1560 English Protestant exiles in Geneva print the Geneva Bible.

1500-1599 Christianity reaches Thailand, Cambodia, Korea, South America and Africa through Catholicism. Protestant missionaries are rare for the next two hundred years.

1611 King James of England commissions the King James Version Bible. It takes fifty four scholars six years to use Greek and Hebrew manuscripts, and the Bishops and Tynsdale's Bibles, to complete this Bible. It is initially unpopular, but then becomes the most popular version for three hundred years.

1620-30's The Mayflower sets sail for America, bringing separatists that no longer agree with the Church of England. Puritans come later, with the intent of cleansing the church.

1692 Christianity is allowed in China by the emperor, eventually resulting in three hundred thousand conversions.

1698 Protestants begin organizing missionaries.

1600-1699 Christianity enters Taiwan, Uruguay, Laos, Antigua, Virgin Islands, Bermuda, Belize, Polynesia, Chad, Bahamas and Micronesia.

1706 The first Presbyterian Church is established in America.

1738 John and Charles Wesley convert to Christianity and establish Methodism—concentrating on specific spiritual disciplines each week.

1740 George Whitefield leads the Great Awakening in New England, which spreads within colonial America.

1741-2 Handel writes the music to the Messiah.

1764 "Amazing Grace" is written by a former slave trader, John Newton.

1769 Father Junipero Serra begins building the first of nine missions in California.

1773 The Black Baptist church comes into being in America.

1780 Robert Raikes invents "Sunday School" for the urban poor in England.

1792 New England is overcome for thirty years by the Second Great Awakening.

1795 America's churches divide over their positions on slavery.

1797 Methodists form their own denomination and break away from the Church of England.

1700-1799 Christianity spreads to Tonga, Nepal, the Seychelles Islands, the Falkland Islands, the Turks and Caicos Islands and Sierra Leone.

1804 Napoleon declares himself emperor, invades Rome and takes the pope prisoner.

1807 England abolishes slave trading as led by William Wilberforce. He also affects changes in the areas of child labor, illiteracy, prison conditions, education and civil rights for minorities.

1816 Richard Allen founds the African Methodist Episcopal Church (AME) in Philadelphia.

1836 The first faith orphanage is created in England by George Muller.

1844 Christianity is introduced to large urban groups in England through the creation of the YMCA and the YWCA. William Miller begins the Adventist Movement.

1854 Charles Spurgeon preaches to such huge numbers in England that a new church is built for him.

1855 Revivalism is started by Dwight L. Moody and others, holding revival meetings for urbanites.

1859 The Origin of the Species is written by Darwin.

1870 Papal infallibility is declared by the First Vatican Council.

1875-9 Jehovah's Witnesses and Christian Science begin, and deny that Christ is the Son of God.

1878 Methodist preachers (William Booth and Catherine Munford, his wife) found the Salvation Army to serve the poor and needy.

1895 The Turks kill three hundred Christians in Armenia.

1800-1899 Christianity covers Somalia, Botswana, Zambia, Rwanda, Liberia, Madagascar, Uganda, Hong Kong and Samoa.

1904-5 The Welsh Revival sweeps Scotland.

1906 Pentecostalism—Spirit baptism and speaking in tongues—begins at the Azusa Street Revivals in Los Angeles. Out of this movement, the Four-Square, Assemblies of God and Church of God denominations would begin.

1917 Communism attacks Christian ideology in schools and churches in Europe, Asia and Latin America. Millions are taken captive or murdered.

1925 The Baseball Preacher (Billy Sunday) leads revivals. The Scopes (Monkey) Trial addresses the teaching of evolution.

1934 Wycliffe Bible Translators is organized, and will grow Bible translations from six hundred in 1914 to sixteen hundred in 1980.

1933-45 Nazis kill six million Jews and millions of Christians in World War II.

1945 A Lutheran pastor, Dietrich Bonhoeffer, is hung for planning Hitler's assassination.

1948 The Dead Sea Scrolls (c. 100) are discovered by a shepherd boy.

1949 Organized Christianity reaches every country except Saudi Arabia, Tibet and Afghanistan.

1954 The Unification Church and Scientology are created, renouncing that Jesus is the Son of God.

1962 The Second Vatican Council encourages mass to be preached in the common language instead of Latin.

1970 International crusades and charismatic movements begin: Luis Palau, Campus Crusade, the Jesus Movement and Billy Graham among them.

1998 Over five million people have viewed the evangelistic "The Jesus Film" over the past twenty years.

2004 Mel Gibson creates The Passion of the Christ movie in Christ's original Aramaic, with subtitles, and record numbers see the death and resurrection of Christ on film. Christianity arrives in the Antarctic. There is still a need for two thousand people groups to have the Bible translated into their own language and dialect.

Glossary

Acropolis	Ancient fortified hilltop
Agora	Market area and gathering place of an ancient Greek city
Amphora	A two-handled jar for oil or wine
Basilica	In Roman architecture, a large covered hall; later, a style of Christian church developed in the fourth century with three or five aisles
Byzantine Empire	Greek-speaking Christian state, ruled from Constantinople (modern Istanbul), after the eastern Roman Empire divided from the west (fourth century)
Byzantium	Original name for Constantinople
Cavea	Auditorium seating of a Greek theater
Citadel	Fortress
Classical	Art of the fifth to fourth century BC in Greece
Corinthian column	A column with an ornate capital decorated with scrolls and acanthus leaves
Forum	Market area of a Roman-era city
Hellenism	Spread of Greek culture
Hippodrome	Course for chariot races
Icon	Greek; eikon, "image, likeness"; a sacred picture, usually on a panel
Ionic column	A column of uniform thickness, with ornamental base and volute capital
Minoan culture	Culture on the island of Crete from 2600-1100 BC.
Narthex	Vestibule of a church
Nave	Central lengthwise aisle of a church
Necropolis	Cemetery (literally, "city of the dead")
Neos, Nea, Neo	"New"; common part of a town name
Paleos, Palea, Paleo	"Old"; common part of a town name
PanHellenic	"All Greece," games or festivals

Peristyle	A covered colonnade surrounding a building; or an inner court with a colonnade
Portico	A colonnaded porch, with a roof supported on at least one side by columns
Stadium	A measure of length, six hundred feet, or a running track of the same length; also *stadion*

Suggested Resources: General

Books:

101 Hymn Stories, Kenneth Osbeck

Anticipate; Experience; Reflect (mission trip devotionals/journals)

Christ in Youth, ©2007, Christ in Youth, Standard Publishing

Called, Challenged, Changed (mission trip devotionals/journals)
Standard Publishing, ©2000

The Christian Travel Planner Kevin J. Wright, ©2008, Thomas Nelson

Rose Book of Bible and Christian History Timelines ©2018, Rose
Publishing

The Works of Josephus, Flavius Josephus/William Whiston, ©1980

APPENDIX: ISRAEL: THE HOLY LAND

Major Archaeological Finds: New Testament
Jesus' Teachings, in Biblical Order
Jesus' Parables, in Biblical Order
Jesus' Miracles, in Biblical Order
Jesus' Disciples
Resurrection Appearances
Harmony of the Gospels by Region
Jerusalem Occupiers: Old Testament and New Testament
Suggested Resources: The Holy Land
Map: First Century Israel
Map: Modern Israel Today
Map: Ancient Jerusalem

Major Archaeological Finds, New Testament

Site or Artifact	Location	Related Scripture
Herod's temple	Jerusalem	Luke 1:9
Herod's winter palace	Jericho	Matthew 2:4
The Herodium (possible site of Herod's tomb)	Near Bethlehem	Matthew 2:19
Masada	Southwest of Dead Sea	Luke 21:20
Early synagogue	Capernaum	Mark 1:21
Pool of Siloam	Jerusalem	John 9:7
Pool of Bethesda	Jerusalem	John 5:2
Pilate inscription	Caesarea	Luke 3:1
Inscription: Gentile entrance of Temple sanctuary	Jerusalem	Acts 21:27–29
Skeletal remains of crucified man	Jerusalem	Luke 23:33

| Peter's house | Capernaum | Matthew 8:14 |
| Jacob's well | Nablus | John 4:5-6 |

Jesus' Teachings, in Biblical Order

Teaching	Location	Related Scripture
Beatitudes*	Mount of Beatitudes (northwest corner of the Sea of Galilee, near Capernaum)	Matthew 5:1–12
Sermon on the Mount*	Mount of Beatitudes (northwest corner of Sea of Galilee, near Capernaum)	Matthew 5:1–20
Lord's Prayer	Mount of Beatitudes northwest corner of Sea of Galilee, near Capernaum)	Matthew 6:5–15
Sending out the twelve	Possibly Capernaum	Matthew 10:1–42
Wealth	Perea (Jordan)	Matthew 19:16–30
Greatest Commandment	Jerusalem	Matthew 22:34–40
Giving to Caesar	Jerusalem	Mark 12:13–17
Golden rule	Plateau above Sea of Galilee	Luke 6:31
Worry	By Sea of Galilee	Luke 12:22–24
Discipleship	Believed to be Perea	Luke 14:25–35
Born again	Jerusalem	John 3:1–21
Living water	Sychar in Samaria	John 4:1–26
Bread of life	Sea of Galilee	John 6:25–29
Good shepherd	Jerusalem	John 10:1–21
The way to life	Jerusalem	John 14:1–7
True vine	Jerusalem	John 15:1–17
* New law, like the old law (Exodus 19:3) given from a mountain		

Jesus' Parables, in Biblical Order

Parable	Location	Matthew	Mark	Luke
Lamp under a bowl	Mount of Beatitudes (Sermon on the Mount)	5:14–16	4:21–25	8:16–18 11:33–36
The son's request (1)	Mount of Beatitudes	7:9–11		11:11–13

Wise and foolish builders	Mount of Beatitudes (Sermon on the Mount)	7:24–27		6:47–48
Bridegroom	Capernaum	9:14–15		
New cloth on an old coat	Along the Sea of Galilee	9:16	2:21	5:36
New wine in old wineskins	Along the Sea of Galilee	9:17	2:22	5:37–39
Fisherman's net	Boat along the Sea of Galilee	13:47–50		
Mustard seed	Boat along the Sea of Galilee	13:31–32	4:30–32	13:18–19
Pearl of great price (2)	Boat along the Sea of Galilee	13:45–46		
Parable of the sower	Boat along the Sea of Galilee	13:1–23	4:3–20	8:4–15
Weeds	Boat along the Sea of Galilee	13:24–30		
Yeast	Boat along the Sea of Galilee	13:33		13:20–21
Lost sheep (1)	Capernaum	18:10–14		15:3–7
Hidden treasure (2)	Boat along the Sea of Galilee	13:44		
Owner of a house	Boat along the Sea of Galilee	13:52		
Growing seed	Boat along the Sea of Galilee		4:26–29	
Unmerciful servant	Capernaum	18:21–36		
Debtors and money lender (1)	Pharisee's house, Capernaum		7:36–50	
Workers in the vineyard (1)	Jordan (a.k.a. Perea or Transjordan)	20:1–6		
Two sons	Temple in Jerusalem	21:28–32		
Vineyard and the tenants (4)	Temple in Jerusalem	21:33–46	12:1–12	20:9–19
Wedding banquet (1)	Temple in Jerusalem	22:1–14		
Fig tree	Jerusalem	24:32–35	13:28–31	21:29–33
Talents and ten minas(4)	Mount of Olives, Jerusalem	25:14–30		19:11–27
Watchful servants (4)	Mount of Olives, Jerusalem		13:32–37	12:35–40
Good Samaritan	Judea			10:25–37
Friend in need (1)	Judea			11:5–8

Rich fool (2)	Judea		12:16–21
Faithful and wise steward (4)	Judea	24:45–51	12:42–48
Barren fig tree	Judea		13:6–9
Lowest seat at feast	Perea		14:7–14
Great banquet (1)	Perea		14:15–24
Cost of being a disciple (2)	Perea		14:25–33
Lost coin (1)	Perea		15:8–10
Prodigal son (1)	Perea		15:11–32
Shrewd manager (3)	Perea		16:1–13
Rich man and Lazarus	Perea		16:19–31
Master and servant (4)	Perea		17:7–10
Persistent widow	Perea		18:1–8
Pharisee and tax collector	Perea		18:9–10
Ten virgins	Mount of Olives, Jerusalem	25:1–13	
Sheep and goats (4)	Mount of Olives, Jerusalem	25:31–46	
Stewardship Parables: The Generosity of God The Value of the Kingdom of God The Proper Use of Money The Charge to Faithful Stewardship		Note: Not one parable was recorded in the Gospel of John, the shortest Gospel of Jesus' public ministry, the longest of Passion Week.	

Jesus' Miracles, in Biblical Order

Miracle	Location	Type	Matt.	Mark	Luke	John
Man with leprosy	Down from Mt. of Beatitudes	Healing	8:1–4	1:40–45	5:12–13	
Centurion's servant healed	Capernaum	Healing	8:5–13		7:1–10	
Heals Mary, Peter's mother-in-law on Sabbath	Capernaum	Healing	8:14–15	1:29–31	4:38–39	

Demonic men healed (pigs in Decapolis)	Sea of Galilee, Gadara six miles southeast/Gerasa thirty-five miles southeast	Healing	8:28–34	5:1–20	8:26–39	
Jesus calms the storm	Sea of Galilee	Nature	8:23–27	4:35–41	8:22–25	
Two blind men healed	Capernaum	Healing	9:27–31			
Jairus's daughter raised	Capernaum	Raised from death	9:18–19, 23–26	5:22–43	8:41–42, 49–56	
Mute and possessed man healed	Capernaum	Healing	9:32–33			
Paralytic healed	Capernaum	Healing	91–8	2:1–12	5:17–26	
Woman's issue of blood healed	Capernaum	Healing	9:20–22	5:25–34	8:43–48	
Man's withered hand healed on Sabbath	Galilee	Healing	12:9–13	3:1–6	6:6–11	
Feeding of the 5,000*	Tabgha	Nature	14:13–21	6:30–44	9:10–17	6:1–15
Jesus walks on water	Sea of Galilee	Nature	14:22–27	6:45–52		6:16–21
Canaanite girl healed	Tyre/Sidon	Healing	15:21–28	7:24–30		
Feeding of the 5,000	Decapolis, southeast of Sea of Galilee	Nature	15:29–39	8:1–21		
Boy healed from demon	Mt. Hermon, northeast of Caesarea Philippi (after Transfiguration)	Healing	17:14–18	9:14–29	9:37–43	

Temple tax provided, coin in catfish mouth	Capernaum	Nature	17:24–27			
Blind men receive sight	Jericho	Healing	20:29–34	10:46–52	18:35–43	
Fig tree withers	Road from Bethany to Jerusalem	Nature	21:18–22	11:12–14, 20–25		
Man with evil spirit healed on Sabbath	Capernaum	Healing		1:21–28	4:31–37	
Deaf and mute man healed	Decapolis, southeast of Sea of Galilee	Healing		7:31–37		
Blind man's sight restored	Pools of Bethsaida	Healing		8:22–26		
Jesus goes unseen	Nazareth	Nature			4:28–30	
Catch of fish	Lake of Gennesaret, a.k.a. Sea of Galilee or Sea of Tiberius	Nature			5:1–11	
Widow's son raised	Nain	Raised from death			7:11–17	
Blind, mute demoniac healed	By Sea of Galilee	Healing	12:22–30		11:14–23	
Crippled woman healed on Sabbath	Judea	Healing			13:10–17	
Man's dropsy healed on Sabbath	Perea (Samaria/ Galilee border)	Healing			14:1–6	
Ten lepers healed	Perea (Samaria/ Galilee border)	Healing			17:11–19	

Malchus's (high priest's) servant healed	Perea (Samaria/ Galilee border)	Healing			22:50–51	
Water made into wine (first miracle)	Cana in Galilee	Nature				2:1–11
Official's son healed	Capernaum and Cana	Healing				4:46–54
Healing at the pool on Sabbath	Pools of Bethesda	Healing				5:1–9
Man born blind healed on Sabbath	Jerusalem	Healing				9:1–41
Lazarus raised from the dead	Bethany, two miles from Jerusalem	Raised from death				11:1–44
Catch of fish	Sea of Tiberias (Sea of Galilee)	Nature				21:1–14

Jesus warns three cities that they have seen many miracles, yet do not believe, in Matthew 11:21–24:

"Woe to you, Chorazin! Woe to you, Bethsaida! For if the miracles that were performed in you had been performed in Tyre and Sidon, they would have repented long ago in sackcloth and ashes. But I tell you, it will be more bearable for Tyre and Sidon on the day of judgment than for you. And you, Capernaum, will you be lifted to the heavens? No, you will go down to Hades.

For if the miracles that were performed in you had been performed in Sodom, it would have remained to this day. But I tell you that it will be more bearable for Sodom on the day of judgment than for you."

Chorazin, Bethsaida and Capernaum were all within three miles of each other. Capernaum is on the northern shore of the Sea of Galilee and Chorazin and Bethsaida are nearby in the hillsides. Though the Bible does not specify a location for the Sermon on the Mount, Chorazin is a possibility as it was "up on a mountainside" somewhere in the region of Galilee. Ten miracles are recorded in Capernaum, by far the most in any town, yet they rejected Him.

Not just one, but actually seven miracles were performed on the Sabbath.

*The Feeding of the 5,000 is the only miracle recorded in all four Gospels.

Jesus' Disciples

Disciple means "follower" or "learner."

Apostle means "one who is sent out."

While Jesus was on earth, the Twelve, including Judas Iscariot, were called disciples. After the Ascension when Jesus sent them out to be His witnesses, they were called apostles (Matthias having replaced Judas Iscariot, though some view the Apostle Paul as the true twelfth apostle).

From Scripture, we only know about the deaths of Judas Iscariot and James (Acts 12:2) The most extensive and early source for the traditions is Eusebius (a.k.a "the Father of Church History"), the Bishop of Caesarea in Palestine in the early fourth century, who wrote in Greek. For proclaiming Jesus' Resurrection, the disciples were beaten, imprisoned, and killed. Five were crucified, three stoned, two speared, one beheaded, and John died of old age. All they needed to do to escape was to denounce their faith. If the Gospel message was a lie, why would they have chosen to die such horrible deaths?

The original twelve disciples were all from the region of Galilee, except for Judas Iscariot, who was from Judea near Jericho. The eleven disciples were present for the Great Commission and the Ascension (Matthew 28:16–20).

The Twelve Tribes of Israel were blessed *"to be a blessing to all nations."* Also, the twelve disciples were sent out to bless all nations. Today, we followers of Christ are also commanded to go out and make disciples (not just converts) of all nations!

Name	Andrew	Bartholomew	James, son of Alphaeus
Other names		Nathaniel	James the Younger, James the Less
Born	Bethsaida	Ptolemais	
Lived	Capernaum	Cana of Galilee	
Died	Crucified on an X-shaped Cross for 2 days in Achaia (Greece)	Beaten, flayed with knives, then crucified upside down and buried in Armenia	Stoned in Jerusalem, body cut into pieces, buried by the Temple
Family	Son of John, brother of Simon Peter		Possible brother of Matthew
Writing			James
Vocation	Fisherman		
Background	First disciple of John the Baptist; first to follow Jesus (John 1:35–40)		Confused with James, the brother of Jesus, or James, the brother of Joseph, possibly a Zealot
With Jesus	Told Jesus of boy with five loaves and two fish (John 6:8–9); witnessed Jesus being taken up into Heaven (Acts 1:8–9)	Ate breakfast with Jesus after miraculous catch of fish after Resurrection. along with Peter, Thomas, the sons of Zebedee and two others (John 21:2–14)	Present when Jesus appeared after the Resurrection to all except Thomas (John 20:19–25)
After Jesus	Might have preached in Scythia (Ukraine today) and Thracia (Bulgaria today)	Armenian church claims him as their founder, possibly served in India also	

Name	James, son of Zebedee	John, son of Zebedee	Judas Iscariot
Other names	Son of Thunder, James the Elder	Son of Thunder, the disciple whom Jesus loved	Son of Simon, Judas the Betrayer
Born	Bethsaida	Bethsaida	Judea, near Jericho
Lived	Capernaum	Capernaum	Judea
Died	First to be martyred, beheaded by Herod Agrippa I (Acts 12:2), buried in Judea	Last to die, only one not martyred, died of old age in exile in Ephesus circa 100 AD	Hung himself (Matt 27:5)
Family	Brother of John, son of Zebedee and Salome	Brother of James, Son of Zebedee and Salome	
Writing		John, 1/2/3 Gospel of John, Revelation	
Vocation	Fisherman	Fisherman	
Background	Partner with John and Peter (Luke 5:10)	Possibly 2nd disciple of John the Baptist, partner with James and Peter (Luke 5:10)	Believed to be in Zealot assassin sect
With Jesus	One of three core disciples. Requested to sit at Jesus' sides in the Kingdom (Mark 10:35–45). Witnessed Transfiguration (Mark 9:2–8).		Treasurer and thief (John 12:5–6, 13:29). Criticized Mary for anointing Jesus with expensive perfume (John 12:4–8), Betrayed Jesus (Matthew 26:14–16, 47–50). Jesus referred to him as the devil (John 6:70–71)
After Jesus	Pillar of Jerusalem Church (Galatians 2:9)		Replaced by Matthias (Acts 1:26)

Name	Matthew	Philip	Simon Peter
Other names	Levi		Cephas ("Rock"), Simon bar Jonah Simon
Born	Capernaum	Bethsaida	Bethsaida
Lived	Capernaum	Capernaum	Capernaum
Died	Speared in Parthia (near Tehran today) or India	Crucified upside down or hanged from a Temple (in eastern Turkey today)	Crucified by request upside down by Nero in Rome
Family	Possible brother of James, also son of Alphaeus		Son of John, brother of Andrew, married (Mark 1:30)
Writing	First Gospel, Matthew (in Hebrew)		1/2 Peter
Vocation	Tax collector in Galilee	Fisherman	Fisherman
Background		Confused with Philip the Evangelist (in Acts), the third disciple called (John 1:43)	Jesus named him Cephas/ Peter/ Rock (John 1:41–42), partner with James and John (Luke 5:10).
With Jesus	Invited Jesus to dine with him and his corrupt friends (Matthew 9:9–13)	Brought Bartholomew to Jesus (John 1:45–51) Jesus tested him about the feeding of the 5,000 (John 6:5–7)	One of three core disciples. Witnessed Transfiguration (Mark 9:2–8). With Jesus in the Garden of Gethsemane (Matthew 26:36–46).
After Jesus	Possibly ministered in Asia	Possibly preached in Scythia (Ukraine today)	Pillar of Jerusalem Church. Wrote Gospel from Peter's testimony. Founded Rome church with Paul. Preached, healed and ministered to Jews after Pentecost.

Name	Simon the Zealot	Thaddeus	Thomas	Matthias
Other names	Simon the Canaanite	Jude, Judas son of James (Luke 6:14, Acts 1:13)	Didymus, Judas Thomas, Doubting Thomas	
Born	Canaan		Galilee	
Lived				
Died	Crucified	Stoned	Speared and buried in India	Stoned
Family		Son of James	Twin	
Writing				
Vocation	Fisherman		Possibly a carpenter	
Background	Zealot	Confused with Judas, the brother of Jesus, Judas Barsabbas and Judas Iscariot. Some say Zealot		
With Jesus	Possibly the bridegroom at wedding in Cana		Doubted Resurrection (John 20:25), then affirmed Jesus was God (John 20:28)	
After Jesus	Some say Missionary to Persia		Founded church in India	Replaced Judas Iscariot (Acts 1:26)

Resurrection Appearances

Event	Location and date	Matt.	Mark	Luke	John	Acts	1 Cor
At the empty Tomb	Jerusalem, Early Sunday Morning	28:1–10	16:1–8	24:1–12	20:1–9		
To Mary Magdalene at the Tomb	Jerusalem, Early Sunday Morning		16:9–11		20:11–18		
To two travelers on the road to Emmaus	Sunday at midday			24:13–32			
To Peter	Jerusalem, during the day on Sunday			24:34			15:5
To the ten disciples in the Upper Room	Jerusalem, Sunday evening		16:14	24:36–43	20:19–25		
To the eleven disciples in the Upper Room	Jerusalem, one week later				20:26–31		15:5
To the seven disciples fishing	Sea of Galilee, one day at dawn				21:1–23		
To the eleven disciples on the mountain in Galilee	Galilee, sometime later	28:16–20	16:15–18				
To more than 500	Sometime later						15:6
To James (stepbrother)	When and where unclear						15:7
At the Ascension on the Mount of Olives	Forty days after the Resur-rection			24:44–49		1:3–8	

Harmony of the Gospels by Region

Event	Matthew	Mark	Luke	John
Bethany				
Christ's raising of Lazarus				11:1
Retirement to Bethany	21:17	11:11		
Visit to Mary and Martha			10:58	
The supper in Simon's house	26:6–13	14:3–9		12:1
Mary anoints Jesus	26:7	14:3		12:23
Warning of the betrayal	26:1			
Ascension		16:19	24:50–51	
Bethlehem				
Birth of Jesus			2:1–7	
Adoration by shepherds			2:8–16	
Circumcision	1:25		2:21	
Adoration by the wise men	2:1–12			
Massacre of the innocents	2:16–18			
Bethsaida				
The miracle of the feeding of the 5,000	14:13	6:30	9:12	6:1
Healing blind man		8:22		
Cana				
First miracle				2:1–11
Christ's return to Cana				4:43–46
Christ's healing of nobleman's son				4:46–54
Capernaum				
Visit to Capernaum				2:12
Christ's preaching at Capernaum	4:13		4:31	
Call of Andrew, Peter, James, and John	4:18–22	1:16		
Casting out a devil		1:21–28	4:31–37	
Healing Peter's mother-in-law	8:14–15	1:29–31	4:38–39	
Healing many sick and diseased		1:32	4:40	
Healing of paralytic man	9:1–8	2:1–12	5:17–26	
Call of Matthew (Levi), supper and discourse	9:9	2:13–18	5:27–33	
The miracle of the withered hand	12:10	3:1	6:6	

Event	Matthew	Mark	Luke	John
Opposition of Herodians	12:14	3:6	6:11	
Retirement for prayer		3:13	6:12	
Ordination of twelve apostles	10:2–4	3:14	6:13	
Sermon in the Plain of Gennesaret (near Capernaum)			6:17–49	
Healing centurion's servant (near Capernaum)	8:5–13		7:1–10	
Message from John the Baptist; Christ's testimony	11:2–7		7:17–24	
Warning to Chorazin, etc.	11:20–28			
Mary Magdalene			7:36	
Healing of a demoniac	12:22			
Blasphemy against the Holy Ghost	12:24	3:22		
The unclean spirit	12:43			
The interruption of his relatives	12:46	3:31		
The parable of the bridegroom	9:14–15			
The parables of the new cloth and new wine	9:16–17			
The miracle of Jairus's daughter and bleeding woman	9:18–26	5:22–43	8:41–56	
The miracle of two blind men	9:27–31			
The miracle of the dumb spirit	9:32–33			
Discourse on the plain and in the synagogue	14:34			6:22–70
Discourse on defilement	15:1–20	7:1–23		
The miracle of the Temple tax coin in the fish's mouth	17: 24–27			
Decapolis				
The miracle of the healing of the deaf and dumb man		7: 32		
The miracle of the healing of many sick	15:29			
Emmaus (Modern-Day El-Qubeibeh or Amwas)				
Christ appears to the two disciples going to Emmaus		16:12	24:13	
Gadara				
Christ suffers devils to enter the swine	8:28	5:1	8:27	

Event	Matthew	Mark	Luke	John
Galilee				
The Sabbath; plucking corn	12:1	2:23	6:1	
Through Galilee		3:19	8:1–3	
Predictions of his Passion	17:22	9:30	9:43	
Mission of the seventy			10:1–17	
Appearance of Christ to eleven apostles on the mountain	28:16			
The Garden				
A guard placed at the door, which was sealed	27:65–66			19:39–42
Women carry spices to the Tomb	28:1	16:2		
An angel had rolled away the stone	28:2			
The women return to the Tomb			24:1	
Peter and John run to the Tomb			24:12	20:3
The women return to the Tomb			24:1	
Christ appears to Mary Magdalene		16:9–10		20:14
Christ appears to the women returning home	28:9			
Gennesaret				
Sermon on the Mount (hills above Gennesaret)	5:7–27			
Sermon in the boat; miraculous draught of fish			5:1	
The parable of the sower	13:1–9, 18–23	4:1, 14–20	8:4, 11–15	
The parable of the tares	13:24			
The parable of the mustard seed	13:31	4:30		
The parable of the candle		4:21	8:16	
The parable of the treasure	13:44			
The parable of the pearl	13:45			
The parable of the net	13:47			
Christ calms the storm (sea of Gennesaret)	8:24	4:37	8:23	
The miracle of the issue of blood	9:18	5:22	8:41	
The miracle of the feeding of the 4,000	15:32	8:1		
The parable of the leaven	13:33, 16:5	8:14		

Event	Matthew	Mark	Luke	John
Gethsemane				
The agony	26:37	14:33	22:39	18:1
His prayer (repeated thrice)	26:39–44	14:36–39	22:42	
His sweat and the angel's comfort			22:43–44	
The sleep of the disciples	26:40–45	14:37–41		
Betrayal by Judas	26:47–50	14:43–44	22:47	18:2–4
Peter smites Malchus	26:51	14:47	22:50	18:10
Christ heals the ear of Malchus			22:51	
Christ forsaken by his disciples	26:56	14:50		
Golgotha				
They give Him vinegar and gall	27:34	15:23	23:36	
Nailed Him to the Cross	27:35		23:38	19:18
The superscription	27:37	15:26	23:38	19:19
"Father, forgive them"			23:34	
His garments parted and vesture allotted	27:35	15:24	23:23–34	19:23
Passersby mock, the two thieves revile	27:39–44	15:29–32	23:35	
The penitent thief			23:40	
"Today you will be with Me in Paradise"			23:43	
"Woman, here is your son . . ."				19:26–27
The darkness	27:45	15:33	23:44	
"My God, My God, why hast thou forsaken Me?"	27:46	15:34		
"I thirst"				19:28
The vinegar	27:48	15:36		19:29
"It is finished"				19:30
"Father, into your hands I commit My spirit"			23:46	
Testimony of the centurion	27:54	15:39	23:47	
Watching of the women	27:55	15:40	23:49	
Piercing His side				19:31
Taking down from the Cross and burial by Joseph of Arimathea and Nicodemus	27:57–60	15:46	23:53	19:38
Hebron				

Event	Matthew	Mark	Luke	John
The visit of Mary to Elizabeth			1:39–55	
Jerusalem				
Annunciation of the birth of John the Baptist			1:5–25	
Presentation and purification			2:22–29	
With the doctors in the Temple			2:46–50	
First Passover; first cleansing of Temple				2:13–23
Second Passover				5:1
Discourse with Nicodemus				5:1–21
Miracle at Bethesda				5:2–47
The Feast of Tabernacles				7:2–10
Discourses				7:10–46
Officers sent to arrest Him				7:30, 46
The adulteress				8:3
Discourses				8:12
Threatened with stoning				8:59
Healing of the blind man and discourses				9:1
Christ the Door				10:1
Christ the Good Shepherd				10:11
Feast of dedication				10:22
Christ's oneness with the Father				10:30
Parable of The Good Samaritan			10:1–17	
The dumb spirit			11:14	
The rich fool			12:16	
God's providence to birds and flowers			12:22–30	
The barren fig tree			13:6	
The woman with an infirmity			13:11	
The mustard seed			13:18	
Healing the man with dropsy			14:1–4	
Lesson on humility			14:7	
Parables:				
The great supper			14:12	
The lost sheep and piece of silver			15:1	

Event	Matthew	Mark	Luke	John
The prodigal son			15:11	
The unjust steward			16:1	
The dogs and Lazarus			16:19	
Importunate widow			18:1	
Pharisee and publican			18:9	
Rich young man	19:16	10:17	18:18	
Laborers in the vineyard	20:1			
Ten minas			19:12	
Triumphal entry into the Temple	21:1–17	11:1–11	19:29–41	12:12–20
Cleansing the Temple	21:12	11:15	19:45	
Discourses in the Temple:				
The father and two sons	21:28			
The wicked husbandmen	21:33	12:1	20:9	
The wedding garment	22:1			
Tribute money	22:15	12:13	20:20	
The Sadducees and Resurrection	22:23	12:18	20:27	
The great commandment	22: 34	12: 28		
The widow's mite		12: 41	21: 1	
The eight woes	23			
Destruction of Jerusalem and of the world	24:1	13:1	21:5	
The counsel of the Sanhedrin	26:3	14:1	22:1	
Judas' betrayal	26:14	14:10	22:3	
Preparation of the Passover	27:17	14:12	22:7	
Washing the disciples' feet				13:1-7
The breaking of bread	26:26	14:22	22:19	
"He who shared my bread has turned against Me"			22:21	13:18
"Surely you don't mean me, Rabbi?"	26:22–25	14:19		
The giving of the sop: "What you are about to do, do quickly"				13:26–27
Departure of Judas				13:30
The blessing of the cup	26:28	14:24		

Event	Matthew	Mark	Luke	John
The hymn	26:30	14:26		
Peter warned	26:34	14:30	22:34	13:36
The discourses after the supper				14:16
Christ's prayer for his disciples				17
Christ led to Annas				18:12
Christ tried by Caiaphas	26:57	14:53	22:54	18:15
Peter follows Christ	26:58	14:54	22:55	18:15
The high priest's adjuration	26:63	14:61		
Christ condemned, buffeted, mocked	26:66–67	14:64–65	22:63–65	
Peter's denial of Christ	26:69	14:66	22:55–59	18:17–27
Christ before Pilate	27:1	15:1	23:1	18:28
Repentance of Judas	27:3			
Pilate comes out to the people				18:28
Pilate speaks to Jesus privately				18:33
Pilate orders him to be scourged	27:26	15:15		19:1
Jesus crowned with thorns	27:29	15:17		19:2
Jesus exhibited by Pilate: "Ecce Homo!"				19:5
Jesus accused formally	27:11	15:1	23:2	
Jesus sent by Pilate to Herod, mocked, arrayed in purple			23:6–11	
"Here is your king!"				19:14
Pilate desires to release Him	27:15	15:6	23:17	
Pilate receives a message from his wife	27:19			
Pilate washes his hands	27:24			
Pilate releases Barabbas	27:26			
Pilate delivers Jesus to be crucified		15:15	23:25	19:16
Simon of Cyrene carries the Cross	27:32	15:21	23:26	
Rending of the veil	27:51	15:38	23:45	
Opening of graves, and resurrection of saints	27:52			
Women announce the Resurrection	28:8			20:1–2
The guards report it to the chief priests	28:11–15			
Appearance of Christ after His Resurrection				

Event	Matthew	Mark	Luke	John
To Peter (also in 1 Cor 15:5)			24:34	
To ten apostles in the Upper Room			24:36	20:19
To the eleven apostles in the Upper Room		16:14		20:36
Mount of Olives				
The Lord's Prayer	6:9–13		11:2–4	
The parable of the importunity of a friend			11:5	
Cursing the fig tree	21:18	11:12		
The withered fig tree and its lesson		11:20		
The parable of the ten virgins	25:1			
The parable of the talents	25:14			
The parable of the sheep and the goats	25:31			
Mount Tabor (or Hermon)				
Transfiguration	17:1	9:2	9:28	
Nazareth				
Espousal of Virgin Mary	1:18		1:27	
The Annunciation of the birth of Jesus			1:26–38	
Joseph's vision	1:20–25			
Return to Nazareth	2:19–23		2:39	
Childhood of Jesus			2:40	
Youth of Jesus			2:51	
Christ's preaching at Nazareth		6:1	4:15–30	
Perea				
Christ's retreat across the Jordan				10:40
Samaria				
Christ's rejected by the Samaritans			9:53	
The ten lepers			17:11	
Tiberias				
Christ appears to seven apostles at the Sea of Tiberias				21:1–24
Wilderness of Judea				
Temptation of Jesus	4:1–11	1:12–13	4:1–13	

Jerusalem Occupiers: Old Testament and New Testament	
Canaanites 3000–1000 BC	Abraham, Isaac, Mount Moriah "God will provide" Egypt Moses Joshua Judges Saul United Kingdoms David "City of David," Ark of Covenant, Temple Mount
Israelites 1000–900 BC	Solomon: First Temple religious and political center Rehoboam and Jeroboam North: Israel, South: Judea
600 BC	Hezekiah: Assyrian exile for Israelites Nebuchadnezzar: Babylonian exile for Judeans—50 years (Psalm 137:5–6); burned Temple
500–300 BC	Cyrus, the Persian king allowed their return, only some returned. Second Temple and city rebuilt: Ezra and Nehemiah
Hellenists 300–150 BC	Alexander the Great captures Jerusalem from Persians Hanukkah celebrates recapture and purification of Temple
Hasmoneans 150–60 BC	Independent rule
Romans 60 BC–325 AD 37–4 BC 66–70 AD	Pompey, head of Roman army, captured Jerusalem King Herod reconstructed and extended Temple Mount, Great Revolt, Titus, Temple destroyed 70 AD
Byzantines 300–600 AD	Christian rule under Constantine, emperor of Byzantium Monasteries, churches, pilgrimages
Persians 600–630 AD	Occupied by Persians, then Byzantines regained and massacred Jews
Early Muslims 640–1100 AD	Caliph Omar captured, not mentioned in Koran; Dome of the Rock, 691 AD
Crusades 1100–1200 AD	Christian Europe's religious revival; Jerusalem captured in 1099, Crusades massacred Muslims and Jews; Muslims recaptured it in 1187 and converted churches to mosques; 1229 agreement: Muslims keep Temple Mount and Crusaders the rest—15 years
Mamelukes 1250–1500 AD	Turks ruled Egypt; now third holiest Muslim site.

Suggested Resources—The Holy Land

Books:

The Arab–Israeli Wars, Chaim Herzog, ©1982, Random House

The Christian Traveler's Guide to the Holy Land, Charles H. Dyer and Gregory A Hatteburg, ©2006, Moody Publishers

Exodus, Leon Uris, ©1958, Doubleday

Hebrew Christianity, Dr. Arnold G. Fruchtenbaum, ©1974, Canon Press

Hiking the Jesus Trail, Anne Dintaman and David Landis, © 2010, 2013, Village to Village Press

The Holy Land Today, M. Basilea Schlink; ©1975, Evangelical Sisterhood of Mary

Jesus, David Flusser, ©2001, The Hebrew University Magnes Press

Jesus the Jew, Geza Vermes, ©1973, First Fortress Press

Jesus Was a Jew, Dr. Arnold G. Fruchtenbaum, ©1981, Broadman Press

My Life, Golda Meir

The New Encyclopedia of Archaeological Excavations in the Holy Land, Volume 2,

Claire Epstein; Israel Exploration on Society and Carta, © 1993

Our Father Abraham, Marvin Wilson, ©1989, Eerdmans

Lawrence of Arabia, T.E. Lawrence

The Source, James Michener

Tracts:

The Twelve Disciples, ©2014, Rose Publishing

Biblical Archaeology Review magazine, Biblical Archaeology Society

Videos:

"The Gospel According to Matthew," © 1993, Visual Bible, Visual Entertainment

"In the Footsteps of Christ" (5 DVDs), ©2005, Madacy Entertainment Group

"That the World May Know: Series, Ray Vander Laan, Focus on the Family, ©2005, TMC Entertainment

Map: First Century Israel

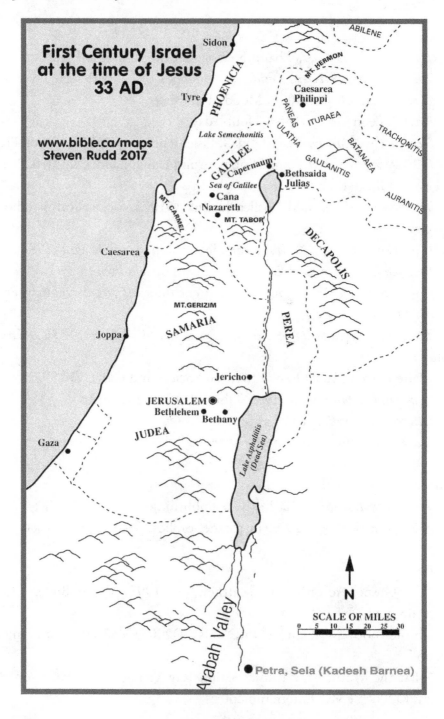

Map: Modern Israel Today

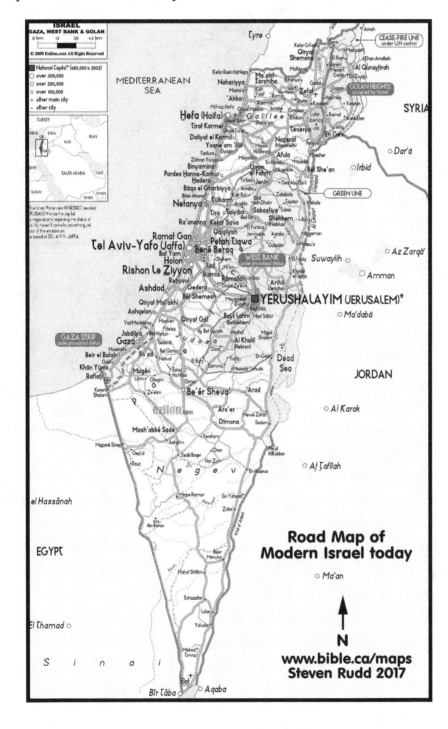

Map: Ancient Jerusalem

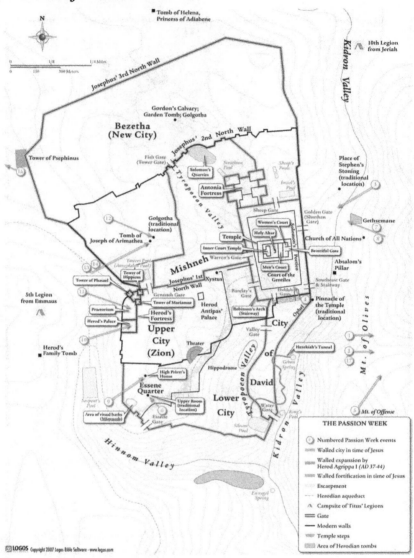

APPENDIX: PAUL'S JOURNEYS

Letters Written by Paul, in Order of Writing Date
Themes of Letters Written by Paul, in Biblical Order
Paul's Traveling Companions
Major Archaeological Finds: New Testament
Roman Emperors During the Biblical Period
Timeline of Paul's Life and Journeys
Biblical References to Places in Greece, Turkey and Cyprus
Suggested Resources: Paul's Journeys
Map: Paul's First Missionary Journey
Map: Paul's Second Missionary Journey
Map: Paul's Third Missionary Journey
Map: Paul's Trip to Rome

Letters Written by Paul, in Order of Writing Date

Letter/ Key Verses	To	Where Written	When	Message
Gal. 5:22–23	Church in Galatia	Antioch in Syria	48–55 AD	Freedom in Christ versus Legalism; Paul's Authority
1 Thess. 5:16–23	Church in Thessaloniki	Corinth	49–54 AD	New Christians, Commit to God Until Christ Returns
2 Thess. 3:4–6	Church in Thessaloniki	Corinth	50–54 AD	Persevere Until Christ Returns
1 Cor. 13:4–5	Church in Corinth	Ephesus	56 AD	Addresses Division and Immorality in the Church
2 Cor.12:9	Church in Corinth	Philippi	56 AD	Paul's Authority Against False Teachers
Romans 12:1–2	Church in Rome	Corinth	57 AD	Law, Faith, Salvation, Righteousness
Eph. 2:8–9	Church in Ephesus	Rome (prison)	60–64 AD	Living in Christ
Col. 2:9–10	Church in Colossae	Rome (prison)	60–64 AD	Heretical Teachings; Christ is Enough

Phil. 17–19	Philemon, a friend in Colossae	Rome (prison)	60–61 AD	Brothers in Christ, Forgive Slave (Onesimus)
Phil. 2:14–15	Church in Philippi	Rome (prison)	60–64 AD	Paul's Love for Philippians; Joy; Humility
1 Timothy 4:12–13	Timothy, leader of Church in Ephesus	Rome	62–64 AD	False Teachings; Church Leadership
Titus 3:4–7	Titus, leader of Church in Crete	Rome	63–64 AD	Living in Faith; Good Works
2 Timothy 3:15–17	Timothy, leader of Church in Ephesus	Rome (prison)	65–67 AD	Paul's Last Words, Encouraging Timothy

Themes of Letters Written by Paul, in Biblical Order

Romans	Paul shares his insights into his understanding of the faith as he addresses the two different types of house-churches: those primarily Jewish and the larger with those primarily Gentile. In Romans 1, he states: "**I am not ashamed of the Gospel . . . for in the Gospel the righteousness of God is revealed . . . the righteous will live by faith.**" Whether Jew or Gentile, "**all have sinned and fall short.**" Salvation is offered to all, not because of merit or ethnicity.
1 Corinthians	Paul reminds the quarreling Corinthians that, through Christ's Resurrection, they have new life now, one that is to be characterized by love, not by division among believers. Christians in community cannot have immorality, lawsuits, disharmony, and insensitivity to needs within.
2 Corinthians	Just as we are ambassadors, representatives of our homeland, Paul relates that, as Christians, we are Christ's ambassadors, representatives of our God. Paul challenged them and us to **aim for perfection, being of one mind and living in peace**.
Galatians	The Galatians had fallen for the trap we also conveniently do at times: check off a "Do and Don't" list to feel we are good enough. He reminds them they are a new creation by saying: "**I am astonished that you . . . are turning to a different gospel—which is really no Gospel at all**" (Galatians 6:7). It is about transformation, not about following rules.
Ephesians	Paul's message to his beloved church in Ephesus is to live a unified life worthy of the calling. He famously proclaims: "**It is by grace you have been saved, through faith . . . it is the gift of God, not by works**" (Ephesians 2:8–9).

Philippians	This letter is simply about joy and that we have it because we are united with Christ, because we have fellowship with each other, and because we know our "**Citizenship is in Heaven**."
Colossians	Paul emphasized Christ's supremacy here, that He is one with God and Creation, Head of the Church. Because our sins are forgiven and the Law is fulfilled in Him, "**whatever you do, whether in word or deed, do it all in the name of the Lord Jesus**"(Colossians 3:17).
1 Thessalonians	Persecution by man and spiritual attack by the enemy are to be expected because of our faith that opposes the world's ways. We are to stay the course, knowing that one day He will return to end suffering and death forever for us.
2 Thessalonians	Continuing the theme of Christ's return, Paul says to replace anxiety with hope and encouragement, to trust Christ's protection from all harmful forces.
1 Timothy	Paul continued to instruct his young protégé in the faith. Just as Paul was his example of being grounded in sound doctrine that guided his heart and mind, he wants Timothy to be such an example.
2 Timothy	Paul's last letter is a plea for Timothy—and us—to remain strong and to preach the Word, so that we may endure inevitable hardships and be equipped for good works.
Titus	Titus served the longest with Paul: twenty years! He later became the first bishop on the island of Crete, where he instructed the elders to be examples, above reproach. Paul encourages his friend that one of our highest callings is to "**devote ourselves to doing what is good**."
Philemon	Philemon's slave, Onesimus, had run away and then accepted Christ. As all relationships are transformed in Christ, Paul personally asks Philemon to accept Onesimus as a brother in the Lord.

Paul's Traveling Companions

Barnabas	Joseph, a Levite from Cyprus, was called Barnabas ("Encourager") by the apostles. Paul and Barnabas shared their First Missionary Journey to Asia Minor, before they went separate ways over Mark, each powerfully spreading the Word to the world.
John Mark	The early church met in his mother's home; the place Peter first visited after his release from jail. When he departed the First Missionary Journey with Paul and Barnabas early, he caused them to split, and joined Barnabas on his subsequent travels. He later reconciled with Paul and joined Peter in Rome.

Luke	A Greek physician prior to conversion, Luke joined Paul in Troas on the Second Missionary Journey, and went by ship with him to Rome after the Third Missionary Journey and Paul's imprisonment. He wrote the Gospel of Luke and The Acts of the Apostles after Paul died.
Priscilla and Aquila	Expelled from Rome in 49 AD by emperor Claudius, they ended up in Corinth as fellow tent makers, where they extended hospitality to Paul. They later joined him during his years in Ephesus.
Silas	He traveled with Paul for three years on the Second Missionary Journey, ministered in Corinth after Paul departed to Ephesus, and later joined Peter in Rome.
Timothy	This young man from Lystra in Asia Minor (Greek father, Jewish mother) accompanied Paul and Silas on the Second Missionary Journey. Paul wrote 1 and 2 Timothy to his protégé.
Titus	He traveled with Paul for twenty years. As he was born a Gentile and uncircumcised, Jerusalem Christians wanted him to be circumcised. Paul vehemently defended Titus's right to remain uncircumcised. Titus later became the first bishop on the island of Crete and received Paul's personal letter describing the qualities of a church leader.

Major Archaeological Finds: New Testament

Site or Artifact	Location	Related Scripture
	TURKEY/ASIA MINOR	
Derbe Inscription	Kerti Huyuk	Acts 14:20
Sergius Paulus inscription	Antioch in Pisidia	Acts 13:6–7
Altar of Zeus (Some call it Satan's throne)	Pergamum	Revelation 2:13
Fourth Century BC walls	Assos	Acts 20:13–14
Artemis temple and altar	Ephesus, Turkey	Acts 19:27–28
Ephesian theater	Ephesus	Acts 19:29
Silversmith shops	Ephesus	Acts 19:24
Artemis statues	Ephesus	Acts 19:35
	GREECE	
Erastus inscription	Corinth	Romans 16:23
Synagogue inscription	Corinth	Acts 18:4
Meat market inscription	Corinth	1 Cor 10:25

Cult dining rooms (in Asclepius and Demeter temples)	Corinth	1 Cor 8:10
Court (bema)	Corinth	Acts 18:12
Marketplace (bema)	Philippi	Acts 16:19
Starting gate for races	Isthmia	1 Cor 9:24,26
Gallio inscription	Delphi	Acts 18:12
Egnatian Way	Kavalia (Neapolis), Philippi, Apollonia, Thessalonia	Acts 16:11–12, 17:1
Politarch inscription	Thessalonia	Acts 17:6

Roman Emperors During the Biblical Period

Augustus	27 BC–14 AD	Vitellius	69
Tiberius	14–37 AD	Vespasian	69–79
Gaius Caligula	37–41	Titus	79–81
Claudius	41–54	Domitian	81–96
Nero	54–68	Nerva	96–98
Galba	68–69	Trajan	98–117
Otho	69	Hadrian	117–138

Timeline of Paul's Life and Journeys

Activity	Approximate Date AD
Paul is called (conversion experience)	32–33
Preaching in Arabia and Damascus	33–36
First visit to Jerusalem	36
Mission to Syria, Cilicia, and Galatia; return to Antioch	36–49
Second visit to Jerusalem; Jerusalem Council	49
Mission to Asia Minor, Macedonia, and Achaia, (including Corinth)	
Paul in Corinth	50–52
Writes 1 Thessalonians	50
Returns to Antioch	52
Mission to Galatia, Ephesus, Macedonia, and Corinth	53–56
Paul in Ephesus	53–55

Writes Galatians	53
Writes 1 Corinthians and portions of 2 Corinthians	54–55
Perhaps writes Philippians and Philemon	55
Travels to Macedonia	56
Writes remainder of 2 Corinthians	56
Travels to Corinth	56
Writes Romans	56
Third visit to Jerusalem; arrested and sent to Caesarea as a prisoner	59
Imprisonment in Rome (house arrest) Perhaps writes Philippians and Philemon	60–62 60–62

Biblical References to Places in Greece, Turkey, and Cyprus

Greece	
Greece	Daniel 8:21; 10:20; 11:2; Zechariah 9:13; Acts 20:2; see also Joel 3:6
Achaia	Acts 18:12,27,19:21; Romans 15:26; 1 Corinthians 16:15; 2 Corinthians 1:1; 9:2, 11:10; 1 Thessalonians 1:7,8
Amphipolis	Acts 17:1
Apollonia	Acts 17:1
Athens	Acts 17:15,16, 18:1; 1 Thessalonians 3:1; see also Acts 17:22
Berea	Acts 17:10,13, 20:4
Cauda	Acts 27:16
Cenchreae	Acts 18:18; Romans 16:1
Chios	Acts 20:15
Corinth	Acts 18:1, 19:1; 1 Corinthians 1:2; 2 Corinthians 1:1, 23; 2 Timothy 4:20; see also Acts 18:8; 2 Corinthians 6:11
Kos	Acts 21:1
Crete	Acts 27:7, 12, 13, 21; Titus 1:5; see also Acts 2:11; Titus 1:12; possibly the meaning of "Caphtorim" in Genesis 10:14; Deuteronomy 2:23; 1 Chronicles 1:12; and "Caphtor" in Jeremiah 47:4; Amos 9:7
Fair Havens	Acts 27:8
Lasea	Acts 27:8
Phoenix	Acts 27:12
Salmone	Acts 27:7

Macedonia	Acts 16:9, 10, 12, 18:5; 19:21–22; 20:1,3; Romans 15:26; 1 Corinthians 16:5; 2 Corinthians 1:16, 2:13, 7:5, 8:1, 11:9; Philippians 4:15; 1 Thessalonians 1:7–8, 4:10; 1 Timothy 1:3; see also Acts 19:29, 27:2; 2 Corinthians 9:2,4
Mitylene	Acts 20:14
Neapolis	Acts 16:11
Nicopolis	Titus 3:12
Patmos	Revelation 1:9
Philippi	Acts 16:12, 20:6; Philippians 1:1; 1 Thessalonians 2:2; see also Philippians 4:15
Rhodes	Acts 21:1; likely the meaning if "Rodanim" in Genesis 10:4 and 1 Chronicles 1:7
Samos	Acts 20:15
Samothrace	Acts 16:11
Thessaloniki	Acts 17:1, 11, 13; Philippians 4:16; 2 Timothy 4:10; see also Acts 20:4, 27:2; 1 Thessalonians 1:1; 2 Thessalonians 1:1
Turkey	
Adramyttium	Acts 27:2
Antioch of Pisidia	Acts 13:14, 14:19,21; 2 Timothy 3:11
Antioch of Syria	Acts 6:5, 11:19, 20, 22, 26, 27, 13:1, 14:26, 15:22, 23, 30, 35, 18:22; Galatians 2:11
Ararat	Gen 8:4; 2 Kings 19:37; Isaiah 37:38; Jeremiah 51:27
Asia (province)	Acts 2:9, 6–9; 19:10, 22, 26–27; 20:16, 18, 21:27, 24:19, 27:2; Romans 16:5; 1 Corinthians 16:19; 2 Corinthians 1:8; 2 Timothy 1:15; 1 Peter 1:1; Revelation 1:4,11; see also Acts 20:4
Assos	Acts 20:13,14
Attalia	Acts 14:25
Bithynia	Acts 16:7; 1 Peter 1:1
Cappadocia	Acts 2:9; 1 Peter 1:1
Carchemish	2 Chronicles 35:20; Isaiah 10:9; Jeremiah 46:2
Cilicia	1 Kings 10:28 (called Kue); Acts 6:9, 15:23, 41, 21:39, 22:3, 23:34, 27:5; Galatians 1:21
Cnidus	Acts 27:7
Colossae	Colossians 1:2

Derbe	Acts 14:6, 20, 16:1, 20:4
Ephesus	Acts 18:19, 21, 24; 19:1, 17, 26, 35; 20:16, 17; 1 Corinthians 15:32, 16:8, 1 Timothy 1:3; 2 Timothy 1:18; 4:12; Revelation 1:11, 2:1; mentioned in some ancient manuscripts of Ephesians 1:1; see also Acts 19:28
Galatia	Acts 16:6, 18:23; 1 Corinthians 16:1; Galatians 1:2; 2 Timothy 4:10; 1 Peter 1:1; see also Galatians 3:1
Haran	Genesis 11:31–32, 12:4–5, 27:43, 28:10, 29:4; 2 Kings 19:12; Isaiah 37:12; Ezekiel 27:23; Acts 7:2, 4
Hierapolis	Colossians 4:13
Iconium	Acts 13:51, 14:1, 19, 21, 16:2; 2 Timothy 3:11
Laodicea	Colossians 2:1; 4:13, 15–16; Revelation 1:11; 3:14
Lycaonia	Acts 14:6; see also Acts 14:11
Lycia	Acts 27:5
Lydia	Possibly identified with some or all references to "Lud" or Ludim" in Genesis 10:13, 22; 1 Chronicles 1:11, 17; Isaiah 66:19; Ezekiel 27:10; 30:5
Lystra	Acts 14:6, 8, 21; 16:1–2; 2 Timothy 3:11
Miletus	Acts 20:15, 17; 2 Timothy 4:20
Myra	Acts 27:5; mentioned in some ancient manuscripts of Acts 21:1
Mysia	Acts 16:7
Pamphylia	Acts 2:10, 13:13, 14:24, 15:38, 27:5
Patara	Acts 21:1
Perga	Acts 13:13, 14, 14:25
Pergamum	Revelation 1:11; 2:12
Philadelphia	Revelation 1:11; 3:7
Phrygia	Acts 2:10, 16:6, 18:23
Pisidia	Acts 13:14; 14:24
Pontus	Acts 2:9, 18:2; 1 Peter 1:1
Sardis	Revelation 1:11, 3:1, 4; in Obadiah 20, "Sepharad" may be a reference to Sardis
Seleucia Pieria	Acts 13:4
Smyrna	Revelation 1:11, 2:8
Tarsus	Acts 9:11, 30, 11:25, 21:39, 22:3
Thyatira	Acts 16:14; Revelation 1:11; 2:18, 24

Troas	Acts 16:8, 11, 20:5–6; 2 Corinthians 2:12; 2 Timothy 4:13
Trogyllium	Mentioned in some ancient manuscripts of Acts 20:15
Cyprus	
Cyprus	Acts 4:36, 11:19–20, 13:4, 15:39, 21:3, 16, 27:4; likely the meaning of "Kittim" in Genesis 10:4 and 1 Chronicles 1:7; possibly the meaning of Elishah in Genesis 10:4; 1 Chronicles 1:7; and Ezekiel 27:7
Paphos	Acts 13:6, 13
Salamis	Acts 13:5

SUGGESTED RESOURCES: PAUL'S JOURNEYS

Books:

Ancient Greece, a Concise History, Peter Green, © 1979, Thames and Hudson

Ancient Turkey, a Traveler's History, Seton Lloyd, © 1999, Thames and Hudson

Archaeology and the New Testament, John McRay, © 1991, Baker Books

Faith Lessons in the Dust: Becoming a Disciple, Ray Vander Laan, © 2006, That the World May Know

Faith Lessons of the Early Church: Conquering the Gates of Hell, Ray Vander Laan, © 2000, That the World May Know

A Guide to Biblical Sites in Greece and Turkey, Clyde E. Fant and Mitchell G. Reddish, © 2003, Oxford University Press

In the Steps of St. Paul, H.V. Morton, © 2002, Da Capo Press

The Journal Time of Paul, David Sparks, © 1998, Footsteps Ministries

Paul, Apostle of the Heart Set Free, Frederick Fyvie Bruce, © 2000, Eerdmans

Paul, the Jewish Theologian, Brad Young, ©1997, Hendrickson

Paul, a Man of Grace and Grit, Charles R. Swindoll, © 2002, The W Publishing Group

Paul for Everyone (Commentary on 1 Corinthians), N.T. Wright, ©2004, Westminster John Knox Press

Paul, a Novel, Walter Wangerin Jr. , © 2000, Zondervan Publishing House

The Pillars of Hercules, Paul Theroux. © 1995, Cape Cod Scriveners Company, Fawcett/Random House

To Live is Christ, Embracing the Passion of Paul, Beth Moore, © 2001, Broadman and Holman

Tracts:

"The Life of the Apostle Paul," ©2006, Rose Publishing

Videos:

St. Paul in Greece ©2013, Blue Sky Productions

St. John in Exile © 1996, DJ Productions

Apostle Paul and the Earliest Churches ©2004, B and N Productions

Odyssey of St. Paul Paul L. Maier, © 2003, Tobias Communications

Map: Paul's First Missionary Journey

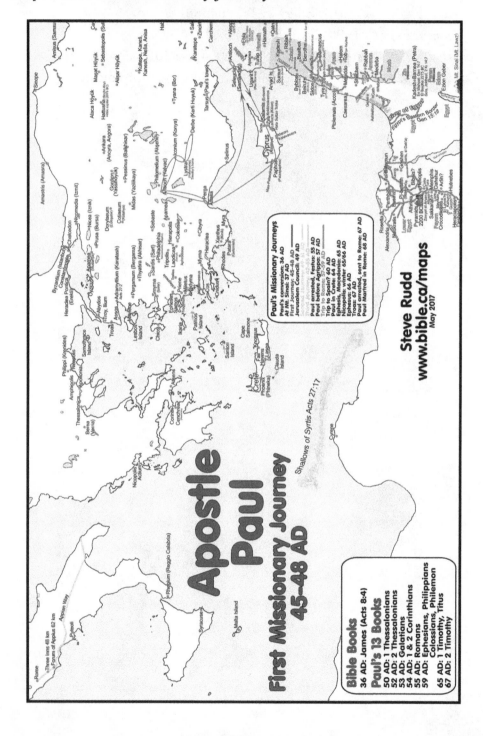

Map: Paul's Second Missionary Journey

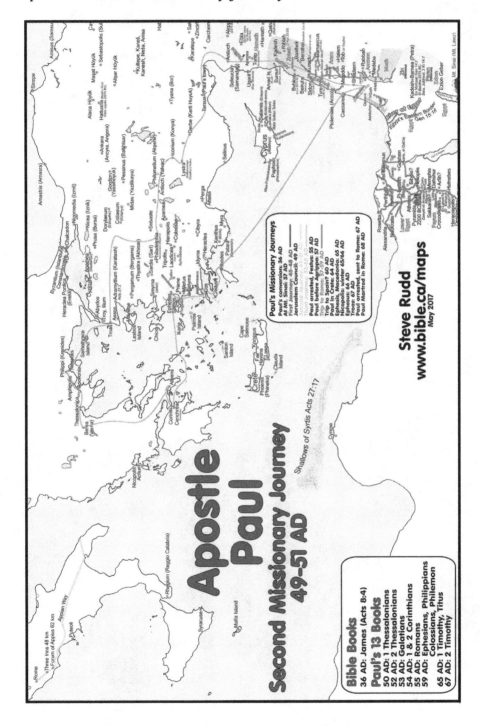

Map: Paul's Third Missionary Journey

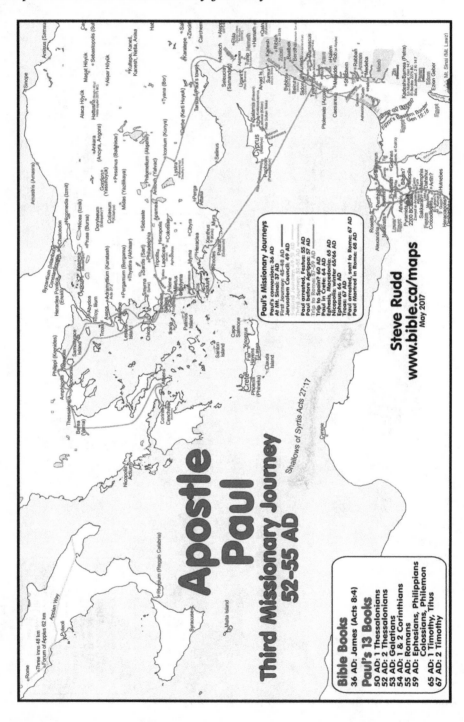

Map: Paul's Trip to Rome

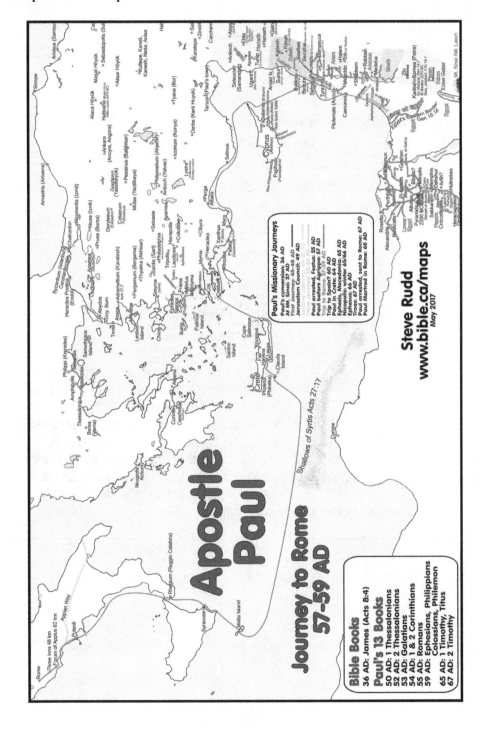

APPENDIX: THE REFORMATION

Key Figures of the Reformation
Key Timeline of the Reformation
Bible Translation Timeline
Church Branches and Denominations Timeline
Arminianism versus Calvinism
Five Solas of the Reformation
Luther's 95 Theses
Suggested Resources: The Reformation

Key Figures of the Reformation, in Chronological Order

1320–1384	John Wycliffe, (also Wyclif and Wycliff), morning star of the Reformation, priest. Completed the first hand-written English Bible manuscript from the Latin Vulgate in 1384; Oxford scholar, philosophy professor, theologian; opposed non-Biblical Catholic teachings such as transubstantiation. Wycliffe was condemned by the Council of Constance (along with Jan Hus) in 1414–1418 and by pope Gregory XI in 1377; his followers were derisively known as "Lollards"; forty-four years after the death of Wycliffe, pope Martin V ordered that his writings be burned and his bones dug up, burned and scattered in the River Swift. Wycliffe was the precursor to the English Reformation led by William Tyndale and Myles Coverdale.

1369–1415	**Jan Hus (Huss),** early reformer, theologian, author of **De Ecclesia.** Religious thinker in Bohemia (now Czech Republic); started a movement using Wycliffe's teachings; ordained priest; a professor in Prague; excommunicated four times; his followers were known as Hussites. In 1405, pope Innocent VII effectively placed the entire city of Prague under an interdict due to Hus's teachings and followers. Hus defended his beliefs in 1415 at the Council of Constance, then was tried and burned at stake as a heretic for his views on the sale of indulgences, and immoralities in the Church—after the pope and emperor had promised him safe conduct. The myth is that he said, "In one hundred years, God will raise up a man whose call for reforms cannot be suppressed" (102 years before Luther's 95 Theses); due to his prophecy and his name meaning "goose," a swan (along with Luther's rose) is a traditional symbol of many Lutheran congregations; Hus was a precursor to the Swiss Reformation led by John Calvin and Ulrich Zwingli.
1395–1468	**Johann Gutenberg** ("Beautiful Mountain" born Genfleisch), inventor of the printing press. Invented printing press with movable type in Mainz, Germany, considered the most important event of the modern world. The first printed book was a Latin Vulgate Bible in 1455; each was colorfully hand-illuminated. Gutenberg was left in poverty by unscrupulous business associates, but his invention was essential to the Reformation. His other trades were blacksmith and goldsmith.

1463–1525	**Frederick the Wise**: Luther's benefactor. Frederick, a very large man, ruled the Electorate of Saxony from 1486–1525; As his primary home, he built a residential castle in lieu of a military fortress in Wittenberg. He protected Luther—who he had never met—for political, not spiritual, reasons, as he sought to weaken the powers of the pope and the emperor. He earned the moniker, "The Wise," for his success in avoiding military conflict. On his deathbed, he received sacraments, a late commitment to the Reformation he had contributed to. Upon Frederick's death in 1525, his brother, John the Steadfast, became Elector. John was friendly with the Reformers, and led the town of Torgau to become the political center of the Reformation. In 1526, the League of Torgau was founded. John was followed in 1532 by his eldest son, John Frederick the Magnanimous, who completed Hartenfels Castle with its incredible staircase, soaring like a spindle without support over two stories. While a supporter of the Reformation, his poor political skills led to the Schmalkaldic War.
1466–1536	**Desiderius Erasmus:** scholar, priest, theologian, social critic, humanist, teacher. Educated at Cambridge; published Greek-Latin Parallel New Testament—an instant best-seller—in 1516 in Basel, Switzerland. Sourced directly from the more reliable, original Greek New Testament rather than from the corrupt, inaccurate Latin Vulgate (translated later into German by Luther). The Roman church continued to threaten to kill anyone who read Scripture in any language other than Latin, even though the originals were written in Hebrew and Greek. He remained a Roman Catholic, recognized the pope's authority and kept his distance from Luther and Melanchthon. Erasmus died in Basel. Johann Froben, who had taken possession of the Amberbach printing establishment, agreed with Erasmus to print his Latin translation in return for Erasmus's editorial work on the Greek text. The texts were to be printed side by side in a single volume. It required a great deal of courage to print a Latin translation that was not the Vulgate, since the Vulgate translation was then considered nearly infallible.

1472–1553	**Lucas Cranach the Elder,** appointed court painter by Frederick the Wise. Famous for portraits of Electors of Saxony and Reformers, though he still worked for Catholic clients. Luther's German translation of the Bible in 1522 included Cranach's illustrations. He passed his workshop on to his son, Lucas Cranach the Younger, who became equally famous; world's largest collection of their work is in the Dresden State Art Collections; the Museum of Fine Arts in Leipzig also has an extensive collection.
1473–1570	**Thomas Wolsey,** Lord Chancellor of England, Cardinal: King Henry VIII's chief advisor; burns Lutheran books; replaced by Sir Thomas Moore in 1529 for failing to get the pope's approval for Henry's annulment from Catherine of Aragon so that Henry could marry Anne Boleyn (Moore is later beheaded by Henry for his opposition).
1483–1546	**Martin Luther:** Father of the Reformation. Born and baptized in Eisleben; attended the University in Erfurt from 1501–1505. He called out to St. Anne for help in 1505 when caught in a severe thunderstorm, and vowed to become a monk. He entered a monastery in 1505 and was ordained in 1507 in Erfurt. Luther visited Rome in 1509; he became disillusioned and sermonized against the selling of indulgences, posting his **95 Theses** to the door of All Saints Church in Wittenbergb, Germany on October 31, 1517. He defended his position to Augustinians in Heidelberg and met with cardinal Cajetan from Rome in Augsburg in 1518. In 1520, Luther burned the papal bull threatening his excommunication if he did not recant. Luther was many things: law student, monk, theology professor; taught grace alone, faith alone, Christ alone, Scriptures alone, glory of God alone; authored first common German Bible; translated Erasmus's New Testament into German in 1522 and the entire Bible in the 1530s. Following the Diet of Worms in 1521, Luther was excommunicated by pope Leo X and exiled. Luther was hidden in Wartburg Castle by Frederick the Wise after a fake kidnapping. Protected by Frederick the Wise, he preached from the New Testament in the Block Cloister in Wittenberg, wrote many hymns including "A Mighty Fortress" (1527), and wrote against Jews in 1538. Luther married Katherine von Bora in 1525 at the age of 42, putting the seal of approval on clerical marriage. Luther died on a trip to Eisleben and is buried in Castle Church in Wittenberg where he nailed the **95 Theses** years earlier.

1484–1531	**Ulrich Zwingli,** Father of the Swiss Reformation Zwingli, who was born in Wildhaus, believed in simple theology based on literal, explicit Biblical beliefs and practices. As an ordained priest, he denounced music, paintings, and sculptures in church, opposed Luther's belief in transubstantiation in the Lord's Supper and never reconciled those differences with Luther. Like Luther, he preached sermons from the New Testament. Switzerland was not a country but a confederation of thirteen city-states (cantons), the most powerful being his home canton of Zürich. In 1519, Zwingli used his most powerful ecclesiastical position in the city, that of "People's Priest," in order to encourage dissent. In 1523 Zürich became the first Protestant state outside of Germany after he took on the city council, arguing his own sixty-seven-point thesis and replacing the mass with a simple service. Zwingli was killed in the Swiss civil war that he had encouraged, to force the remaining cantons to accept Protestants.
1488–1569	**Myles Coverdale,** Printer of the First Complete English Bible. Disciple of Tyndale, Coverdale finished translating the Old Testament (using Luther's German text) into English and printed first complete English Bible, the Coverdale Bible, in 1535. He published the "Great Bible" for Thomas Cranmer and Henry VIII in 1539 and dedicated it to Henry and his ex-wife Anne Boleyn; fled to the Church at Geneva with John Foxe in 1554.
1489–1556	**Thomas Cranmer,** archbishop of Canterbury. Named Archbishop in 1533 as a married man (so Anglican clergy were no longer required to be celibate, similar to the effect of Luther's 1525 marriage in Germany). In 1539, at king Henry VIII's bidding, Cranmer hired Myles Coverdale to publish the "Great Chained Bible," fourteen inches tall, to be distributed and chained to the pulpit of every church in England, with a reader provided so the illiterate could hear the Word in their own language for the first time; only seven editions were ever printed. Part of the White Horse Tavern Bible study group with fellow Cambridge scholars (including William Tyndale), Cranmer was burned at the stake by Mary Tudor (Bloody Mary) in 1556 after he was removed as Archbishop in 1555.

1491–1547	**Henry VIII,** king of England, 1509–1547 (From 1542 also king of Ireland). Inherited the throne in 1509 at age eighteen, second in the Tudor dynasty. Henry formed the (Anglican) Church of England and named himself its head when the pope refused his annulment from Catherine of Aragon to marry his mistress, Anne Boleyn. He broke relations with the Roman church in 1529 and pressured the clergy to submit to the king (not the pope) as supreme spiritual authority in 1532. Henry married the already pregnant Anne Boleyn and crowned her queen after his marriage to Catherine was voided in 1533; neither Catherine nor Anne produced a male heir. Henry executed two of his six wives (including Anne); dissolved hundreds of nunneries and monasteries in 1536; named himself Head of the Irish Church in 1541. Henry was succeeded by Edward VI (who died six years later and was succeeded by Mary I, known as Bloody Mary).

1494–1536	**William Tyndale,** Author of First Printed English New Testament. Born near Gloucestershire, Tyndale, an Oxford/Cambridge scholar, began at age twelve in 1506 reading the Bible in English to fellow students at Magdalen College, Oxford, eleven years before Luther wrote his **95 Theses.** Tyndale, a theologian, genius, fluent in eight languages, and Master's degree holder, refused monastic orders as a newly ordained priest. Part of the White Horse Tavern Bible study group with fellow Cambridge scholars (including Thomas Cranmer); Tyndale was a spiritual leader and Captain of the Army of Reformers; referred to as "Father of the English Bible," and "Architect of the English language"—some say even more than Shakespeare. Tyndale escaped to Germany in 1525 with only parts of his English New Testament, and finished translating the New Testament into English in Worms before completing its printing in 1526. Subsequent printings were often elaborately hand illustrated. The Church confiscated and burned as many copies as they could. Privately they found no errors, but publicly declared that it contained thousands of errors. If the people could read Scripture in their own language, and understand Salvation through faith, not works or donations, the Church would lose power and income, e.g. , no longer selling indulgences for forgiveness of sins, or for the release of loved ones from a church-manufactured purgatory. Only two known copies remain today of Tyndale's first edition. The king and the Church confiscated every available copy to burn, but Tyndale was funded to print even more. He was betrayed by a friend, imprisoned for fifteen months and finally strangled and burned at the stake. Two of his followers, Coverdale and John Rogers, submitted a New Testament in English in 1538, that was virtually identical to Tyndale's translation, which became the "Chained Bible" approved by the same king who had Tyndale killed seventeen years earlier. The first English Bible drawn directly from Hebrew and Greek texts; Tyndale, who had been influenced by Erasmus and Luther; had his writings banned and condemned as heresy. Tyndale was condemned to death by Henry VIII, and ordered to be strangled and burned at the stake in 1521.
1497–1560	**Philipp Melanchthon,** A Leader of German Reformation. Second to Luther in Lutheran Reformation; Melanchthon was a scholar, humanist, and a Greek professor at the University of Wittenberg with Luther. He wrote and presented the Augsburg Confession on then-outlawed Luther's behalf, at the 1530 Diet of Augsburg.

1499–1552	**Katherine von Bora,** Luther's wife. Birthplace and birthdate unknown (perhaps in Lippendorf, south of Leipzig on January 29, 1499), she was placed in a convent at age six upon her mother's death. Katherine entered the Cistercian Marienthron convent in 1509 in Nimbschen near Grimma; Luther helped her and eleven other nuns escape the convent in 1522. She then lived with artist Lucas Cranach's family until marrying Luther in 1525 in the Black Cloister in Wittenberg. Together they raised six children and four orphan children. She was a devoted wife (he called her "my Lord Katie") and a great manager of the household despite limited funds and many guests. Katherine died in Torgau, where she had fled due to the plague in Wittenberg, six years after Luther died.
1501–1536	**Anne Boleyn,** Queen of England. Lady-in-waiting to Henry VIII's first wife, Catherine of Aragon, she married Henry after his controversial divorce. She was the second of his six wives, and one of two that he executed.
1505–1572	**John Knox,** Father of the Scottish Reformation. Founder of Presbyterianism and the Calvinist Scottish Reformation in 1541, John Knox had attended St. Andrews College, became a Catholic priest, was made a French galley-slave, worked in England, taught with Calvin in Geneva, and returned to Scotland where he was born in Haddington. He formed the Reformed Church in 1560.
1509–1564	**John Calvin,** Swiss Reformer. Born in Noyon, France, Calvin was a humanist, lawyer, pastor, and theologian. Calvin had a sudden conversion from Catholicism in 1533. He went on to systematize the Reformed tradition in agreement with Luther's views on predestination; taught strict sobriety, thrift, and self-denial. In 1536, Calvin authored possibly the most influential theological book ever, **Institutes of the Christian Religion.** Calvin introduced Protestantism to France; escaping Paris in 1533 after being called a heretic by Catholics. He then moved to Geneva, previously intending to only stay one night on his way to Strasbourg. In 1538 he was banished by Geneva's city council over differences and moved to Strasbourg, France, to pastor a church; returned to Geneva in 1541 to create a theocracy, a "City of God"; established University of Geneva in 1559.

1516/17–1587	**John Foxe,** Publisher of **Actes and Monuments** (commonly known as **Foxe's Book of Martyrs**). Fled to the Church at Geneva in 1554 with Myles Coverdale; authored the only exhaustive reference work on the persecution/martyrdom of early Christians and Protestants from the first through the mid-sixteenth centuries.
1703–1791	**John Wesley,** Cofounder of Methodist Church with brother Charles Wesley.
1707–1788	**Charles Wesley**, Composer of 4,500 Hymns, Cofounder of Methodist Church with brother, John Wesley. "Jesus, Lover of My Soul," published in 1740, was his most famous hymn: translated into more languages than any other. Initially rejected by his brother John Wesley as too sentimental, the hymn is now lauded with "People will sing that hymn until the end of time and then on our lips in Heaven." Out of 188 words, 156 are one syllable. Christ is portrayed as lover, healer, refuge, fountain, pilot and all-sufficient. Multiple tunes have been used with his words; "Christ the Lord is Risen Today": published in 1739 for Wesleyan Chapel's first service, originally called "Hymn for Easter Day," composer unknown, added a joyous "Hallelujah" at end of each line, from an ancient Hebrew worship service (see **One Hundred and One Hymn Stories** by Kenneth Osbeck).

Key Timeline of the Reformation

Pre-Reformation (1215–1515)	
1215	Magna Carta signed, in which English aristocrats pushed king John to state their rights, the founding document of English (and eventually American) liberties.
1290	King Edward I expels Jews from England.
1295	Edward I summons England's first Parliament, the first representative form of government which allowed someone other than royalty to make legislation.
1302	Pope Boniface VIII declares that popes have authority over every person and civil authority, that there is only one true Church (the only path to Salvation).
1306	England expels100,000 remaining Jews.
1309	The pope Clement V establishes the papal court in his country of France (in Avignon, until 1377).

1320	John Wycliffe is born.
1337	Hundred Years War between France and England begins.
1347–1351	The bubonic plague kills up to two-thirds of the population in parts of Europe.
1369	Jan Hus is born.
1370	John Wycliffe, an English priest, known as "The Morning Star of the Reformation," opposes doctrines such as transubstantiation, proclaims Scripture should be in everyone's heart language, and proposes limits to the pope's powers.
1377	The pope Gregory XI releases five bulls (declarations sealed for authentication) condemning Wycliffe, puts him under house arrest and returns the papal court from Avignon to Rome.
1378	Two opposing papal elections (Urban II in Rome versus Clement VII in Avignon) divide Catholics until 1413.
1382	Wycliffites (or Lollards) complete the first translation of the Bible from Latin (not Biblical Hebrew or Greek) into English.
1384	Wycliffe dies.
1395	Johann Gutenberg is born.
1405	The pope Innocent VII issues an interdict over the entire city of Prague due to support for Hus's teachings and followers.
1408	English law forbids translating or reading the Bible in English without a bishop's permission.
1413	Jan Hus codifies Wycliffe's teachings by writing **De Ecclesia.**
1415	Wycliffe is denounced (thirty-one years **after** his death) at the Council of Constance in Germany on 267 counts of heresy. He is burned at the stake when he will not recant his beliefs.
1428	Pope Martin I orders Wycliffe's writings burned and his remains unearthed, burned, and tossed into the River Swift, forty-four years after his death.
1447–1450	The Renaissance period begins (through 1521).
1453	Hundred Years War ends.
1455	The printing press (with movable metal type) is invented in Mainz, Germany; Johann Gutenberg prints the first non-handwritten book in Europe, the Latin Vulgate or Bible.
1466	Desiderius Erasmus is born.
1468	Johann Gutenberg dies.

1483	Martin Luther (founder of the German Reformation) is born in Eisleben, Germany, on November tenth and is baptized at the Church of St. Peter and St. Paul.
1484	Ulrich Zwingli (founder of the Swiss Reformation) is born in Wildhaus (Toggenburg), Switzerland.
1488	Myles Coverdale is born.
1491	Henry VIII is born.
1494	William Tyndale is born in Gloucestershire, England.
1495	Leonardo da Vinci paints the "Last Supper."
1497	Philip Melanchthon is born.
1501	Music is printed by movable type.
1505	John Knox (leader of the Scottish Reformation) is born in Haddington, Scotland; while caught in a severe thunderstorm, Luther vows to be a monk.
1506	William Tyndale reads the Bible in English at Oxford (age twelve, at Magdalen College; eleven years before Luther's **95 Theses**); St. Peter's Cathedral in Rome is begun.
1507	Martin Luther celebrates his first Mass as a newly ordained priest.
1508	Michelangelo begins painting of Sistine Chapel ceiling.
1509	John Calvin, leader of the Swiss Reformation, is born in Noyon, France. Henry VIII becomes king in England at age eighteen and weds Catherine of Aragon. Luther visits Rome.
1515	William Tyndale, a newly ordained priest with his Master's degree, refuses to enter monkhood; Thomas Wolsey becomes Lord Chancellor of England.
Reformation: 1516–1563	
1516	Erasmus issues his New Testament translation from Greek into Latin, the foundation of future Luther, Tyndale, and King James translations.
1517	Martin Luther nails his **95 Theses** to the door of the Church of All Saints in Wittenberg, Germany, challenging the Church on selling indulgences, papal authority, penance and other issues; seven people burned at stake by the Roman Catholic Church for teaching their children to recite the Lord's Prayer in English rather than Latin.
1518	Luther defends his positions to Augustinians in Heidelberg and meets with cardinal Cajetan from Rome at the Imperial Diet in Augsburg; his protector, Frederick the Wise, prevents Luther's imprisonment by Rome after he refuses to recant his theology.

1519	Luther debates the claimed infallibility of popes and begins teaching from the New Testament, as does Zwingli, birthing the Swiss Reformation.
1520	Luther publicly burns the papal bull that threatened excommunication if he did not recant.
1521	Luther is excommunicated. He attends the Diet of Worms, again will not recant, is condemned as a heretic, which at the time was punishable by death by the civil authorities, and is hidden at Wartburg Castle by Elector Frederick the Wise after a fake kidnapping. The Catholic Church bans everyone from possessing or reading any of his writings. Luther begins his thirteen-year translation of the Bible into German. The first Protestant communion is served, in Wittenberg. William Tyndale is charged with heresy due to his teaching, and forms a study group with fellow Cambridge scholars (including Thomas Cranmer) at the White Horse Tavern.
1523	Zürich becomes the first Protestant state outside of Germany, under Ulrich Zwingli.
1525	William Tyndale escapes from England with only part of his English New Testament, later completing it in Worms; Anabaptists (later Brethren and Mennonites) proclaim baptism for believers and separation of church and state; Martin Luther and Katherine von Bora marry in the Black Cloister in Wittenberg, putting the seal of approval on clerical marriage.
1526	Tyndale prints the New Testament (the first in English and the first from the Biblical Greek) in Worms. Copies are then smuggled into England. Henry VIII's chief advisor, Cardinal Wolsey, burns Lutheran books. Protestant churches start in Denmark and Sweden.
1527	Luther writes the great hymn, "A Mighty Fortress"; he disagrees with Zwingli's teachings; the first Protestant university is started, in Germany; the purchase and burning of Tyndale's testaments ironically funds his second New Testament edition; the plague hits Wittenberg.
1529	King Henry VIII and Parliament break relations with the Roman church; Luther's followers are called "Protestants" for the first time at the Diet of Speyer, based on beliefs including: justification by faith alone, the Bible as the only source for truth and the priesthood of all believers; Sir Thomas Moore is appointed to replace Wolsey as Lord Chancellor for failing to get the pope's approval of Henry VIII's annulment from Catherine (to marry Anne Boleyn).
1530	Copies of Tyndale's Pentateuch (first five books of the Old Testament), printed in Worms, arrive in England; the Diet of Augsburg results in the Augsburg Confession, Lutheran beliefs presented on (outlaw) Luther's behalf by his friend, Philipp Melanchthon.

1531	Tyndale declines Henry VIII's offer to come back to England; Ulrich Zwingli is killed in the Swiss civil war he encouraged, to force Catholics to accept Protestants.
1532	Henry VIII pressures the Church to submit to the king (not the pope) as the supreme spiritual authority; John Calvin introduces Protestantism to France.
1533	Calvin escapes Paris after being called a heretic by Catholics; Thomas Cranmer, a widower, replaces William Warham as archbishop of Canterbury, signifying Anglican clergy no longer need to be celibate. Luther's 1525 marriage in Germany had also shown approval for clerical marriage. Henry VIII's marriage to Catherine is voided and Anne Boleyn is crowned queen.
1534	The Act of Supremacy makes the king the head of the Church of England. Luther finishes his thirteen-year translation of the Bible into German. The Society of Jesus (Jesuits) was formed in Paris by Catholic priest Ignatius Loyola to counter the Reformation. Tyndale's revised New Testament is printed.
1535	Tyndale is imprisoned for heresy, in part due to challenging Henry's divorce from Katherine of Aragon, on behalf of king Henry VIII near Brussels, Belgium. Myles Coverdale completes translating Tyndale's Bible, the first complete Bible in English, and ironically dedicates it to Henry and his consort, Anne Boleyn. Anabaptists are killed by Catholics in Germany (and later commit to pacifism); Thomas Moore is beheaded for opposing Henry VIII.
1536	Tyndale is strangled and burned at the stake after fifteen months in jail. Luther fails to reconcile disagreements with the Swiss Zwinglians over the Lord's Supper. Norway and Denmark become Lutheran. Henry VIII dissolves hundreds of convents and monasteries. Calvin publishes **Institutes of the Christian Religion** and moves to Geneva.
1538	Calvin is banished by Geneva's city council over differences and moves to Strasbourg, France, pastoring a French speaking congregation for three years. Luther writes against Jews.
1539	Henry VIII authorizes the archbishop of Canterbury, Thomas Cranmer, to commission Myles Coverdale to publish the "Chained Bible," a large Bible to be chained to the pulpit of every church in England-the first English Bible for public use-with a reader provided for the illiterate. Only seven editions were ever printed.
1540	The Jesuit order is recognized by the pope and increase their role in Counter-Reformation and evangelism; the Worms and Hagenau (Haguenau) Conferences are unable to reconcile Catholic and Protestant doctrinal differences.

1541	Calvin returns to create a theocracy in Geneva. John Knox founds the Calvinist Scottish Reformation, known as Presbyterians, due to being under the authority of a group of presbyters (elders) vs. that of a single leader. The Regensburg Conference also is unable to reconcile Catholic and Protestant differences. Henry VIII names himself Head of Irish Church.
1544–1545	The Council of Trent opens in Italy to reform the Catholic Church (ongoing through 1563). Catholic Counter-Reformation disapproves of nepotism, selling indulgences, immoral clergy . . . and Protestants.
1546	Martin Luther dies and is buried in Eisleben.
1547	Henry VIII dies and is succeeded by Edward VI.
1549	**The Book of Common Prayer** forges a compromise between Protestantism and Catholicism.
1553	Edward VI dies, succeeded by Mary I ("Bloody Mary").
1554	Henry VIII's daughter, Mary I (Tudor), persecuted Protestants. After Tyndale's assistant is burned, along with 300 others including bishops, priests, and women, many flee to Calvin; Myles Coverdale and John Foxe among them.
1555	Peace of Augsburg Treaty lets each regional ruler in Germany choose between Lutheranism and Catholicism; Thomas Cranmer is removed as archbishop of Canterbury.
1556	Thomas Cranmer is burned at the stake.
1558	Mary I dies and is succeeded by Elizabeth I (reign 1558–1603); Elizabeth names herself Supreme (not Head, a male term) Governor of the Church of England and tries to reconcile differences between Protestants and Catholics.
1560	The first Bible divided into verses is completed, with margin notes: The Geneva Bible, by the Church of Geneva, for the English families exiled there. John Knox in Scotland forms the Reformed Church; Philipp Melanchthon dies.
1562–1563	The most major Protestant statement of doctrine, the Heidelberg Catechism, is established.
Post–Reformation (1564–1698)	
1564	Protestants trying to purify the Church of England of non-Biblical traditions are called "Puritans"; John Calvin dies.
1570	Elizabeth is excommunicated by the Church of Rome and persecutes Catholics.
1572	John Knox dies.

1601	Calvinism (predestination, that God predetermines our entrance into Heaven) is disputed by Arminianism (man chooses Christ as our entry into Heaven) by Dutch Reformed theologian Jacobus Arminius, based on the book of Romans—see Five Points each of Arminianism and of Calvinism in Appendix.
1603	Elizabeth I dies, succeeded by James VI and I.
1605	Guy Fawkes, along with fellow Catholics, fail to assassinate James I and blow up London's Parliament in the hope it would result in England having a Catholic king ("Gunpowder Plot").
1611	The King James Version of the Bible is released after six years of work by fifty-four scholars. This became the most-used Bible until the mid-1900s. Much of the text was from Tyndale's translations.
1620	Pilgrims leave the Church of England. Pilgrims on Mayflower voyage land at Cape Cod in Massachusetts Bay Colony. They founded Plymouth Colony and are later followed by the Puritans who start the first colonies.
1642	Puritan Parliamentarian Oliver Cromwell wins the civil war over Charles I and protects Protestants.
1647	The Westminster Confession of Faith, defining Presbyterianism in England and Scotland, is drafted at Westminster Abbey. George Fox establishes the Quakers.
1648	The Thirty Years War ends allowing equality between Protestants and Catholics through most of the remaining Roman empire (Peace of Westphalia). Some say this was the end of the Reformation.
1665	Great Plague hits London.
1666	Great Fire takes place in London.
1689	Constitutional monarchy and Bill of Rights created in England, barring Catholics from the throne. Dissenters given freedom to worship by the Toleration Act.
1698	Protestants establish missionaries.

Bible Translation Timeline

The Bible was written over the course of 1,600 years of history, in sixty-six books, by forty different authors from all walks of life. It was written in different locations, from the thrones of kings to the dungeons of the imprisoned, on three different continents—Asia, Africa, and Europe. It was written in three different languages—Aramaic, Hebrew and Greek. Yet the inspired, breathed Word of God is consistent in facts and theology and is as relevant today as when it was written.

Nearly one-fourth of the Bible includes prophecies, including 300 in the Old Testament about Christ, written from 450 to over 2000 years before He came and fulfilled every one of them.

We celebrate the many mostly unnamed church fathers who, often at the risk of loss of their freedom and lives, protected, hand-copied, translated, printed, published, and distributed not only original manuscripts, but copies and translations in so many heart languages, that we may read God's sixty-six love letters to us today.

1400 BC	Ten Commandments given to Moses, God's first written Word.
500 BC	Completion of all original Hebrew manuscripts, representing the eventual thirty-nine books of the Old Testament.
200 BC	Completion of the Septuagint Greek manuscripts of the thirty-nine Old Testament books plus fourteen Apocrypha books (intertestamental books written hundreds of years before Christ) by seventy scholars.
1st Century AD	Completion of all original Greek manuscripts, representing the eventual twenty-seven books of the New Testament.
315	The twenty-seven books of the New Testament are identified by the Bishop of Alexandra, Athanasius.
382	Completion of Jerome's Latin Vulgate manuscripts containing eighty books: thirty-nine Old Testament, fourteen Apocrypha and twenty-seven New Testament. Jerome was a zealous promoter of monastic life.
500	Scriptures have been translated into over 500 languages.
600	Latin is deemed the sole language authorized for Scripture.
1384	John Wycliffe produces first hand-written manuscript of the eighty-book Bible into English, from the Latin Vulgate.
1455	Johann Gutenberg invents the movable-type printing press, the first non-handwritten book printed is the Bible, in Latin (Vulgate).
1516	Erasmus completes a Greek/Latin Parallel New Testament.
1522	Martin Luther completes first German New Testament including illustrations by Lucas Cranach the Elder.
1526	William Tyndale completes first English New Testament in Worms, Germany; it is also the first translated from the Biblical Greek; copies smuggled back into England.

1534	Luther completes his thirteen-year translation of the complete Bible into German; Tyndale's revised New Testament is printed.
1535	Myles Coverdale completes (Tyndale's) first complete English Bible (eighty books) and dedicates it to king Henry VIII and his second wife, Anne Boleyn.
1539	The Great Bible (a.k.a. the Chained Bible) is printed, the first in English authorized for public use. A large copy was to be chained to the pulpit of every church in England, with a reader provided for the illiterate; only seven editions were ever printed.
1560	The Geneva Bible (a.k.a. the Breeches Bible) is printed in Geneva for the English exiles, the first English Bible with numbered verses and margin notes. The Geneva Bible is quoted hundreds of times in Shakespeare's plays; it was the preferred English Bible for over 100 years. Printed in 144 editions, and retaining over ninety percent of Tyndale's original English translations, it was the Bible of the Protestant Reformation. The Geneva Bible was also the first taken to America and used by the Puritans and Pilgrims.
1582	Roman Catholic Church prints the Rheims New Testament (along with the Douai Old Testament in 1609), surrendering their "Latin only" fight, but still using the corrupt and inaccurate Latin Vulgate as the source, despite Erasmus's exposure seventy-five years earlier of its thousands of errors; up to today, Catholic Bibles still contain the fourteen Apocryphal books.
1611	The King James Bible is printed (eighty books), much from Tyndale's translations and not widely used until decades later; despite the accuracy and commentary of the widely accepted Geneva text. King James I (also James VI of Scotland) authorized this Bible without its controversial margin notes (e.g. , calling the pope an antichrist); the translation to end all translations; over seven years by forty-seven scholars; most Protestants do not realize it is actually Anglican designed to compete with the Protestant Geneva Bible; the most printed book in history (over five billion copies).
1782	The first English Bible (KJV) is printed in America by Robert Aitken, the only Bible ever authorized by the U.S. Congress; needed due to the embargo of imported English goods during the Revolutionary War.
1808	The first English Bible (KJV) printed by a woman, Jane Aitken (Robert's daughter).
1833	Noah Webster, after publishing his Dictionary, prints a KJV revision.
1885	The English Revised Version (ERV) removes the fourteen Apocryphal books (with no widely accepted reason for doing so). It is the first major English revision to replace the KJV.

1901	The American Standard Version (ASV) is printed, the first major American revision, in response to the ERV.
1971	The New American Standard Version (NASB, NASV, or NAS) is printed, the most accurate word-for-word English translation, nearly identical to the ASV; direct and literal, but not conversational.
1973	The New International Version (NIV) is printed, a phrase-for-phrase English, junior high reading level translation; the best-selling modern English translation.
1982	The New King James Version (NKJV) is printed, in modern English maintaining the KJV style, by Thomas Nelson Publishers; never taken seriously by scholars.
2002	The English Standard Version (ESV) is printed, to bridge the gap between the NASB's precise accuracy and the NIV's simple readability.

Church Branches and Denominations Timeline

Roman Catholics				
1517	Lutherans			
	1525	Anabaptists		
		1537	Mennonites (USA 1725)	
		1693	Amish	
	1536	Calvinists/ Reformed/ Presbyterians		
		1607	Congregationalists	
		1607	Baptists	
			1801	Church of Christ
			1844	Seventh Day Adventists
			1845	Southern Baptists
			1924	American Baptists
	1950	Evangelical Free		

1534	Church of England/ Anglican/ Episcopal			
	1738	Methodists		
		1814	African Methodist Episcopal (AME)	
		1880	Salvation Army	
		1908	Nazarenes	
		1901	Pentecostals	
			1907	Pentecostal Assembly
			1914	Assemblies of God
			1927	Foursquare Gospel
			Charismatics	
			1965	Calvary Chapel
			1983	Vineyard

Five Points of Arminianism:

1. Free will or human ability: Free will consists of our ability to choose good over evil; we have the power to cooperate with God's grace or to resist it.

2. Conditional election: God's choice (election) determined by knowledge of what man would do (foreseen faith). *Our* choice of God, not *God's* choice of us, is cause of Salvation.

3. Universal redemption or general atonement: Jesus' death and Resurrection made it possible for all to be saved, but is effective only for those who choose to accept it.

4. Resistible grace: Our free will limits the Holy Spirit's ability to draw us toward Salvation; God's grace can be resisted.

5. Falling from grace: Salvation can be lost, as it requires our cooperation.

Five Points of Calvinism:

1. Total depravity (inability): Sin affects every part of human nature, resulting in our inability to choose good over evil. We must be regenerated by the Holy Spirit in order to believe.
2. Unconditional election: God's choice (election) determined not by our foreseen response (faith); rather, faith and repentance are also gifts given by God. *God's* choice of us, not *our* choice of God, is the cause of Salvation.
3. Limited atonement: Jesus' death and Resurrection actually saved the elect; it guarantees everything necessary for Salvation, including the gift of faith.
4. Irresistible grace: The Holy Spirit is called irresistible; God's grace never fails to result in Salvation for those to whom it is extended.
5. Perseverance of the saints: Salvation cannot be lost, as it is completely powered by God; thus, the elect will persevere (be preserved) to the end.

Five Solas of the Reformation:

1. *Sola Scriptura:* Scripture Alone; the Bible alone is the sole authority, not fallible men.
2. *Soli Deo Gloria:* For the Glory of God Alone; all that we are, say, and do subsequent to our Salvation should be for His Glory only.
3. *Solo Christo (or Christus):* By Christ's Work Alone are We Saved; Jesus finished the work on the Cross.
4. *Sola Gratia:* Salvation by Grace Alone; *our* works only mater *after* our redemption (Eph 2:8–9).
5. *Sola Fide:* Justification by Faith Alone; faith is a gift, also not by virtue of our works.

Solo Christo summarizes Sola Fide, Sola Scriptura, and Sola Gratia into one primary principle.

Luther's 95 Theses

1. When our Lord and Master Jesus Christ said, "*Repent*" (Matthew 4:17), He willed the entire life of believers to be one of repentance.

2. This word cannot be understood as referring to the sacrament of penance, that is, confession and satisfaction, as administered by the clergy.

3. Yet it does not mean solely inner repentance; such inner repentance is worthless unless it produces various outward mortification of the flesh.

4. The penalty of sin remains as long as the hatred of self (that is, true inner repentance), namely till our entrance into the kingdom of Heaven.

5. The pope neither desires nor is able to remit any penalties except those imposed by his own authority or that of the canons.

6. The pope cannot remit any guilt except by declaring and showing that it has been remitted by God; or, to be sure, by remitting guilt in cases reserved to his judgment. If his right to grant remission in these cases were disregarded, the guilt would certainly remain unforgiven.

7. God remits guilt to no one unless at the same time He humbles him in all things and makes him submissive to the vicar, the priest.

8. The penitential canons are imposed only on the living, and, according to the canons themselves, nothing should be imposed on the dying.

9. Therefore the Holy Spirit through the pope is kind to us insofar as the pope in his decrees always makes exception of the article of death and of necessity.

10. Those priests act ignorantly and wickedly who, in the case of the dying, reserve canonical penalties for purgatory.

11. Those tares of changing the canonical penalty to the penalty of purgatory were evidently sown while the bishops slept (Matthew 13:25).

12. In former times, canonical penalties were imposed not after but before absolution, as tests of true contrition.

13. The dying are freed by death from all penalties, are already dead as far as the canon laws are concerned, and have a right to be released from them.
14. Imperfect piety or love on the part of the dying person necessarily brings with it great fear; and the smaller the love, the greater the fear.
15. This fear or horror is sufficient in itself, to say nothing of other things, to constitute the penalty of purgatory, since it is very near to the horror of despair.
16. Hell, purgatory, and Heaven seem to differ the same as despair, fear, and assurance of salvation.
17. It seems as though for the souls in purgatory fear should necessarily decrease and love increase.
18. Furthermore, it does not seem proved, either by reason or by Scripture, that souls in purgatory are outside the state of merit, that is, unable to grow in love.
19. Nor does it seem proved that souls in purgatory, at least not all of them, are certain and assured of their own salvation, even if we ourselves may be entirely certain of it.
20. Therefore the pope, when he uses the words "plenary remission of all penalties," does not actually mean "all penalties," but only those imposed by himself.
21. Thus those indulgence preachers are in error who say that a man is absolved from every penalty and saved by papal indulgences.
22. As a matter of fact, the pope remits to souls in purgatory no penalty which, according to canon law, they should have paid in this life.
23. If remission of all penalties whatsoever could be granted to anyone at all, certainly it would be granted only to the most perfect, that is, to very few.
24. For this reason, most people are necessarily deceived by that indiscriminate and high-sounding promise of release from penalty.
25. That power which the pope has in general over purgatory corresponds to the power which any bishop or curate has in a particular way in his own diocese and parish.

26. The pope does very well when he grants remission to souls in purgatory, not by the power of the keys, which he does not have, but by way of intercession for them.

27. They preach only human doctrines who say that as soon as the money clinks into the money chest, the soul flies out of purgatory.

28. It is certain that when money clinks in the money chest, greed and avarice can be increased; but when the Church intercedes, the result is in the hands of God alone.

29. Who knows whether all souls in purgatory wish to be redeemed, since we have exceptions in St. Severinus and St. Paschal, as related in a legend.

30. No one is sure of the integrity of his own contrition, much less of having received plenary remission.

31. The man who actually buys indulgences is as rare as he who is really penitent; indeed, he is exceedingly rare.

32. Those who believe that they can be certain of their salvation because they have indulgence letters will be eternally damned, together with their teachers.

33. Men must especially be on guard against those who say that the pope's pardons are that inestimable gift of God by which man is reconciled to Him.

34. For the graces of indulgences are concerned only with the penalties of sacramental satisfaction established by man.

35. They who teach that contrition is not necessary on the part of those who intend to buy souls out of purgatory or to buy confessional privileges preach unchristian doctrine.

36. Any truly repentant Christian has a right to full remission of penalty and guilt, even without indulgence letters.

37. Any true Christian, whether living or dead, participates in all the blessings of Christ and the Church; and this is granted him by God, even without indulgence letters.

38. Nevertheless, papal remission and blessing are by no means to be disregarded, for they are, as I have said, the proclamation of the divine remission.

39. It is very difficult, even for the most learned theologians, at one and the same time to commend to the people the bounty of indulgences and the need of true contrition.

40. A Christian who is truly contrite seeks and loves to pay penalties for his sins; the bounty of indulgences, however, relaxes penalties and causes men to hate them—at least it furnishes occasion for hating them.

41. Papal indulgences must be preached with caution, lest people erroneously think that they are preferable to other good works of love.

42. Christians are to be taught that the pope does not intend that the buying of indulgences should in any way be compared with works of mercy.

43. Christians are to be taught that he who gives to the poor or lends to the needy does a better deed than he who buys indulgences.

44. Because love grows by works of love, man thereby becomes better. Man does not, however, become better by means of indulgences but is merely freed from penalties.

45. Christians are to be taught that he who sees a needy man and passes him by, yet gives his money for indulgences, does not buy papal indulgences but God's wrath.

46. Christians are to be taught that, unless they have more than they need, they must reserve enough for their family needs and by no means squander it on indulgences.

47. Christians are to be taught that their buying of indulgences is a matter of free choice, not commanded.

48 Christians are to be taught that the pope, in granting indulgences, needs and thus desires their devout prayer more than their money.

49. Christians are to be taught that papal indulgences are useful only if they do not put their trust in them, but very harmful if they lose their fear of God because of them.

50. Christians are to be taught that if the pope knew the exactions of the indulgence preachers, he would rather that the Basilica of St. Peter

were burned to ashes than built up with the skin, flesh, and bones of his sheep.

51. Christians are to be taught that the pope would and should wish to give of his own money, even though he had to sell the Basilica of St. Peter, to many of those from whom certain hawkers of indulgences cajole money.

52. It is vain to trust in salvation by indulgence letters, even though the indulgence commissary, or even the pope, were to offer his soul as security.

53. They are the enemies of Christ and the pope who forbid altogether the preaching of the Word of God in some churches in order that indulgences may be preached in others.

54. Injury is done to the Word of God when, in the same sermon, an equal or larger amount of time is devoted to indulgences than to the Word.

55. It is certainly the pope's sentiment that if indulgences, which are a very insignificant thing, are celebrated with one bell, one procession, and one ceremony, then the gospel, which is the very greatest thing, should be preached with a hundred bells, a hundred processions, a hundred ceremonies.

56. The true treasures of the Church, out of which the pope distributes indulgences, are not sufficiently discussed or known among the people of Christ.

57. That indulgences are not temporal treasures is certainly clear, for many indulgence sellers do not distribute them freely but only gather them.

58. Nor are they the merits of Christ and the saints, for, even without the pope, the latter always work grace for the inner man, and the Cross, death, and hell for the outer man.

59. St. Lawrence said that the poor of the Church were the treasures of the Church, but he spoke according to the usage of the word in his own time.

60. Without want of consideration we say that the keys of the Church, given by the merits of Christ, are that treasure.

61. For it is clear that the pope's power is of itself sufficient for the remission of penalties and cases reserved by himself.

62. The true treasure of the Church is the most holy Gospel of the glory and grace of God.

63. But this treasure is naturally most odious, for it makes the first to be last.

64. On the other hand, the treasure of indulgences is naturally most acceptable, for it makes the last to be first.

65. Therefore the treasures of the Gospel are nets with which one formerly fished for men of wealth.

66. The treasures of indulgences are nets with which one now fishes for the wealth of men.

67. The indulgences which the demagogues acclaim as the greatest graces are actually understood to be such only insofar as they promote gain.

68. They are nevertheless in truth the most insignificant graces when compared with the grace of God and the piety of the Cross.

69. Bishops and curates are bound to admit the commissaries of papal indulgences with all reverence.

70. But they are much more bound to strain their eyes and ears lest these men preach their own dreams instead of what the pope has commissioned.

71. Let him who speaks against the truth concerning papal indulgences be anathema and accursed.

72. But let him who guards against the lust and license of the indulgence preachers be blessed.

73. Just as the pope justly thunders against those who by any means whatever contrive harm to the sale of indulgences.

74. Much more does he intend to thunder against those who use indulgences as a pretext to contrive harm to holy love and truth.

75. To consider papal indulgences so great that they could absolve a man even if he had done the impossible and had violated the mother of God is madness.

76. We say on the contrary that papal indulgences cannot remove the very least of venial sins as far as guilt is concerned.

77. To say that even St. Peter if he were now pope, could not grant greater graces is blasphemy against St. Peter and the pope.

78. We say on the contrary that even the present pope, or any pope whatsoever, has greater graces at his disposal, that is, the gospel, spiritual powers, gifts of healing, etc., as it is written, 1 Corinthians 12:28.

79. To say that the cross emblazoned with the papal coat of arms, and set up by the indulgence preachers is equal in worth to the Cross of Christ is blasphemy.

80. The bishops, curates, and theologians who permit such talk to be spread among the people will have to answer for this.

81. This unbridled preaching of indulgences makes it difficult even for learned men to rescue the reverence which is due the pope from slander or from the shrewd questions of the laity.

82. Such as: Why does not the pope empty purgatory for the sake of holy love and the dire need of the souls that are there if he redeems an infinite number of souls for the sake of miserable money with which to build a church? The former reason would be most just; the latter is most trivial.

83. Again, "Why are funeral and anniversary masses for the dead continued and why does he not return or permit the withdrawal of the endowments founded for them, since it is wrong to pray for the redeemed?"

84. Again, "What is this new piety of God and the pope that for a consideration of money they permit a man who is impious and their enemy to buy out of purgatory the pious soul of a friend of God and do not rather, because of the need of that pious and beloved soul, free it for pure love's sake?"

85. Again, "Why are the penitential canons, long since abrogated and dead in actual fact and through disuse, now satisfied by the granting of indulgences as though they were still alive and in force?"

86. Again, "Why does not the pope, whose wealth is today greater than the wealth of the richest Crassus, build this one Basilica of St. Peter with his own money rather than with the money of poor believers?"

87. Again, "What does the pope remit or grant to those who by perfect contrition already have a right to full remission and blessings?"

88. Again, "What greater blessing could come to the Church than if the pope were to bestow these remission and blessings on every believer a hundred times a day, as he now does but once?"

89. "Since the pope seeks the salvation of souls rather than money by his indulgences, why does he suspend the indulgences and pardons previously granted when they have equal efficacy?"

90. To repress these very sharp arguments of the laity by force alone, and not to resolve them by giving reasons, is to expose the Church and the pope to the ridicule of their enemies and to make Christians unhappy.

91. If, therefore, indulgences were preached according to the spirit and intention of the pope, all these doubts would be readily resolved. Indeed, they would not exist.

92. Away, then, with all those prophets who say to the people of Christ, "*Peace, peace*," and there is no peace! (Jeremiah 6:14).

93. Blessed be all those prophets who say to the people of Christ, "Cross, Cross," and there is no Cross!

94. Christians should be exhorted to be diligent in following Christ, their Head, through penalties, death and hell.

95. And thus be confident of entering into Heaven through many tribulations rather than through the false security of peace (Acts 14:22).

Note: This document was originally made available to the Internet by Bob Van Cleef, converted to HTML format by Jonathan Hall Barlow.

SUGGESTED RESOURCES:
THE REFORMATION

Book:

Real Marriage, Mark Driscoll, © 2011, On Mission LLC

Tract:

Reformation Time Line, ©2006, Rose Publishing

Film:

Luther: The Life and Legacy of the German Reformer, Director Stephen McCaskill, ©2017

GRATITUDES

———

We are so grateful for such professional, generous and kind assistance from so many people and from so many sources we researched.

First, thanks to the Author of Life. This project of obedient love, which has blessed us each so much, individually and collectively, comes courtesy of the inspiration from our God, from Jesus and from the Holy Spirit.

Thanks to Bob Shank of The Masters Program and The Barnabas Group, who facilitated the Dream Master retreat weekend in the year we were married (2004) that started this shared dream adventure together to write such a book.

Thanks to former Pastor Kenton Beshore of Mariners Church for showing us the possibilities and promises of a faith-based trip that moves beyond just great *head knowledge* to deep, life-application, *heart experience*. Four of the Defining Moments in the Israel section, which incubated the dozens of other Defining Moments throughout the book, started from our trip with him.

Thanks to Pastor Eric Heard, who beautifully lives the team shepherd role we prioritize in the book. We brought him to Greece and Turkey as we led a group through Paul's Journeys, and were able to test out some of our Defining Moment opportunities together with him and with David and Elizabeth Sparks of Footstep Ministries, who facilitate such trips in such a rich way that also includes experiencing the local culture.

Thanks to our early adopters, those who so generously endorsed this book in draft form.

Thanks to Jennifer Harshman & the rock-star team at Harshman Services for superb and very resourceful line editing, copy editing, proofreading and test reading.

Thanks to so many at Morgan James Publishing, who have educated, encouraged and served us so lavishly from Founder David Hancock to Publisher Jim Howard to Margo Toulouse, our Author Relations Manager and to the entire Author Support Team of Nickcole Watkins, Jessica Burton-Moran, Amber Parrott, Taylor Chaffer, and Heidi Nickerson.

ABOUT THE AUTHORS:

DefiningMomentsbook.com

Rick and Susan McCarthy have a deep love of the Lord, each other (he always calls her his "bride" and gets her door) and traveling together. Rick has traveled to over 80 countries and Susan to over 70 countries . . . so far. They travel about 140 days each year together for pleasure and ministry (which is also quite pleasurable to them), none for business, including serving biannually with Un Jour Nouveau in eastern D.R. Congo.

Susan is the author of "*Captive to Captivated*," which shares her faith journey of being set free from the captivity of lies to being captivated by God's love, told through the lens of her Kingdom purpose—"To set the captives free." Her misunderstanding of God as a terrifying punisher transforms into a revelation of God's true being. A Christian for over twenty years now, the Lord has made up for lost time, and Susan now shares a loving, wondrous relationship with her Savior. Her next book, "*Redeemed to Redeeming*", shifts the story from her to others, how the Holy Spirit uses her now being Redeemed to Redeeming others who are stuck in areas of their lives and faith journeys. She also has a calling to pray with ministry leaders and give them a safe place to process hard places on their journeys. She also mentors women through spiritual direction and intercession.

Rick has been self-employed as a CPA in private practice since 1978. He serves numerous ministries, including The Sheepfold, The Master's Program, The Barnabas Group, Standing Stone Ministry, Africa New Day/Un Jour Nouveau, Pacific Justice Institute and Evangelical Christian Credit Union.

An Honors graduate from Cal State University, Fullerton, Rick taught Taxation for the American Institute for Philanthropic Studies. He served many roles at Mariners Church since 1984, from usher to elder.

Rick loves to write and edit—from editing his high school newspaper, to his Orange County Business Journal opinion column "To the Point," to his Monday-morning handwritten letters to his son, Patrick (starting in college and continuing periodically for years after), to his ongoing love, memories and affirmation journal postings to Susan, to his political emails, to his outlining his next book on asking great questions (sharing how the greatest teachers ever, Jesus and Socrates, taught through great questions, out of curiosity), to the farewell letter he wrote decades ago and updates annually to be read at his eventual memorial (talk of "always having the last word"!). He is also notorious for irritatingly writing in small print.

Rick also is an avid reader, an info junkie, who loves to pass along gems he discovers to others. He has read the entire fiction works of an eclectic mix of over 25 authors so far. Rick is also an inviter who loves to share new possibilities with others, whether it be through his love of questions or through inviting people to family reunions, high school reunions, unique experiences, concerts/plays, Christian movies/events/fundraisers, travel/dining ideas or just fellowshipping over a meal and a bottle of wine.

His personal mission statement is: *To use my gifts, including Holy Spirit, discernment, capacity, and humor, to lovingly equip and Influence the Influencers, by challenging their thinking and behaviors and by connecting them with growth and service opportunities, to achieve God's will.*

Rick's varied experience in helping clients achieve their business, personal, and ministry goals along with his passion for helping leaders raise the bar on their walk with Christ led him through Bob Shank's *The Master's Program*, to the convergence of his *career* (as a CPA helping leaders grow their organizations) and *calling* (helping men in accountability relationships) as a Convene Chair—mentoring marketplace and nonprofit leaders one-to-one, and on a Biblical-wise counsel advisory board.

Rick and Susan have a son, Patrick, who preceded them to Heaven and to whom this book is dedicated. Their daughter, Jennifer, lives in Palm Desert, California with her daughter, June. They reside in Newport Beach, California, and have a shared passion to mentor couples, whether in ministry or through various life stages like courtship, engagement, early marriage, or whether in healthy or troubled marriages.

LIKE THIS BOOK?

Consider sharing it with others!

Share or mention the book on your social media platforms.
Use the hashtag **#DefiningMomentsBook**

Write a book review on your blog or retailer site.

Pick up a copy for friends, family, colleagues, pastors or even strangers!

Share this message on Twitter or Facebook.
"I loved #DefiningMomentsBook by @McCarthyRick and @ McSusan123"

Recommend this book for your church, small group, workplace, book club or class.

Follow us on social media and tell us what you like.

Facebook.com/Rick.McCarthy.180/
Facebook.com/Susan.McCarthy.923/

@McCarthyRick
@McSusan123

DefiningMomentsBook

LinkedIn.com/in/RickMcCarthy1/

Check out our substantial free Resources and more on our website:
DefiningMomentsBook.com

CPSIA information can be obtained
at www.ICGtesting.com
Printed in the USA
JSHW032009121020
8729JS00001B/1